D0991269

AVENGING PEARL HARBOR

THE SAGA OF AMERICA'S BATTLESHIPS IN THE PACIFIC WAR

KEITH WARREN LLOYD

Guilford, Connecticut

To the crew of the USS Arizona

An imprint of Globe Pequot, the trade division of
The Rowman & Littlefield Publishing Group, Inc.
4501 Forbes Blvd., Ste. 200
Lanham, MD 20706
www.rowman.com

Distributed by NATIONAL BOOK NETWORK

British Library Cataloguing in Publication Information available

Library of Congress Cataloging-in-Publication Data available

ISBN 978-1-4930-5866-2 (cloth : alk. paper)
ISBN 978-1-4930-5867-9 (electronic)

∞™ The paper used in this publication meets the minimum requirements of American National Standard for Information Sciences—Permanence of Paper for Printed Library Materials, ANSI/NISO Z39.48-1992.

CONTENTS

Preface iv
Chapter 1: Wai Momi 1
Chapter 2: The Philosopher 9
Chapter 3: Rising Sun 15
Chapter 4: Dreadnought 22
Chapter 5: Games of Chance 30
Chapter 6: The Fleet at Pearl 37
Chapter 7: A Date Which Will Live in Infamy 49
Chapter 8: Second Wave 70
Chapter 9: Short War, Long War 78
Chapter 10: A Fortunate Choice 94
Chapter 11: Refloating the "Cheer Up Ship" 102
Chapter 12: Raising the Prune Barge 107
Chapter 13: Resurrecting the Wee Vee 117
Chapter 14: *Kantai Kessen* 124
Chapter 15: The View from the Sidelines 141
Chapter 16: "Commence firing" 163
Chapter 17: "Give the bastards hell" 176
Chapter 18: Catchpole, Hailstone, and Forager 202
Chapter 19: "A thorough working over" 227
Chapter 20: *Sho-Go* 243
Chapter 21: Revenge of the Dreadnoughts 265
Chapter 22: Epilogue 296
Acknowledgments 307
Sources 308
Index 317

PREFACE

THIS IS THE STORY OF THE EIGHT DREADNOUGHT-ERA BATTLESHIPS OF the United States Pacific Fleet that were present in Pearl Harbor, Hawaii, on December 7, 1941, specifically the *Arizona*, *California*, *Maryland*, *Nevada*, *Oklahoma*, *Pennsylvania*, *Tennessee*, and *West Virginia*. It chronicles the events leading up to the Japanese surprise attack which plunged America into the Second World War, and tells of the enormous courage and sacrifice displayed by the battleship sailors of the Pacific Fleet on that fateful day.

Of this much has already been written by many gifted researchers and authors over the intervening eighty years. This account, however, goes beyond the events of December 7 to describe the heroic firefighting and search-and-rescue operations that occurred in the immediate aftermath of the attack, as well as the effort to salvage the heavily damaged battleships, an immense undertaking which lasted well into the year 1943. It tells the story of the dirty, difficult, and often dangerous work of the salvage officers, divers, and skilled technicians, both military and civilian, who were responsible for raising the battered dreadnoughts from the mud of Pearl Harbor so they could be repaired and returned to the fight.

The book then delves into the extensive modernization of the six surviving battleships that took place in the naval shipyards of Pearl Harbor, Puget Sound, and Hunters Point, the re-manning, shakedown, and training periods that followed, and their subsequent return to the fleet and participation in the Pacific Campaign. The contribution of these older battleships and their stalwart crews to final victory in the Pacific, which took place in far-flung locales with names like Attu, Tarawa, Kwajalein, Saipan, Peleliu, the Philippines, Iwo Jima, and Okinawa, has often been overlooked. This particular narrative will culminate with the epic sea battle of Surigao Strait, where the resurrected battleships of Pearl Harbor played a key role in a decisive victory over the Imperial Japanese Navy.

The story is not just about the battleships themselves, of course, but also the officers and men who commanded and sailed them. While providing an overall strategic view of the Pacific War, it also endeavors to describe the often indescribable, that being the violent fury of naval combat.

The war in the Pacific was unparalleled in terms of the numbers of ships, airplanes, and personnel involved, the vast distances over which it was fought, its horrifying destructiveness, and in the vitriol and savagery displayed by both sides. That being said, the author would like to ask in advance for the reader's patience and understanding with regard to certain direct quotations used in the text, containing expressions and epithets which some might find disturbing. The omission or altering of these quotations was certainly considered, but in the end, the decision was made to include them. It was felt that any effort to omit or sanitize the words used by those who fought in the Pacific to express the visceral hatred the two sides felt for one another would result in an unrealistic misrepresentation of history.

The remarkable, if not miraculous, process of healing and the cultivation of partnership and trust that has occurred between the United States and Japan in the eight decades following the war has certainly shown us that the abandonment of such hatred is possible.

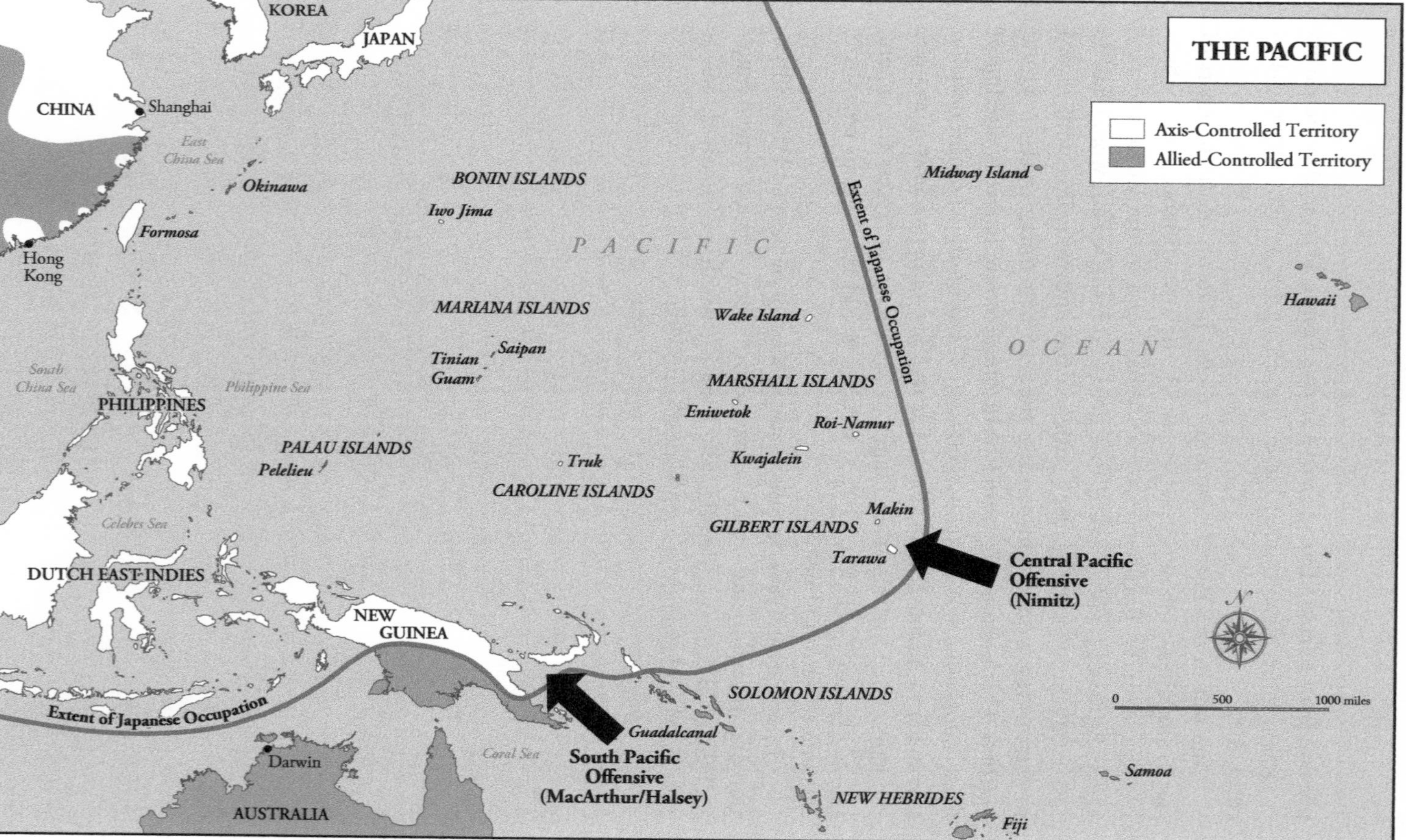
THE PACIFIC
Axis-Controlled Territory
Allied-Controlled Territory
KOREA
JAPAN
CHINA
Shanghai
East China Sea
Okinawa
Formosa
Hong Kong
BONIN ISLANDS
Iwo Jima
PACIFIC
OCEAN
Midway Island
Extent of Japanese Occupation
Hawaii
MARIANA ISLANDS
Saipan
Tinian
Guam
South China Sea
Philippine Sea
PHILIPPINES
Wake Island
MARSHALL ISLANDS
Eniwetok
Roi-Namur
Kwajalein
PALAU ISLANDS
Pelelieu
Truk
CAROLINE ISLANDS
Makin
GILBERT ISLANDS
Tarawa
Central Pacific Offensive (Nimitz)
Celebes Sea
DUTCH EAST INDIES
NEW GUINEA
SOLOMON ISLANDS
0
500
1000 miles
Extent of Japanese Occupation
Guadalcanal
Darwin
Coral Sea
South Pacific Offensive (MacArthur/Halsey)
Samoa
NEW HEBRIDES
AUSTRALIA
Fiji

CHAPTER 1
WAI MOMI

Darkness falls quickly in the tropics.

It had been a beautifully languid afternoon on the island of Oahu. Fragrant trade winds gently swayed the loulu palms along the beaches and glided smoothly over the emerald mountains, carrying with them the familiar scents of passion flower and jasmine along with the faint, sweet smell of smoke from the fires of the late-year sugarcane harvest.

Reflecting the deep cobalt blue of the brilliantly lit sky, the sea pounded ashore at Waikiki. Tourists sunned themselves on the warm sand or sipped tropical drinks on the lanai of the Moana Hotel, having made the passage from San Francisco on the Matson steamship line to escape the winter cold of the mainland, an unmistakable sign that the economic despair of the past decade was finally on the wane. Among the displays of Aloha sport shirts and colorful *pareaus* in the windows of the shops along King Street, *Mele Kalikimaka* decorations had begun to appear, featuring a Santa Claus festooned with flower leis in an outrigger canoe towed by a team of dolphins. Many hundreds of happy locals streamed past on their way to Honolulu Stadium to watch the Rainbow Warriors of the University of Hawaii face the Willamette Bearcats of Oregon in the annual Shriner Classic football game.

A few miles to the west were the cloud-topped hills of Aiea Heights, their pineapple and sugarcane fields a deep green cross-hatched by roads of red dirt, sloping gently downward to the sprawling blue lagoon that native Hawaiians called *Wai Momi*, or "waters of pearl." An abundance of pearl-bearing oysters was once harvested here, one of the finest natural harbors in the world and home to the ancient Hawaiian shark goddess *Ka'ahupahau*. Amid its placid waters lay the silent gray battleships of the United States Pacific Fleet.

In late November, the battle fleet had put to sea for a series of training exercises in the waters surrounding the island of Maui. Those sun-washed days had been filled with tactical formation drills, the launching and recovering of seaplanes, air defense and antisubmarine exercises, and an extensive amount of gunnery practice. At night the fleet would lie at anchor off Maui's Lahaina Roads, with the battleship crews taking their evening chow, listening to *hapa haole* music broadcast from Honolulu's NBC affiliate KGU, and preparing to repeat the same series of drills the following morning.

The fleet had returned to Pearl Harbor in time for the first full liberty weekend following the US Navy's monthly payday. As the battleships entered the anchorage the tireless harbor tugboats went to work, nudging each immense dreadnought into position to face south along the eastern edge of Ford Island in the center of the harbor, against a line of white concrete mooring quays that had become known as Battleship Row. Under the orders of Admiral Husband E. Kimmel, Commander-in-Chief Pacific Fleet, the ships were poised in this manner so as to be aimed toward the harbor entrance.

Amid a stream of messages from Washington, warning of an imminent conflict with the increasingly belligerent Empire of Japan, Admiral Kimmel wanted his capital ships to be in a position to sortie immediately should a hostile force approach the islands. From Kimmel's offices on the second floor of the submarine base headquarters building in Pearl Harbor's southeastern loch, a splendid view could be had of Battleship Row.

It was truly an awe-inspiring sight. To view one of these magnificent steel behemoths at rest and up close, let alone eight of them, would render speechless even the most passionate and pacifistic of isolationists. Marvels of early-twentieth-century engineering and technological innovation, they served as stirring symbols of the wealth, prestige, and power of a still-young nation. They were emblematic of the upstart agrarian republic that had grown to become an industrial giant through adventurism, toil, and conquest, to take its place among the great economic and military powers of the world.

Although there were four different classes of battleships present in Pearl Harbor that afternoon, all shared similar characteristics. Any sleek or graceful lines they possessed were there by pure coincidence, for they were of the most utilitarian design. Even their handsome clipper bows were contoured for keeping their foredecks dry while plowing through heavy seas. Modern battleships were built to fulfill a singular purpose: to locate, close with, and destroy an enemy fleet through the use of overwhelming firepower, supplied by the huge rifles with which each ship fairly bristled, weapons capable of hurling an 1,800-pound shell nearly 20 miles.

At the quay numbered Fox Three at the forward point of Battleship Row lay the USS *California.* First launched in 1916 and a stalwart of the Pacific battle fleet since the early 1930s, she flew the flag of Vice Admiral William Pye, the commander of Battle Force Pacific Fleet. The *California* was known to the US Navy as a "standard-type battleship," and like the rest of her companions in Pearl Harbor she was over 600 feet long, nearly 100 feet at the beam, and displaced some 33,000 tons. To her crew, however, she was affectionately known as the "Prune Barge," a reference to the enormous number of plums grown and harvested in the state of California.

Lying off the *California*'s stern was the *Maryland*, or "Old Mary" to her crew, with the truly old *Oklahoma,* a veteran of thirty years' service, tied to her port side. Moored behind the *Maryland* was the *Tennessee*, sister of the *California*, with the "Wee Vee," the *West Virginia,* standing outboard. Tied to quay Fox Seven, just 75 feet astern of the *Tennessee*, was the proud flagship of Rear Admiral Isaac Kidd's Battleship Division One, the *Arizona*. Moored singly at the tail end of Battleship Row lay the *Nevada*. In Dry Dock Number One across the channel rested the Pacific Fleet flagship *Pennsylvania*, in the midst of an overhaul, with three of her four huge bronze screws removed.

To serve aboard a battleship in the United States Navy was a distinct honor. With most of the world already at war, the battleship force was viewed as the primary means of fulfilling the navy's mission of projecting American power and deterring foreign aggression. They were the core of the Pacific Fleet: The cruisers, destroyers, submarines, aircraft, and auxiliaries were all there to facilitate bringing the big guns of the "battlewagons" into position to do their deadly work. Discipline in the battleship navy was notoriously strict, and standards for performance were extraordinarily high. As a result, the battleship crews were well-drilled and fiercely proud.

On the weather decks of each battleship, lean and brown young sailors of the deck divisions labored in the bright Hawaiian sunshine. Teakwood decks were onerously scrubbed with holystones until gleaming, gun barrels were swabbed and oiled, brightwork polished, and ubiquitous gray paint daubed onto hundreds of scraped steel surfaces. Mail boats, garbage lighters, officers' gigs, and dozens of other small craft sped back and forth between Battleship Row and the Navy Yard to the southeast, the waters of the narrow channel left heaving in their wake. Repair vessels and oilers were tied up alongside, and skilled workmen were tending to the hundreds of items that required maintenance aboard a battleship. Fuel bunkers were topped off with oil for firing the huge boilers of the ships; the *Arizona* alone took on 1,500 tons in preparation for another round of training exercises scheduled to begin on Monday morning.

Accommodations on Oahu were sparse and expensive, and since the relocation of the fleet from the West Coast to Pearl Harbor, very few navy men had been able to have their wives and families join them in Hawaii. Unless they occupied a billet in one of the shore installations most sailors lived aboard their ships, which were expected to be manned with the appropriate watches standing around the clock. Liberty for the crew was therefore granted by section. Sailors berthed on the port side of the ship would usually have liberty on the first day of making port, while the starboard section had the following day off.

Chief Petty Officer Joe Karb of the *Arizona* was one of the lucky ones. In early summer his wife and daughter had arrived from the mainland and Joe was spared from having to stand watch over the weekend while the ship was in port. Feeling guilty that the unaccompanied Chief William Tisdale had the duty while he was ashore with his family, Joe returned to the *Arizona* on Saturday morning.

"What the hell's the matter? Your wife throw you out?" Tisdale teased. "We don't want you here—get off the ship!"

Not everyone went ashore during their liberty hours. A few chose to remain aboard to write letters or catch up on their sleep after standing the grueling all-night midwatch. Signalman Robert Boulton decided that he would stay aboard and take in the movie being shown that night in the fresh air of the *California*'s quarterdeck, away from the stifling steel compartment where he lived. Ensign Jim Miller planned to go to bed early in his two-man stateroom aboard the *Arizona*. With the repair ship *Vestal* tied alongside to perform routine upkeep, Miller was anticipating a long work day ahead for his Third Division.

For unmarried men below the rank of petty officer second class, it was a "Cinderella liberty." On the quarterdeck of each battleship, enlisted sailors stood inspection in their undress white uniforms before queuing up for the liberty boats, anxious to get ashore for a few hours of frivolity before having to report back on board by midnight. Taking the advice of the old salts, a few of the younger sailors stashed a dime in the square knot of their black silk kerchief, so they would not return to the ship flat broke.

Spilling out of liberty boats and across the planks of Merry Point Landing, some sailors would choose to grab their first cold beer at a nearby honky-tonk like the Pearl City Tavern or the Tin Roof. Others headed for the sound of big band music drifting across the water from the new Bloch Recreation Center, where musicians from each of the battleships were warming up for the Battle of the Bands. Seventeen-year-old Edmund Chappell looked forward to an afternoon of swimming and relaxation on the beach before having to return to the *Maryland* for mess duty the following morning. Ensign Everett Malcolm of the *Arizona* invited his girlfriend Marian to join him for a round of golf at the Ala Wai links.

Most would press on, beyond the main gate where the "Wahoo Cannonball," the liberty bus, sat waiting along with several enterprising taxi drivers to take them into downtown Honolulu. The bus lines from Pearl Harbor, Fort Shafter, Wheeler Field, Schofield Barracks, Kaneohe Bay, and every other military installation on Oahu all ended at the Army-Navy YMCA, a handsome white three-story building at the corner of Richards and Hotel Streets. For those lucky enough to have scored an overnight pass, "The Y" promised a hot dog, a Coca-Cola, a cot, and a blanket for fifty cents. Across the bustling street was the famous and perpetually crowded Black Cat Cafe, where a porterhouse steak with mushrooms served by a sassy and voluptuous Portuguese waitress could be ordered for a dollar.

A brief and ethereal Hawaiian sunset quickly gave way to a night sky lit by thousands of luminescent stars. In the sultry air along Hotel Street, which spanned Chinatown and the downtown district, rushing streams of khaki converged with the flood tide of navy white as sailors, soldiers, and marines crowded into the local watering holes. The crew of the *Arizona* trended toward Smith's Union Bar, an old sailors' dive near Hotel Street and Nu'uanu Avenue. The *Nevada* men would often gather at Shanghai Bill's, while sailors from the *Maryland* frequented the Four Aces Tavern. Not everyone made it into the bars. After encountering the hard, piercing glares of huge Polynesian bouncers guarding the doorways, many underage sailors felt compelled to seek their entertainment elsewhere.

The cinema offered a welcome distraction, as it had in their childhood during the Great Depression. That weekend saw the island's premiere of *A Yank in the RAF*, starring Tyrone Power and Betty Grable, at the Waikiki Theater. Charlie Chaplin's *The Great Dictator* was playing at the Princess on Fort Street, while the Liliha showed the latest installment of the Bing Crosby and Bob Hope *Road to* comedy series, with a stunning Dorothy Lamour joining them in *Road to Zanzibar*.

Bill Guerin was eighteen years old and striking for a gunner's mate rating aboard the *Arizona*. "I had my first date with a beautiful Hawaiian-Portuguese girl that I met in the skating rink," Bill remembered. "That was my first real date—and that was the end of it. I never saw her again."

"There are almost no white girls whom the sailors can meet," stated an article in the October 1940 edition of *Life* magazine spotlighting the US fleet in Hawaii, "and since the average of enlisted men are high school–trained, ambitious and self-respecting, they do not want to have dates with native girls or underworld whites."

Contrary to this high-toned and bigoted rhetoric, one would have had difficulty locating an American sailor in Hawaii at the time who was willing to forsake the charms of a doe-eyed young wahine. Not many of them were above seeking the comforts of an "underworld white" either, especially after a few weeks at sea. For those wishing to get "stewed, screwed and tattooed," as the time-honored navy expression goes, one had to look no further than that section of downtown Honolulu bordered by River and Fort Streets to the north and south, and between Hotel and Kukui Streets to the east and west.

The ramshackle buildings along these narrow streets were home to that certain variety of entrepreneurship commonly found close to military bases. There were the usual barbershops, shooting galleries, and predatory pawn shops. There were the kind of trinket kiosks that cater to servicemen everywhere, pedaling pocketknives, cigarette lighters embossed with army and navy insignia, and cheap souvenirs "from the South Seas." Tattoo parlors featured the type of unimaginative, standard-issue artwork one might expect, that of exotic women, swooping eagles, coiled cobras, and fouled anchors. For ten cents, a sailor could have his photograph taken in the arms of a busty, grass-skirted maiden before an inexpertly rendered and horribly tacky backdrop of Diamond Head, flanked by potted palm trees. Finally, there were no fewer than twenty establishments like the Palace, the Ritz Rooms, and the New Senator Hotel; the names never fooled anyone, regardless of how dignified the proprietors tried to make them sound.

On liberty weekends, Honolulu's red-light district did a brisk and profitable business. By early afternoon the front parlors of the various cathouses, staffed by attractive young women recruited from mainland cities, were crowded shoulder to shoulder with men in uniform. Services were provided for ten furious minutes at the rate of three dollars, or roughly 10 percent of the monthly pay then earned by a junior enlisted soldier or sailor. In the interest of safeguarding the greater good and keeping the wandering servicemen contained in the downtown area, the Honolulu police tended to look the other way so long as the houses were kept clean, forbid the sale or consumption of alcohol on the premises, and the girls received regular examinations from a physician.

"Such liberties were the true test of health and stamina," Ted Mason of the *California* would record in his memoirs. "Every block held its dangers, in the form of shore patrol, police or bouncers; merchants, bar girls, or cabbies; occasional roving bands of island toughs, or other sailors, soldiers or marines carried away by inter-ship or inter-service rivalries."

This particular evening, however, was remembered as being rather unremarkable and quiet in Honolulu. As the Cinderella hour approached, the Shore Patrol made their usual sweep through the downtown to police-up any inebriated or disheveled personnel left behind. Not many were found, and there were only a couple of inane fistfights to break up. It seemed that few men wanted to risk arriving aboard ship after midnight and having to explain themselves at Captain's Mast the following morning.

Years later, many who served aboard the battleships in Pearl Harbor would be hard-pressed to recall exactly where they went or what they were doing on this particular day. Robert Duncan from the *Tennessee* would have difficultly remembering whether he went ashore at all. Some would recall the usually festive mood of downtown Honolulu as being somewhat subdued, replaced by a certain intangible tension that hung thickly in the humid night air.

"We knew for some time that we were going to get mixed up in something, but this particular night it just felt a little uneasy," Russell Lott from the *Arizona* would remember. Since Russell and his buddy had the duty the following morning, they returned to the ship early from liberty.

"Just the whole atmosphere in the town," Lott recalled. "It just didn't feel right."

The date was Saturday, December 6, 1941.

CHAPTER 2
THE PHILOSOPHER

It was in the summer of 1886 that a distinguished-looking gentleman, having just arrived from his home in New York City, first ascended the steps of a stately two-story stone building that was surrounded by well-manicured lawns and overlooked the calm waters of Narragansett Bay in Newport, Rhode Island. Forty-five years old, approaching complete baldness and possessing a pair of brooding blue eyes and a neatly trimmed gray beard, he carried himself with something more of a professorial air than with the commanding presence of a naval officer. His name was Captain Alfred Thayer Mahan, the newly appointed president of the United States Naval War College.

The news of the appointment undoubtedly caused some eyebrows to be raised among the members of the navy's officer corps, for Mahan's career to that point had been anything but estimable. Perhaps because the newly established Naval War College had yet to earn the prestige of a highly regarded research institute and renowned center for the professional development of naval and military officers, it must have seemed like a safe place to install the hapless Captain Mahan.

Some thirty years earlier, and despite the objections of his father, a well-respected professor of civil engineering at the US Military Academy at West Point, young Alfred had applied for and was accepted to the US Naval Academy after spending two years at Columbia College in New York.

"He told me he thought me much less fit for a military than for a civilian profession, having watched me carefully," Alfred would write. "I think myself now that he was right." Although he graduated second in the Class of 1859, it soon became apparent that seamanship was not Alfred Thayer Mahan's strong suit.

"I am not very smart in this sort of work," Mahan would admit to the pages of his diary while serving aboard the screw schooner USS *Iroquois*. Early in his career he struggled mightily with basic navigation and ship handling, and over the years Mahan had been responsible for a number of maritime embarrassments while serving aboard various naval vessels.

Mahan was in command of the USS *Wasp* on its mission to chart the South American coast when the sidewheel gunboat ran aground in the Rio de la Plata estuary. On another occasion the unfortunate *Wasp* collided with a harbor lighter. When he neglected to inquire into the dimensions and depth of the dry dock at Montevideo, Mahan managed to get the *Wasp* hopelessly lodged. Captain Mahan was at the conn when his last seagoing command, the elderly screw sloop-of-war *Wachusett*, collided with a merchant sailing ship off the coast of Peru, badly damaging both vessels.

"Why, the Pacific Ocean wasn't big enough for us to keep out of the other fellow's way," one of Mahan's officers quipped.

Overtly vain, sanctimonious, and ill-tempered, Mahan was rather unpopular among the officers of the various wardrooms to which he belonged and with the enlisted sailors in his charge. Disenchanted and bored by the relentless tedium of his profession, he was at the same time plagued by a persistent paucity of confidence and an abundance of self-doubt. These factors, along with Mahan's capacity for accidents, contributed to a serious disdain for sea duty.

"I found myself perplexed by my pretty strong conviction that the employments to which I am forced are a waste of time, and by the opposite fact that I am bound to obedience and submission," Mahan would write. Later he would admit: "I have found myself very subject to nervousness and excitability, a frequent trouble when business presses."

While at sea Mahan was something of an introvert; when he wasn't performing his official duties he would often sequester himself in his cabin, where he would read voraciously. Consuming volume after volume of naval and military history, he became particularly enamored of the writings of Antoine-Henri Jomini, the French general and military theorist of the Napoleonic era. In 1883, while assigned to the pedestrian billet of navigation officer for the Brooklyn Navy Yard (his duties included supervising the inventory of signal flags), Mahan published his first book, *The Gulf and Inland Waters*, which examined the role of the Union Navy in the Civil War.

It was therefore the mind of Alfred Thayer Mahan, not his popularity or proficiency as an officer, that inspired Rear Admiral Steven Luce to invite him to join the faculty of the Naval War College. Luce had been commanding officer of the Naval Academy's sailing frigate *Macedonian* during Mahan's posting to Annapolis as an instructor in 1863. Admiring Mahan's devotion to the study of history and noting their shared advocacy of naval reform, Luce thought Mahan would be ideal for a professorship in history and tactics. In June 1884, Steven Luce won approval for Mahan, then patrolling the Pacific coast of South America aboard the *Wachusett*, to be assigned to the Naval War College.

Mahan accepted the appointment with enthusiasm, all too happy to be relieved from his inglorious command. "I ought to go home at once and be given till at least next summer to get up the work," he wrote to Admiral Luce.

Following the decommissioning of the tired *Wachusett*, Mahan did indeed return home to New York and began assembling a series of lectures on naval history. Before this task could be completed, however, Admiral Luce would accept one final seagoing command prior to reaching the age of mandatory retirement. In June 1886 Luce took over the navy's North Atlantic Squadron, and his nominal second-in-command, Captain Mahan, replaced him as college president.

As it would turn out, Mahan's career had only just begun, his true brilliance yet to reveal itself. In a relatively short period of time Alfred Thayer Mahan would become one of the most celebrated and influential military philosophers in world history, as much so as Sun Tzu or von Clausewitz.

In a series of now-famous lectures delivered to the Naval War College, Mahan would declare that it was essential to the survival and prosperity of any nation-state geographically positioned on a seacoast to develop a thriving maritime trade and build a strong navy to protect it. "The ships that thus sail to and fro must have secure ports to which to return," Mahan would write, "and must as far as possible, be followed by the protection of their country throughout the voyage."

Using the history and development of the British Empire as an example throughout many of his lectures, Mahan stressed the importance of the establishment of overseas territories and trade routes for the export of manufactures and the import of critically needed resources. The navy, rather than functioning solely as a protector of its own shores and harbors, must assure free and unfettered navigation of the seas for the "peaceful commerce and shipping from which alone a military fleet naturally and healthfully springs, and on which it securely rests."

The mission of protecting seaborne trade should be supported by advanced bases and fortified coaling stations for the battle fleet in ports acquired along commercial shipping lanes, Mahan would advocate. These bases would also serve as a means for the navy to project power abroad and expand the nation's sphere of influence in a given region. Between those bases "there must be reasonably secure communication, which will depend on military control of the intervening sea," Mahan would explain. "This control must be exercised by the navy, which will enforce it by clearing the sea in all directions of hostile cruisers, thus allowing the ships of its own nation to pass with reasonable security."

In time of war, this robust network of advanced bases would serve not only as a "defense in depth" but also would aid the fleet in carrying the fight to the enemy, far from the shores of its home country. A concentrated fleet of modern battleships working in concert with numerous cruisers and destroyers, augmented by an adequate force of auxiliaries such as colliers and ammunition vessels, would then destroy the enemy's fleet and its seaborne commerce through superior firepower. The mere presence of such a formidable naval force, Mahan further theorized, would likely discourage a potential enemy from starting a war in the first place.

Mahan's argument for a strong navy to fulfill the mission of assuring safe navigation of the seas not only resonated strongly with officers attending the Naval War College, it also served as the doctrinal basis for the US Navy's efforts to re-man and modernize an aged and anemic fleet suffering from two decades of neglect following the Civil War.

Mahan's influence, however, would soon spread far beyond the Navy Department. In 1890, Mahan's lectures were published in the book *The Influence of Sea Power upon History*, which immediately found an enthusiastic audience among expansionists intent on establishing American hegemony in the Western Hemisphere and the Pacific, and for whom the concept of "Manifest Destiny" did not stop at America's shoreline.

"My dear Captain Mahan," Theodore Roosevelt would write. "During the last two days I have spent half my time, busy as I am, in reading your book; and that I found it interesting is shown by the fact that having taken it up I have gone straight through and finished it."

In part, it had been Mahan's strategic vision that inspired President Benjamin Harrison, along with his progressive Navy Secretary Benjamin Tracy, to launch the United States Navy into the age of steam and steel. The first move toward a "new navy" was the Naval Appropriations Act of 1891, which saw the authorization of three modern battleships, the *Indiana*, *Massachusetts*, and *Oregon*. Although modernization of the US Navy would briefly stall during the second administration of Grover Cleveland, it would resume with great vigor after the election of William McKinley in 1897.

Mahan and Roosevelt first met in 1888, when the young politician had been a guest lecturer at the Naval War College following the publication of his book *The Naval War of 1812*. It had been the start of an intellectual collaboration between the two men that would continue long after Roosevelt's appointment as Assistant Secretary of the Navy under McKinley.

"We need a large navy," Roosevelt would state, echoing Mahan's principles, "composed not only of cruisers, but containing also a full proportion of powerful battleships, able to meet those of any other nation."

During his brief tenure in that office, Roosevelt often consulted with Mahan through confidential correspondence. As war with Spain drew near, Roosevelt allowed the president of the Naval War College to study the navy's deployment plan for the anticipated campaign in the Caribbean. Upon receiving Mahan's comments, Roosevelt replied: "There is no question that you stand head and shoulders above the rest of us! You probably don't know how much your letter has really helped me clearly to formulate certain things which I had only vaguely in my mind. I think I have studied your books to great purpose."

Victory in the Spanish-American War of 1898 saw the establishment of American naval facilities in Cuba's Guantanamo Bay, Puerto

Rico, Guam, and the Philippines. Efforts to annex the Hawaiian Islands as a United States territory and secure Pearl Harbor as a permanent naval base, the benefits of which Mahan and Roosevelt had discussed at length, would come to fruition the following year. Mahan would lend his by-then considerable influence with policy makers to the argument for a trans-isthmus canal in Central America, and during Roosevelt's presidency the United States would take over the failed Panama Canal construction project.

More than anything else, the modern US Navy would come to represent the "big stick" in Roosevelt's famous aphorism regarding American foreign policy. "I wish to see the United States the dominant power on the shores of the Pacific Ocean," the president announced.

In 1907 Roosevelt would send the "Great White Fleet" of sixteen new battleships and their supporting vessels, each painted a sparkling white, on a grand tour that circumnavigated the globe and visited over twenty foreign ports in a prodigious display of American sea power. By that time the United States Navy had risen from its decrepit state to become the third-largest battle fleet in the world behind those of Britain and France.

Not only would the work of Alfred Thayer Mahan help to inspire an American naval renaissance, it would receive significant critical acclaim from a global audience. Mahan would be received by Queen Victoria of England, honored with degrees from Oxford and Cambridge, and celebrated by British navalists for the soundness of his strategic doctrine and the eloquence of its presentation. The highly impressionable Kaiser Wilhelm II, according to historian Barbara Tuchman, was "bewitched by Mahan," seeing an expansive naval construction program as a means to achieve parity with what he conceived to be Germany's most dangerous rival, Great Britain. After he had "devoured" Captain Mahan's book, the Kaiser ordered a copy to be placed in the wardroom of every German warship.

The Influence of Sea Power Upon History would, in fact, become required reading for the officers of many foreign navies after being translated into several languages . . . including Japanese.

CHAPTER 3
RISING SUN

In 1869, Lieutenant Commander Mahan was serving as executive officer of the USS *Iroquois* on her cruise to the Far East when the American warship called upon several ports in Japan, including Yokohama and Nagasaki. At that time the island nation was in the final throes of a vicious civil war, which brought an end to the feudal Tokugawa shogunate and saw the restoration of imperial rule.

As he sought to consolidate his power and establish political control over the Japanese Home Islands, Emperor Meiji would turn to the West for assistance in modernizing his nation's infrastructure, including port facilities, railroads, mines, factories, and telegraph communications. Having borne witness to the subjugation of China and Korea by Western empires and determined that Japan should never become the vassal state of a European power, the Meiji government adopted the phrase *Fukoku kyōhei* as a national byword, meaning "Enrich the Nation, Strengthen the Military."

It was the destiny of the Empire of Japan, they believed, to become the dominant economic and military power in Greater East Asia. This would require an assertive foreign policy to counter the encroachments of Britain, France, and Russia, backed by a highly trained and disciplined army equipped with the latest weaponry. A modern navy powerful enough to contend with the Asiatic squadrons of Western nations would also be needed, not only to protect mainland Japan from invasion but also to support the expeditionary forces of the army.

Until the military and industrial base of Japan could be developed to challenge that of rival nations, however, the expertise, technology, and resources required to establish a modern army and navy would have to be imported from those very same rivals. The British Royal Navy, master of the seas for well over a century, would provide the template for the organization and doctrine of what would become the Imperial Japanese Navy.

In 1873, a British delegation led by Sir Archibald Douglas trained the first class of thirty Japanese naval officers. Douglas would remain in Japan until 1879 as an instructor at the new Naval Academy in the Hiroshima Prefecture. Several of his graduates would in turn journey to Great Britain to study engineering, gunnery, propulsion, naval architecture, and other technical disciplines. In 1888, the Japanese would establish their own naval war college in Tokyo's Tsukiji district.

For the construction of its first modern warships and naval bases, the Empire of Japan would turn to the French as well as the British. French engineers would design four major naval stations in the port cities of Sasebo, Maizuru, Yokosuka, and Kure. For fiscal as well as strategic reasons the Japanese would at first adhere to the *Jeune École,* or "young school" concept of naval defense, which advocated the use of fast protected cruisers and numerous small, speedy torpedo boats to perform deadly hit-and-run attacks on an approaching enemy fleet, a system that the French Navy had employed with some success in past conflicts. Since the Japanese did not yet possess the technical ability or industrial capacity to produce state-of-the-art warships, the keels of these first combatants were laid in French and British shipyards. The Imperial Japanese Navy would accumulate a dozen protected cruisers and some two dozen torpedo boats by 1894, when it steamed into combat for the first time.

The Battle of the Yalu would see the new Japanese Navy soundly defeat the Beiyang Fleet of China's Qing Dynasty. Even though the Chinese possessed two ironclad battleships and theoretically had the advantage, the superb training and discipline of the Japanese crews, the higher quality and condition of their warships, and their clearly superior tactical command and gunnery carried the day. While half of the ships of the Japanese Combined Fleet sustained considerable damage, five Chinese ships were sunk and over eight hundred Chinese sailors lost. This decisive action was the knockout punch required for the Japanese to gain control of the seas surrounding the Korean peninsula, contributing greatly to their overall victory in the First Sino-Japanese War.

Although wounded himself, Lieutenant Tetsutaro Sato had assumed command of the steam gunboat *Akagi* after her captain was killed by a Chinese shell during the Battle of the Yalu. After the war Sato was sent to Great Britain and the United States to study naval tactics and strategy, and upon his return he reported to the Naval War College to serve as an instructor. In 1901 Sato wrote a position paper for the Navy Ministry entitled *On the Defense of the Empire*, applying several lessons from the work of Alfred Thayer Mahan to the strategic situation faced by Japan in the early twentieth century. Specifically, Sato argued that it was not enough for the navy to maintain command of the seas close to the Home Islands; it must also be able to project a superior offensive capability abroad. The best way to safeguard the Empire, Sato wrote, was to be able to destroy an enemy fleet long before it reached Japan.

In the decade that followed, Tetsutaro Sato would continue lecturing at the Naval War College between tours of sea duty, all the while developing a thesis for yet another groundbreaking document that would greatly shape the future of Japanese naval doctrine. While the strategic tenets discussed in *The Influence of Sea Power Upon History* and subsequent writings by Alfred Thayer Mahan would remain central to Sato's work, he would examine and draw conclusions from a number of significant events that would occur in the opening years of the new century.

Just before midnight on February 8, 1904, four Japanese destroyers launched a surprise torpedo attack against the Russian battle fleet anchored in Port Arthur, Manchuria, the opening salvo in a war fought over the conflicting imperial aspirations of both nations in the Far East. The attack—initiated three hours prior to a formal declaration of war by Japan—heavily damaged two Russian battleships and a protected cruiser.

By this time the Imperial Japanese Navy, having dispensed with *Jeune École* concepts in favor of a strictly offensive Mahanian philosophy, had grown well beyond a plucky coastal defense force. At the center of the Japanese Combined Fleet under Admiral Heihachiro Togo was a squadron of six modern steel battleships, each constructed in British shipyards and displacing between 12,000 and 15,000 tons, powered by coal-fired triple-expansion steam engines and armed with main batteries of 12-inch guns. Although the following morning the Japanese were driven off by Russian shore batteries, they managed to keep the Russian ships bottled up in Port Arthur and maintained the initiative over the following seventeen months of the conflict.

The Russian Pacific Squadron would make several unsuccessful attempts to break the Japanese blockade of Port Arthur. The final attempt was made on August 10, 1904, and resulted in the Battle of the Yellow Sea, a fourteen-hour-long pitched battle between two fleets of armored steamships, the first in world history. When the smoke had cleared all six of Togo's battleships were damaged and over three hundred of his men were dead, but the Russians, having suffered a similar number of casualties, were forced to return to Port Arthur.

Czar Nicholas II then ordered the Russian Baltic Fleet under Admiral Zinovy Rozhestvensky to set sail for the Pacific from its base at St. Petersburg, with the mission of relieving Port Arthur. The decision was made at the urging of the instigatious Kaiser Wilhelm II, who implored his cousin Nicholas to destroy the "Yellow Peril" that threatened the existence of European colonialism in Asia. Rozhestvensky's orders would change in January 1905, while the Baltic Fleet was still en route to the Far East. Port Arthur had fallen. The destruction of the Russian Pacific Squadron had come, ironically, at the hands of the Imperial Japanese Army, after they seized the heights overlooking Port Arthur and directed artillery fire onto the anchorage below.

Rozhestvensky's fleet finally arrived at Cam Rahn Bay in French Indochina on the last day of March, after an arduous 16,000-mile voyage around Africa's Cape of Good Hope. Exhausted after seven months at sea, suffering from rampant sickness and near-mutinous morale, the Russians spent the entire month of April in Indochina taking on coal and attempting to reorganize, to the great annoyance of the French colonial government. Rozhestvensky's fleet finally departed on the first day of May with the new mission of joining forces with the Russian naval squadron in the port of Vladivostok and then finishing the Japanese once and for all. As the Russian vessels passed in column through the Tsushima Strait on the afternoon of May 27, 1905, they found the Japanese Combined Fleet lying in wait.

The previous night two Russian hospital ships, not observing blackout conditions like the warships they were trailing, had remained illuminated "like bright stars" as they neared the tip of the Korean peninsula. In another historical first, the wireless telegraph would greatly affect the outcome of a naval engagement, when alert Japanese pickets relayed the position of the Russian armada to Admiral Togo.

From the bridge of his flagship *Knyaz Suvorov*, Rozhestvensky signaled his twelve battleships to form a line abreast, but the maneuver was so lamely executed that the fleet commander abandoned the attempt and countermanded the order. The result was two ragged, parallel columns of Russian vessels steaming northeast toward the Japanese, who were 7 miles ahead and in a single column moving west. At eight minutes after two o'clock, the *Suvorov* opened fire at a range of 7,000 yards and the Japanese were soon enveloped in a withering barrage from the Russian fleet.

The Japanese were down to four battleships, having lost both the *Hatsuse* and the *Yashima* to Russian mines off Port Arthur on May 15. Their absence would have little effect on the outcome of the battle, other than to underscore the brilliance of what would be a very one-sided Japanese victory. In an act that would earn him the nickname "the Japanese Nelson," Heihachiro Togo sent the signal "*[T]he Empire's fate depends on the result of this battle, let every man do his utmost duty*," and ordered his flagship *Mikasa* to turn sharply to port. The remainder of the Japanese battle line followed in *Mikasa*'s wake, making a countermarch to the east in front of the Russian vanguard, effectively "crossing the T" of the enemy columns. This allowed the Japanese vessels to fire broadsides at the oncoming Russians, who could bring only their forward-facing gun turrets to bear. Only then did Togo hoist the signal to open fire.

With frightening accuracy, Japanese gunfire soon decimated the Russian battle line. Within minutes the *Suvorov* was a blazing wreck, hundreds of her crew were dead, and the ship's captain and Rozhestvensky were badly wounded. A fire aboard the *Borodino* quickly spread to an ammunition magazine; a young able seaman would be the sole survivor of her 728-man crew when the battleship blew up and sank. Her sister ship, the *Imperator Aleksandr*, was lost with all hands after she sustained several direct hits, took on water, and capsized. The battleship *Oslyabya* was holed by dozens of shells and plunged to the bottom of the Tsushima Strait an hour into the battle. The onslaught continued throughout the night, as Japanese destroyers and torpedo boats pressed home repeated, aggressive torpedo attacks on the beleaguered Russians. After losing two more battleships and two cruisers, the remnants of the Russian fleet surrendered the following morning.

Over four thousand Russians had died and nearly six thousand were taken prisoner. Twenty-one Russian warships had been sunk. Seven vessels, including four battleships, would end up in the hands of the Japanese. A half-dozen ships fled to neutral ports, where they were interned along with their crews for the duration. Only three ships of the Russian fleet escaped the slaughter to arrive safely in Vladivostok. Against this, the Russian Navy destroyed but three Japanese torpedo boats and inflicted some seven hundred casualties.

The Battle of Tsushima Strait would be a national humiliation for Imperial Russia, contributing greatly to the eventual downfall of Czar Nicholas II. Facing a rising tide of social and political unrest at home following Russia's stunning defeat, Nicholas would welcome the offer of American president Theodore Roosevelt to negotiate a peace treaty with Japan.

During the battle, Tetsutaro Sato had served on the staff of Vice Admiral Kamimura aboard his flagship, the armored cruiser *Izumo*. In 1906 Sato would return to the Naval War College to resume his work, armed with a wealth of new information and lessons learned from the Russo-Japanese War. The experience at Tsushima Strait served to validate a number of strategic precepts taught by Alfred Thayer Mahan as well as the operational planning of the Japanese Navy General Staff. Japan had benefited greatly from its investment in ships of high quality and in new technologies such as modern optics and range-finding equipment, wireless telegraphy, and improved munitions.

The enemy had been completely outclassed by Japan's efficient fleet maneuvering and superior gunnery, disciplines that could only be maintained through relentless drill and fleet exercises. The attrition strategy of night attacks by destroyers and torpedo boats against a much larger enemy fleet had proven to be highly successful and would become a mainstay of Japanese tactical doctrine.

In his 1902 work *Retrospect and Prospect*, Mahan wrote that one of the fundamental principles of naval warfare was "that defense is insured only by offense, and that the one decisive objective of the offensive is the enemy's organized force, his battle fleet." Considered incontrovertible in the halls of the Naval War College in Tokyo, adherence to this Mahanian catechism had been the key to Japanese victory. Admiral Togo had courageously sought the all-important *kantai kessen*, the decisive battle, where the enemy fleet had been soundly beaten by the superior gunfire of Japanese capital ships. Thereafter, the Japanese would view the *decisive fleet engagement* as the single most critical objective in naval combat, with an emphasis bordering on obsession. It would dominate strategic thinking in the Imperial Japanese Navy for the remainder of its existence.

Even as Tetsutaro Sato began a new series of lectures at the Naval War College using these examples to expand upon his earlier work, another momentous event occurred that not only would be a major turning point in the development of sea power—it would also have far-reaching geopolitical effects and touch off a massive naval arms race in the years leading up to the First World War.

CHAPTER 4
DREADNOUGHT

AT PORTSMOUTH DOCKYARD ON FEBRUARY 10, 1906, THE ROYAL NAVY launched the powerful HMS *Dreadnought.* The brainchild of First Sea Lord Admiral Sir John "Jackie" Fisher, in a single stroke the British established an entirely new standard for capital ship design and rendered obsolete every other battleship afloat.

At over 500 feet long and 80 feet at the beam, she displaced just over 18,000 tons. The *Dreadnought* was the first battleship to be propelled by steam-driven turbines, making her capable of an impressive 21 knots and thus the fastest battleship in the world. The importance of speed was just one of the lessons Jackie Fisher and the *Dreadnought*'s design team gleaned from the reports of British naval officers who had observed the Battle of Tsushima Strait and noted just how quickly Togo had outmaneuvered the slower ships of the Russian fleet.

The *Dreadnought* would be known as the first "all big gun" battleship, mounting five turrets of double 12-inch guns utilizing the latest fire control technology and capable of a range of over 20,000 yards, all but assuring that the Royal Navy would dominate any decisive fleet encounters like Tsushima in the foreseeable future. For protection against enemy shells and torpedoes, much of the *Dreadnought*'s Krupp-designed armor was nearly a foot thick. So revolutionary was her design that future battleships incorporating these advanced features became known as "dreadnoughts," while the now-antiquated battleships that came before her would be referred to as "pre-dreadnoughts."

The design and launching of the *Dreadnought* had come after the first of several naval appropriations acts were rammed through the German Reichstag by Kaiser Wilhelm II and his tenacious naval chief, Grand Admiral Alfred von Tirpitz. The Royal Navy, Tirpitz had assumed, with its ongoing commitment to safeguarding Britain's worldwide empire and communication of its seaborne commerce, would be able to concentrate only about two-thirds of its strength in European waters to confront the German High Seas Fleet in the event the two nations went to war.

The so-called Tirpitz Plan, therefore, called for the steady construction of capital ships until the navy of Imperial Germany was at least two-thirds as strong as that of the British. In this light the *Dreadnought* came to represent not only a quantum leap in the evolution of battleship design but also a dramatic raising of the stakes in a time of increasing Anglo-German hostility. Along with British insistence on adhering to a "Two Power Standard" of naval defense, which was defined as the Royal Navy maintaining a number of capital ships equal to a combination of the next two most powerful foreign fleets, the debut of the *Dreadnought* would lead Tirpitz to call for a further increase in German naval spending of 35 percent.

The first of Germany's dreadnoughts, the SMS *Nassau*, was laid down in Wilhelmshaven the following year. In response, British navalists would take up the cry "We Want Eight and We Won't Wait," demanding the construction of eight more dreadnoughts in the midst of the Liberal government's campaign to implement social welfare reform.

"The Admiralty wanted six ships, the economists offered four, we finally compromised on eight," First Lord of the Admiralty Winston Churchill would lament.

The shipyards of France, Russia, Austria-Hungary, and Italy were soon laying the keels of their own dreadnought battleships as the world's navies scrambled to maintain parity with potential enemies. Brazil ordered three dreadnoughts from British shipbuilding firms, prompting a decade-long naval arms race with South American rivals Argentina and Chile. In December 1906 the United States began construction on its first two dreadnoughts, the *South Carolina* and the *Michigan*. The first of a dozen standard-type battleships of the US Navy, the USS *Nevada*, would be laid down in 1911. These "super-dreadnoughts" were armed with 14-inch guns, powered by oil-fired steam turbines and featured an "all or nothing" armor scheme, where heavy armor protected the vital portions of the ship with the remaining sections receiving minimal protection.

In 1907, naval architects began drawing up plans for the dreadnoughts *Kawachi* and *Settsu*, among the first modern warships to be laid down in Japan rather than ordered from foreign shipyards. That same year, Captain Tetsutaro Sato would complete a new collection of lectures entitled *History of Naval Defense*, a publication that would greatly influence a generation of Japanese naval officers and the development of naval theory in Japan.

Expanding upon his earlier lectures and writings, which had greatly angered the leadership of the Japanese Army as they grappled with the navy for a greater slice of the Diet's military budget, Sato once again declared that the navy must be considered the island nation's first line of defense. Only by establishing naval dominance in the Pacific Basin could the Japanese Home Islands and overseas holdings be considered secure. Moreover, for the Empire to expand into overseas territories and secure vital strategic resources (into Southeast Asia, for example), the navy must be able to ensure the safe navigation of the intervening seas.

"Now is the time for our Empire to attempt world-wide expansion, and our world-wide expansion must of necessity depend on oceanic expansion," Sato wrote in a Mahanian fashion. "Japan must control world trade, and for this purpose it is absolutely necessary to obtain command of the sea." Japanese hegemony in Greater East Asia, in other words, was reliant upon the strength of the navy.

It would therefore be prudent, Sato would advocate, to identify the powers that may seek to deny such regional influence and control to Japan, or who may potentially threaten Japan itself. The planning of future naval construction and operations should focus on a potential confrontation with this *hypothetical enemy*. Following the defeat of Russia, the signing of an Anglo-Japanese alliance, and the American acquisition of Hawaii, Guam, Wake, and the Philippines, the selection of this hypothetical enemy was rather simple, as far as Sato and others in the Japanese naval hierarchy were concerned. There was only one potential enemy capable of challenging Japanese supremacy in the Pacific or posing an existential threat to Japan: the United States Navy.

"The infernal fools in California, and especially in San Francisco, insult the Japanese recklessly," President Theodore Roosevelt would write to his son Kermit. "However, I hope to keep things straight. I am perfectly willing that this nation should fight any nation if it has got to, but I would loathe to see it forced into a war in which it was wrong."

An October 1906 decision by the San Francisco school board to place all students of Japanese descent into a segregated Oriental School, to prevent "white children from being placed in any position where their youthful impressions may be affected by association with pupils of the Mongolian race," ignited a storm of anti-American outrage in Japan.

The "Yellow Peril" ideology that had swept through Europe in the late nineteenth and early twentieth centuries, trumpeted by the German Kaiser and others, expressed the belief that the unchecked expansion of Asian power and influence posed a danger to the way of life and security of the Western world. Many would point to the 1900 Boxer Rebellion in China as a frightful example, where gangs of anti-imperialist Chinese embarked upon a campaign of violence against foreigners, burning Christian churches and murdering missionaries across the country before plundering the city of Beijing and laying siege to the International Legation Quarter. A coalition of troops from six European nations, the United States, and Japan had to fight their way through the streets of Beijing to rescue their trapped diplomats and their families. Japan's trouncing of a major European power in the Russo-Japanese War had shocked the world, which Yellow Peril theorists considered another illustration of dark forces on the rise in Asia.

In America, Yellow Peril racism manifested itself in the alienation of Asian immigrants, along with riots and lynchings of Chinese laborers in several West Coast communities. Many white Americans feared and resented the Asian "coolies" who had "invaded" the country, especially for their willingness to work for much lower wages than their white neighbors, a visceral bias stoked by the leaders of the American Federation of Labor and other unions. This resulted in the Chinese Exclusion Act of 1870 and the Naturalization Act of 1906, which mandated that immigrants must speak English in order to obtain citizenship. The Japanese became the target of such American xenophobia after the annexation of Hawaii, when thousands of Hawaiian residents of Japanese descent migrated to California seeking work.

An ardent belief in the supremacy of the Japanese people over those of other Asian races, propagated by officials of the Imperial government to justify Japan's forced subjugation of Formosa and Korea, caused many Japanese political elites to become greatly offended by the actions of the San Francisco school board. The Americans had, after all, treated Japanese students with the same regard as the children of Chinese and Korean immigrants. With fervent nationalism and militarism on the rise in Japan following their recent triumph over Russia, some claimed that the American affront to Japanese honor was cause for war.

This was not the first time Theodore Roosevelt had incurred the wrath of the Japanese. When the Treaty of Portsmouth ended the Russo-Japanese War without an expected financial indemnity from Russia, the Japanese delegation placed the blame squarely on Roosevelt's shoulders, causing spirited anti-American demonstrations in many Japanese cities. Roosevelt was well aware of this and worked quickly to bring a satisfactory end to the Japanese immigration crisis, encouraging officials in San Francisco, the Republican governor, and California's congressional caucus to pressure the school board into reversing their policy. The damage, however, had already been done. Throughout Japanese society, a deep antipathy for the United States had already taken root.

The flames of the California crisis had barely reduced to a smolder before the Emperor granted his approval to the *Teikoku kokubo hoshin*, the Imperial National Defense Policy of 1907. Tetsutaro Sato and his colleague at the Naval War College, Captain Saneyuki Akiyama, were the chief architects of the naval portion of the document, which officially recognized the United States as a hypothetical enemy, ostensibly for determining the required strength of the Imperial Japanese Navy.

At that time the US Navy possessed eighteen battleships and twenty-seven cruisers (with four additional dreadnoughts under construction), a number of capital ships that the Japanese shipbuilding industry could never hope to match, even if Imperial coffers were able to provide the means. The Sato-Akiyama scheme, which resembled the Tirpitz Plan for challenging the immense strength of the Royal Navy, called for an "Eight-Eight Fleet," or a minimum of eight dreadnoughts and eight cruisers, with the eventual goal of achieving a force level equivalent to 70 percent of that maintained by the American Navy.

In the event of war with the United States it was assumed that the US Navy, with its strength divided over two oceans, would at first sortie its units in the Pacific to attack Japan. The 70 percent ratio would ensure that the Japanese had an adequate force of capital ships to defeat the Americans in a decisive battle before reinforcements from the US Atlantic squadron could arrive. Austerity measures and political wrangling with the Japanese Diet would frustrate the Navy Ministry's attempts to establish an Eight-Eight Fleet over the next decade and a half; in 1910 the first of several compromises was reached, resulting in orders for the construction of one battleship and four cruisers.

The battleship *Fuso* was laid down in 1912, a year after construction began on the battlecruiser *Kongo* at the Vickers shipyard in Great Britain. The *Kongo* would be the last Japanese capital ship to be built by a foreign nation; her sister ships, *Hiei*, *Kirishima*, and *Haruna*, would be completed by the Yokohama Naval Arsenal and the Mitsubishi and Kawasaki companies. The *Fuso* and the four battlecruisers, which were eventually converted into fast battleships, would join the Japanese fleet in time for its limited participation in the First World War.

When Great Britain declared war on Germany in August 1914 the Japanese wasted little time invoking the Anglo-Japanese Alliance, using the agreement as a pretext for their own declaration of war and snapping up German possessions in the Marshalls, Marianas, and Caroline Islands. Included in this windfall were the future Japanese fleet anchorage of Truk and the islands of Kwajalein, Saipan, Tinian, and Peleliu, destined to become the scenes of savage battles in the Pacific War.

The swift and nearly bloodless occupation of German colonies was an important first step in establishing a chain of advanced bases in the Central Pacific in preparation for a future war with the United States. Many senior officers in the Japanese Navy had begun to view a war with America as inevitable, given the rising acrimony between Japan and the United

States over "Open Door" trade practices in China. American expansion into Chinese markets, being conducted with an increasing level of assertiveness, was seen as a serious threat to Japanese economic prosperity and overall hegemony in the region. In an earlier memorandum to the Navy Ministry, Tetsutaro Sato would declare that the Americans were "determined to monopolize all interests in China," and that "the United States is actively oppressing Japan to bring us to our knees."

In November 1921 the major naval powers of the world were invited to the Washington Naval Conference, what would be the first arms limitation talks in history and convened in no small part to curb Japanese militarism and bring a measure of stability to the situation in the Far East. This resulted in the Washington Naval Treaty of 1922, which limited the total tonnage of capital ships that each signatory nation was allowed to maintain. A fixed ratio of 5:3:3 for battleship tonnage was settled upon, or what equated to 525,000 tons each for Britain and the United States, 315,000 tons for Japan, and 175,000 tons for Italy and France. The treaty stipulated that construction of new battleships would have to be discontinued or existing battleships scrapped in order to meet these limits.

The debut of naval aviation in the Great War had led to the development of an entirely new category of capital ship: the aircraft carrier. By 1921 the British had already commissioned two aircraft carriers, the *Furious* and the *Argus*. The United States had converted the hull of a former collier into its first aircraft carrier, the *Langley*. While the Washington conference was getting under way, the Japanese laid down what would be the first ship to be built from the keel up as an aircraft carrier, the *Hosho*. Carriers were limited by the Washington Naval Treaty to 135,000 tons for Britain and the United States, 81,000 tons for Japan, and 60,000 tons for Italy and France.

Cruisers of all nations were limited to 10,000 tons, with main batteries having a maximum caliber of 8 inches. Having borne the brunt of the German U-boat campaign during the war, the British called for the submarine to be banned as a weapon of war, but in the end no limits on submarine construction were imposed. In what was seen as an important victory for the Japanese, the future fortification of British, American, and Japanese bases in the Pacific would be prohibited.

The limitations imposed on Japan by the Washington Naval Treaty would cause deep and vitriolic divisions within the officer corps of the Imperial Japanese Navy. Those who had aligned themselves with the steadily growing ultra-nationalist, virulently militaristic, and expansionist movement within Japanese society viewed the terms of the treaty as a tremendous insult, just another device that Britain and the United States would use to suppress Japanese power and influence in the Pacific Basin. The vociferous band that would come to be known as the "Fleet Faction" was composed of mostly younger, mid-level officers but included many strong personalities, such as the recently retired but still influential Rear Admiral Tetsutaro Sato. Members of the Fleet Faction were enraged by their delegation's apparent acquiescence with regard to the 5:3:3 ratio, which allowed the Japanese to amass only 60 percent of the strength of the US Navy.

The group of Japanese officers supporting the ratification of the Washington Naval Treaty—which was appropriately termed the "Treaty Faction" and included the hero of Tsushima, Heihachiro Togo—believed that the restraint of heretofore unchecked American naval growth was a clear victory for Japan. The 60 percent limitation had been counterbalanced by the article prohibiting the fortification of American advanced bases. A "well-fortified Guam," argued Japan's chief negotiator, Navy Minister Tomosaburo Kato, would be an "impregnable" base for the American fleet in the western Pacific.

The Treaty Faction would further argue that America's Naval Act of 1916, signed into law by President Woodrow Wilson, had authorized a huge increase in naval construction: ten super dreadnought battleships, six cruisers, fifty destroyers, and thirty submarines—numbers the Japanese could never hope to emulate. Japan lacked the economic capacity, industrial might, and access to strategic resources to match such a naval buildup. By signing the Washington Naval Treaty, the Americans would have to scrap or discontinue the construction of nearly thirty capital ships.

"Anyone who has seen the automobile factories of Detroit or the oil fields of Texas knows that Japan lacks the power for a naval race with America," commented a young officer of the Treaty Faction. That officer was Isoroku Yamamoto.

CHAPTER 5
GAMES OF CHANCE

RESPLENDENT IN THEIR DRESS WHITE UNIFORMS, THE CREW OF THE *Nagato* manned the rails as a motor launch flying an admiral's pennant approached the anchored dreadnought from across the waters of Wakanoura Bay. The shrill tones of a bosun's pipe pierced the still August air and the staff of the Combined Fleet snapped to attention as their new commander-in-chief nimbly ascended an accommodation ladder and stepped onto the quarterdeck of the flagship.

The admiral paused to render a smart salute to the Rising Sun ensign at the *Nagato*'s stern. He was a small man, even by Japanese standards, at just 5 feet, 3 inches tall and weighing 130 pounds. Despite his diminutive stature, Isoroku Yamamoto nevertheless radiated confidence and a professional military bearing. He was certainly not without his share of detractors, who both feared and despised him, and his career had not been without controversy. But his reputation of being a man of surpassing intelligence, an efficient administrator, and inspirational leader had preceded him. Yamamoto would quickly enjoy the respect and devotion of the officers and sailors of his new command.

He had been born Isoroku Takano in the city of Nagaoka, on the northern coast of the Japanese main island of Honshu, in the spring of 1884. In the Japanese language *Isoroku* is a spelling-out of the number fifty-seven, the age of the boy's father, a former samurai, at the birth of his son. Isoroku was given up for adoption into the Yamamoto family; at that time Japanese male infants were often given away to parents incapable of producing an heir to continue the family bloodline.

Yamamoto graduated from the Naval Academy in 1904 and was assigned as gunnery officer aboard the armored cruiser *Nisshin*. During the Battle of Tsushima, the *Nisshin* had been singled out for special punishment by Russian gunners and received several direct hits. An explosion in the forward turret, which may have resulted from a malfunction of the guns, showered young Ensign Yamamoto with steel fragments and severed two fingers from his left hand. Later in life, the Tokyo geishas who performed his manicures would tease him with the nickname "Eighty Sen," or eight-tenths of one yen, with one yen being the price of a manicure for a person with all ten fingers.

In his youth Yamamoto would often attend Christian services offered by missionaries in his home prefecture, and though he kept a Bible, there is little evidence to suggest that he ever converted to Christianity. He was known to be sentimental at times and given to composing verse whenever the mood struck him. He drank very little, having learned at a young age that he was incapable of holding his liquor. He enjoyed fine cigars but eventually gave up smoking. While it was not uncommon for Japanese gentlemen to visit geishas for companionship and entertainment, Yamamoto took the rare step of keeping a geisha for a mistress after the cooling of his rather desultory marriage, which had produced four children.

Few things piqued his interest like a game of chance. Behind the calm, impassive, even cherubic face ticked the mind of a spirited gambler. Yamamoto *loved* to gamble, whether the contest was over a hand of poker, a rubber of bridge, or a game of *shogi*, the Japanese version of chess. He preferred to strike suddenly, with bold and audacious opening moves designed to unnerve his opponent, and he would often play with his fellow officers late into the night. Though he sometimes met his match at the gambling table, he was seemingly undeterred by loss and consistently employed an aggressive strategy. Isoroku Yamamoto had, as a contemporary once described him, "a gambler's heart."

In 1919 Yamamoto was sent to the United States to attend Harvard University and would return in 1926 to serve as naval attaché in Washington. During his tour as attaché he traveled extensively across America, an experience that allowed Yamamoto not only to observe American society but also to gain a firsthand appreciation for the economic power, industrial might, and vast natural resources available to the United States.

Though he never learned to fly an airplane, Yamamoto became an early proponent of naval aviation. Upon his return from the United States he would assume command of the aircraft carrier *Akagi*.* In subsequent years he would serve in various technical posts within the navy's aeronautics department, supervising the development of various carrier-based aircraft and weapons systems, and in 1935 became Vice Admiral in charge of Navy Aeronautics.

The following year Yamamoto was appointed to the post of Deputy Navy Minister, at a time when Japanese nationalism and the fierce political rivalry between the Imperial Army and Navy was at its height. The Japanese had already occupied Manchuria, and a clash between Chinese Nationalist soldiers and Japanese troops stationed near Beijing, the so-called "China Incident," soon erupted into another Sino-Japanese War. During the seizure of Nanking, which saw the massacre of hundreds of thousands of Chinese civilians at the hands of the Japanese, the river gunboat USS *Panay* was sent to evacuate the American consular staff from the beleaguered city. Japanese naval aircraft attacked and sank the *Panay*, killing three Americans and wounding a dozen more. The fliers professed to have not seen the horizontal US flags prominently displayed on the deck of the vessel, a claim the American press found highly dubious. Yamamoto himself delivered the official apology for the *Panay* sinking to American ambassador Joseph Grew, offering a $2 million indemnity and expressing Japan's regret over the incident.

Though he was a loyal officer devoted to the service of his Emperor, Isoroku Yamamoto was no fire-breathing ultra-nationalist. He was pragmatic and unapologetically blunt in his criticism of the war on China, which he viewed as a quagmire that consumed manpower and resources, and of Japan's contemplation of a military alliance with Nazi Germany and Fascist Italy. Viewed as defeatist and unpatriotic by right-wing fanatics, Yamamoto began receiving death threats with enough frequency that he was assigned a protection detail from the army's military police, whom he dubbed "wolves in sheep's clothing," sent to spy on him as much as protect him.

Tensions between the United States and Japan, already greatly exacerbated by Japanese aggression in China and the *Panay* incident, would

* Unlike the US Navy, the Japanese Navy did not require its aircraft carrier captains to be qualified aviators.

only worsen after Yamamoto left the Navy Ministry to assume command of the Combined Fleet. The Home Islands yielded precious little in the way of natural resources. Having to meet the voracious energy demands of the army's campaign in China, the oil-fired ships of the world's third-largest navy, an expansive merchant marine, and an industrial base now operating on a war footing, the Japanese had become completely dependent on the import of foreign oil, over 80 percent of which came from the United States.

Japanese eyes had already turned south, toward the British and Dutch possessions in Malaya and the East Indies, a region rich in oil, rice, tin, rubber, and other vital strategic resources. Forcing these territories into Japan's declared "Greater East Asia Co-Prosperity Sphere" would certainly mean war with Britain and the Netherlands and most likely with the United States, requiring the neutralization of British and American military bases in Singapore, Hong Kong, and the Philippines.

"A war between Japan and the United States would be a calamity for the world," Yamamoto would write, "and for Japan it would mean, after several years of war already, acquiring yet another powerful enemy—an extremely perilous matter for the nation.

"It is necessary therefore," he concluded, "that both Japan and America should seek every means to avoid a direct clash, and Japan should under no circumstances conclude an alliance with Germany."

Unfortunately, the decision to enter into the Tripartite Pact with Germany and Italy was out of Yamamoto's hands. Signed on September 27, 1940, the agreement pledged that the three nations "would assist one another with all political, economic and military means if one of the Contracting Powers is attacked by a Power at present not involved in the European War or in the Japanese-Chinese conflict."

In an effort to check further Japanese aggression, President Franklin D. Roosevelt had already ordered the US fleet to move from bases on the West Coast to Pearl Harbor. The move had little effect; the same month that the Tripartite Pact was signed, Japanese forces occupied parts of Vichy-controlled French Indochina, the eventual springboard for their planned invasion of British Borneo and the Dutch East Indies. The Americans responded with painful economic sanctions, denying the use of the Panama Canal to Japanese shipping and banning the export of scrap metal to Japan, a severe blow to Japanese war production. Not surprisingly, Japan's right wing howled even louder for war with the United States.

"At this stage," Yamamoto wrote in a letter to a colleague, "to profess shock and indignation at American economic pressure is either childishly impetuous or suggests an extraordinary inattentiveness to recent events."

During an audience with Prime Minister Prince Fumimaro Konoe, the Commander-in-Chief of the Combined Fleet was characteristically frank when asked for an opinion of how the Imperial Japanese Navy would fare in a war with the United States.

"If we are ordered to do it," Yamamoto replied, "then I can guarantee to run wild for six months. After that, I have no expectation of success."

For the next year, Japan and the United States would continue down the slippery slope toward war. In the summer of 1941, Japanese bombers were flown into airfields in southern Indochina in what was viewed as a direct threat to British Malaya, the Dutch East Indies, and Australia. The Americans then imposed a complete oil embargo on Japan along with the freezing of Japanese financial assets in the United States. The British and the Dutch Colonial Government of the East Indies quickly followed suit, moves that would soon cause the Japanese economy—and with it, their military campaigns on the Asian mainland—to grind to a halt. With only eighteen months of oil stocks in reserve, the Japanese were suddenly faced with two choices: submitting to American demands, or seizing the oil fields of Southeast Asia and going to war with the Netherlands, Britain, and the United States.

Prime Minister Konoe's ambassador to the United States, retired Admiral Kichisaburo Nomura, had spent much of 1941 in negotiations with American Secretary of State Cordell Hull in an attempt to salvage peace between the two nations. Nomura urged President Roosevelt to meet with Konoe as the premier faced mounting criticism from the Japanese right wing for failing to end the embargo crisis, but Roosevelt refused to do so until the negotiations had reached an agreement. Konoe tendered his resignation on October 16 and was replaced by General Hideki Tojo, the fiercest war hawk in all of Japan and an outspoken proponent of war with the United States and Britain.

On November 20, Nomura put forth the following proposal: Japan would agree to withdraw from Indochina and cease further expansion into Southeast Asia, in return for the lifting of sanctions and the approval of the purchase of 1 million gallons of aviation gasoline. The reply from Secretary of State Cordell Hull, what became known as the "Hull Note," demanded that "The Government of Japan will withdraw all military, naval, air and police forces from China and Indochina," as well as enter into a nonaggression pact "among the American, British, Chinese, Japanese, the Netherlands and Thai Governments." The Japanese must also agree to make "no agreement with any third powers to conflict with the fundamental purpose of this agreement," essentially ordering Japan to denounce the tripartite alliance with Germany and Italy. The Hull Note further demanded that the Japanese must respect the territorial rights of their neighbors, and a new trade agreement with the United States would be required. Only after satisfying these terms would the oil spigot be turned back on.

For the Japanese, the American proposal required an unacceptable loss of face. After reading the text of the Hull Note to his cabinet on November 26, Tojo would conclude: "[T]his is an ultimatum."

Despite his profound reservations, Admiral Yamamoto spent the whole of 1941 preparing the Combined Fleet for war with the US Navy. In order to ensure the success of the "Southern Plan," as the military expedition into the East Indies was being called, the destruction of American airfields and naval units in the Philippines and the eventual seizure of the archipelago was a critical necessity. The American response, it had long been assumed, would be to sortie the Pacific Fleet, now based in Pearl Harbor, to relieve its beleaguered forces in the Philippines.

Japanese naval doctrine called for attacks on the westbound American ships by submarines and bombers operating from advanced bases in the Marshall Islands, systematically chipping away at the strength of the American naval force until it could be met by the Combined Fleet in a *kantai kessen*, a decisive battle, most likely in the waters surrounding the Marianas. What remained of the American fleet would then be sunk by the "big ships and big guns" of the Japanese battle line.

As an officer serving under Togo at Tsushima, and as a student of Sato at the Naval War College, Yamamoto was a true believer in the concept of the *kantai kessen.* As Commander-in-Chief, however, he was not in favor of following the long-held Japanese naval strategy of sitting in an idle position and waiting for the Americans to steam into an ambush, a scenario that had been played ad nauseam on the war game tables of the Naval Academy, the Naval War College, and during fleet exercises for many years.

The Southern Plan would be considered a success only with the seizure of the Dutch East Indies and the eventual safe return of oil and other vital resources to the Japanese Home Islands along commercial shipping routes. And *that* could only be achieved, as Alfred Thayer Mahan would have insisted, upon gaining control of the intervening seas, something the Combined Fleet could never guarantee with an eastern flank exposed to the battleships of the American Navy. The required reduction in the strength of the US Pacific Fleet would therefore have to be achieved quickly, preferably in a single, bold stroke: an audacious first move, calculated to shock and dismay the opponent.

It would indeed be the greatest gamble that Admiral Isoroku Yamamoto, and the Empire of Japan, would ever make.

CHAPTER 6

THE FLEET AT PEARL

The White House of Franklin Delano Roosevelt was notorious for serving dreadful food. When the First Family moved into the executive mansion in January 1933, Eleanor Roosevelt offered the job of Head Housekeeper to her fifty-nine-year-old unemployed neighbor from Hyde Park, Henrietta Nesbitt. In the days before the White House employed an executive chef, the Head Housekeeper had the responsibility of supervising the kitchen, an area in which Mrs. Nesbitt had little talent or expertise.

The beginning of Nesbitt's tenure coincided with the darkest days of the Great Depression. With thirteen million Americans out of work, the First Lady knew that it would be imprudent for the architect of the New Deal to be seen dining on the sort of epicurean fare usually served to heads of state. Eleanor Roosevelt, therefore, decreed that the presidential pantry should be managed with an eye toward frugality. This instruction, when combined with Henrietta Nesbitt's distinct lack of culinary aptitude, led to many thousands of aberrant and tasteless meals being served by the White House kitchen over the next dozen years.

Sandwiches made with only bread and butter, stuffed eggs in a thin tomato sauce, fried chicken liver in gravy, overcooked mutton, pasta with boiled carrots, prune pudding, gelatin salads—dignitaries and guests who had once been honored to dine at the White House began to accept the invitation with a sense of dread. "Eat before you go" was the advice offered to first-time invitees by those who had experienced dinner with the Roosevelts. Ernest Hemingway once declared that the meal he was served at the White House in 1937 was the worst he'd ever had in his life. Despite being an enthusiastic lover of fine food, the president himself apparently approved of, or at least tolerated, his wife's program of austerity and Mrs. Nesbitt's dreary recipes.

On a crisp autumn afternoon in October 1940, Admiral James O. Richardson watched as White House mess stewards served lunch to President Roosevelt, Admiral William Leahy, and himself, knowing that the task that lay before him would prove to be as unpalatable as the food. The Commander-in-Chief of the United States Fleet was visiting Washington for the second time since June to discuss the president's order to relocate the Pacific Battle Force to Pearl Harbor, a move which he vehemently opposed.

One senses that a study of his official navy portrait, taken in a dress blue uniform with gold braid, tells the observer everything he needs to know about James Otto Richardson. Studious wire-rimmed spectacles cannot hide the steely gaze that accompanies the firmly set and stern jaw. The arms are folded in a posture that suggests vexation or impatience, as if the pose were struck just after growling something like *Go on, explain yourself* to a trembling young ensign. He appears to be every inch the no-nonsense Texan that he, in fact, was. After spending a tour of duty as chief of the Bureau of Navigation, Richardson served for six months as Commander, Battle Force, before being promoted to Commander-in-Chief of the United States Fleet in January 1940, a post that oversaw both the Pacific and Atlantic fleets, at the time named Battle Force and Scouting Force, respectively.

In March 1940 the ships of the Battle Force departed from their bases on the West Coast for Hawaiian waters to participate in Fleet Problem XXI, a series of exercises focused on preparing the navy for a possible war with Japan. Throughout the month of April, intensive training was conducted in carrier task force and line-of-battle formations, convoy escort, reconnaissance, antisubmarine warfare, night destroyer tactics, underway refueling and replenishment, and fleet defense against air attack. At the conclusion of Fleet Problem XXI, Richardson received a message from the Chief of Naval Operations, Admiral Harold R. Stark, ordering the Pacific Battle Force to remain in Hawaii at the direction of the President of the United States.

"Basing the Fleet at Pearl Harbor in May of 1940 was undertaken under a completely false premise, in my opinion," Richardson would later write. "The false premise was that the Fleet so positioned would exercise a restraining influence on the actions of Japan."

The following month Richardson boarded the Pan American Clipper in Honolulu for the first leg of a journey to Washington. He would visit the Navy and War Departments, Capitol Hill, and the White House, speaking with Admiral Stark, Army Chief of Staff General George C. Marshall, Secretary of State Cordell Hull, Senator James Byrnes of South Carolina . . . essentially anyone of influence who would listen to him reel off the list of reasons why the Battle Force did not belong at Pearl Harbor—and the list was lengthy—before finally visiting President Roosevelt.

Richardson's trepidation was caused, first and foremost, by the fleet's vulnerability to attack in Hawaiian waters. The approaches to Pearl Harbor and the Maui anchorage were both "2,000 miles closer to Japanese submarine bases." The nightmare scenario of his burning capital ships plunging to the bottom of Lahaina Roads after a concentrated attack by a wolfpack of Japanese submarines was Richardson's overriding concern, although Admirals Harry Yarnell and Ernest King had both demonstrated—during war games conducted in 1932 and 1938—that Pearl Harbor was also highly vulnerable to surprise attack from carrier-based aircraft.

As home port to the entire Pacific Battle Force, Richardson would argue, Pearl Harbor would quickly become congested with so many large vessels being based there. A narrow channel leading to the Pacific provided the only egress, raising the possibility that the channel could be blocked and the vessels in port perilously trapped. Pearl Harbor lacked adequate berthing, repair, fueling, and training facilities. Transporting personnel, supplies, and munitions to the Hawaiian Islands would be time-consuming and expensive. As for the officers and men who manned the fleet, their morale would surely suffer due to long periods of time away from the mainland and their families, making many experienced sailors reluctant to reenlist and creating a serious retention problem in an already undermanned fleet.

"I am sure it will come as something of a shock to the Honolulu Chamber of Commerce," Richardson wrote, "and it might not be true today, but in 1940, the Commander, Battle Force Destroyers stated 'Enlisted men, on the whole, do not desire duty in the Hawaiian area.'"

Unlike the civilian government of the United States, the military government of Japan was already operating on a war footing, Richardson would argue further, and rather than serving as a deterrent to plans of expanding their empire by brutal conquest, the Japanese were more likely to view the American fleet in Pearl Harbor as a target of opportunity. Having participated in the formulation of War Plan Orange, the joint army and navy plan for a possible war with Japan, Richardson had arrived at this conclusion after a great deal of consideration and study of his potential enemy's motives and tendencies. President Roosevelt, however, had refused to budge. In October 1940, Admiral Richardson would return to the White House to plead his case once again.

"I can be convinced of the desirability of retaining the battleships on the West Coast," FDR told Richardson over their dismal lunch, "if I can be given a statement which will convince the American people, and the Japanese government, that in bringing the battleships to the West Coast we are not stepping backward."

Richardson would later state that the discussion "waxed hot and heavy." Finally, the admiral would look his commander-in-chief in the eye and state emphatically: "Mr. President, I feel that I must tell you that the senior officers of the Navy do not have the trust and confidence in the civilian leadership of this country that is essential for the successful prosecution of a war in the Pacific."

Roosevelt's face fell. The statement, purposefully blunt but delivered after a great deal of deliberation, was intended to shock the president into reassessing his position. Roosevelt was not only shocked by Richardson's words, he was deeply hurt. Like his distant cousin Theodore, FDR had once served as Assistant Secretary of the Navy and possessed a long-held affection for the sea service. Few things brought Roosevelt joy like a visit to the fleet, and many senior naval officers were his close friends and trusted advisors. The man who would succeed him, Harry S. Truman, would say of the White House: "When Roosevelt was here this place was like a damned wardroom."

"It seemed to me that the President's great love for the navy led him, on occasion, to rationalize that, since he loved the navy as much or more than the naval officers with whom he was dealing on naval matters, this love raised his technical judgement in regard to these matters to a par or above that of his really informed advisors," Richardson would remark.

Admiral Richardson would receive a shock himself in January 1941, when he was suddenly relieved of his command. He was replaced by Rear Admiral Husband E. Kimmel, commander of the cruiser force in the Pacific. The change of command took place on February 1, 1941, the same day that General Order 143 went into effect, establishing the separate Pacific and Atlantic Fleets. Kimmel would receive four stars and assume the role of Commander-in-Chief, Pacific Fleet, or CINCPAC. He would also hold the title of Commander-in-Chief, United States Fleet, in the unlikely event the Atlantic and Pacific forces were combined.

Husband E. Kimmel was a tall, blond-haired, blue-eyed Kentuckian who had graduated thirteenth in the Naval Academy Class of 1904. Historians will often note that Kimmel once served as an aid to Assistant Secretary of the Navy Franklin Roosevelt and had been promoted to the CINCPAC post over fifty admirals more senior, but there is nothing in Kimmel's official record to indicate that he was unworthy or incapable of the command. Known as "Hubby" during his time at Annapolis and thereafter nicknamed "Kim" by his associates, he personified the consummate "battleship navy" officer.

As a young ensign, Kimmel had sailed aboard the pre-dreadnought battleship *Georgia* for the world tour of the Great White Fleet in 1907, and had been wounded during the amphibious landings at Veracruz in 1914. After America entered the First World War, the navy dispatched Battleship Division Nine to reinforce the Royal Navy's Grand Fleet, with Kimmel aboard the flagship *New York* as senior gunnery officer. He would serve as executive officer of the *Arkansas* and captain of the *New York* before obtaining flag rank and eventually becoming Commander, Battle Force Cruisers. His reputation was that of a highly efficient, detail-oriented, and hardworking officer.

Admiral Kimmel was in the unenviable position of having to provide for the defense of a network of American installations scattered across the world's largest ocean, while at the same time having to ensure the readiness of a fleet that was disconcertingly unprepared for combat. With President Roosevelt's declaration of an "Unlimited National Emergency" in May 1941, the ranks of the Pacific Fleet were soon swollen with reserve officers and sailors recalled to active duty. These were soon accompanied by thousands of apprentice seamen fresh from boot camp and recent college graduates who had completed a three-month Direct Commissioning Program, the notorious "Ninety-Day Wonders."

"Due to these circumstances and through no fault of my predecessor," Admiral Kimmel would write, "the fleet was not ready for war. I set out to make it ready. This required an intensive training program. In carrying out this program we were handicapped by the constant detachment in large numbers of qualified officers and enlisted men to meet the demands of the expanding procurement and training agencies on shore, and to supply trained personnel to man new ships."

As for the new arrivals to the fleet, Kimmel would remark: "Excellent material, but they required training and indoctrination, which takes time and effort. In the meanwhile the ships they manned were not ready to fight. More than half the officers of the fleet were newly commissioned reserve officers. There were times when three-fourths of the men in a ship had never heard a gun fired."

That would soon change. Under Husband Kimmel the Pacific Fleet would embark upon a rigorous training schedule, with ships staying in Pearl Harbor just long enough to refuel, rearm, and repair before getting under way once again. "In addition to individual ship training," Kimmel wrote, "I had to provide for coordinated training of ships, divisions and squadrons as part of the fleet as a whole."

Cruisers ranged far ahead of the fleet on scouting missions. Flanked by destroyers and directed by reconnaissance seaplanes, battleships maneuvered to bring their big guns to bear on towed target sleds. Carrier-based aircraft performed simulated strike missions and provided air cover for the surface fleet. Aircraft carriers worked in concert with their own screening destroyers and antiaircraft cruisers, exercises that led to the development of the fast carrier task forces that would be used with deadly effectiveness against the Japanese Navy in the coming Pacific War. "Our training activities were not just *routine* training or *peacetime* training," Kimmel would state. "They were intensified training activities indispensable to the creation of fighting efficiency in the fleet."

Maintaining this aggressive tempo of operations, critical for providing the kind of workups the fleet sorely required, would have been an immense challenge for any fleet commander and his staff under normal conditions. But there were many more obstacles on the Pacific Fleet's route to preparedness, some logistical in nature, others bureaucratic. US naval intelligence had long suspected that the Japanese were fortifying their bases in the Central Pacific in direct violation of their League of Nations mandate. Airfields and extensive port facilities had been constructed on Kwajalein, Saipan, Palau, and Truk, a threat to the American bases on Guam, Wake, and Midway, which needed to be reinforced with marine defense battalions, artillery, and aircraft.

War Plan Orange, for two decades the template for operations in a war with Japan, had since been superseded by the Rainbow series of war plans drawn up by the joint army and navy planning committee. The most current of these, Rainbow Five, anticipated that Britain and the United States would be allied in a war against Germany and anticipated joint offensive operations in Europe and the Mediterranean. In 1940, CNO Admiral Stark issued his famous Plan Dog memo, which called for a "Europe first" strategy in the event of a two-ocean war with the German-Italian-Japanese Axis, and the employment of a defensive strategy in the Pacific.

In late April 1941, Stark ordered the transfer of the aircraft carrier *Yorktown*, the battleships *New Mexico*, *Idaho*, and *Mississippi*, three light cruisers, and a dozen destroyers to the Atlantic Fleet to augment the Neutrality Patrol guarding merchant shipping lanes between Great Britain and North America. This reduced the striking power of the Pacific Fleet, already greatly outnumbered and outgunned by the Japanese, by an astounding 25 percent. Two months later, while on an official trip to Washington, Admiral Kimmel learned that the Navy Department planned to transfer an additional carrier, another division of three battleships, four heavy cruisers, and two squadrons of destroyers to the Atlantic. The normally affable Kimmel launched into a vigorous protest, and on this particular occasion the commander of the Pacific Fleet was heard. The moves were canceled.

As for the defense of the fleet base at Pearl Harbor, Rainbow Five assigned the responsibility to the army's Hawaiian Department, commanded by General Walter C. Short, and to Admiral Claude C. Bloch's

Fourteenth Naval District. Admiral Kimmel joined the two area commanders in their requests for more resources with which to defend the Hawaiian Coastal Frontier, specifically more personnel, aircraft, antiaircraft weapons, and radar, to which Washington responded with empty promises or delays. The Army Air Corps in Hawaii, for example, was allotted nearly two hundred B-17 Flying Fortresses, aircraft that could be employed for long-range reconnaissance. By November only a dozen of the strategic bombers had been delivered to Hickam Army Airfield on Oahu, and only six of those were in a flyable condition due to a lack of spare parts. The Fourteenth Naval District had received none of the one hundred additional patrol aircraft they were promised.

During the fateful ten months that Husband E. Kimmel would serve as Commander-in-Chief, Pacific Fleet, he repeatedly asked the Navy Department for yet another critical resource: timely intelligence data. Like everything else he requested from Washington, the information stream had arrived in a trickle, largely due to an ongoing turf battle between the Office of Naval Intelligence (ONI) and Rear Admiral Richmond Kelly Turner, head of the War Plans Division, over *who* was responsible for the dissemination of intelligence to fleet commanders and for determining *what* the admirals needed to know. Shortly after taking command, Kimmel posted a letter to Stark on the subject.

"I do not know that we have missed anything," Kimmel wrote, "but if there is any doubt as to whose responsibility it is to keep the Commander-in-Chief fully informed with pertinent reports that should be of interest to the fleet, will you kindly fix this responsibility so that there will be no misunderstanding?"

Subsequent investigations have supported the assertion that Kimmel was significantly shortchanged when it came to receiving meaningful intelligence from Washington. A decoding apparatus earmarked for Station HYPO, the Combat Intelligence Unit of the Fourteenth Naval District in Pearl Harbor, would have allowed signals intelligence cryptanalysts to decipher the Japanese "Purple" diplomatic code, but the machine was instead sent to England in exchange for a British-designed device used for decoding German messages. Sometime after July 1941 Washington stopped sharing the "Magic" intercepts of decoded Purple messages with

Station HYPO "for security reasons." If Kimmel's staff had been privy to Japanese diplomatic traffic, the Commander-in-Chief, Pacific Fleet would have known that spies posing as diplomats from the Japanese consulate in Honolulu were sending frequent messages to Tokyo, reporting on the type, number, and status of American warships in the Pearl Harbor anchorage.

Admiral Kimmel's intelligence officer was thirty-eight-year-old Commander Edwin Layton, an accomplished Japanese linguist who had served for three years as naval attaché to the American embassy in Tokyo. During his time in Japan, "Eddie" Layton had even become friendly with Admiral Isoroku Yamamoto. Layton's job of providing accurate intelligence estimates for his boss would be made considerably more difficult by the dearth of Purple intercepts.

"The lack of this high-level diplomatic information seriously hampered our ability to assemble all the pieces of the intelligence jigsaw puzzle," Layton would write.

Another reason for Washington's failure to provide information needed by fleet commanders, as the official US Navy historian Samuel Eliot Morison has observed, was the sheer volume of intercepted Japanese diplomatic and military radio traffic and the time required to decipher, analyze, and prioritize each intercept for dissemination. In short, messages were flooding in faster than they could be processed. By the autumn of 1941 American economic sanctions were gradually placing a stranglehold on Japan's military ambitions, negotiations in Washington were nearing an impasse, and tensions between the two nations were strained to the breaking point. Multiple intercepts indicated that a "surprise aggressive movement" by Japanese forces was on the horizon; the question was *where*. Both Admiral Stark and General Marshall believed the Philippines or Guam would be attacked to facilitate a Japanese advance against the Malay Peninsula or the Dutch East Indies, while Admiral Turner insisted that the Japanese were poised to attack Russia in support of their German allies.

On November 27, the Chief of Naval Operations sent the following message to Admiral Kimmel in Pearl Harbor and to Admiral Thomas C. Hart in Manila:

```
This dispatch is to be considered a war warning.
Negotiations with Japan looking toward stabili-
zation of conditions in the Pacific have ceased
and an aggressive move by Japan is expected in
the next few days. The number and equipment of
Japanese troops and the organization of naval
task forces indicates an amphibious expedition
against either the Philippines Thai or Kra Pen-
insula or possibly Borneo. Execute an appropri-
ate defensive deployment preparatory to carrying
out the tasks assigned in WPL 46.
```

"As for the Hawaiian commands," an officer serving with the Pacific Fleet would later write, "some people observed that they were 'fed up' on alarms, alerts, rumors, and an overdose of pressures and cautionary messages. Fleet operations were at times subordinate to alerts and defensive drills, and suffered accordingly. The cry of 'wolf' had become so customary that it no longer made an impact."

Kimmel's forces on the islands of Guam, Wake, Johnston, and Midway were already on alert. Marines had been sent to shore up the defenses of Midway and Wake, and submarines and aircraft had been ordered to conduct patrols from those outposts. On November 28, Vice Admiral William F. Halsey's *Enterprise* task force weighed anchor and steamed for Wake Island to deliver a dozen F4F Wildcats from Marine Fighter Squadron 211. The *Lexington* group would soon depart for Midway on a similar mission. The battleships of the Pacific Fleet, which were considerably slower than the carriers and their screening vessels, were ordered to remain in Hawaii. Antisubmarine patrols by destroyers and aircraft had been increased in Hawaiian waters, especially near the Pearl Harbor entrance. These measures, and whether or not they constituted "an appropriate defensive deployment," would later be subjected to an intense degree of scrutiny, and at the highest levels of government.

Eddie Layton's December 2, 1941, intelligence summary to Admiral Kimmel would contain an ominous note: The three Japanese aircraft carrier divisions in the Pacific had gone silent. Their disposition, therefore, was unknown. For several days, it appeared that the carrier groups had neither sent nor received any radio signals, leaving no clues with regard to their whereabouts for the analysts of Station HYPO.

The picture was clouded further by a stream of Japanese radio traffic believed to consist of false messages and a change of radio call signs that had recently taken place. Layton suspected that the carrier divisions were in Japanese home waters, though the possibility existed that they were in the vicinity of the mandates in the Central Pacific or moving south to support a new Japanese thrust into Southeast Asia. It was anyone's guess.

"You mean to say that you, the intelligence officer, don't know where the carriers are?" Kimmel asked pointedly.

"No, sir, I don't," Layton admitted.

"You mean they could be rounding Diamond Head, and you wouldn't know it?" the admiral demanded.

"Yes, sir. But I hope they'd have been sighted before now."

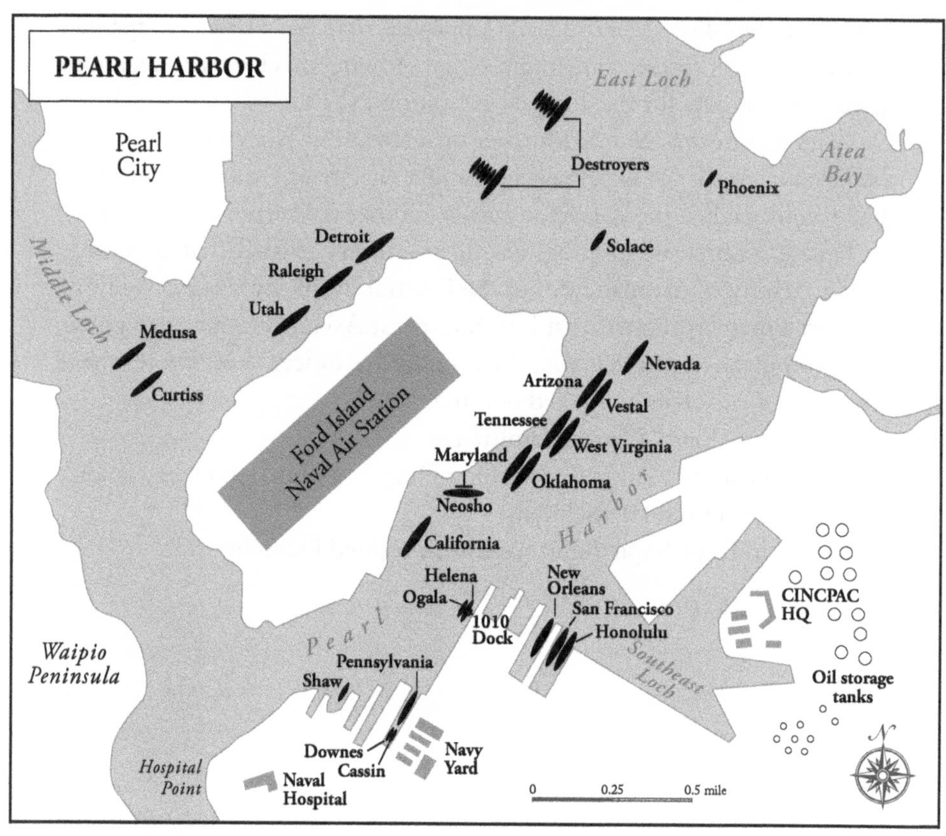

PEARL HARBOR
Pearl City
East Loch
Destroyers
Phoenix
Aiea Bay
Solace
Detroit
Raleigh
Utah
Middle Loch
Medusa
Curtiss
Ford Island Naval Air Station
Nevada
Arizona
Vestal
Tennessee
West Virginia
Maryland
Oklahoma
Neosho
California
Harbor
Helena
Ogala
1010 Dock
New Orleans
San Francisco
Honolulu
Southeast Loch
CINCPAC HQ
Oil storage tanks
Pearl
Waipio Peninsula
Pennsylvania
Shaw
Downes
Cassin
Navy Yard
Hospital Point
Naval Hospital
0
0.25
0.5 mile
N

CHAPTER 7
A DATE WHICH WILL LIVE IN INFAMY

THE PIECES OF THE JIGSAW PUZZLE, AS EDDIE LAYTON DESCRIBED IT, had still not fallen together by the morning of Sunday, December 7, 1941. At 6:30 a.m., as sunlight brightened the eastern sky and filtered through the white cumulus scudding across the saw-toothed peaks of the Koʻolau mountains, the destroyer USS *Ward* sent an urgent wireless message to the headquarters of the Fourteenth Naval District in Pearl Harbor.

> Attacked, fired on, depth bombed and sunk submarine operating in the defensive sea area.

A Japanese two-man midget submarine, attempting to sneak through open antisubmarine gates and into the Pearl Harbor channel in the wake of the cargo ship *Antares*, had been spotted by a PBY patrol plane operating from Naval Air Station Kaneohe Bay. The *Ward*, on patrol duty at the harbor entrance, fired a 4-inch shell into the submarine's exposed conning tower, then dropped several depth charges to finish its destruction. Admiral Bloch and the staff officers of the Fourteenth Naval District, inclined to believe the report to be another false alarm triggered by an over-eager destroyer captain, deliberated for several minutes before asking the *Ward* to confirm the message.

Shortly after the *Ward* engaged the midget sub, Private Joseph Lockard telephoned the Information Center at Fort Shafter from the US Army's mobile radar station at Opana, on the northern tip of Oahu. The excited young soldier had insisted on speaking with the duty pursuit officer, Lieutenant Kermit Tyler. A large blip had appeared on the oscilloscope, Lockard explained, indicating a flight of several aircraft on a bearing northeast of Oahu, now at a distance of 74 miles and approaching fast. Lockard added that the contact was the biggest he had yet seen. Lieutenant Tyler was aware that a dozen of the long-promised B-17 Flying Fortresses were inbound from California and due to arrive at Hickam Field around 0730.

"Don't worry about it," Tyler told Lockard.

The sailors of Battleship Row had been awake since the call to reveille and "up hammocks" was sounded at five o'clock. "Sweepers, man your brooms" followed twenty minutes later, and at 7:30 a.m. the crews were piped to breakfast. "Rig for church" and "liberty call" were the only anticipated events of what promised to be a typically relaxed Sunday routine in port. Just before the eight o'clock hour, as the tolling of church bells in Pearl City echoed across the placid lochs and buglers sounded "first call," details of sailors and marines on each ship prepared to hoist the national colors.

On the fantail of the *Nevada*, the ship's band began to play "The Star-Spangled Banner." The band of the *Arizona* had been allowed to sleep late, their reward for placing second in the previous night's Battle of the Bands at the recreation center. The musicians of the *Pennsylvania* had taken top honors, with many in the departing crowd grumbling that the judges had been biased toward the band of the Pacific Fleet flagship—the *Arizona* band clearly should have won.

Aboard the *West Virginia*, twenty-three-year-old ensign Roman Brooks watched as a burst of fire erupted from a seaplane hangar on the southern end of Ford Island, followed by the stunning shock of an explosion. From his vantage point on the quarterdeck, the Officer of the Deck at first believed that an accident had befallen the *California*, moored by herself at Fox Three and well forward of the *West Virginia*.

"*Away Fire and Rescue Party!*"

Brooks's sudden announcement across the 1MC caused hundreds of *West Virginia* crew members to scramble topside, with several cursing the overly enthusiastic officer who had ordered an emergency drill on a peaceful Sunday morning. Hours later, many of these same men would realize that Brooks's initial misinterpretation of events had, in fact, saved their very lives. As the first Japanese Aichi "Val" dive-bombers flattened from their descent and roared across the harbor, more bombs exploded among the parked PBYs on Ford Island, and the *West Virginia*'s klaxon sounded again, followed by an even more startling call.

"This is not a drill! This is not a drill! General Quarters, General Quarters: All hands man your battle stations! All hands man your battle stations!"

The commanding officer of the *West Virginia*, Captain Mervyn Bennion, emerged from his cabin to be informed by the first sergeant of the ship's marine detachment that the Japanese were bombing Pearl Harbor.

"Well, this is certainly in keeping with their history of surprise attacks," Bennion coolly remarked as he headed for the conning tower.

Howard Juhl was thinking the same thing. A member of the construction and repair gang on the *California*, he was at breakfast when a shipmate told him that the planes over the harbor had "red spots" on their wings. Juhl had just finished reading a book about the Japanese surprise attack on Port Arthur in 1904.

"I knew right then and there that this was it," Juhl would state.

Not everyone did. Confusion would reign over Battleship Row for the first several seconds. Some of the men believed that US Army Air Corps or Marine aviators were staging a rather realistic mock raid on the fleet. There were those who stared in wonder at the Rising Sun emblems on the wingtips of the Japanese aircraft. There were still others who, even as they began to realize that they were targets of an actual air attack, thought the whole scene had a surreal, motion picture–like quality. All were quickly shaken from their reverie as the first attackers concluded their bombing runs and raked the massed superstructures of Battleship Row with machine-gun fire. If any doubts existed among the men aboard the *Oklahoma*, they were quickly dispelled by a rather succinct announcement issued over the ship's loudspeaker: "Man your battle stations! This is no shit!"

Milton Thomas had stepped into the bright sunshine on the *Arizona*'s quarterdeck to have a cigarette. "The first bit of excitement I noticed was the Officer of the Deck and the Junior OD standing near the admiral's gangway, pointing and looking west toward Ford Island. Out of curiosity

I went over to the life line to see what everyone was looking at. I saw a large column of smoke going up into the air. At this time the Officer of the Deck told the Boatswain of the Watch to sound general alarm which he did on the double."

The young aviation's mate third class began to wonder if a fire had broken out aboard one of the other ships or at the Naval Air Station. "I watched several planes sweep over Ford Island and when one went over our fantail I saw the red spot on the wings," Thomas remembered. "Our guns opened up then and it first struck me that we were being attacked."

On the *Maryland*, a gunner's mate named Stanley Gruber had been reading the Honolulu newspaper in a topside workshop when he remarked to a companion: "Gee, it seems like there's an awful lot of planes flying around." Gruber thought this was particularly odd for a Sunday.

"They're holding bombing practice," his friend replied. With so many military planes based on Oahu, the drone of aircraft motors over Pearl Harbor was commonplace. So was the faraway, thumping sound of gunfire and explosions that often accompanied practice missions. But Sundays were usually quiet.

Still holding his newspaper, Gruber stepped outside to witness the first bombs fall upon the Ford Island seaplane ramp and saw the red circle on the wings of the dive-bombers. Gruber dashed down a midship ladder to alert his fellow antiaircraft gunners. As he passed a shipmate named Bill Anderson, Gruber yelled for the sailors nearby to man their battle stations. Anderson just laughed at him.

"Bill—*the Japs are bombing us!*" Gruber exclaimed, and bounded back up the ladder to the workshop to retrieve the firing lock for his 5-inch gun.

Edmund Chappell and several of his fellow cooks climbed a ladder topside from the *Maryland*'s galley. Someone had said that army pilots were performing mock bombing runs on Battleship Row, and the cooks went to see for themselves. Just as they emerged onto the weather deck, Chappell saw an airplane pull from a dive and pass over the ship. There was no mistaking the Rising Sun on the fuselage.

"He was so close that I saw the pilot very vividly and had I had a rock, I could perhaps [have] hit him with it," Chappell said. "But as he went over us, he strafed us and I can still recall the deck being gypped up alongside of us and we all made a dive for the hatch to get back down where we came from."

Concluding a wide sweeping turn around the perimeter of Hickam Field, four groups of Nakajima "Kate" torpedo planes from the carriers *Akagi* and *Kaga* zoomed downward to just a few scant feet above the waters of Southwest Loch, the wash from their propellers leaving a swirling wake of spray as they tore past the docks of the Navy Yard and raced for Battleship Row.

On the quarterdeck of the *West Virginia*, Gunner's Mate Bill Hardeman stood waiting for the first liberty boat of the day in his dress whites, on his way to meet his girlfriend at the Blaisdell Hotel in Honolulu for breakfast. When General Quarters was sounded he sprinted to his battle station and began pulling the canvas covers from antiaircraft guns.

"I was standing over by the splinter shield, by the forward gun on the port side, and I watched these planes come in over the fleet landing," Hardeman recalled. "They were in arrow formation, one leader and two wing men, one on each side. I saw the lead man drop his torpedo, and it was running straight for the ship. It looked like it was going to hit exactly right under me."

As far back as January 1941, the Chief of Naval Operations had corresponded with Admirals Richardson and Bloch over the possible danger of an aerial torpedo attack against the fleet in Pearl Harbor and the possible need for anti-torpedo countermeasures. The question was raised after British torpedo planes from the HMS *Illustrious* launched a successful attack against the Italian fleet in the port of Taranto the previous November, sinking a battleship and heavily damaging two others.

Kimmel had received a memorandum from Stark on the subject, shortly after becoming CINCPAC in February 1941. In order to successfully drop a torpedo, Stark wrote, an aircraft had to descend below 250 feet, and a minimum depth of 75 feet of water was required. The hills surrounding Pearl Harbor, Stark had concluded, would make it difficult for attacking airplanes to descend to such a low altitude to start their torpedo runs, especially in the face of antiaircraft fire from the fleet. Since Pearl Harbor was only about 30 feet deep in most places, and because heavy and cumbersome anti-torpedo nets would interfere with the fleet's ability to maneuver in the harbor, the Navy Department had concluded that such protections were unnecessary.

Lieutenant Commander John N. Opie III had been an American observer aboard the *Illustrious* during the Taranto raid and had transmitted a four-page summary on the battle from the American embassy in Cairo, decrying the effectiveness of shipboard antiaircraft guns against low-flying torpedo planes. John Opie—a Naval Academy classmate of Ed Layton's—had offered to travel to Hawaii to brief the staff of the Pacific Fleet on the lessons of Taranto, a suggestion that was ignored by his superiors. In June, a report from the ONI about the Taranto attack quoted Lieutenant Albert Morehouse, an American naval attaché serving aboard the HMS *Ark Royal*, stating that the specifications of the British Mark 12 weapon "indicate that this torpedo can be dropped in water as shallow as 4 fathoms," or 24 feet. The ONI report, a copy of which was sent to Admiral Kimmel, apparently went unread.

In May 1941 Isoroku Yamamoto had ordered a naval mission to Italy led by Rear Admiral Hiroaki Abe. The Japanese, according to their Italian hosts, "showed great interest in the aerial torpedo attack against the ships anchored at Taranto." The Japanese had already begun to practice aerial torpedo attacks in shallow anchorages, and in 1939 experimented with the installation of breakaway wooden fins on their Type 91 aerial torpedoes during test runs in Kagoshima Bay. The rather crude modification had proven to be a cheap and simple solution to a complex problem: The fins reduced the torpedo's speed during the drop, thereby limiting its depth as it plunged into the water.

Two such torpedoes darted across the shallow channel and slammed into the *Oklahoma*, moored outboard from the *Maryland* on a direct line with the mouth of Southwest Loch. Within minutes, *Oklahoma* would be struck by seven more. Six torpedoes crashed into the *West Virginia*; a seventh tore away the ship's rudder. Even as a torpedo ripped into the bow of the *Nevada*, sailors manning both fore and aft machine guns opened fire, shooting down one of the bombers as it roared past. The Japanese plane smacked into the water about 100 yards from the *Nevada*'s port quarter.

Seaman First Class Leslie Short had just finished breakfast and was sitting in the fresh air of the *Maryland*'s forward superstructure addressing

Christmas cards. A gunner's mate striker, Short just happened to be beside his battle station, a gun tub containing a .50 caliber Browning.

"Suddenly I noticed planes diving on the naval air base nearby," Short would remember. "At first I thought they were our own planes in a practice dive bombing attack, but when I saw smoke and flames rising from a building, I looked closer and saw that they were not American planes. I broke out ammunition nearby, loaded my machine gun and opened fire on the torpedo planes coming in from the east, which had just dropped two torpedoes. Flames and smoke burst from the first plane I aimed at, and it veered off to the left falling toward the hospital."

Depictions of the attack on Pearl Harbor often lead one to believe that the American response was chaotic, the manning of antiaircraft defenses desperately improvised, and the return of fire sporadic at best. Multiple after-action reports indicate that, generally speaking, this was not the case. Several officers of the fleet recalled their men acting in a calm and professional manner as they manned their battle stations and performed their duties, even though nearly all of them were under enemy fire for the first time in their lives.

While in port the ships of the Pacific Fleet had been ordered to maintain Readiness Condition Three, which required one-quarter of their antiaircraft guns and directors to be in a ready state. At least one .50 caliber machine gun was constantly manned aboard each warship, and the ready service lockers alongside antiaircraft batteries were stocked with ammunition. Where ammunition stores were padlocked, with the keys in the pocket of the Officer of the Deck, fire axes or heavy crowbars provided immediate access.

Upon witnessing Japanese bombers attack the airfield on Ford Island, several ships sounded General Quarters and began returning fire with machine guns almost immediately. In most cases 5-inch antiaircraft guns were firing within four minutes. The crew of the port broadside 5-inch gun on the *Nevada* would score a direct hit on one of the fast-approaching torpedo planes, the aircraft disintegrating before dropping its weapon. Even the humble seaplane tender *Curtiss* proved her mettle as a fighting ship and gave a good account of herself, shooting down two Japanese planes and scoring two direct hits on another midget submarine that had slipped into the harbor. The Japanese might have achieved complete surprise on a peaceful Sunday morning, but the bluejackets of the Pacific Fleet managed to hurl some 280,000 rounds of ammunition at their attackers.

"As my group made its bomb run, enemy anti-aircraft suddenly came to life," the leader of the first wave of the attack, Commander Misuo Fuchida, would comment years later. "Dark gray bursts blossomed here and there until the sky was clouded with shattering near misses which made our plane tremble. Shipboard guns seemed to open fire before the shore batteries. I was startled by the rapidity of the counterattack which came less than five minutes after the first bomb had fallen."

It was not enough. It would require interceptors to repel a determined attack of such size, and most of the Curtiss P-40 Warhawk fighter planes of the army's Hawaiian Department were already in a blazing heap on the tarmac of Wheeler Army Airfield, 13 miles to the north. In the preceding days General Walter Short had also received dispatches from Washington warning that an outbreak of war in the Pacific was imminent, but that the first blow by Japanese forces was expected to fall upon Guam or the Philippines. With regard to the security of the American military installations in Hawaii, Short was more concerned with a "fifth column" of saboteurs being among the 150,000 Hawaiian residents of Japanese descent. He had, therefore, ordered his aircraft to be removed from their revetments and hangars and parked in the open, wingtip to wingtip, where they would be easier to guard—and sitting ducks for strafing Zero fighters and plunging Val dive-bombers.

Wheeler Field, the bomber base at Hickam, and the Marine Corps Air Station at Ewa, as well as NAS Kaneohe Bay and Bellows Army Air Field on the island's windward shore, were all struck within minutes of the first bombs falling on the airstrip on Ford Island, an effort calculated to neutralize Oahu's air defenses and prevent the Americans from pursuing the retiring strike force. A stunning 86 percent of the American aircraft based on the island—some 347 planes—would be heavily damaged or completely destroyed. Only a handful of American fighter pilots managed to get aloft, shooting down eleven of the twenty-nine Japanese planes lost during the raid.

In the very front of the battleship queue, the *California* was hammered by two torpedoes and began flooding uncontrollably as water poured through manholes that had been left uncovered. When General Quarters is sounded aboard a naval vessel, standard procedure calls for the crew to set Material Condition Z, or "Condition Zed" in the parlance of the day, where all hatches, doors, and fittings marked with a "Z" symbol are slammed shut and dogged tight. On the *Oklahoma*, there was no time to finish setting Condition Zed and ensure the watertight integrity of the ship, no time to conduct counterflooding that might have kept her from capsizing. In less than two minutes the *Oklahoma* was struck by five torpedoes and immediately began listing heavily to port. The executive officer and the senior man aboard, Commander Jesse Kenworthy, had not yet reached his battle station in the ship's conning tower before the list steepened to 35 degrees. As more torpedoes tore into the hull of the old battlewagon and the list increased even further, oil surged upward from her fuel bunkers to cover the weather decks.

"It was now obvious that the ship was going to continue to roll over and I climbed over the boat deck toward the starboard side," Kenworthy would report. "Men were beginning to come up from below through hatches and gun ports and from them it was learned that the ship was filling with water in many spaces below." Jesse Kenworthy quickly decided the *Oklahoma* was beyond saving and that his responsibility had shifted: He had to get as many men to safety as possible. Kenworthy issued the order to Abandon Ship.

Seaman Erwin Mitschek was manning a starboard antiaircraft battery on the *Oklahoma* when Kenworthy's order was passed. "I secured my gun and I went down on the boat deck, and there was a two-inch hawser between the *Oklahoma* and the *Maryland*. That's how we were tied up together. And I decided, well, hey, I gotta get off of here. So I started to climb hand over hand, you know, like Tarzan does."

Just astern of the capsizing *Oklahoma*, the captain and crew of the *West Virginia* were working fast to save their ship from a similar fate. The first four torpedoes to strike her port side had impacted against a belt of defensive armor. The strengthened bulkheads immediately behind the armor had been distorted but nevertheless held, a testimony to the sturdiness of the anti-torpedo protections built into the *Colorado*-class battleships. However, the joints of several steel hull plates above the belt were fractured; below the armor a huge split in the hull flooded the ship's fire rooms. The resulting list allowed the next two torpedoes to strike above the armor belt nearly amidships, and the waters of Pearl Harbor poured into the jagged, blasted gaps. The *West Virginia* was in serious trouble.

After making sure that his antiaircraft batteries were manned and firing, Lieutenant Claude Ricketts, the senior gunnery officer aboard, dashed to his battle station in the fire control tower. As the deck lurched and tilted beneath his feet, Ricketts, who had once served as the *West Virginia*'s damage control officer, sought out Captain Bennion in the adjacent conning tower.

"Captain! Shall I go below and counterflood?" he asked.

"Yes, do that!" the captain responded.

Ricketts quickly descended to "Times Square" on the main deck, an open space amidships where the fore-to-aft and port-to-starboard passageways intersected. There he came upon Garnett Billingsley, a veteran boatswain's mate first class who was skilled at damage control. Together they raced to the starboard side of the ship, down ladders and through escape scuttles to the third deck.

"The ship was now listing so heavily that on the linoleum decks it was impossible to walk without holding on to something," Ricketts later reported. "I reached the third deck by the ladder at frame 87 starboard and went forward to the first group of counterflood valves. Billingsley went aft and got a crank for operating the valves. When he came back, Rucker and Bobick, shipfitters from Repair Three, came with him. Billingsley and I started counterflooding while the other men assisted at other valves."

Behind the steel skin of the *West Virginia*'s hull there was a 4-foot-wide void space. Beyond the void lay a fuel oil bunker, followed by yet another void space. Behind the armored bulkheads of the inner void lay the ship's interior work and living spaces. These robust outer layers were designed to absorb and distribute the energy of exploding torpedoes. As Billingsley and the two shipfitters cranked opened the valves, seawater rushed in to fill the starboard voids and the *West Virginia* slowly began to right herself.

"When I was assured that counterflooding was well under way, I told Rucker to counterflood everything on the starboard side until the ship was on an even keel," Ricketts stated. "It was not long before the excessive list to port began to decrease."

Nothing further could be done to stop the battleship from settling into the shallow water of Pearl Harbor, but the action had saved her from capsizing like the unfortunate *Oklahoma* and allowed the "Wee Vee" to be raised and repaired to fight again another day. The steep list to port had caused the hulls of the *West Virginia* and *Tennessee* to slam together, pinning the *Tennessee* against the concrete mooring quay on her starboard side. This caused even further damage to both ships, but it had the effect of slowing the progress of the *West Virginia*'s list and kept her from turning over before she could be counterflooded.

Even as the *Oklahoma*, *West Virginia*, and *California* were shuddering from the impacts of torpedoes, a formation of forty-nine more Kate torpedo planes, these carrying armor-piercing bombs, appeared some 3,000 feet above Battleship Row. Five of these 800-kilogram projectiles, which were actually converted 16-inch naval artillery shells, rained down upon the *Arizona*. One plunged into the water so close to her port bow that many believed the ship had been struck by a torpedo; another caromed off the armor of the Number Four Turret and smashed through the starboard portion of the quarterdeck. Two more bomb hits would ravage the *Arizona* before the last—and most catastrophic—struck forward, near Turret Number Two.

In mere seconds, flames rolled into magazines that stored black powder used for the launching charges of the *Arizona*'s seaplane catapults and smokeless powder for the 14-inch main guns, touching off an explosion so horrendous that several eyewitnesses, including a dumbfounded Admiral Kimmel watching from his neighbor's yard in Aiea Heights, claimed that the bow of the great battleship actually lifted from the surface of Pearl Harbor. Residents of Oahu would recall the sound of the horrific thunderclap that signaled the destruction of the *Arizona* for the rest of their lives. A few can still hear it to this day. In the blink of an eye, the lives of

Rear Admiral Isaac Kidd, Captain Franklin Van Valkenburgh, and over a thousand officers, sailors, and marines of the *Arizona* were suddenly and forever extinguished.

Roscoe Hillenkoetter, the *West Virginia*'s executive officer, was thrown from his feet by the concussion of the blast. The flames erupting from the *Arizona* were "higher than the foretop. Burning debris of sizes from a fraction of an inch to five inches in diameter rained on the quarterdeck of the *West Virginia*."

Across the harbor, Radioman Ray Daves was hurrying ammunition to the crew of a .30 caliber machine gun on the roof of the submarine base headquarters building when he witnessed the explosion. Daves had a buddy on the *Arizona*, George Maybee.

"I could actually feel the concussion," Daves recalled. "It was like a small earthquake, and the man next to me was yelling 'That's the *Arizona*!' I thought I was going to be sick. I doubled over and dropped to my knees and all I could say was 'No! Oh no!' The *Arizona* was a giant fireball. I couldn't imagine how George or anyone else on that ship might have survived."

George Maybee did not survive. Neither did Chief Bill Tisdale, who on Saturday morning had jokingly ordered his friend Joe Karb to "get off the ship" and return home to his wife. But others aboard the *Arizona* somehow lived. Gunner's Mate Second Class Jack McCarron was manning a 5-inch gun on the boat deck when the forward magazines exploded "[a]nd I was blown off the ship. Or I'd like to think that one of God's angels picked me up. I can remember being on the mount and the next thing I knew, I was in the water."

Herbert Buehl, an electrician's mate striker, had just arrived at his battle station on the fourth deck near the Number Three Turret when the first bombs struck the *Arizona*. Buehl suddenly found himself in total darkness, so he climbed a nearby ladder to the passageway between the Number Three and Four turrets. There he hesitated.

"I just stood there because I hadn't been given any permission to leave my battle station, and as I stood there, there was this terrific explosion," Buehl would state. "And it was just like a tornado had gone through the ship and it just pushed me from the top of the ladder to the bottom. And I have no idea how I got down there. All I know is that I was standing on the bottom of the ladder and so I just took my hands and I rubbed my body all over, and checked my arms and legs to see if I had any broken bones, or was bleeding, and I wasn't." After several minutes Buehl and other members of his division were able to grope their way topside to find that the entire forward portion of the ship was demolished and heavily involved in fire.

"There just wasn't anything left of it," Buehl said.

The *Arizona* had been turned into a floating inferno. Thousands of gallons of fuel oil gushed from her ruptured bunkers to float upon the surface of the water where it was readily ignited. The flaming oil drifted forward to threaten the *Tennessee*, where under the relentless strafing of Japanese planes, sailors deployed fire hoses to keep their ship from catching fire.

Another of the armor-piercing bombs was dropped upon the port side of the *West Virginia*, crashing through the superstructure and main decks to lodge itself on the second deck. Though it caused an enormous amount of damage, the huge shell fortunately did not explode. A second bomb struck the armored roof of Number Three Turret and broke apart. This bomb also failed to detonate but demolished two OS2U Kingfisher seaplanes perched atop the turret. One of the wrecked Kingfishers was hurled from its catapult, spilling burning gasoline across the main deck.

Machinist's Mate Gery Porter and another man had just taken cover from a strafing Japanese plane in the doorway of the ship's library, just forward of Number Three Turret, when the bomb hit.

"We stepped back out on the quarterdeck, and what had been a fairly clean quarterdeck when we went in was now a mess; one of our planes that had been sitting in the catapult on top of number three turret, was laying on the quarterdeck burning," Porter said. "And we realized we'd been hit right there. I didn't know for maybe a year or two what it was. It was a 500-pound projectile with fins fitted on it. It was a direct hit on number three turret and didn't go off. And I guess we were within fifty or sixty feet of it. We might've been in the same position as the *Arizona* had it gone off."

The *Tennessee*, moored inboard of the *West Virginia* and thus far spared any battle damage, was then targeted by the horizontal bombers.

She was also hit atop the Number Three Turret by a bomb that broke apart without exploding. The next bomb, however, struck the center gun of the Number Two Turret and detonated.

Standing in the doorway of the *West Virginia*'s starboard bridge wing, Captain Mervyn Bennion was struck down by a large metal fragment hurled from the terrific explosion that rocked the *Tennessee*. Having reappeared on the bridge, Lieutenant Ricketts called for Chief Pharmacist's Mate Leslie Leak to render aid to Bennion. The captain, Leak noted as he applied a battle dressing, had been eviscerated by the big piece of shrapnel and was rapidly spiraling into deep shock.

Upon learning that Captain Bennion had been grievously wounded, the *West Virginia*'s communications officer, Lieutenant Commander Doir Johnson, headed for the bridge along with Doris Miller, an African American mess steward and the ship's heavyweight boxing champion. Johnson had selected Miller to accompany him because the sailor was "a very powerfully built individual, having in mind that he might pick the captain up and carry him below." Mervyn Bennion knew he was dying, however, and protested against efforts to place him on a makeshift litter and lower him to safety.

"The Captain deserves the highest praise for his noble conduct to the last," Ricketts would state. "Although in great pain he kept inquiring about the condition of the ship, and whether or not we had any pumps running. He was particularly concerned about the fires on board and the oil on the surface of the water. I assured him that everyone was doing everything possible to fight the fire and control the damage. He did not want to be moved and after the fire started kept insisting that we leave him and go below. For a short time after he was wounded it would have been possible to lower him down, but his wound was so serious I knew that he would be better off with as little handling as possible."

As gently as they could, the sailors moved Captain Bennion to the port side of the navigation bridge, away from the thick black smoke that was beginning to envelop the foremast. Chief Leak would remain by his side while the other men returned to the fight. Ensign Victor Delano found that the .50 caliber machine guns mounted on the platform forward of the conning tower had not yet been manned, and directed two of the sailors to begin returning fire on the Japanese. Although he had never been trained to operate a machine gun, Cook Third Class Doris Miller was soon blazing away at the low-flying strafers.

"It wasn't hard," Miller said later. "I just pulled the trigger and she worked fine. I had watched the others with these guns. I guess I fired her for about fifteen minutes. I think I got one of those Jap planes. They were diving pretty close to us."

For the next several minutes Claude Ricketts busied himself with directing the firefighting efforts on the boat deck below the bridge. Water pressure was lacking, dense black smoke and intense heat soon made their position untenable, and it became clear that the men of the *West Virginia* were fighting a losing battle. Word came from Damage Control Central Station to abandon ship, and soon Chief Leak would emerge from the smoke to report: "Mr. Ricketts, the captain is about gone."

"As Commanding Officer of the USS *West Virginia*," the posthumous Congressional Medal of Honor citation would read, "after being mortally wounded, Captain Bennion evidenced apparent concern only in fighting and saving his ship, and strongly protested against being carried from the bridge."

Steadfast devotion to duty.

The phrase is frequently used by the sea services when rendering honors to those who have displayed unwavering courage in the face of great adversity. The virtue for which it stands had never been found in greater abundance than at this time, the most desperate hour in the history of the United States Navy.

Twenty-six-year-old Robert Raymond Scott was a machinist's mate first class aboard the *California*. He was at his battle station in the compressor room, providing the compressed air necessary for the operation of the ship's antiaircraft guns, when seawater began to flood the compartment from one of two torpedo strikes. It was a scenario for which the men had drilled countless times; all of the machinists save for one quickly exited through a hatchway. Scott, however, was still inside the compartment and refusing to leave.

"This is my station," Scott said, "and I will stay and give them air as long as the guns are firing." He then directed his shipmate to slam and dog the hatch.

Lieutenant Junior Grade (j.g.) Aloysius Schmitt, a Roman Catholic chaplain, was holding confession when the first torpedoes struck the *Oklahoma*. Father Schmitt and his parishioners found themselves trapped in their compartment belowdecks as the ship rapidly took on water and capsized. Without a thought for himself, the priest pushed a dozen men to safety through a small porthole before he drowned in the quickly rising flood of seawater that filled the space.

On the *Maryland*, gun captain Stanley Gruber had smashed open the locker containing the firing lock for his 5-inch antiaircraft gun and soon had the weapon in action, thumping away at the Japanese planes approaching low over Ford Island. The gun was usually served by a crew of eight, but Gruber had only one man to help him. In their rush to get the gun firing the two men had not taken the time to don hearing protection, and after several blasts from the muzzle of the 5-incher, Gruber's companion cried: "My ears! My ears!"

"To hell with your ears!" Gruber yelled back at him. "This is your ass!"

The destroyer *Monaghan* had cast off from her berthing in the East Loch and was under way, having already been dispatched to assist the *Ward* at the harbor entrance before the air raid began. Alerted to the presence of a midget submarine by the seaplane tender *Curtiss*, skipper William Burford unhesitatingly ordered the *Monaghan* to ram the intruder at flank speed, killing the two Japanese occupants.

Twenty-one-year-old Joseph Taussig Jr. was the son of an admiral and the grandson of another. A newly minted ensign, having graduated from the Naval Academy Class of 1941, Taussig was standing the forenoon watch as Officer of the Deck aboard the *Nevada*. One of her boilers had been providing steam for the turbines and power for the ship while in port. Taussig decided to have a second boiler lit, intending to shift the workload from one boiler to another around eight o'clock. He was on the quarterdeck, concerned with choosing an American flag of the proper size for the morning color ceremony, when the Japanese appeared over Pearl Harbor.

"Personal involvement in historical happenings creates vivid, life-long memories for the participant, but rare is the man who, at the moment, can visualize the entire forest being destroyed—he is far too busy ducking the trees that are falling all around him," Taussig would write. "As an individual, then, my view was restricted to what was going on in my immediate vicinity."

While bombs exploded on Ford Island, torpedoes crashed into Battleship Row, and the *Nevada*'s guns opened fire on the zooming Japanese planes, the young ensign ran from the quarterdeck and scurried topside, ascending six different ladders before arriving at his battle station in the starboard antiaircraft director.

"As I climbed through the door of the director, I was conscious that the cross hairs on my check sight were on an airplane, and I saw that it was hit almost immediately and went down trailing smoke," Taussig recalled. "The director was slewing around for another target when I was hit by a missile which passed completely through my thigh and through the case of the ballistic computer of the director which was directly in front of me. There was no pain, and because I was clutching the sides of the hatch as the director slewed around, I did not fall down. My left foot was grotesquely under my left armpit, but in the detachment of shock, I was not aware that this was particularly bad."

The dazed Ensign Taussig looked to the startled petty officer standing beside him.

"That's a hell of a place for a foot to be," he remarked.

Like Captain Bennion of the *West Virginia*, Joseph Taussig refused to be taken below. His badly mangled left leg was later amputated.

"They carried me into the Sky Control structure between the two AA directors, and laid me out on the deck. Eventually a hospital corpsman arrived with a basket stretcher, administered a shot of morphine, and got me into the stretcher. The rest of the morning was spent 'observing' the battle of Pearl Harbor through the eyes of the enlisted personnel who remained with me."

On the blazing *Arizona*, it seemed like Lieutenant Commander Samuel Fuqua was everywhere. The ship's damage control officer and first lieutenant, now the senior surviving officer aboard, had been momentarily knocked unconscious but was soon on his feet and leading the firefighting effort, hoping to buy enough time to get the few remaining survivors off the sinking battleship.

After the order to Abandon Ship had been passed, Gunner's Mate Third Class James Lawson found himself standing on the main deck near the *Arizona*'s Number Four Turret. A very frightened young member of Lawson's gun crew, one of the newly mobilized reservists, stood by his side. With flames rapidly consuming the ship, the two men realized they were going to have to jump overboard and swim for Ford Island while trying to avoid the thick layer of burning oil on the surface of the water. The problem was made even more daunting by the fact that the terrified novice couldn't swim. As they prepared to jump, Lawson suddenly realized that Commander Fuqua was standing next to him, telling Lawson that he had better get over the side.

"Where he came from I haven't any idea," Lawson would recall. "He just appeared from nowhere, like Jesus Christ. All of a sudden he was there."

"We've gotta go!" Lawson shouted, and shoved the young sailor into the water before jumping in after him.

Fuqua then located the admiral's barge, which was damaged but still operable. Boatswain's Mate Second Class John Anderson helped Fuqua load a dozen severely burned men into the barge. When they were finished, Fuqua ordered: "Get in, Andy."

"I can't go," Anderson replied, "my brother's up there."

Anderson gestured to the burning boat deck, where his twin brother Jake had been manning one of the antiaircraft batteries.

"He's gone," Fuqua told Anderson. "He couldn't have made it. You've got to go, otherwise you're going to go with him." In time Anderson would learn that Fuqua was correct; Jake had in fact perished, along with most of his gun crew.

"So he gave me a shove," Anderson remembered. "That's how I got in. I wasn't going in there, but he shoved me."

Not a strong swimmer himself, James Lawson had thrown an arm across the chest of his companion and tried to pull the young man along in an effort to reach Ford Island, but the current was steadily carrying them toward a mass of burning oil. Out of the smoke Sam Fuqua appeared suddenly before Lawson once again, this time in the admiral's barge loaded with wounded men. Someone extended a T-shirt for Lawson to grasp, and the two struggling men were towed to safety. Commander Fuqua would use the barge to pluck several more oil-drenched and wounded sailors from the water under the intense strafing of Japanese planes.

Across the channel, the *New Orleans* had been receiving power and lighting from shore lines at the Ten-Ten Dock while undergoing repairs to her turbines. A Japanese bomb landed alongside the heavy cruiser, injuring several members of the crew and dousing the lights. With no power to operate the ammunition hoists, sailors quickly formed a "daisy chain," a staggered double column, to pass ammunition by hand from the magazines to the antiaircraft batteries. The chaplain of the *New Orleans*, Lieutenant Howell Forgy, rushed back and forth from the galley to the ammunition lines in the dim light and stifling heat, bringing pitchers of drinking water and shouts of encouragement to the hardworking sailors muscling the heavy shells topside.

"Well, Chaplain, I guess we're not having church this morning," one of the sweating young sailors remarked.

Forgy shrugged and responded with a one-liner that would soon become famous: "Praise the Lord and pass the ammunition."

The hapless repair ship *Vestal* had been in the wrong place at the wrong time, hit by two bombs intended for the *Arizona* tied alongside. One bomb exploded in the stores hold and started a fire after smashing through three decks; the second struck the starboard side and passed completely through the bottom of the ship, leaving a gaping 5-foot hole. When the forward magazines of the *Arizona* exploded, the tremendous shock wave hurled over a hundred *Vestal* sailors into the harbor, including the captain, Cassin Young. Soaking wet and furious, his skin blackened by fuel oil, Commander Young climbed back aboard the *Vestal* to find the remainder of his crew gathering at the starboard rail.

"Where in the hell do you think you're going?" the captain demanded.

"We're abandoning ship, sir!" one of the men replied.

"Get back to your stations!" Young admonished. "You don't abandon ship on me!"

Over the next two hours the crew of the *Vestal* would rescue dozens of severely burned survivors from the *Arizona* and deliver them to the hospital ship *Solace* at anchor in the East Loch before Young beached his stricken vessel on a shoal near the Aiea Landing.

"Throughout the entire action," Roscoe Hillenkoetter of the *West Virginia* would write, "and through all the arduous labors which followed, there was never the slightest sign of faltering or of cowardice. The actions of the officers and men were all wholly commendable; their spirit was marvelous; there was no panic, no shirking nor flinching, and words fail in attempting to describe the truly magnificent display of courage, discipline, and devotion to duty of all officers and men."

A tranquil and majestic setting just moments before, Battleship Row had been quickly transformed into a scene from a hellish nightmare. Deep crimson flames and billowing pillars of jet-black smoke rolled high into the blue tropical sky from fires raging aboard the *West Virginia*, the *Tennessee*, and what was left of the devastated *Arizona*, which was settling rapidly by the bow. Flaming slicks of oil were drifting far southward to the Fox Three quay where the crew of the *California* struggled to correct their ship's heavy list and keep her afloat. After the *California* had been hit by two torpedoes, a near miss from the horizontal bombers tore a large hole in her port bow; another bomb had landed on her main deck to start a fire. The *Oklahoma* was a truly horrifying sight; only the bottom of her shattered hull and two blades from one of her giant propellers remained visible above the surface.

Scattered across the water were hundreds of men, some floating facedown and motionless, some horribly burned, others clinging to kapok jackets or paddling furiously to get clear of the blazing oil. Tugs, launches, and whaleboats came to the rescue, weaving through the smoke and debris. In the bow of one of the whaleboats was Doris Miller, hauling aboard every wounded and half-drowned survivor he could reach. Chief Boatswain's Mate Lenard Jansen and his crew would become the most unlikely of heroes when their low-born garbage lighter *YG-17* was pressed into service as a fire and rescue boat, taking station off the port quarter of the *West Virginia* and directing hose streams onto the roaring flames.

After the crew of the *West Virginia* were ordered to abandon ship, dozens of men climbed aboard the *Tennessee* to help fight fires, tend to the wounded, pass ammunition, and man the antiaircraft guns. Men from the capsized *Oklahoma* did the same aboard the *Maryland*, as did a handful of refugees from the *Arizona* once they reached the nearby *Nevada*. To the astonishment of everyone in the harbor, this last battleship in the column was on the move.

CHAPTER 8
SECOND WAVE

REAR ADMIRAL WILLIAM FURLONG WAS THE SOPA—SENIOR OFFICER Present Afloat—in Pearl Harbor on December 7. When the first Japanese torpedo planes roared past his flagship, the elderly minelayer *Oglala* moored at the Ten-Ten Dock, Furlong ordered the signal *ALL SHIPS SORTIE* to be hoisted.

Thanks to the foresight of Ensign Taussig, rather than having the requisite single boiler lit while in port, the *Nevada* had two of her six boilers online, allowing her to build enough steam to be under way within forty minutes. After the first wave of Japanese attackers winged their way north toward their carriers, the *Nevada* slowly backed away from quay Fox Eight and stood out for the channel, passing through the smoke from the burning *Arizona* and the treacherous oil fires. It was a remarkable feat of ship handling, considering it was performed without the aid of tugboats, a harbor pilot, or her captain, and with a reserve officer in command.

Lieutenant Commander Francis Thomas, a graduate of the Naval Academy, Class of 1925, had been working as an engineer at Republic Steel in his hometown of Buffalo, New York, when he was recalled to active duty in February 1941 and assigned to the *Nevada* as damage control officer. With the captain, the XO, and the next five officers in the chain of command ashore on a Sunday morning, the thirty-seven-year-old reservist suddenly found himself in command of a battleship under attack.

Fortunately for Commander Thomas, the *Nevada* had many capable junior officers and chiefs on board to assist him, men who proved to be competent, solid professionals under fire. Chief Boatswain's Mate Ed Hill clambered down to Fox Eight to cast off the *Nevada*'s mooring lines before diving into the oily water and swimming back to the ship. Chief Quartermaster Bob Sedberry, the man who had ordered the engine room to raise steam when the attack began, was behind the ship's wheel. Lieutenant Lawrence Ruff, the communications officer, had been attending church services aboard the hospital ship *Solace*. Speeding back to the *Nevada* in a motor launch, Ruff joined Thomas on the bridge to act as navigator.

The *Nevada* had been struck by a torpedo at frame 41 between the first and second turrets, tearing open the outer blister, rupturing joints between several steel plates, and flooding many portside compartments. Thomas promptly ordered counterflooding which corrected the 5-degree list. Despite her wounds, and having already knocked four Japanese planes out of the air, the oldest battlewagon in the fleet was headed out to sea. Even amid the chaos going on around them, people all across Pearl Harbor stopped what they were doing to watch the spectacle.

As the *Nevada* steamed past the Ten-Ten Dock, more Japanese planes appeared over Pearl Harbor. The second wave of the attack, launched thirty minutes after the first, consisted of fifty-four Kate torpedo planes, seventy-five Val dive-bombers, and thirty-four Zero fighters, the bombers carrying 250-kilogram general-purpose bombs. It soon became apparent to everyone—including the Japanese—that if the *Nevada* were to be sunk in the harbor inlet she would become a serious hazard to navigation, perhaps even trapping the ninety-odd vessels in the anchorage and rendering Pearl Harbor useless as a naval base for months to come.

The full fury of the second attack then descended upon the *Nevada*, but the old girl steamed defiantly on, her antiaircraft guns hammering away at the swirling dive-bombers. A bomb exploded and started a fire on the boat deck; another struck the portside antiaircraft director and crashed through the navigation and signal bridges before exploding on the Number 6 gun casement.

Radioman Third Class Ted Mason had spent the last hour dodging Japanese machine-gun fire at his battle station in the *California*'s maintop. From this vantage point he would have an eagle's-eye view of the attack on Pearl Harbor and bear witness to the *Nevada*'s epic sortie in its entirety.

"All her antiaircraft guns were firing," Mason would write, "some in the very midst of fire and smoke. At her stern, the Stars and Stripes flew proudly from the flagstaff. I had never seen anything so gallant. I choked with emotion as she came bravely on. A Val was hit and plunged into the water at full dive. In the maintop, we gave the crew of the *Nevada* our shouted encouragement and our prayerful curses and our great vows of vengeance. Some of us were crying unashamed tears."

Admiral Furlong had an urgent signal flashed to the *Nevada*: Do not attempt to exit the harbor; proceed to the Middle Loch on the north side of Ford Island and drop anchor. As she moved to comply, three more bombs struck the *Nevada*'s forecastle, one of them destroying the anchor windlass and capstans and twisting the two vertical shafts of the anchor engine. It also killed most of the anchoring detail, including the valiant Chief Hill, who was blown overboard by the explosion.

The *Nevada* had been hit by one torpedo and at least five bombs. Fires were breaking out everywhere. Damage to pumps and fire mains resulted in little water pressure being available for fighting the flames, and the *Nevada* was taking on water and traveling low by the bow. Now unable to drop anchor, Commander Thomas ordered Chief Sedberry to beach the *Nevada* off Hospital Point to keep her from sinking. The action would save the ship, allowing her to be salvaged, refitted, and returned to combat. Two and a half years later, the thunder of the *Nevada*'s 14-inch main guns would be heard off the Cherbourg Peninsula of France as she provided fire support for the invasion of Normandy.

"I'm the only officer ever to be awarded the Navy Cross for running a ship aground," Thomas would remark to a newspaper reporter many years later.

Through the smoke and gunfire a motor launch roared across the harbor, cut its engine, and drifted alongside the beached battleship. Standing in the bow of the launch was the *Nevada*'s commanding officer, Captain Francis Scanland, who had been on liberty in Honolulu when the attack began. Fearing that Pearl Harbor's strong current might still dislodge his ship and carry it into the channel, Scanland directed the minesweeper *Avocet* and the district harbor tug *Hoga* to nudge the *Nevada* across the narrow inlet and ground her firmly, stern first, onto the eastern shore of the Waipio Peninsula.

The *Nevada*'s brave attempt to exit the harbor would inadvertently benefit the *Pennsylvania*, having the effect of drawing many Japanese aircraft of the second wave away from the CINCPAC flagship as it sat upon blocks in Dry Dock Number One. Also perched side by side in the dry dock just forward of the *Pennsylvania* were two *Mahan*-class destroyers under repair, *Cassin* and *Downes*. The commanding officer of the *Pennsylvania*, Captain Charles Cooke Jr., witnessed a large flight of Japanese bombers approach the dry dock, when suddenly "about two-thirds appeared to swerve to the left" to pursue the *Nevada*.

The remaining bombers in the formation released their ordnance, passing over the dry dock in five separate high-altitude attacks. A bomb exploded on the dock alongside the battleship; another crashed into the *Downes*. A sister ship of the two destroyers, the *Shaw*, was struck three times while at rest in a nearby floating dry dock. Then the *Pennsylvania* herself was hit, a bomb passing through the boat deck and exploding in a 5-inch gun casement, killing nearly thirty personnel, including the first lieutenant and the ship's physician.

"I never even heard anything go off," recalled Seaman Everett Hyland, who was helping pass ammunition to the 3-inch gun position on the *Pennsylvania*'s fantail when the bomb exploded. "The first thing I knew I'm flat on my face and my arms were out in front of me and my skin is all peeled and curled and I'm bleeding. So I picked myself up and I'm wondering where the gun crew went. There didn't seem to be anybody around. One of the nice things, if that's what you want to call it, when you get hit real badly, you don't feel anything for a while. There isn't any pain. For some reason you get pretty numb." His limbs badly burned and torn by shrapnel, Hyland would spend the next nine months in the hospital.

Oil flowing from the ruptured fuel tanks of the *Downes* was soon ablaze. Sailors and yard workers rushed to stretch fire hoses, even while enemy planes continued their strafing attacks, but the explosion on the dock had damaged the water main, resulting in pitifully underpowered hose streams. According to Cooke, by the time the gates of the dry dock were opened in an effort to drown the flames, somewhere around 9:20 a.m., "both destroyers ahead were on fire from stem to stern." As seawater quickly filled the dry dock, burning oil spread across its surface to threaten the *Pennsylvania*. The *Cassin*, with several hull plates removed to facilitate repairs, quickly took on water and capsized, rolling onto the blazing *Downes*.

Ten minutes later, the harbor was shaken by yet another massive explosion as fire reached the forward magazines of the *Shaw*. Torpedo warheads aboard the *Cassin* and *Downes* also began to explode as they were enveloped in flames. A large fragment weighing nearly half a ton, what was later discovered to be a torn segment of torpedo tube, wobbled through the air and smashed onto the *Pennsylvania*'s forecastle. Power was finally restored to the fire pumps aboard the battleship, and over the next hour the flames were gradually brought under control.

Admiral Kimmel witnessed the disaster unfold before his eyes as he stood on the second floor of the headquarters building at the submarine base, where his staff had hastily assembled. Officers were working the phones, sending and receiving messages, consulting maps and intercepts, working feverishly to discover where the attacking planes had come from. Japanese radio signals had provided clues, but direction-finding equipment had obtained only a bilateral bearing on their source. The Japanese carriers, therefore, were either due north or due south of Hawaii. Having only a fifty-fifty shot at locating the Japanese fleet and striking back, Kimmel ordered Bill Halsey's *Enterprise* task force, on their return voyage from Wake Island, to steam south. They would find only a vast and empty expanse of ocean.

As the admiral watched the antiaircraft guns of his fleet open fire on the planes of the second attack wave, a spent machine-gun bullet crashed through the office window, thumping harmlessly off his chest.

"It would have been more merciful had it killed me," Kimmel told one of his staff officers.

Yamamoto's objective of destroying the battleships of the US Pacific Fleet, allowing the Japanese to "run wild" in the Pacific, had been realized. The route to the coveted oil fields of the Dutch East Indies and Borneo—via Hong Kong, the Philippines, Guam, Wake, Singapore, and Malaya—was now wide open, with little to fear from the American Navy. At some time around 10:00 a.m. Hawaiian time—approximately two hours after the first bombs fell upon Ford Island—the last Japanese attacker escaped to the northwest.

Battleship Row was an utter shambles. The *California* was on fire and sinking, with 98 members of the crew killed and 61 wounded. The overturned *Oklahoma* reported 429 officers and men killed or missing. The *West Virginia* had also sunk but on an even keel, and 106 of her crew would be listed as killed in action. By comparison the two battleships moored inboard had gotten off easy: the *Maryland* and *Tennessee* had each sustained two bomb hits and lost 4 crewmen. The *Nevada* would suffer 60 men dead and over 100 wounded, while 27 men were killed aboard the *Pennsylvania*. The casualty list from the *Arizona* alone would account for nearly half of the Americans killed at Pearl Harbor: 1,177 members of her 1,512-man crew were dead.

The navy had suffered the most from the Japanese surprise attack: 2,008 naval personnel were killed and 711 wounded. The marines would list 109 killed and 69 wounded, while the army reported 218 killed and 364 wounded.

Civilians also lost their lives, 68 all told, including 3 members of the Honolulu Fire Department who had responded to fight the fires at Hickam Field. The firefighters would receive the Order of the Purple Heart, an honor that had once been reserved only for military personnel. Mervyn Bennion, Samuel Fuqua, Edwin Hill, Isaac Kidd, Robert Scott, Franklin Van Valkenburgh, Cassin Young, and eight other American sailors at Pearl Harbor would receive the Medal of Honor. Francis Thomas, Doris Miller, and Joseph Taussig would be awarded the Navy Cross.

Eighteen ships had been sunk or heavily damaged. The elderly battleship *Utah*, stripped of her heavy guns and converted into a target ship, had been tied to one of the quays on the north shore of Ford Island, usually reserved for aircraft carriers. The unfortunate *Utah* rolled over and sank after being hit by two torpedoes. The cruiser *Raleigh* had been torpedoed, as had the *Helena* in her berth at the Ten-Ten Dock, the underwater concussion damaging the nearby minelayer *Oglala* so severely that she also took on water, capsized, and sank. The cruiser *Honolulu* had been damaged by a near miss; one of the Japanese planes gunned down by the

Curtiss had crashed into the crane on her fantail, and three minutes later the seaplane tender had been hit by a bomb.

Firefighting and rescue operations were already well under way. Damage control teams worked to shore up dished bulkheads, secure leaks, and pump water from flooded compartments. Fire and rescue parties from the battleships and civilian workers from the Navy Yard swarmed over the hull of the *Oklahoma*, tapping away with heavy tools, listening desperately for any signs of life, trying to locate the dozens of men trapped inside.

Hundreds of shocked, burned, and wounded men were being rushed to hospitals. On the *Solace* and at the dispensary on Ford Island, hospital corpsmen and physicians from the battleships, some of them wounded themselves, pitched in to help medical personnel treat the overwhelming number of casualties. Corpsmen from the fleet auxiliary *Argonne* set up a casualty collection point on the Ten-Ten Dock. A mobile field hospital was hastily erected in the Navy Yard. By nightfall, the 250-bed Naval Hospital Pearl Harbor would have a patient census of 960. Emergency rooms at Tripler Army Hospital and Queen's Hospital in Honolulu were soon crowded with wounded servicemen and civilians alike.

On Ford Island, in the Navy Yard, at Hickam Field, and at military installations across the island, warehouses and armories were unlocked and helmets, gas masks, weapons, and ammunition were doled out. The likelihood of another Japanese attack, perhaps even an invasion, was on everyone's mind.

James Jones, who would one day pen the splendid novel *From Here to Eternity*, was a rifleman with the 25th Infantry Division based at Schofield Barracks. Within hours of the Japanese attack, Jones's company received orders to move out. On the way to occupy defensive positions on the southern beaches of Oahu, the long column of army trucks passed Pearl Harbor. In his reminiscences of December 7, Jones would speak for an entire generation of Americans.

"We could see the huge rising smoke columns high in the clear sunny Hawaiian air for miles before we ever got near Pearl," Jones wrote. "I shall never forget the sight as we passed over the lip of the central plateau and began the long drop down to Pearl City.

"I remember thinking, with a sense of the profoundest awe, that none of our lives would ever be the same," Jones continued, "that a social, even a cultural watershed had been crossed which we could never go back over, and I wondered how many of us would survive to see the end results. I wondered if I would. I had just turned twenty, the month before."

There was one man at Pearl Harbor, however, who had little doubt what the future held for him, for the next several months at least. Captain Homer N. Wallin was the material and salvage officer for Battle Force, United States Pacific Fleet.

CHAPTER 9
SHORT WAR, LONG WAR

On Ford Island, American sailors and marines were digging fighting holes and filling sandbags while oily black smoke from fires on the *Arizona* and *West Virginia* drifted over them. Aboard the damaged *Maryland* and *Tennessee*, the only two battleships remaining afloat, antiaircraft directors and batteries were fully manned and the guns restocked with ammunition. Sailors from the beached *Nevada*, many of them carrying Springfield rifles for the first time since boot camp, stood guard in the cane fields of Waipio Point. Soldiers from Fort DeRussy were stringing barbed wire and sighting machine guns along the sands of Waikiki.

The few undamaged reconnaissance aircraft that were left, a mere handful of PBY Catalinas, took to the air to perform long-range searches. At Wheeler Field, bulldozers worked to clear the wreckage while mechanics and armorers made ready the remaining P-36 and P-40 fighter planes that were still flyable. Cruisers, destroyers, and submarines stood out from Pearl Harbor to counter any potential seaborne threats.

"No enemy was sighted by the special search to the southwestward . . . it appeared from radio intelligence that all of the enemy striking force had been to the northward and retired northwestward to about 750 miles," one of Admiral Kimmel's staff officers recorded in the CINCPAC Running Estimate and Summary. He added: "Of course they might soon return."

As the afternoon wore on and darkness began to fall upon the island of Oahu, members of the US Armed Forces braced for another Japanese attack. It never came. The question of *why* Admiral Chuichi Nagumo chose to withdraw his task force left American naval and military strategists scratching their heads in the aftermath of the Pearl Harbor raid, and has continued to confound historians ever since.

On the eve of the assault, Nagumo had conferred with his staff aboard the flagship *Akagi*, reviewing the latest intelligence data on the disposition of the United States Pacific Fleet in Pearl Harbor. A submarine had reported that no American ships were in Lahaina Roads. According to spies operating from the Japanese consulate in Honolulu, the eight battleships of the Pacific Fleet were in port. Someone speculated that the three American aircraft carriers then operating in the Pacific, *Enterprise*, *Lexington*, and *Saratoga*, all of which had been absent from Pearl Harbor, might be returning to their base in the next twenty-four hours.

"If that happens," said Captain Minoru Genda, the air operations officer, "I don't care if all eight of the battleships are away."

"As an airman, you naturally place much importance on carriers," replied Nagumo's senior staff officer, Commander Tomatsu Oishi. "Of course it would be good if we could get three of them, but I think it would be better if we get all eight of the battleships."

Not only had the opportunity to sink the US Navy's aircraft carriers been missed, when the main effort of the Japanese raid was concentrated on Battleship Row, the sprawling bulk fuel storage facility just east of the submarine base was left untouched. Had a Japanese third wave struck the tank farm and set ablaze the four and a half million gallons of fuel oil being stored there, the American fleet would have been forced to withdraw to the West Coast and rendered incapable of conducting any serious combat operations in the Pacific for months.

The expansive repair facilities of the Navy Yard were also left unscathed, ensuring Pearl Harbor's continued viability as a major naval base. The Navy's Bureau of Yards and Docks had been steadily improving Pearl Harbor's shore establishment throughout the late 1930s with a series of public works projects, a program that had shifted into high gear after the fleet moved to Hawaii in 1940. In that year alone, more than four thousand skilled laborers had been recruited from the mainland and brought to Oahu to work in the Navy Yard. New administration buildings, barracks, and a supply depot had been constructed; work had already begun on new mooring facilities, two additional dry docks, and a new powerhouse that had been approved by Congress in the 1941 defense budget.

These new installations, along with the numerous welding, electrical, fabrication, and machine shops; the marine railway; the repair basin; and the Yard's 200-ton hammerhead crane were intact at the end of the Japanese raid. Six months later, the badly damaged carrier *Yorktown* would be repaired by a force of 1,400 Navy Yard personnel and returned to sea within seventy-two hours of limping into Pearl Harbor, in time to contribute to the decisive American victory at the Battle of Midway. CINCPAC headquarters had also been completely ignored by the planners of the attack, as had the submarine base, which would serve as the nerve center for a relentless undersea warfare campaign that systematically wiped out the Japanese merchant marine over the course of the next three years.

Isoroku Yamamoto had gambled on the concept of a "short war," of dealing a blow so swift and devastating that it would shock and demoralize the American population, breathing new life into the American isolationist movement and compelling the political leadership of the United States to sue for peace. The Pearl Harbor operation and its desired outcome, the Commander-in-Chief of the Combined Fleet told the officers on his staff, had become "an article of faith," language meant to soothe the nerves of those who had expressed apprehension over the enormous risks involved in the undertaking. One wonders if Yamamoto actually believed that the Americans would so readily capitulate. It is nothing short of incredible that an astute officer of his education and experience would be capable of such a horrible miscalculation, that a man who had spent so much time among the American people could so underestimate their resiliency and resolve.

The preeminent Pearl Harbor historian Gordon W. Prange has observed that Yamamoto's misconceptions were indicative of just how poorly the Japanese and Americans understood one another in the mid-twentieth century. Another possibility exists: In light of Yamamoto's remark to Prince Konoe—that he would "run wild for six months" at the beginning of a war with the United States, and after that, "have no expectation for success"—one might surmise that the admiral had only hoped to cripple the American fleet long enough to secure the eastern flank and consolidate the gains of the Southern Plan operations, and that the stated goal of forcing the United States into a favorable peace settlement represented what he knew to be an unlikely best-case scenario.

For his part, Admiral Nagumo, the officer in tactical command, believed that the goals of the Pearl Harbor operation had been achieved. All eight of the battleships had been sunk or damaged. Now that the enemy had been aroused, he did not want to incur any further risk to his carriers so far from Japanese waters. Despite the vigorous protests of Misuo Fuchida, Nagumo ordered his task force brought about on a northwest heading, without launching the planned third attack wave.

In their effort to crush the US Pacific Fleet's battle line and ensure a short war, the strategy and tactics chosen by the leadership of the battleship-centric Imperial Japanese Navy guaranteed that the war would be a very long and costly one.

The *Oklahoma* had rotated 175 degrees to port, stopping only when her masts and stack sank into the mud of the harbor floor. Lieutenant Commander William Hobby stood on the overturned hull near the bow, watching the last of his shipmates slide into the water and begin paddling to the *Maryland* or toward Ford Island. The forty-two-year-old native of Georgia had served on the "Okie" once before, as a newly commissioned ensign following his graduation from Annapolis in 1923. Over the next fifteen years of his naval career, Hobby would serve in the submarine service and command the destroyer *Anderson*. In March of 1941 he reported for duty aboard the *Oklahoma* once again, this time as damage control officer and first lieutenant.

Satisfied that he was the last man remaining on the hull of the capsized battleship, Hobby kicked off his shoes and stripped down to his skivvies, preparing to jump clear of the ship himself. Suddenly one of the *Oklahoma*'s motor launches appeared off the bow with Boatswain's Mate Adolph Bothne at the helm, motioning for Hobby to climb aboard. He did, but instead of heading ashore Hobby directed the boat to join the makeshift flotilla of rescue craft ranging along Battleship Row, pulling survivors from the water amid the oil fires and the strafing. When it appeared that the Japanese attack had waned and there was no one left in the water to rescue, Commander Hobby had Bothne proceed to the Mine Dock near the submarine base.

At the receiving station Hobby was issued the only clothing they had left on hand: a set of blue dungarees, black leather shoes, and a white sailor's hat. Returning to the dock, the underdressed Hobby managed to convince the coxswain of another boat that he was, in fact, an officer. He then ordered the man to whisk him back across the harbor to the Fox Five berth, where he would find an array of small craft surrounding the *Oklahoma* and several men now reconvened on the exposed hull. Among them was Bothne, who had returned with some two dozen *Oklahoma* sailors from the Ford Island landing.

The fact that men were still alive aboard the overturned battleship was confirmed when a young sailor suddenly breached the surface of the water alongside the wreckage, his chest heaving violently as he gulped in air. Daniel Weissman, a teenager from Brooklyn who claimed that he had never learned to swim, explained to the rescuers that he had been at his battle station in the lower ammunition handling room on the starboard side near the Number Four Turret when the ship capsized and began to flood. Weissman had been able to make it into a nearby escape trunk, but that space also began to quickly fill with seawater. Weissman then dove into the water and swam—*downward*—over 20 feet to the hatch that led to the main deck. The young seaman first class reported that men were still alive in compartments adjacent to the Number Four Turret.

"With several men I went over the hull discussing possibilities of salvaging those still alive inside," William Hobby stated. The sailors fanned across the hull, working their way along the length of the *Oklahoma*, tapping with hammers and listening intently for any response. Soon they heard the forlorn banging of steel on steel in return, often in the pattern of "three dots, three dashes, three dots," the Morse Code "SOS" distress signal.

Hobby and his men were soon joined by Commander Edgar Kranzfelder, who had been dispatched by Vice Admiral Walter Anderson to lead the *Oklahoma* rescue effort. As Commander Battleships, Battle Force, Pacific Fleet, Admiral Anderson had assumed control of the firefighting and rescue operations in Pearl Harbor. Anderson was not only concerned with keeping the fires aboard the battleships, particularly those of the

West Virginia and *Arizona*, from hampering rescue teams and causing even more widespread damage, he also worried that their towering smoke columns would provide a navigational beacon for the pilots of a third Japanese attack. Anderson had already ordered the minesweeper *Tern* and the submarine rescue vessel *Widgeon* to reinforce the resolute crew of the garbage scow *YG-17* in their struggle to bring the fires on board the *West Virginia* under control. Later they would be joined by the minesweeper *Bobolink* and the seagoing tugboat *Navajo.*

Through dense, turbulent black smoke, the smaller craft nosed into the burning dreadnought. Sailors operating firefighting monitors were able to look down upon the *West Virginia*'s immense gun turrets as she rested on the bottom of the harbor with her main decks awash. Shipboard fires often burn well in excess of 1,000 degrees Fahrenheit; the heat of the fire on the *West Virginia* was so intense that portholes were found melted into drooping, oblong shapes. The ad hoc squadron of fireboats would remain alongside until 2:30 the following afternoon, when the last flames aboard the *West Virginia* were finally extinguished. The main firefighting effort was then shifted to the sad heap of blackened wreckage that was the *Arizona*, which would continue burning into the early afternoon of December 9.

Commander Kranzfelder had arrived on the *Oklahoma*'s hull clutching a set of the ship's engineering blueprints and was soon directing the fire and rescue parties from the *Maryland* and *Tennessee* to aid in what would prove to be an extensive and complicated extrication problem. Kranzfelder decided to establish a command post aboard the *Maryland* and designate William Hobby as on-scene leader, with the two men communicating over a sound-powered telephone line.

Commander Hobby would remain on the hull of the *Oklahoma* without rest for the next sixty hours.

Kranzfelder ordered the destroyer tender *Rigel* to assist with her complement of repair and salvage personnel and sent for divers from the submarine base. Despite having gone through hell themselves, enduring the worst of the Japanese attack and with their own ship badly damaged, salvage crews from the *Vestal* also arrived on the scene to lend their expertise. Julio "Lefty" DeCastro, a native of Honolulu and a leadingman caulker and chipper at the Pearl Harbor Navy Yard, quickly organized a team of civilian shipfitters on his own initiative. After loading their industrial cutting equipment onto a barge, they also headed for the *Oklahoma.* The Navy Yard personnel would remain on the overturned hull until the early-morning hours of December 9, working ceaselessly and at great risk to themselves.

The rescue teams knew full well that they were in a race against time, but holes could not be indiscriminately burned into the hull to reach the trapped sailors.

"I know that they were very careful," recalled Floyd Welch, an electrician's mate third class who came over from the *Maryland* to help. "They got the blueprints and went over the hull very carefully so that they would not burn through into a fuel void. And I recall the tappings of the men and their looking on the prints, trying to find what compartments to go through safely, and where those tappings might be coming from."

Entry points were made in the *Oklahoma*'s outer torpedo blister, and additional soundings located two sailors trapped in a pump compartment amidships. Using an oxyacetylene torch, a Navy Yard worker was directed to burn an 18-inch opening through the steel plate to release the men, only to find them dead—the jet of flame from the torch and the burning slag had ignited insulating cork in the bulkhead, filling the compartment with smoke. The men had died from asphyxiation.

George Kahanu was one of the Navy Yard personnel helping to get the heavy cruiser *San Francisco* ready to go to sea. At one of the repair shops in the Yard, George encountered a friend with whom he had worked on many salvage jobs.

"Hey, Red!" George called out. "I thought you went out to the *Oklahoma*?"

Red's eyes welled up with tears.

"What's the problem?" George asked.

The man replied that he had been the one to burn the hole into the pump compartment with the oxyacetylene torch.

"I killed those guys," Red told George.

"Hey boy, you know you're not responsible," George told him. "They told you to do it and you did what you were told."

"But still yet, you know, I'm the guy," the distraught Red had replied.

A costly lesson had been learned, but there was little time to mourn; the work of rescuing the trapped sailors still aboard the *Oklahoma* had to go on. DeCastro ordered the use of torches discontinued and air lines for pneumatic tools were stretched to the hull. Around 1:30 in the afternoon another gasping sailor, Howard Roberts, popped out of the water and was hauled aboard a 50-foot motor launch from the hospital ship *Solace* that had been keeping station alongside the *Oklahoma*'s hull. Roberts had exited through the same escape hatch that Weissman had, and reported that there were "twenty guys trapped down there."

Water had been steadily rising in the handling rooms of the Number Four Turret and the escape trunk. After Roberts's departure, eleven men retreated into Compartment D-57, known to the sailors as the "Lucky Bag," where the *Oklahoma*'s master-at-arms stored "gear adrift" or lost-and-found items collected about the ship. The space also served as stowage for hammocks and the heavy woolen peacoats that were issued to every enlisted sailor but not needed for duty in the tropics. The compartment led to nowhere—there was only one way in or out—but it was at least dry.

The sailors settled down in the darkness to wait, using the peacoats as cushions. Before long, Seaman First Class Stephen Young heard voices through one of the bulkheads and received an answer when he called out. Six radiomen were still alive within an air pocket in the adjacent Radio IV compartment. They in turn had been communicating with another eight men trapped in the Steering Aft Compartment.

"Is there any chance of someone trying to rescue us?" Young asked.

"No, none that we know of," was the reply. "It looks bad. We're just sitting around in here. Same with steering aft. Can you see?"

"We have a light; we keep it turned off to save it."

"Let us know if you hear anything."

"Yeah, sure. You, too."

After what was surely the longest night of their young lives, at 8:00 a.m. on December 8 the six men in Radio IV were freed by Lefty DeCastro's Navy Yard personnel. By the time power drills began to breach the adjacent bulkhead, water from the trunk space was already leaking into the Lucky Bag. When the first opening was made, air began escaping to the outside with a disconcerting hiss. As it did, water at the bottom of the compartment began to rise.

"Hurry up! Burn us out! The water's coming up!" the men shouted.

"We can't. You'd suffocate in there," their rescuers replied.

"Jesus, we'll drown if you don't! The water's coming up to our knees!"

"Calm down, boys," Lefty said reassuringly. "We're going to get you out."

It had become not only a battle against time, but against the laws of physics. Navy Yard shipfitters working feverishly with pneumatic chipping hammers made a hole large enough for a man to crawl through, and at 11:00 a.m. all eleven sailors emerged unharmed from the aptly named Lucky Bag. Three hours later, five souls were freed from a 5-inch ammunition handling room, and the eight men in Steering Aft were saved around 4:00 in the afternoon. At 2:30 in the morning, the last of thirty-two trapped survivors was rescued from the capsized *Oklahoma.*

Homer Wallin's office was underwater.

As material officer on the staff of Vice Admiral William S. Pye, Commander of Battle Force, Pacific Fleet, Wallin's place of business had been aboard Pye's flagship, *California*, which had been slowly settling to the bottom of Pearl Harbor despite the crew's best efforts to keep her afloat. Within three days, the *California*'s quarterdeck would be 17 feet beneath the surface. Admiral Pye, Wallin, and the rest of the Battle Force staff, having salvaged what they could of their material belongings, moved across the harbor and into the offices of CINCPAC at the submarine base.

Homer Norman Wallin was born and raised in the town of Washburn, a tiny farming community on the Missouri River in the south-central portion of North Dakota, which in 1913, the year Wallin entered the US Naval Academy, listed just 650 residents. Due to his Midwest Nordic heritage he was quickly assigned the nickname of "Swede" by his fellow midshipmen.

"Common sense is his long suit—essentially practical in everything—and this ability to use his bean will follow him into the Service and give us a shipmate of the first water," were the words the authors of the annual for the Class of 1917 used to describe Homer Wallin. "May we never lock horns, Swede, because you are a better man than most of us."

After his graduation, Wallin reported aboard the pre-dreadnought battleship *New Jersey*, which spent the First World War in service as a training ship, and after the Armistice transported doughboys home from France. The navy soon recognized that Wallin's talents lay in the technical rather than the tactical disciplines of the service, and after the war he was transferred to the Construction Corps and sent to the Massachusetts Institute of Technology for postgraduate studies.

After obtaining a master's degree in naval architecture in 1921, Wallin reported for duty to the New York Navy Yard, then served for four years with the Bureau of Construction and Repair, the forerunner of the Bureau of Ships, in Washington, DC. During the 1930s he would serve in various design, construction, repair, and salvage billets with BuShips in Washington and at the naval shipyards in Philadelphia and Mare Island, California. In early 1941, Wallin would join Admiral Pye's staff in Pearl Harbor as the material officer in charge of repairs and alterations to the battleships of the Pacific Fleet.

Within hours of the surprise attack on Pearl Harbor, Wallin was busy performing an assessment of the destruction wreaked by the Japanese and submitting a series of preliminary damage reports to CINCPAC headquarters. Even as the wounded were being cared for, fires were still being fought, and rescuers were laboring to free trapped crew members aboard the *Oklahoma*, a salvage unit was being formed under the auspices of the Pearl Harbor Base Force commanded by Rear Admiral William Calhoun, with Commander James Steele as the leading salvage officer. While still serving on Admiral Pye's staff, Wallin pitched in to help with organizing the initial salvage work. Their first priority was to support the search, rescue, and firefighting operations already being conducted, providing essential equipment such as small craft, submersible pumps, cutting torches, and auxiliary lighting. In order to be closer to the work being performed, within a week of the attack the members of the new Salvage Division moved into a contractor's shack in the Navy Yard.

"It was very unpretentious but served satisfactorily," Wallin would write. The Salvage Division staff began the work of sorting out which repair jobs were the most critical and allocating their available resources. Construction and Repair units of each ship were reinforced by specialists from the repair ships *Vestal* and *Medusa*, as well as Navy Yard personnel.

On December 9, Admiral Kimmel received a message from the Chief of Naval Operations: "Because of the great success of the Japanese raid on the seventh, it is expected to be promptly followed up by additional attacks in order to render Hawaii untenable as naval and air bases, in which eventuality it is believed Japanese have suitable forces for initial occupation of islands other than Oahu, including Midway, Maui and Hawaii . . . [I]n expectation of further air raids and inadequacy of defenses Oahu, CNO considers it essential that wounded vessels able to proceed under own power should be sent to West Coast as soon as possible with due regard to safety from current raiding forces and very great importance of effective counter attacks on these raiders by you."

Amid the looming possibility of invasion, the salvage group began focusing their attention on ships that had been undergoing maintenance before the attack and could be quickly readied for service, or those that had suffered light damage and could be easily repaired. The rush was on to get as many warships as possible out of Pearl Harbor and back at sea, and not only because of Stark's urgent warning that Hawaii could be the target of further attacks. All across the Pacific, the Japanese had indeed begun to "run wild."

On December 8 and again on December 9, Japanese bombers operating from advanced bases in the Marshalls struck Wake Island, causing heavy damage to the airfield. Far from being "well-fortified" or "impregnable," the lightly defended Guam fell to the Japanese on December 10. The following morning, the US Marine garrison on Wake drove an amphibious assault by the Japanese into the sea, inflicting heavy losses on the landing force and sinking two enemy destroyers. Task forces were needed to aid in the defense of Wake and to patrol the defensive line between the islands of Midway, Johnston, and Palmyra. Also considered a likely target of the Japanese, American Samoa had to be protected, and convoys traveling to and from the West Coast required antisubmarine escorts.

The repair of the *San Francisco* serves as an example of the fast and furious work being performed by the Navy Yard in the days that followed the attack. On December 7 the heavy cruiser had been alongside her sister ship *New Orleans* at the Navy Yard's Baker 21 berth. Though she came through the attack without sustaining any damage, an immense amount of work was necessary to get her under way. The ammunition for her 5-inch guns and 8-inch main battery had been offloaded, and the job of replacing the obsolete 3-inch antiaircraft guns with rapid fire 1.1-inch guns in quadruple mounts was incomplete. Her badly fouled bottom was scheduled to be descaled and her engineering plant was in pieces, in the midst of an overhaul.

It would take six hours for Navy Yard machinists and welders to mount and level each of the *San Francisco*'s new 1.1-inch guns, a project that would have required a week's time under normal circumstances. Her magazines were reloaded, work in the engine room expedited, and the descaling job put off for a later time. The *San Francisco* was ready for service by December 14. Two days later, she would sail with Admiral Frank Jack Fletcher's *Saratoga* task force bound for Wake Island. Repairs to the *New Orleans* were also hastily completed and within days she was at sea, escorting troop convoys to reinforce Palmyra and Johnston Atoll.

As for the battleships, those that could be quickly restored to a seaworthy condition were to be sent to navy yards on the West Coast for permanent repairs. The *Pennsylvania* and *Maryland* were determined to be the least damaged. Their shipboard construction and repair teams had gone to work in the immediate aftermath of the attack, later assisted by technicians from the Navy Yard and the repair ships *Vestal* and *Medusa*. Salvage personnel assigned to the *Tennessee* found themselves faced with an exacting challenge: Bomb damage to the ship was relatively light, but she was still tightly wedged against the concrete quay by the hull of the *West Virginia.* A method of freeing the 33,000-ton dreadnought would have to be devised before she could be brought to the Navy Yard for temporary repairs, and then set sail for the mainland.

The *California* and *Nevada* were both heavily damaged and would require extensive dewatering and repairs, if repairing them was even possible. With a hull pierced by a half-dozen torpedoes, her upper works crumpled from bomb hits and blackened by fire, the prospects for recovering the sunken *West Virginia* did not look promising. Even Captain

Wallin, who would earn a reputation as an enduring optimist during the Pearl Harbor salvage operations, at first believed the *West Virginia* would have to be stripped of everything of military value and declared a total loss. There was no question with regard to the status of the shattered *Arizona* and the overturned *Oklahoma*, however. Both were listed as "beyond repair."

The single 250-kilogram general-purpose bomb that struck the *Pennsylvania* had blown a 400-square-foot hole in the starboard boat deck, damaging one of the 5-inch antiaircraft guns and its ammunition hoist, destroying the 5-inch broadside gun in the Number Nine Casement, and blowing out the casement bulkhead. The bomb that struck Dry Dock Number One also peppered the starboard hull of the battleship with steel fragments. Except for the charring of paint on her bow, the *Pennsylvania* escaped any significant damage from the intense fire that swept through the *Cassin* and *Downes* lying forward in the dry dock.

Work to get the *Pennsylvania* under way began as early as 2:00 p.m. on December 7. In order to free up the dry dock for more heavily damaged vessels, the Pacific Fleet flagship was made a first priority. Motor launches made several trips across the harbor to the West Loch Ammunition Depot to replenish stocks of ammunition. A legion of Navy Yard workers descended upon the *Pennsylvania*, realigning and reinstalling her huge bronze screws and patching the gaping hole in the boat deck. Members of the *Pennsylvania* crew steered a barge across the channel to the partially submerged *West Virginia*, where they unbolted a 5-inch / 25 caliber antiaircraft mount and a 5-inch / 51 caliber broadside weapon from her scorched decks to replace their own wrecked guns. The *Pennsylvania* left dry dock just five days after the attack and was immediately replaced by the light cruiser *Honolulu*, which had received hull damage and flooding from a near-miss. On a cold and cloudy December 29, the *Pennsylvania* passed beneath San Francisco's Golden Gate Bridge under her own steam. Two days later she entered the dry dock at Hunter's Point.

Two of the converted 16-inch naval artillery armor-piercing shells dropped by Kate bombers had struck the forward portion of the *Maryland.*

Fortunately for "Old Mary," both bombs had a low order of detonation and the damage they caused was fairly light. The first had smashed through the forecastle, wrecking the anchoring gear and two access trunks below. The second bomb penetrated the main deck and exploded in Compartment A-103-A, where canvas sheeting and life jackets were stored. The blast blew a hole in the starboard hull 22 feet below the waterline, flooding several compartments. Splinters sprayed across the *Maryland*'s superstructure caused damage to radio antennae and the radar array. No one was quite sure if the glass shrouds on the spotlights and the windows of the flag bridge and pilothouse were shattered by enemy machine-gun fire, shell fragments, or the concussion of the *Maryland*'s own guns.

Aided by personnel from the repair ship *Medusa*, the ship's complement set to work setting watertight boundaries around the damaged areas and dewatering the flooded spaces, replacing deformed structural members and broken windows, patching the 18-inch-by-20-inch hole in the shell, and restoring power and lighting. On December 19 the *Maryland*'s skipper, Captain Donald Godwin, reported to CINCPAC headquarters that "much other structural work beyond the capacity of the ship's force is required to place that section of the ship in condition for its designated use. It is considered that, barring additional damage to the shell, what water the ship may take on completion of repair work this date can be controlled by the secondary drainage pumps forward."

On December 20 the *Maryland* departed Pearl Harbor for Puget Sound Navy Yard.

In early 1941 Metalsmith First Class Edward Raymer transferred from the crew of the *Vestal* to the Destroyer Repair Unit in San Diego, California, where he was trained as a salvage diver. At two o'clock in the afternoon on December 7, Raymer and eight other divers were informed that they had a little over two hours to pack their sea bags and report to Naval Air Station Coronado.

The team of divers would soon find themselves as passengers aboard a huge four-engined PB2Y Coronado flying boat, following the setting sun across the Pacific. Their final destination, the men were told, was classified.

As the lead petty officer of the group, Raymer was given a sealed envelope containing their orders. He was also placed in charge of the team's service and pay records, a sure indicator that, wherever they were going, their assignment would not be of a short duration. Two days later, the navy divers were at work in the dark and murky depths of Pearl Harbor, tapping along the hulls of sunken vessels to locate any trapped survivors.

On the morning of December 16, five members of the team were concluding the job of sounding the outer shell of the *West Virginia*, while Raymer and two other men finished drilling holes into the concrete of the quay numbered Fox Six, where the *Tennessee* was still firmly lodged. Dynamite was placed into the holes, the quay covered with sandbags, and the charges detonated. Freed from her predicament, "the Rebel" was pushed and pulled to the Navy Yard by tugboats, and four days later she sailed for Puget Sound along with the *Maryland* and *Pennsylvania.*

Standing on the shores of Ford Island, the Secretary of the Navy took in the devastation of Battleship Row. The sight of the capsized *Oklahoma* was only slightly less appalling than the smoldering wreck of the *Arizona*, now a tomb for over a thousand men. A thick, sickening stench from numerous fires, spilled fuel oil, and dead bodies hung in the warm tropical air. The Secretary would admit to being at first shocked and horrified, then motivated to furious anger as he watched the charred corpses of American sailors being prepared for a mass grave.

William Franklin Knox was no stranger to war. At the age of twenty-four, he had enlisted in the Rough Riders and fought alongside Theodore Roosevelt during the charge on San Juan Hill. Twenty years later he would be back in an army uniform, serving as an artillery officer amid the misery and carnage of the Western Front in the First World War. After nearly thirty years in the newspaper business, Frank Knox had witnessed his share of disasters, both natural and human-caused. Nothing in his long experience had prepared him for what he saw on December 11 when he toured Pearl Harbor.

At the submarine base, Knox found Admiral Kimmel busily drafting plans for an expedition to relieve the beleaguered defenders of Wake

Island, centered around Fletcher's *Saratoga* task force. Kimmel was also planning on sending Vice Admiral Wilson Brown's *Lexington* group to raid the Japanese base on the island of Jaluit in the Marshalls, a move that would serve as a diversion to the Wake operation. Though leaning forward and anxious to strike back at the Japanese, it was obvious that Kimmel and his staff were thoroughly rattled by the sudden attack on Pearl Harbor and the destruction it had wrought. In 1941 the community of professional naval officers was still fairly small and intimate, and numerous close friends had been lost. The deaths of over two thousand officers and men under their command weighed heavily. The fact that someone would eventually have to answer for the fleet being caught flat-footed by the Japanese on December 7 was an unspoken certainty that hung over CINCPAC headquarters like a dark cloud.

Knox would meet with General Walter Short before departing for Washington, having spent just twenty-four hours in Hawaii. A day later he was at the White House submitting his report to President Roosevelt.

"The Japanese air attack on the Island of Oahu on December 7th was a complete surprise to both the Army and the Navy," the secret report would state. "Its initial success, which included almost all the damage done, was due to a lack of a state of readiness against such an air attack, by both branches of the service. This statement was made by me to both General Short and Admiral Kimmel, and both agreed that it was entirely true."

After a lengthy conference with a tired and dejected President Roosevelt, Knox returned to his offices at the Navy Department, where he summoned the Chief of the Bureau of Navigation, Rear Admiral Chester W. Nimitz.

"How soon can you be ready to travel?" Knox asked Nimitz.

"It depends on where I'm going and how long I'll be away," the admiral replied.

"You're going to take command of the Pacific Fleet," Knox told him, "and I think you will be gone for a long time."

CHAPTER 10
A FORTUNATE CHOICE

"Several times in recent weeks I have been quoted—correctly—that 'as bad as our losses were at Pearl Harbor on 7 December 1941, they could have been devastatingly worse,' had the Japanese returned for more strikes against our naval installations, surface oil storage and our submarine base installations," Chester W. Nimitz wrote to the present Chief of Naval Operations, Admiral David L. McDonald, in a letter dated April 3, 1965.

"Such attacks could have been made with impunity as we had little left to oppose them. Furthermore, I have been correctly quoted in saying that it was God's divine will that Kimmel did not have his fleet at sea to intercept the Japanese Carrier Task Force that attacked Pearl Harbor on 7 December 1941. That task force had a fleet speed at least two knots superior to our speed, and Kimmel could not have brought the Japanese to a gun action unless they wanted it. We might have had one carrier but I doubt if the *Lexington* could have joined in time.

"Picture if you can: six Japanese carriers working on our old ships which would be without air cover or, had the Japanese wanted to avoid American air attacks from shore, they could have delayed the action until out of range of shore based air. Instead of having our ships sunk in the shallow protected waters of Pearl Harbor they could have been sunk in deep water and we could have lost all of our trained men instead of the 3,800 lost at Pearl Harbor."

Chester W. Nimitz left his childhood home in Fredericksburg, Texas, just after the turn of the century upon receiving an appointment to the US Naval Academy at Annapolis. His father having died before he was born,

Nimitz was raised by his paternal grandfather, a German immigrant and former merchant seaman.

"The sea, like life itself, is a stern taskmaster," his grandfather once told him. "The best way to get along with either is to learn all you can, then do your best and don't worry—especially about things over which you have no control."

Nimitz graduated seventh in the Class of 1905 and was soon on his way to the Philippines for duty with the Asiatic Squadron. He would serve aboard the ill-fated gunboat *Panay* and later, though still holding the rank of ensign, would be given command of the elderly destroyer *Decatur*. One dark night while steaming through Batangas harbor at a dead-slow speed, the young officer managed to run the *Decatur* onto a mud bank.

"I tried to back the *Decatur* down, but she was stuck for good," Nimitz later wrote. "On that black night somewhere in the Philippines, the advice of my grandfather returned to me: 'Don't worry about things over which you have no control.' So I set up a cot on deck and went to sleep."

Ensign Nimitz was found guilty of "hazarding a ship of the United States Navy" during a court-martial aboard the cruiser *Denver* and issued a letter of reprimand. Afterward he applied for transfer to a battleship but was instead sent to submarine school. Over a ten-year period he would command the submarines *Plunger*, *Snapper*, *Narwahl*, and *Skipjack*. Like his future adversary, Yamamoto, Nimitz proved incapable of keeping a full complement of fingers, losing one while assisting in the maintenance of a diesel engine. His injuries might have been worse had his Annapolis class ring not jammed the moving parts of the machinery. Of the many ribbons on his chest was a plain band of sky blue, representing a Coast Guard Silver Lifesaving Medal for the rescue of a drowning sailor.

"In those days I was beginning to develop my theories of leadership: namely that leadership consists of picking good men and helping them to do their best for you," Nimitz would reflect. "The attributes of loyalty, discipline and devotion to duty on the part of subordinates must be matched by patience, tolerance and understanding on the part of superiors."

When America entered the First World War, Lieutenant Commander Nimitz served on the staff of COMSUBLANT—Commander

Submarines Atlantic. Afterward he would return to the surface navy to skipper the cruisers *Chicago* and *Augusta,* then went on to start the navy's first Reserve Officer Training Corps unit at the University of California Berkeley. Achieving flag rank in 1938, Nimitz served as commander of Battleship Division One before reporting to the Navy Department in Washington for a tour of duty as BuNav chief. Like Kimmel, Nimitz bypassed the rank of vice admiral and was advanced to the four-star rank of admiral when he was given command of the Pacific Fleet, over the heads of several flag officers more senior.

During his forty years in the navy, Nimitz had earned a reputation as a pragmatic and unassuming officer who tended to lead, rather than drive, the men under his command. His lack of pretension is evidenced by the fact that, upon assuming the role of CINCPAC, his quiet change-of-command ceremony was conducted before a mere handful of onlookers and with little flourish or fanfare on the foredeck of the submarine *Grayling*, not only because he was an old submariner himself, but because it was the closest naval vessel to his new office in Pearl Harbor.

Of Nimitz, Homer Wallin would write: "He was a fortunate choice for the position. Although he was unknown to the public at that time, his appointment restored public confidence in the abilities of the United States Navy. He not only got along with all elements of a unified command but proved a strong commander in his quiet sort of way . . . a plain man who had no use in wartime for furbelows and ruffles. He was non-argumentative, but used his common sense to arrive at decisions which had to be made. He was a good listener, but used his own judgment in making decisions. Here was a man who in due time gained the confidence of all by the sheer demonstration of ability and good will."

Nimitz would inherit a staff whose morale was "at a low ebb." Admiral Stark had ordered Kimmel relieved on December 17 and command of the fleet had been temporarily placed into the hands of Vice Admiral William Pye until Nimitz could make the journey from Washington. On December 22, Pye signaled the Chief of Naval Operations that the "gallant defense of Wake has been of utmost value but hereafter Wake is a liability. In view [of] extensive present operations I am forced to conclude that risk of one task force to attack enemy in vicinity of Wake is not justifiable." Pye then ordered Fletcher and his *Saratoga* group to withdraw, a decision that would haunt him for the remainder of his life.

The following day the Japanese attacked Wake once again and in greater force; this time the Americans were unable to hold them back. Japanese cruisers and destroyers along with planes from the carriers *Soryu* and *Hiryu* spent the day pounding the island with airstrikes and naval gunfire. At 2:30 in the morning another Japanese landing force was sent ashore which outnumbered the exhausted defenders, a composite unit of marines, sailors, and stranded civilian construction workers, by a margin of three to one. The furious combat continued all night long, and by dawn the fighting was hand to hand. Wake Island would finally fall to the Japanese that afternoon.

The situation in the Far East was looking even worse. Hong Kong had been attacked and would soon be captured. Thailand and Malaya had been invaded, and the Japanese were driving toward the British bastion of Singapore. The Royal Navy's *Prince of Wales* and *Repulse* were sunk by Japanese bombers in the South China Sea. Japanese forces had landed in the Philippines after decimating General Douglas MacArthur's air force and wrecking the Asiatic Fleet base at Cavite. Outnumbered, surrounded, lacking air cover and naval support, MacArthur was ordering his American and Filipino troops to begin a fighting withdraw to the Bataan Peninsula and the island fortress of Corregidor. The Japanese Southern Plan was moving along right on schedule, and the US Navy could do very little to stop it.

It had been a grim Christmas at CINCPAC headquarters. Edwin Layton was among the many staff officers who believed that he had failed Admiral Kimmel and fully expected to be reassigned. After Nimitz took over, Layton requested relief and a transfer to destroyers. The admiral "smiled understandingly" and suggested that by staying on as his intelligence officer Layton would, in effect, be responsible for the killing of more Japanese from his desk in Pearl Harbor "than you ever could kill in command of a destroyer flotilla." Layton agreed to withdraw the request.

"To restore fleet morale and confidence after America's worst naval defeat, I decided to keep the staff intact," Nimitz would state. "Nobody was transferred, nobody sent home in disgrace, nobody court-martialed. My instincts were right. By giving them a second chance, I restored the self-confidence of those CINCPAC officers. I've never known a harder-working, more dedicated staff, and to them must go much of the credit for the ultimate victory in the Pacific."

"It was Nimitz's ready and infectious smile that offered us reassurance," Ed Layton wrote of the new commander-in-chief. "The twinkling blue of his eyes were heightened by a ruddy complexion and boyish mop of sandy-colored hair. But it was his firm jaw line and incisive thrust of questions that made it clear that he was steeled for the tremendous task he was to assume."

On the final day of 1941, the same day he took command of the Pacific Fleet, Nimitz joined Homer Wallin for a tour of Pearl Harbor. A typical midday Hawaiian rain squall passed over the island as their boat motored along Battleship Row through the thick sludge of fuel oil seeping from the hulk of the *Arizona*. The upper works of the *West Virginia* and *California* were teeming with sailors and workers from the Navy Yard. Seawater cascaded over their charred hulls from several pump discharge hoses; the knocking and whirring of pneumatic hammers and impact wrenches echoed across the harbor; and here and there were showers of sparks from cutting torches. The remaining battleships were being stripped of their antiaircraft guns, which were being moved ashore to aid in Pearl Harbor's defense. The bodies of dead sailors were still being collected as they floated to the surface after being dislodged from the various wrecks by the ocean's currents.

Like Secretary Knox, Nimitz would find it difficult to fight off a sense of shock while viewing the mangled, smoke-stained, and sunken remnants of the powerful battleships that had, until a few days before, formed the seemingly invincible core of the United States Pacific Fleet. Nimitz would share a certain abject pessimism, a rare thing in the first days of his tenure, as he and Wallin discussed the possibilities of salvaging the battlewagons.

"There was a general feeling of depression throughout the Pearl Harbor area when it was seen and firmly believed that none of the ships sunk at Pearl Harbor would ever fight again," Wallin would record. "The scene to the newcomer was foreboding indeed. *Nevada* was near the entrance channel and was a sorry spectacle to greet the eye of the new arrival. Yet she was the best of the lot."

Through the drizzling rain the admiral's barge proceeded slowly west, past the protruding superstructure of the *California* and across the channel to where the *Nevada* was anchored stern-first into the coral of Waipio Point. After viewing the extent of the damage done to the thirty-year-old battlewagon, Nimitz would confess his doubts that the *Nevada* would ever return to the sea.

"What Admiral Nimitz saw was a ship entirely filled with water, with her bridge and forward controls entirely burned out, and with the forecastle wrecked by the bombs which exploded beneath," Wallin recalled. "No wonder he was pessimistic!"

Captain Wallin, however, expressed confidence that the *Nevada*, *California*, and *West Virginia* could be refloated, repaired, and returned to the fight. Nimitz knew that Wallin was speaking from a wealth of technical knowledge and practical experience, and had spent his entire twenty-eight years in the navy preparing for this very moment in history.

On January 9, 1942, Nimitz would transfer the recently promoted Captain James Steele to other duties within the fleet, after awarding him the Legion of Merit for his tireless work as salvage superintendent throughout the dark days of December. The organization Steele had founded would become the Salvage Division of the Navy Yard under the command of Captain Homer Wallin, charged with the herculean task of raising the dreadnoughts of Pearl Harbor.

A vast, daunting, and multifaceted salvage project lay before Captain Wallin and the personnel of his new command. While some operations could be assigned a lower priority and scheduled for a later date, such as the righting of the capsized *Oklahoma*, there was a need for more-critical salvage jobs to be conducted simultaneously. Warships that were lightly damaged needed to be repaired and returned to the fleet as soon as possible; those that could not be saved had weapons and munitions on board that were desperately needed for the long fight ahead.

The *Cassin* and *Downes* presented "a sorry spectacle indeed," as Wallin would state. The two fire-ravaged destroyers needed to be removed from Dry Dock Number One to allow less-damaged vessels to take their place. The *Shaw*, her bow completely blown off by the explosion that had racked her magazines, still rested on top of the swamped Auxiliary Floating Dry Dock Number Two. Although she was a total loss, there was still much salvage work to be done aboard the *Arizona*. Oil leaking from the battleship's bunkers was still fouling the harbor and her after magazines held a number of naval artillery shells that could be removed, reconditioned, and hopefully someday hurled back at her tormentors.

There were numerous pieces of unexploded Japanese ordnance to deal with. One of the large armor-piercing projectiles which had failed to detonate lay entangled in the wreckage of the portside second deck of the *West Virginia*, and buried into the mud banks of Ford Island were unexploded Japanese torpedoes that had missed their targets. Both the *West Virginia* and *California*, with their turboelectric propulsion systems, promised that an entirely new series of technical problems would present themselves once they were dewatered and raised.

Other sunken vessels were presenting a hazard to the movement of ships in the narrow confines of Pearl Harbor or taking up badly needed berthing space. The *Oglala*, for example, had been moored alongside the *Helena* when the light cruiser was struck by an aerial torpedo. While the concussion from the blast ruptured the *Oglala*'s hull and lifted fire-room floor plates, causing her to immediately take on water and capsize, sailors would say that the old minelayer had "died from fright." As the *Oglala* rolled over and her main deck became level with the Ten-Ten Dock to which she was moored, Admiral Furlong had reportedly stepped onto the dock and strode away as coolly as if he were stepping off a streetcar in downtown Honolulu. Nimitz would later place William Furlong in command of the Navy Yard, which oversaw Wallin's Salvage Division. The capsized hulk of Furlong's former flagship was taking up prime harbor real estate, and attempts to right the vessel were already under way.

"Pearl Harbor was noted for shortages," Wallin wrote. "This was a fact of life in a comparatively new fleet base two thousand miles from home."

The problem of material shortages was made worse by the fact that there were already many pressing demands on the navy's logistics and supply system, which only increased as combat operations got under way in both the Atlantic and Pacific theaters of war. In solving the myriad of salvage problems encountered, shortages of critical items such as lumber, fasteners, pumps, and other equipment and materials would force Wallin's men to improvise, innovate, and scrounge, making the best of what they had on hand.

Along with these material shortfalls came a scarcity of skilled manpower for attending to the multitude of salvage jobs. The Hawaiian Islands were scoured for every available civilian engineer, mechanic, carpenter, welder, and electrician that could be enticed or cajoled to go to work for the Navy Yard. The submarine rescue vessel *Ortolan*, with her complement of divers, was ordered to Pearl Harbor from the West Coast. The remainder of Destroyer Repair Unit One from San Diego soon arrived aboard the Matson steamer *Lurline*. Reserve officers and enlisted men with a variety of marine salvage, construction, and repair backgrounds were summoned to Hawaii.

"Things were so bad in Pearl Harbor, even the chiefs were working," a junior sailor from the *Nevada* would remark. Fortunately for Captain Wallin and the navy, a group of highly skilled and experienced civilian construction personnel were already there, and over the next several months they would render an invaluable service.

The contingent of engineers, divers, and technicians from the Pacific Bridge Company had been in Pearl Harbor prior to the Japanese surprise attack, under contract with the Navy Department to assemble the Yard's new dry docks. Pacific Bridge had been in the business of building coastal and maritime structures in the Pacific Northwest region of the United States for over seventy years. The company had not only built many of the bridges spanning the Columbia and Willamette rivers in the Portland area, they had also taken part in the Golden Gate Bridge project in San Francisco, and had poured the footers for the Hoover Dam. Pacific Bridge personnel immediately volunteered to help with rescue operations after the attack, and within days the company was issued a new contract to assist with salvage work in Pearl Harbor. Pacific Bridge divers were soon working alongside their navy counterparts in the effort to bring the *Nevada* off her perch on Waipio Point.

CHAPTER 11

REFLOATING THE "CHEER UP SHIP"

A JAPANESE TORPEDO HAD STRUCK THE USS *NEVADA* ON THE PORT SIDE between the two forward gun turrets and 14 feet above the ship's keel, opening a 48-foot gash in her outer torpedo blister. While the weapon failed to penetrate the armored inner bulkhead, as the naval architects who designed the *Nevada*'s torpedo countermeasures had calculated, the impact pushed the bulkhead inboard "in a well-defined elliptical dish," splitting it open 4 inches at its base. The *Nevada* then began to take on water, listing 5 degrees to port.

While the prompt order to counterflood issued by Lieutenant Commander Francis Thomas had corrected the list, fittings and closures marked *X*, *Y*, and *Z*, supposedly watertight and dutifully closed by the crew after General Quarters was sounded, had nonetheless begun to leak. As the ship sustained more damage from bomb hits, the watertight armored second deck would prove to be anything *but* watertight. Water rushed across the second deck, seeping through closed hatches and ventilation shafts, flooding the fire rooms and dousing the boilers. When bombs crashed through the forecastle the order was given to flood the forward magazines, lest the ship suffer the same fate as the *Arizona*, but in their haste the crew also flooded the after magazines by mistake. This was the dreadful condition in which Admiral Nimitz had found the *Nevada* when he made his gloomy prediction to Homer Wallin: ripped open by a torpedo, shattered by bombs, blackened by fire, and completely flooded with seawater.

The *Nevada*'s captain and most of her crew had already been assigned to other ships and stations. Acting commanding officer Harold

Thompson and twenty members of the crew were retained for the salvage project, assisted by personnel from the *Medusa* and divers from the *Widgeon*, Destroyer Repair Unit One, and Pacific Bridge. Fortunately for those assigned to the *Nevada* salvage project, there were a couple of factors working in their favor. The ship was beached with the interior flooded, not submerged like the other battleships, and much of the salvage work could be commenced from the weather decks, which were still above water. They were also free to go about their work without having to contend with recovering the bodies of *Nevada* crew members killed on December 7, for they had already been removed from the ship.

Navy divers would discover that the hole torn by the torpedo was not the only place where the *Nevada*'s hull had been breached. One of the bombs that struck the forward part of the ship had passed through the hull at the level of the second deck before exploding alongside. Near-misses had also ruptured or dished in the Nevada's hull plates in three other locations.

Measurements were provided to carpenters at the Navy Yard, who went to work on building wooden "window-frame" patches for sealing the holes in the *Nevada*'s outer skin. The upturned hull of the *Nevada*'s sister ship, *Oklahoma*, was used as a template for fabricating a large patch to fit over the gash made by the torpedo. The window-frame patches were to be secured to the hull with J-bolts fitted through holes cut along the outer edges of the damaged areas, burned by divers using underwater cutting torches.

By the first week of January 1942, divers had sealed the bomb hole in the *Nevada*'s port side with a window-frame patch. Other ruptures were covered with wood or welded steel patches. The large patch for the torpedo hole was completed at the Navy Yard's shipfitter shop, loaded onto a floating derrick, and motored out to Waipio Point. Over the next several weeks, crane operators and divers would struggle to install the huge, ungainly wooden appliance, which refused to seat properly. Mud and coral were laboriously dredged from beneath the *Nevada* to enable the patch to be lowered deeply enough to conform to the curvature of the ship's hull. Even a portion of her docking keel, the longitudinal steel member upon which a vessel rests while in dry dock, was removed by divers using dynamite charges. Nothing worked.

It would later be discovered that the skin of the ship's torpedo blister had been forced outward nearly 2 feet by the explosion of the warhead, making it impossible to seal with a rigid wooden patch. After multiple attempts, the assistant salvage officer overseeing the *Nevada* project, Lieutenant (j.g.) George Ankers, received Captain Wallin's permission to abandon the effort to install the big patch over the torpedo hole. Instead, divers would be sent into the *Nevada*'s flooded interior spaces, repairing and shoring the bulkheads of compartments bordering the torpedo-damaged area. Even with the hole from the torpedo strike left open, Ankers calculated that once an interior watertight boundary was set and water was pumped from the remainder of the ship, the *Nevada* should refloat. Navy and Pacific Bridge divers would make over four hundred separate dives in and around the *Nevada*, putting in over fifteen hundred hours of work.

"Once divers entered the interiors of sunken battleships," Edward Raymer would later write, "they experienced a world of total blackness, unable to see the faceplates in their helmets, a scant two inches from their noses. The abundance of sediment, oil, and other pollutants inside the ships rendered diving lamps useless, since the beams of light reflected into the divers' eyes, blinding them."

Groping through the *Nevada*'s pitch-black compartments, divers closed watertight doors and hatches, manipulated valves, and placed suction pumps. Spaces bordering the area of torpedo damage were sealed off but left flooded, allowing water pressure to back up the steel bulkheads. Several suction pumps, the largest being a monster with an impeller housing of 10 inches, gradually began dewatering the remaining flooded compartments.

As the water level slowly decreased, hundreds of rounds of ammunition and powder cans were removed and sent to the West Loch depot. The *Nevada* was lightened by nearly 2,000 tons once her oil tanks were drained into a fuel barge alongside. Equipment, stores, and furniture were carried off the ship, along with the crew's clothing and personal items which were inventoried and warehoused after being allowed to dry. The ship's documents and classified materials were recovered and sent to fleet headquarters. A supply of meat in the galley was discarded, which Wallin would report "was very smelly by this time." After each compartment was dewatered, the long, hard, back-wrenching job of cleaning began. Sailors wearing coveralls and rubber boots scrubbed bulkheads and decks and sprayed them with a hot, caustic solution to remove the oily film left behind.

Electric motors were used for hundreds of applications aboard the battleships, powering all types of machinery, pumps, blowers, and weapons systems. The *Nevada* salvage project would prove that electrical equipment was remarkably resilient to saltwater immersion and could be reused if properly cleaned and dried. A product known as Tectyl—a water-displacing lubricant and corrosion preventive compound developed in 1935 by the Daubert Chemical Company—was used to clean the oil and sludge from the *Nevada*'s electrical appliances before they were sent ashore and reconditioned.

The work of saving the *Nevada* was progressing satisfactorily and at a steady pace. For the remaining members of the original crew still on board, it was beginning to look as if their stubborn old battlewagon would actually float again and steam for the West Coast, where she would receive a complete refitting and maybe someday get back into the war. As their hopes started to rise, they began to call her by an old nickname seldom used in recent years: the "Cheer Up Ship."

Then on February 7, tragedy would once again strike the crew of the *Nevada*. After removing the cap from an air test fitting in the ship's steering engine room, Lieutenant James Clarkson was killed by escaping poisonous gas. Six other men were sickened by fumes during their attempts to rescue Clarkson. One of them, a machinist's mate first class named Peter DeVries, later died at the naval hospital. It was determined that the gas was hydrogen sulfide emitted by the breakdown of organic material—in this case, rotting paper products.

When work resumed, extra safety precautions were taken when entering confined spaces. Procedures were initiated for air sampling and monitoring, ventilation, and the use of respirators where indicated. Yet another tragic and costly lesson had been learned by those working to salvage the battleships of Pearl Harbor.

On the morning of February 18, 1942, sailors and civilians all around Pearl Harbor would pause once again to watch the USS *Nevada* on the move. Battle-scarred and smoke-blackened but nevertheless afloat, the Cheer Up Ship was on her way back up the channel between Ford Island and the Navy Yard with the assistance of harbor tugboats. She was still traveling markedly low by the bow, with her wound from the Japanese torpedo still open to the sea. To allay the apprehensions of Admirals Nimitz and Furlong, Wallin agreed to keep the pumps running during the short journey, lest the battleship become a blockship in the narrow channel.

There was still much work to be done. The gash from the torpedo, of course, needed to be properly sealed. The starboard propeller shaft and rudder, damaged by the stern-first grounding on the coral heads of Waipio Point, had to be repaired and realigned. The flooded boilers required a thorough overhaul. Only then could the *Nevada* depart under her own power for Puget Sound Navy Yard in Bremerton, Washington, for permanent repairs and modernization.

As the Commander-in-Chief of the Pacific Fleet watched, tugboats gently guided the *Nevada* through the gates of Dry Dock Number Two. The remaining *Nevada* crew members, clad in their grimy dungarees and coveralls, were joined by members of the Salvage Division in manning the rails. On the starboard bridge wing, someone had hung a handmade sign.

"WE'LL FIGHT AGAIN," it said.

CHAPTER 12

RAISING THE PRUNE BARGE

On the morning of December 7, 1941, the USS *California* had been tied to quay Fox Three, the southernmost position on Battleship Row, with her bow aimed down-channel toward the entrance to Pearl Harbor. The depth of the anchorage at that location was approximately 40 feet; at the bottom, a layer of mud 90 feet deep lay over a shelf of coral. Directly off the *California*'s stern lay the Ford Island fuel wharf, where the fleet oiler *Neosho* was docked after discharging a quantity of aviation gasoline, just ahead of the next two battlewagons at Fox Five, *Maryland* and *Oklahoma*. General Quarters was sounded aboard the *California* at 0755 when the first Japanese planes appeared over the naval air station and the ship's ready machine guns were quick to return enemy fire.

At 0805 the battleship was hit by two aerial torpedoes that struck almost simultaneously, one impacting her port side between Turret Number Two and the bridge, the second striking aft near Turret Number Three. At twenty years old, the *California* was one of the newer battlewagons in the Pacific Fleet. Her torpedo countermeasures performed as designed and withstood the insult rather well. Unlike the aged *Nevada*, the *California*'s inner bulkheads were distorted but held together without splitting apart at the butts and seams.

An armored dreadnought was expected to absorb this type of punishment and still remain afloat, as long as the appropriate measures were taken to ensure watertight compartmentation. It would be the *California*'s lack of such material readiness that ultimately led to her sinking. Within six of the portside voids, manhole covers had been removed, and others "were found with securing nuts slacked off, all on the port side in way of torpedo damage," seriously compromising the battleship's watertight integrity.

In his after-action report the *California*'s commanding officer, Captain Joel Bunkley, would claim that the voids "were opened in order to inspect for possible leakage from fuel tanks, which had been filled when the ship fueled to 95% capacity." Samuel Eliot Morison would state that the manhole covers had been left open "for an admiral's inspection." The joint congressional committee that investigated the Pearl Harbor attack, however, could not find any evidence of a pending inspection after examining the ship's log and the inspection schedule for the Battle Force.

According to naval historian Dr. Norman Friedman, the presence of the unsecured manholes "was not particularly surprising or alarming; had she been at sea, these covers would have been fastened down." Another analysis of the damage done to the battleships of Pearl Harbor, published in the December 1977 edition of the US Naval Institute's journal *Proceedings*, was less than kind: "The *Oklahoma* and *Nevada* were lost because of design defects, the *West Virginia* was simply overwhelmed by forces her defenses were not meant to thwart, and the *California* was sunk because of the performance of her officers and crew."

In any event, seawater quickly filled the *California*'s outer void spaces and poured through open or loose manholes to flood the third deck. Water then rushed through open doors, ventilation ducts, exhaust trunks, and leaking deck seams and bulkheads. The explosions also ruptured port-side wing tanks, along with a large 8-inch fuel main, adding thousands of gallons of fuel oil to the mix. The main radio compartment, the port-side thrust block room, electrical storerooms, lower handling rooms, and dozens of other spaces were soon charged with oily water. The *California* rapidly took on a steep list to port that "ominously strained" the mooring hausers that secured the ship to her concrete quay.

The senior officer aboard at the time, Lieutenant Commander Marion Little, ordered counterflooding to reduce the list, prevent the mooring lines from parting, and the Prune Barge from turning over. By that time the Japanese horizontal bombers were making their first pass over Battleship Row. One of their converted naval artillery shells penetrated the *California*'s upper and main decks, bounced off the armored second deck, and exploded. Fires broke out, bulkheads were blown open, and hatches sprung, adding further to the *California*'s loss of watertight integrity. Then another projectile landed close along the port side, punching a hole in the outer shell and causing even more flooding.

As if things could not get any worse, around the same time the Japanese bombers were withdrawing at 10:00 a.m., flaming slicks of oil drifting southward from the *Arizona* and *West Virginia* were beginning to surround the embattled *California*. Whirling clouds of foul black smoke and searing heat soon made the decks of the battleship untenable. Captain Bunkley, on board in civilian attire after having rushed back to Pearl Harbor from his liberty weekend at the Halekulani Hotel, gave the order to abandon ship.

Minutes later the order was rescinded after the prevailing wind and currents cleared the burning patch of oil from the ship, but precious time to control the fires and flooding had been lost. In the interval the *California* had once again taken on a list of 8 degrees. While the ship "showed a strong disinclination to sink," there were not enough pumps available in the entire harbor to keep her from settling.

"*California* was well designed," Captain Homer Wallin would later comment. "The holding bulkhead near the torpedo holes was adequate to its task . . . Adequate pumping, if it could have been supplied at the time, would have kept the vessel afloat." Three days later, the Prune Barge had finished sinking into the deep mud of the harbor floor, with her decks canted 5.5 degrees to port. The foredeck was awash by 3 feet while the after portion of the ship was down a full 17 feet, enough to completely submerge the big guns of Turret Number Four.

Lebbeus Curtis was the co-founder of the Pillsbury & Curtis Company, a marine survey and salvage concern based in San Francisco. At the age of sixty, Lieutenant Commander Curtis had been recalled to active duty from the Naval Reserve and happened to be in Pearl Harbor at the time of the attack, while in transit to the Far East to perform salvage work. Rear Admiral Calhoun quickly arranged for a change of orders and retained Curtis to work for the initial Pearl Harbor salvage organization. Before Wallin assumed command of the Salvage Division, Curtis had ordered a quantity of steel sheeting for the construction of a cofferdam to surround the *California* and prevent seawater from entering the ship as she was pumped dry, following a recommendation from the Bureau of Ships.

Engineers from Pacific Bridge, however, believed that a cofferdam made from wood timbers, similar to that placed around bridge pilings during their installation, would be better suited for Pearl Harbor's muddy bottom. Wallin agreed, and the change of plan was readily approved by BuShips. The supply of steel sheeting was retained for use on future salvage projects, and carpenters at the Navy Yard then went to work on the construction of timber cofferdams in 30-foot sections, their gaps sealed with a watertight oakum. The sections of cofferdam were then transported to the *California* by barge, where they were installed by Pacific Bridge divers. The cofferdam timbers extended 5.5 feet above the main deck of the ship, supported by angle iron braces and weighed down by sandbags.

While divers were busy installing the cofferdams, work got under way to lighten the ship. Loose items and debris were cleared, along with the fleet paymaster's heavy safes. The *California*'s huge 14-inch guns, except those remaining in the submerged Number Four Turret, were dismantled and removed by floating derricks. Catapults, cranes, boats, and anchors, along with their massive chains, were also taken off the ship. Studs and tap rivets holding down the conning tower and the flag conning tower were removed and the structures were prepared to hoist away. Even the ship's main mast was being removed.

Several large-diameter electric and gasoline-driven centrifugal pumps, sitting atop hastily constructed scaffolding alongside the ship, operated around the clock to dewater the *California*'s flooded spaces. Navy divers entered the ship to bolt down the offending manhole covers. Where the covers were missing, wooden patches were installed over the manholes. Divers also secured doors, hatches, ventilation shafts, and drains; patched leaking gasoline and oil lines; plugged leaking shrapnel holes with carved wooden wedges; and placed steel blanks over open portholes and gun ports. It was discovered that the armored bulkheads surrounding the areas of torpedo damage were surprisingly intact and watertight. A window-frame patch had already been placed over one of the tears in the hull, but as in the case of the *Nevada*, it was decided that the Prune Barge could be refloated without having to patch the holes blasted by Japanese torpedoes.

With topside weight being removed and pumps working twenty-four hours a day, the water level inside the hull gradually decreased below the level of water inside the cofferdams, and the *California* very slowly began to regain buoyancy and rise from the mud.

Then in the early-morning hours of March 4, 1942, the Japanese nearly succeeded in sinking the *California* for a second time.

Anxious to obtain an assessment of the ongoing American salvage operations, the Japanese admiralty initiated plans for a long-range reconnaissance mission and harassment raid on Pearl Harbor dubbed *Operation K*. Two four-engined Kawanishi H8K "Emily" flying boats were tasked for the purpose, each carrying four 250-kilogram multipurpose bombs. Leaving their base in the Marshall Islands on March 3, 1942, the Emilies rendezvoused with two Japanese submarines near French Frigate Shoals, with each seaplane taking on 3,000 gallons of additional fuel before continuing on the final 560-mile leg of their mission to Pearl Harbor.

The submarine *I-23* had been ordered to maintain a position south of Oahu to report on weather conditions and rescue any survivors from the Emilies should the flying boats be shot down or encounter a mishap. On February 24, the *I-23* transmitted a final progress report to her base on Kwajalein and was never heard from again, apparently having met with an accident of her own. Had the flying boats been able to receive updated weather information from the submarine, the mission would likely have been scrubbed, for on the night of March 3–4, 1942, Oahu was completely socked in by rain clouds.

Forces defending the Hawaiian Sea Frontier had been placed on alert on March 3, after the radio intelligence unit at Station HYPO sniffed out the impending Japanese raid. Unsure of exactly what the enemy was planning, the cryptanalysts suspected that there would be "some kind of offensive against the Hawaiian area, possibly tomorrow, employing large seaplanes and submarines based in the Marshalls." Just after midnight, the intruders were picked up by an American radar station on the island of Kauai at a distance of 204 miles. This time the contact report of the soldier manning the radar scope was taken seriously.

At 12:48 a.m., the Fourteenth Naval District sounded General Quarters in Pearl Harbor, and within the hour four P-40 Warhawks in an alert status at Wheeler Field were scrambled to intercept the bogies. The fighter pilots, however, were unable to visually acquire the Emilies in the darkness and heavy clouds. Correctly assuming that the inbound aircraft were enemy seaplanes, the Naval District ordered PBY Catalinas launched from NAS Kaneohe Bay, armed with torpedoes and tasked with locating and sinking any Japanese seaplane tenders that might be present to support the mission.

After a journey of nearly 2,500 miles, the Japanese aviators were finally able to find Oahu by spotting the lighthouse on Kaena Point, one of the very few lights on the island that had been allowed to remain illuminated. However, with a nearly solid undercast and with the Americans otherwise observing strict blackout conditions, the Japanese were unable to locate their target. One of the Emily pilots released his bombs into the ocean while the other blasted a crater into a hillside north of Honolulu, the explosions shattering windows at nearby Roosevelt High School but inflicting no casualties. Both pilots reported to their superiors that they had successfully bombed Pearl Harbor.

At the naval base, air raid sirens sounded, antiaircraft batteries were manned, and, in accordance with emergency protocol, electric power was shut off to douse any remaining lights. Unfortunately this also killed the power to the electric 12-inch centrifugal pumps at work on the *California*, and their gasoline-powered counterparts were left struggling to make up the difference. Seawater began to flow into the Prune Barge faster than it could be pumped out, and she began to reacquire a list and once again settle toward the harbor floor. The watch standers aboard the *California* had to work fast to restore power and get the electric pumps running again before that could happen.

Every day throughout the month of March, working parties of unassigned seamen from the Pearl Harbor Receiving Station came aboard the *California* to clear debris, remove ammunition and equipment for reconditioning, carry off loose gear and stores, and begin the arduous task of cleaning.

"The Salvage Division never did get enough men to do a satisfactory cleaning job, although men from the Receiving Station were added from time to time to augment the ship's force available," Wallin would report. "The amount of cleaning which is necessary in a sunken battleship is well-nigh incalculable. The maximum number required was about 500 men; at first only 6 officers and 48 men were available."

On March 20, 1942, the diary of the Salvage Division would report: "*California*: Water level lowered below centerline hatches on second deck. Stern of vessel now afloat. Water is still standing on port side of forecastle. Conning towers awaiting removal. Ship's complement and 100 men from the Receiving Station engaged in cleaning operations but unable to keep up with the pumping. Additional men, equipment and accommodations have been requested. 50,000 gallons of loose oil removed in the last 24 hours. Casting loose Turret IV range finder."

The following day, the remains of a fallen *California* crewman were found in one of the flooded compartments. The bodies of some fifty sailors killed in action on December 7 had already been removed from the ship, but many others were still unaccounted for. More bodies were sure to be found as the ship was dewatered, in various states of decay and dismemberment. Concerned about the effect this might have on the young sailors assigned to the working parties, Captain Wallin and his salvage officers devised a method for the discreet removal of the deceased. When bodies were discovered, recovery teams were summoned, entering the space before it was completely drained of seawater. The human remains were then floated into canvas bags and quietly carried from the ship.

"The bags were tightly tied and transported to the Naval Hospital for proper identification and burial," Wallin wrote. "The method was very effective and was undisturbing to the salvage crew." On March 23, fifteen bodies were located and removed; two were found the following day, another eight on March 25, and three on March 26. The final two were recovered on March 29.

By April 1, the draft of the *California* was nearly 40 feet and the ship was steady on an even keel. Machinery spaces and holds were being pumped dry. Some 200,000 gallons of oil were drained from her fuel bunkers; a similar amount of loose oil was also recovered; and 14-inch naval artillery shells were removed and sent to the West Loch. Divers were working to remove the wooden cofferdams.

Then, on April 5, with preparations under way to move the battleship across the channel and into dry dock, the *California* was once again rocked by a sudden explosion. In a compartment on the third deck near the port bow, vapors from a leaking gasoline line had accumulated and quickly found an ignition source: an unprotected electric lightbulb.

Fortunately no one was hurt by the blast, which blew off the window-frame patch covering near-miss bomb damage on the port bow. Pacific Bridge divers and crane operators recovered the patch, which had been distorted by the force of the explosion. The bulkheads surrounding the area of the explosion had held fast, pumps were able to keep up with the additional water that entered the ship, and navy divers secured a newly sprung hatch by welding it shut. This made the damaged section watertight once again, and it was decided that the dry-docking of the *California* could proceed on schedule without taking the time to fabricate and install another patch.

Not quite ready to give up on the notion of spies and saboteurs living among the *nisei* population of Hawaii, the Office of Naval Intelligence soon initiated an investigation into the *California* explosion. No evidence of sabotage was discovered, of course, and the true cause of the blast was quickly ascertained. Despite the ardent beliefs of many senior government and military officials (Navy Secretary Knox was particularly hawkish on the subject), there were no known acts of espionage or sabotage perpetrated by Hawaiians of Japanese descent during the Second World War.

On the morning of April 9, 1942, the Prune Barge was nudged across the channel by tugboats and into the open caisson of Dry Dock Number Two, which had just been vacated by the carrier *Lexington*.

The following day, a forty-two-year-old naval officer by the name of Hyman Rickover arrived in Pearl Harbor.

Rickover would one day go down in history as the "Father of the Nuclear Navy." In 1952 he oversaw construction of the *Nautilus*, the world's first nuclear-powered submarine, and ruled over the US Navy's nuclear propulsion program for three decades. Any submarine officer vying for command of a nuclear boat had to first get past Rickover's famously nerve-racking interview process. Abrasive and autocratic, Rickover was not one to suffer stupidity or incompetence—and would not hesitate to point out such flaws in another man if he felt the need.

Edward Beach, the decorated submarine commander who authored the best-selling thriller *Run Silent, Run Deep*, would refer to Rickover as "a tyrant." Even the soft-spoken and pious former president Jimmy Carter, who once served under Rickover, told the CBS news program *60 Minutes*: "There were a few times, yeah, when I hated him, because he demanded more from me than I thought I could deliver."

To be fair, Admiral Rickover worked as hard as he drove his subordinates, for the simple reason that he "was paid to do it." He was finally forced to retire in 1982 after sixty-three years in the navy, making him the longest-serving member of the armed forces in American history. Shortly thereafter, and still stinging from his dismissal, Rickover was summoned to the White House by President Ronald Reagan, who offered him a job as a special advisor on nuclear technology.

"Mr. President, that's bullshit," Rickover replied, and walked out of the Oval Office.

In the spring of 1942, however, Hyman Rickover was a newly promoted commander, holder of a master of science degree in electrical engineering from Columbia University, and the assistant chief of the Electrical Section of the Bureau of Ships. His mission to Pearl Harbor was to assess the viability of the *California*'s turboelectric propulsion system and, if possible, to get the Prune Barge under way once again under her own power.

Most warships of the day, including the *Pennsylvania*-class and *Nevada*-class battleships, were powered by "direct drive" engines. Oil-fired boilers provided steam to rotate turbines, to which the ship's propeller shafts were directly connected. The battleships of the *Colorado* class, which included the *West Virginia* and *Maryland*, and the *Tennessee* class, to which the *California* belonged, were propelled by a turboelectric transmission designed by the General Electric Company. In this system, steam from the ship's boilers rotated turbines which turned electric generators. The generators were connected by bus bars to electric motors which drove the propeller shafts. Among other advantages, the turboelectric system allowed for more efficient transfer of power and control of the propeller's speed of rotation.

Rickover, who had arrived in Pearl Harbor with representatives from General Electric and the Puget Sound Navy Yard in tow, laid out his plans for the restoration of turboelectric power to the *California* in an April 11 conference with the staff of Wallin's Salvage Division. Rickover and his associates believed that one generator and two electric motors could be cleaned, dried out, and reconditioned in about four months' time, providing sufficient speed for the *California* to make the voyage to Bremerton where she would undergo final repairs.

"Remarkable achievements were common during the war," Edward Beach would write, "but even so, submariners looking across the placid waters of Pearl Harbor at the terribly damaged hulk of the once-proud battleship *California*, inside of which her main drive motors were being cleaned of the encrustation of oil and saltwater that had been there for months, knew this job, this repair, was very special. *California* and her sisters had been built with electric drive—an engineering innovation of its time for ships of their size—and everyone in the Navy had been indoctrinated with the utter destruction that would occur if either oil or saltwater was allowed in the miles of electric windings that constituted their main motors."

Throughout the early summer, while Rickover supervised the extensive overhaul of the *California*'s generator and motors by a force of fifty-three General Electric technicians, the Navy Yard made permanent repairs to her damaged hull and replaced the firebrick in the ship's eight boilers. On the morning of June 7, 1942, while Admiral Nimitz and his staff were receiving and analyzing reports of the smashing American victory over Nagumo's carriers at the Battle of Midway, another triumph was occurring just across the narrow waters of Pearl Harbor's southwest loch. The USS *California* was departing Dry Dock Number Two under her own power.

The *California* would spend the remainder of the summer and the early autumn of 1942 in Hawaii, performing test runs on her patched-together turboelectric drive and having her 14-inch main guns reinstalled by the Navy Yard. On October 10, 1942, escorted by the destroyer *Gansevoort*, the Prune Barge would finally set sail for Puget Sound.

CHAPTER 13
RESURRECTING THE WEE VEE

"RAISING THE *WEST VIRGINIA* WOULD BE FAR MORE DIFFICULT THAN either the *Nevada* or *California* had been," navy diver Edward Raymer would record in his memoirs. "It would test the ingenuity and salvage expertise of every faction involved in the operation."

Six Japanese torpedoes had slammed into the *West Virginia*, leaving two gaping holes: one between frames 43 and 52 below Turret Number Two, and a much larger gash amidships between frames 61 and 97. Roughly half of the Wee Vee's 624-foot hull had been laid open on the port side; only the quick action of her skilled officers and crew had prevented the battleship from turning turtle in the manner of the *Oklahoma*. A seventh torpedo had carried away the ship's rudder, which now lay on the harbor floor.

Two armor-piercing bombs had also struck the ship. Fortunately for the *West Virginia* and her crew, both turned out to be improperly fused duds that did not explode. One was still buried deep within a pile of debris in a compartment on the second deck. The other had broken apart upon striking the armored top of Turret Number Three, but not before tossing a burning Kingfisher seaplane onto the quarterdeck.

The stubborn fire aboard the *West Virginia*, which burned for close to thirty hours, had stymied firefighting crews by breaking out in previously unaffected areas after being extinguished in others. This was due to interior bulkheads being covered with an oil-based paint. Intense heat conducted from burning compartments through steel bulkheads, pipelines, and conduits had ignited painted surfaces in adjacent spaces, which quickly spread to nearby furniture and stores. The shipboard firefighting experience aboard the *West Virginia* would cause the use of oil-based paint to be banned navy-wide, resulting in the development of fire-resistant paints for maritime application.

With her port side open to the sea and interior spaces gutted by fire, the *West Virginia* came to rest on the bottom of Pearl Harbor with a 3-degree list to port, and a draft of 50 feet forward and 40 feet aft. She was a pitiful sight, her crumpled and charred upper works still visible above the surface of the water and strewn with wreckage, the damage "so extensive as to beggar description," as Captain Homer Wallin would report. Later the salvage officer would state: "Here was a ship much more severely damaged than *California* or *Nevada.* Salvage was getting harder as the work progressed. Few there were in the early days after the Japanese attack who believed that *West Virginia* would ever float again, much less be a formidable ship against Japanese sea power."

The two enormous gashes in the *West Virginia*'s hull posed an entirely different and challenging salvage problem than those already encountered. The method used to raise the *California* and *Nevada* would simply not work with the Wee Vee; positive buoyancy would never be achieved by leaving the wounds open and setting internal watertight boundaries. The jagged holes would have to be patched in some way before the ship could be pumped dry and refloated.

Fortunately, Captain Wallin had an ace up his sleeve. For the solution to the *West Virginia*'s dilemma, the salvage officer would turn to general manager Jack Graham and the crew of Pacific Bridge, journeyman builders and artisans who were accustomed to finding innovative ways of overcoming the many varied and complex obstacles encountered in their work. They proposed that cofferdam-style patches be fabricated and installed, each consisting of horizontal 4-inch planks fit snugly together, backed by a grid of steel and heavy timber shoring. The patches would be built in sections 13.5 feet wide and nearly 50 feet tall, extending from above the waterline to the turn of the ship's bilge and attached to the hull by J-bolts, which would be inserted through holes burned by divers using underwater cutting torches. Lead weights would keep the patches from floating away before they could be installed. The joints between the sections would be sealed by gaskets made from discarded rubber fire hoses and brought tightly together by threaded bolts run through lugs installed along the edges of each patch.

Finally, the outer edges and bottom of each completed patch would be sealed with underwater concrete, the mixing and pouring of which being a rare skill in which the Pacific Bridge Company specialized. The Pacific Bridge plan was duly approved, and even while the focus of the Salvage Division was concentrated on refloating the less-damaged *Nevada* and *California*, work got under way on fabricating the patches and preparing the *West Virginia* for her resurrection.

The unexploded bomb was rendered safe by ordnance technicians and, together with the shattered pieces of the other dud projectile, packed off to the Navy Department for examination. Navy divers entered the ship to open doors and hatches to facilitate the placement of deep-well centrifugal pumps; in some cases, holes were burned through decks with torches to accommodate the larger-sized devices. The leaks resulting from the torpedo strike that wrecked the *West Virginia*'s steering gear were isolated behind watertight doors. Distorted portholes were covered by strongback patches; drains and other fittings were closed; and arms and munitions were removed from the ship. Sections of the ship that were still above water were cleared of debris.

"Removal of the debris was a monotonous, back-breaking job," remembered Lieutenant Commander William White. "To keep from exhausting the crew by repeated shoveling at various deck levels, wheel barrows were used for transporting. Holes were burned in each wheel barrow for attaching a wire sling. Air winches equipped with the slings were used at each deck level to effect the hoist. Thus, once a wheel barrow was loaded, the contents were not again moved until the debris was emptied on a barge. All compartments were then steam cleaned. A large tank was constructed on the boat deck to contain a cleaning solution. This solution consisted of 'Turko' plus other magic ingredients added by the chief watertenders. This was then piped throughout the ship along with steam from an ex-tug. The hot mix was applied through hose[s] with control nozzles. This process not only removed the oil but loosened much of the paint so that it peeled off in sheets."

Electric power lines were stretched from Ford Island, and air compressors were brought aboard for the purposes of displacing water in various compartments and adding to the ship's buoyancy. A tent camp was established on Ford Island for the ship's company and a wooden walkway to the ship was constructed. The galley was thoroughly cleaned out and resupplied and was soon serving three meals a day to the remaining crew and workers on board. On March 24, 1942, the *West Virginia*'s detached main mast was lifted away by a floating crane.

On Saturday, April 18, 1942—the same morning that sixteen US Army B-25 medium bombers under the command of Lieutenant Colonel James Doolittle were launched from the carrier *Hornet* on their audacious mission to bomb mainland Japan—the first cofferdam patch for the hull of the *West Virginia* was being maneuvered into place by crane operators and divers from Pacific Bridge. Because the *West Virginia* had settled with a 3-degree list to port, harbor mud had to be jetted away by divers using fire hoses in order for the patch to conform to the turn of the ship's bilge. The patch was successfully placed at frame 61, over the forward edge of the larger torpedo gash amidships.

By May 1, 1942, the work of covering the torpedo wounds with wooden patches was complete, and a barge carrying the Pacific Bridge Company's concrete mixer was brought alongside the *West Virginia*. A crawling crane on the barge lifted yard buckets of concrete from the mixer to a hopper, feeding the rich mixture of cement and aggregate into Tremie pipes, which were applied to the edges of the patched areas by divers.

Within a week, Pacific Bridge completed the work of sealing the patches after mixing and pouring 325 yards of concrete. Several smaller leaks in the hull then revealed themselves, which were plugged by navy divers, and at 10:30 a.m. on May 12, deep-well pumps began dewatering the *West Virginia*. Six days later, the ship that even the chronically optimistic Captain Wallin had at first considered "a total wreck" was rising from the floor of Pearl Harbor.

In mid-April, while working to close a watertight door in the utter darkness of the *West Virginia*'s submerged third deck, a navy diver came across the floating remains of a young sailor killed on December 7. As the ship was gradually dewatered, the bodies of sixty-five more *West Virginia* crew members would be found aboard the sunken battleship. Among them were Louis Costin, Ronald Endicott, and Clifford Olds. Of the countless stories of tragedy to emerge from Pearl Harbor, theirs would be the most heartbreaking of all.

In May 1942, salvage crews were able to enter Compartment A-109, a freshwater pump room, and the adjacent storeroom in Compartment A-111. There they found the bodies of Costin, Endicott, and Olds huddled close together on a shelf. Though the surrounding compartments had been completely flooded as the ship sank, both of these spaces were dry, sealed off behind watertight doors. The manhole cover to the freshwater storage tanks had been removed and emergency rations had been broken out. Spent flashlight batteries littered the deck.

This was gut-wrenching enough, but then the calendar was found. An *X* had been drawn through the date of December 7 and every day on the calendar until December 23, apparently the day that the concentration of oxygen in the space dropped below the level necessary to sustain life. The three bodies were gently slipped into canvas bags and carried from the ship.

The family of twenty-year-old Clifford Olds would request that his body be shipped home to North Dakota for burial; eighteen-year-old Ronald Endicott and twenty-one-year-old Louis Costin would be interred in the National Memorial Cemetery of the Pacific in Honolulu's Punchbowl Crater. All three government-issued headstones would show December 7 as the date of their death. The US Navy would never disclose to their families the circumstances in which the young men died.

Ronald Endicott's parents in Aberdeen, Washington, would go to their own graves believing the typewritten words on the Navy Department telegram they received, which stated that their son had "died at his battle station" on the day the Japanese attacked Pearl Harbor. Louis "Buddy" Costin's younger brother Harlan would also join the navy in late 1942. While serving in the South Pacific, Harlan would learn the truth about his brother's death from a friend on the crew of the *West Virginia*. Harlan could never bring himself to tell his widowed mother Effie or his younger sister, Edna.

"I just wanted to spare them the grief," he would say many years later. The navy had sent Effie a wristwatch found in Buddy's locker, inoperable after being submerged in seawater for many months, intended as a Christmas gift for his mother. Effie had the watch repaired and wore it every day until she died at the age of ninety-two, never having learned what had truly happened to her eldest son. Edna would finally be told a decade later, when she was contacted by a reporter from the *Honolulu Advertiser* writing a feature article about the Pearl Harbor attack.

In 1942, a sailor serving at the Puget Sound Navy Yard, where the *West Virginia* was undergoing repairs, would learn of what had truly happened to his cousin, Clifford Olds. He would share the tragic news with Cliff's brother and two sisters, and together the siblings and their cousin swore an oath of secrecy: Cliff's grieving parents would never be told the horrible truth.

And they never were.

On June 8, 1942, tugboats maneuvered the battered but floating Wee Vee, still down at the stern and with pumps still working hard to shunt water overboard, across the harbor channel and into Dry Dock Number One. Originally she was to have replaced the *California* in Dry Dock Number Two, but it was decided to keep the deeper dry dock available for ships returning from combat.

The *West Virginia* would remain in the Pearl Harbor Navy Yard for the better part of a year while her turboelectric drive was painstakingly cleaned and restored; a tremendous amount of steelwork on her hull was conducted; the rudder was recovered and steering gear mended; interior spaces were scrubbed clean; and thousands of other alterations, replacements, and repairs were performed. On the final day of April 1943, sporting a fresh coat of dark gray paint, the national ensign at her stern unfurled in the tropical breeze, and her crew manning the rails in their dress whites, the USS *West Virginia* stood out from Pearl Harbor under her own steam, bound for Bremerton, Washington, and the Puget Sound Navy Yard.

"Enough cannot be said in praise of the salvage crew," Homer Wallin would write. "They worked hard and earnestly. They soon saw that the results of their efforts exceeded the fondest hopes of their supporters and they were urged on by their successive achievements."

In November 1942, with the Americans and Japanese locked in the brutal combat of the Guadalcanal campaign, Captain Wallin was reassigned to Bill Halsey's South Pacific Area command as the admiral's maintenance officer. Prior to his departure, an award ceremony was conducted in Pearl Harbor upon the deck of the aircraft carrier *Enterprise.* Admiral Nimitz himself would read aloud the citation for Captain Homer N. Wallin's Distinguished Service Medal, recognizing Wallin's outstanding leadership of the Salvage Division of the Pearl Harbor Navy Yard from January to November 1942, which saw the recovery of three sunken American dreadnoughts.

"And for being an undying optimist," Nimitz would add.

CHAPTER 14
KANTAI KESSEN

The destruction of the Pacific Fleet's battle line at Pearl Harbor would have an effect that neither the Americans nor the Japanese could have foreseen. It would force the United States into a change of naval strategy and tactics that would ultimately play to its strengths and be enormously successful in their prosecution of the war against Japan.

As late as April 1940, when the last of the prewar Fleet Problems was conducted in Hawaiian waters, aircraft carriers and their embarked air groups served as supportive adjuncts to the battleships of the Pacific Fleet. The US Navy's scripted battle plans called for heavy cruisers to form the vanguard of the fleet, with squadrons of fast, torpedo-laden destroyers working ahead and alongside the cruisers, functioning more or less like infantry skirmishers. The battleships would follow in the center of the formation, maneuvering to bring their broadsides to bear upon the opposing battle line, while additional destroyers protected their flanks. Aircraft carriers and their own screening vessels were to bring up the rear.

While carrier-based scouting squadrons performed reconnaissance and fighters provided air cover for the battle line, torpedo- and dive-bombers were to strike at approaching enemy capital ships. Once the long-range gunfire of the American battleships decimated the opposing fleet in a decisive surface action, follow-up carrier airstrikes would be launched to sink any damaged or retreating enemy vessels.

At the time of the Pearl Harbor attack, there were three battleship divisions assigned to Battle Force, Pacific Fleet, each consisting of three super dreadnoughts. When the attack was over, there were no American battleships available for combat duty in the Pacific. Two had been completely destroyed; three had been sunk and were in need of salvage and extensive repairs; and three had been lightly damaged and required the services of naval shipyards on the West Coast before they could be fully returned to service. The remaining battleship, *Colorado*, was in the midst of a major refit at the Puget Sound Navy Yard and would not be available until the following April.

The three *New Mexico*–class battleships, transferred to the Atlantic the previous summer to safeguard merchant convoys and counter the threat posed by German battlecruisers, were then ordered to reinforce the Pacific Fleet. The *Mississippi* and *Idaho* left their base in Iceland on December 9, transiting the Panama Canal after a brief stop in Hampton Roads and arriving in San Francisco at the end of January. They would later be joined by *New Mexico* herself, after the battleship had put into Norfolk for repairs following a collision with the freighter *Oregon* south of Nantucket Island. Both vessels had been traveling without running lights in the early-morning hours of December 10 when the accident occurred, which resulted in the sinking of the unfortunate merchant ship.

In the meantime, the US Pacific Fleet, finding itself suddenly bereft of battleships, initiated wartime operations utilizing task forces built around one or more aircraft carriers. The carriers were screened by heavy and light cruisers capable of throwing a curtain of antiaircraft fire into the faces of attacking enemy pilots. Destroyers assisted with antiaircraft defense while fulfilling their traditional antisubmarine role and acting as "plane guards," rescuing aircrews involved in mishaps during takeoffs and landings.

The operating procedures, tactics, and doctrine of what would become known as the Fast Carrier Task Forces had been in development during Kimmel's tenure as CINCPAC, as a means of providing air superiority over the battle line. The carriers and their screening vessels were learning to act as flexible, independent units to support the ultimate goal of destroying the enemy fleet, tasked with performing reconnaissance and strikes against the enemy's carriers, advanced bases, and his train of auxiliary vessels. Their evolution would continue after Nimitz assumed command, with the carrier air group, not the big guns of the battleships, becoming the primary means of projecting the striking power of the United States Navy.

A CINCPAC strategic assessment written in January 1942 outlined "Considerations leading to adoption of offensive courses":

(1) Damage to the enemy, disproportionate if practicable. At shore objectives sufficient facilities might be destroyed to prevent, or at least hinder, the use of these bases by the enemy.

(2) Tendency to divert enemy forces for defense. He might try to cover his territory with forces which he would intend to be stronger than our attacking forces.

(3) Boost to morale of the fleet.

(4) Boost to morale of the nation.

(5) In general, the advantages which go with the initiative.

With the American public and the armed forces reeling from a series of humiliating losses in the Pacific, Admiral Nimitz knew that it was imperative for the United States to strike back. The Pacific Fleet needed to carry the fight to the Japanese, if for no other reason than to shore up its own flagging spirits. Fortunately, Nimitz had just the right man for the job.

As a destroyer skipper during the First World War, William F. Halsey Jr. had been awarded the Navy Cross for "vigorously and unremittingly prosecuting against all forms of enemy naval activity." In order to gain command of the aircraft carrier *Saratoga* in 1934, Halsey completed flight training at NAS Pensacola and became qualified as a naval aviator at the age of fifty-two, the oldest person ever to do so. A gruff, salty old sea dog with a searing hatred for any and all things Japanese, "Bull" Halsey was just the sort of energetic and aggressive commander Nimitz needed to lead his carrier task forces into battle.

On January 11, 1942, Halsey's Task Force 8, composed of the carrier *Enterprise*, three cruisers, and six destroyers, stood out from Pearl Harbor. After rendezvousing with Frank Jack Fletcher's Task Force 17, built around the *Yorktown* recently arrived from the Atlantic, the two carrier groups accompanied a convoy of transports shuttling five thousand US Marines to reinforce the garrison of American Samoa. On January 29, their escort mission completed, the task forces turned northwest and steamed for the Marshall and Gilbert Islands at 30 knots.

On February 1, Halsey's *Enterprise* Task Force attacked the Japanese advanced bases of Kwajalein, Wotje, and Taroa while Fletcher's *Yorktown* group raided the islands of Jaluit, Makin, and Milli. To provide cover for their withdrawal, Wilson Brown's *Lexington* Task Force maintained a ready position in the waters off Kiritimati to the east.

"It was one of those plans which are called *brilliant* if they succeed and *foolhardy* if they fail," Halsey would later remark.

This time it would be the Japanese that were caught completely off guard. While the cruisers *Northampton*, *Salt Lake City*, and *Chester* pounded Japanese installations on Wotje and Taroa with their 8-inch guns, planes from the *Enterprise* bombed and strafed enemy airfields and dockyards and attacked ships in the Kwajalein anchorage. The transport *Bordeaux Maru*, the gunboat *Toyotsu Maru*, and the patrol craft *Shonan Maru* were sunk, while the cruiser *Katori* and eight other ships were badly damaged. Rear Admiral Sukeyoshi Yatsushiro, the commander of the Marshall Islands Defense Forces who chose to ignore a warning from his radio intelligence unit that the Americans were up to something, would be the first Japanese flag officer to die in the Pacific War when an SBD Dauntless dive-bomber from the *Enterprise* scored a direct hit on his headquarters.

HAUL ASS WITH HALSEY flashed from the signal bridge of the *Enterprise* as Task Force 8 wheeled about and raced for Hawaii, easily brushing off a counterattack by Japanese bombers. At Makin atoll there were fewer targets; Fletcher's planes bombed and strafed two Japanese ships and the *Yorktown*'s fighters shot down a flying boat that attempted to follow Task Force 17's eastward retirement.

On the afternoon of February 20, the *Lexington* was steaming toward the island of New Britain in the Solomons, in the company of four heavy cruisers and ten destroyers, intending to raid the newly established Japanese base at Rabaul. The task force was spotted by Japanese search planes as it passed near the island of Bougainville, and just after three o'clock, seventeen Mitsubishi G4M "Betty" twin-engine bombers attacked the *Lexington*. As they were set upon by the *Lexington*'s fighter cover and encountered heavy antiaircraft fire from the screening cruisers and destroyers, the Japanese failed to score any hits on the American ships. All but two of the Betties were splashed by the *Lexington*'s Wildcat fighters, three of them by Lieutenant Edward "Butch" O'Hare, who was later awarded the Medal of Honor. Having lost the element of surprise, Admiral Brown chose to withdraw his task force from the area rather than press on to Rabaul and risk losing one of only three operational American aircraft carriers in the Pacific.

On February 24 Halsey was at it again, with planes from his *Enterprise* group striking the airfield on the now-Japanese-occupied island of Wake, while *Northampton* and *Salt Lake City* bombarded enemy installations on nearby Peale Island. The following day Halsey's forces pummeled the Japanese garrison on Marcus Island, just 999 miles from Tokyo. On March 10, a strike force of 104 aircraft from the *Lexington* and *Yorktown* flew over New Guinea's 13,000-foot Owen Stanley Mountain Range to bomb and strafe the Japanese beachheads at Lae and Salamaua, destroying four transports and causing heavy damage to several other ships.

"The raid against Marcus caused some concern as to the defenses of the Japanese homeland, but the exact amount of diversion from Japanese effort in the southwest cannot be measured at this time," Nimitz would write in a report to his new boss, Admiral Ernest J. King. Surly, iron-willed, and fiercely territorial, King had assumed the dual role of Commander-in-Chief United States Fleet (COMINCH) and Chief of Naval Operations after "Betty" Stark had been sent packing by President Roosevelt.

"When they're in trouble, they send for the sons of bitches," King is said to have uttered upon learning of his appointment, an anecdote which spread like wildfire throughout the navy. When asked about it years later, King replied that he never made such a statement—but if he had thought of it at the time, he would have.

Nimitz was basing his assertion on the undertone of panic and bewilderment that ran through a series of Japanese radio intercepts decoded by Station HYPO. After decimating the Pacific Fleet battleship force at Pearl Harbor, the Japanese had seized Guam, Wake, Hong Kong, and Singapore, and were in the process of neutralizing the remaining American and Filipino resistance on Luzon's Bataan Peninsula and the fortified island of Corregidor. A string of victories over the combined American, British, Dutch, and Australian naval force in the southwest Pacific had accompanied their successful invasion of Borneo and the Dutch East Indies. A bombing raid had been conducted against the port of Darwin in northern Australia. The Japanese were busily consolidating their chain of advanced bases in the Central Pacific to ensure their "long-term invincibility." The next phase of their war plans included an invasion of Port Moresby on the southeastern tail of New Guinea, in order to interdict the critical lines of communication between Australia and the United States.

The audacity of the American hit-and-run carrier raids, and their inability to stop them, appalled a Japanese admiralty that had grown heady with its own success. What was particularly galling was that this unexpected shift in American naval tactics had been brought on by the Japanese themselves. After the losses to Japanese shipping suffered during the *Lexington-Yorktown* raid on Lae and Salamaua, the Port Moresby operation had to be postponed until May 1942.

"The Japanese are flushed with victory," the CINCPAC Running Estimate stated in late April 1942. "Their morale is high. As long as the course of their operations proceeds according to plan, their morale and efficiency will remain high. But when they are forced to improvise because of major setbacks, a lowering of morale and efficiency can be expected. The impression is gained that they have definitely been held up in eastern New Guinea by the losses inflicted by Vice Admiral Brown's force and by persistent bombing from Australia and Port Moresby."

Yamamoto himself was deeply concerned about the American Navy's ability to strike the Japanese homeland. If Halsey could raid Marcus Island and get away scot-free, he could very well do the same to Tokyo. The fears of the Commander-in-Chief of the Combined Fleet would be realized on April 18, 1942, when Jimmy Doolittle's B-25s suddenly appeared over the Japanese capital, having launched from the carrier *Hornet* after Halsey's task force had closed to within 600 nautical miles of the Home Islands. As a strategic bombing raid the Doolittle mission was a pinprick, but it electrified the American home front and caused a tremendous amount of anxiety in Japan. The raid was also an intolerable loss of face for the leadership of the Imperial Japanese Navy and caused significant air and naval resources to be diverted from other operations to conduct a fruitless search for Halsey's retiring task force.

While the early American carrier raids on Japanese advanced bases in the Central Pacific had also achieved very little in a military sense, their successful execution helped to restore the confidence of the officers and men of the Pacific Fleet and provided valuable combat experience as they looked toward future encounters with the Japanese. Desperate for a hero, the American public delighted in the daring exploits of the hell-for-leather Admiral Halsey.

"The reason we brought off these early raids is that we violated all the rules and traditions of naval warfare," Halsey would later explain. "We did the exact opposite of what the enemy expected. We did not keep our carriers behind the battle; we deliberately exposed them to shore-based planes. Most important, whatever we did, we did fast."

On May 8, the day after the fall of Corregidor, Jack Fletcher's carriers would intercept the anticipated Japanese move toward Port Moresby. The Battle of Coral Sea would be a portent of things to come, having the distinction of being the first major naval engagement in history where the opposing fleets never came within sight of one another. Rather than battleships engaging in a long-range gun action, all of the blows would be struck by carrier-based aircraft.

By the time the two-day slugging match was over, the Japanese light carrier *Shoho* was sunk, while the *Shokaku* and *Zuikaku*, veterans of the Pearl Harbor attack, were both rendered combat-ineffective after their air groups sustained heavy losses. Three bomb hits from American SBDs would knock the *Shokaku* out of action for the next seven weeks. A Japanese counterstrike sank the *Lexington* and caused the *Yorktown* to limp back into Pearl Harbor badly damaged. Despite the loss of their beloved "Lady Lex," the Americans could claim a tactical victory after the Japanese invasion force was forced to retreat.

The aggressive and relentless employment of US Navy carrier task forces throughout the spring of 1942 would provide justification for Yamamoto's ambitious plan to capture the American base on Midway Island, a key objective in his "short war" strategy. The Imperial Japanese Army, which had instead favored an invasion of Australia, would execute an about-face and agree to support the Midway operation in the aftermath of the Doolittle Raid. The seizure of Midway was to be performed concurrently with an invasion of the remote Aleutian Islands of Kiska and Attu, in order to secure the northern approaches to mainland Japan.

An attack on Midway would undoubtedly lure the truculent American carrier fleet into battle, where it could be destroyed once and for all. The Japanese would then be free to contemplate a further invasion of the Hawaiian Islands. The vital lifeline between the United States and Australia could then be severed. From newly acquired bases in Hawaii, Japanese carrier strikes against West Coast port cities and the Panama Canal would prevent any reinforcement of the US Pacific Fleet and bring the Americans to their knees.

On May 27, Nagumo's First Carrier Strike Force—composed of the carriers *Akagi*, *Kaga*, *Hiryu*, and *Soryu*, the fast battleships *Haruna* and *Kirishima*, three cruisers, and a destroyer squadron—departed Hiroshima Bay for Midway. The next day the *Kido Butai* was followed by the main body of the First Fleet, made up of three battleships, an escort carrier, two seaplane tenders, and a squadron of destroyers. Yamamoto himself would command this formidable trailing force, flying his flag from the "super battleship" *Yamato.* A flotilla of transports carrying five thousand troops from the Special Naval Landing Force and the army's Ichiki Regiment was also under way from the Marshall Islands, escorted by two battleships, two cruisers, a destroyer squadron, and one light carrier from Vice Admiral Nobutake Kondo's Second Fleet.

Commissioned just after Pearl Harbor, the monstrous *Yamato* and her sister *Musashi* were the largest and most powerful battleships ever to be built, at over 860 feet long and displacing 72,800 tons. Yamamoto's plan for meeting the Americans in a decisive surface action, the importance of which overshadowed even the invasion of Midway itself, called for Nagumo's aircraft to achieve air supremacy in the skies over the battlespace. Then the *Yamato*, firing her massive 18-inch guns from 40,000 yards, would obliterate the American fleet.

Unfortunately for Yamamoto, Nimitz was unwilling to play along and conform to his plans. With the launching of the Midway operation, Yamamoto's earlier prediction to Prime Minister Konoe that he would "run wild for six months" after the commencement of hostilities would prove to be uncannily accurate. On June 4, 1942, five months and twenty-nine days after Pearl Harbor, the Imperial Japanese Navy would finally have their *kantai kessen*, but it was certainly not the one they were expecting.

Ed Layton and his colleague from Station HYPO, Lieutenant Commander Joseph Rochefort, had convinced Admiral Nimitz that the Japanese were planning to invade Midway during the first week of June. Rochefort's team of cryptanalysts, growing increasingly adept at decoding the Japanese Navy's JN-25B radio cipher, intercepted an enemy signal in early May for the "AF Occupation Force" to proceed to Saipan and "wait for the forthcoming campaign." Other Japanese messages referred to equipment and supplies being readied for shipment to "AF" once the mysterious objective was secured. The commander of a seaplane squadron, displaying the sort of brazen overconfidence that was running rampant through the Japanese Navy at the time, had even sent a radio message to Japan asking for his unit's mail to be forwarded to "AF."

The size, type, and number of units and resources being allocated to the future occupation of "AF" indicated that it was a location from which the American military installations of Hawaii would be within range of Japanese land-based bombers. The logical choice, therefore, was Midway, at 1,100 nautical miles from Pearl Harbor. Admiral Nimitz agreed with Layton and Rochefort's assessment, but communications security officers on the staff of the Chief of Naval Operations were skeptical, as was Admiral King himself. Johnston Atoll, though less suitable as an air base than Midway, was nevertheless a possibility. It could all be a feint, with New Caledonia or Samoa being the next target of the Japanese. An officer on Rochefort's staff, Lieutenant Commander Jasper Holmes, then hatched a simple but clever scheme to confirm that "AF" meant Midway.

A communication was sent by means of a secure undersea telephonic cable, the presence of which was unknown to the Japanese. Radio operators on Midway were instructed to broadcast an unencrypted "urgent" message to Fourteenth Naval District Headquarters, advising that the island's freshwater distillation system had broken down. Pearl Harbor then replied that an emergency supply of freshwater would soon be on its way. Hours later, Station HYPO intercepted Japanese radio messages stating that "AF" was suffering from a shortage of freshwater and units assigned to the occupation force should plan accordingly.

On May 26, Bill Halsey was admitted to Naval Hospital Pearl Harbor just after the *Enterprise* made port, his body wracked by severe psoriasis likely caused by the sleepless nights and stress of the past six months. Nimitz chose Rear Admiral Raymond Spruance to replace Halsey as commander of Task Force 16, which consisted of the carriers *Enterprise* and *Hornet*, six cruisers, and two squadrons of destroyers. The selection elicited some surprise and consternation from the community of naval aviators, for Spruance was a "black shoe" admiral, a full-fledged member of the navy's "Gun Club" who had led Halsey's cruiser divisions and never before commanded aviation units or a carrier task force.*

Admiral Nimitz, however, had good reasons for the appointment, aside from Halsey's emphatic recommendation. Quiet, judicious, and calm even when under enormous pressure, Ray Spruance was known to be an intuitive and forethoughtful strategist. Nicknamed "The Electric Brain" by his colleagues, over his thirty-seven-year career Spruance had amassed a great deal of command experience at sea, served for three years on the faculty of the Naval War College, and was considered by many to be one of the smartest officers in the navy. The most telling insight into Spruance's command ability was provided by the admiral himself, when he was quoted as saying: "A man's judgment is best when he can forget himself and any reputation he may have acquired and can concentrate wholly on making the right decisions."

Spruance was ordered to sail his task force to a location 325 miles northeast of Midway, a rally point that had been assigned the tongue-in-cheek designation of "Point Luck" by the CINCPAC staff. There they would rendezvous with Jack Fletcher's Task Force 17 built around the *Yorktown*, back at sea and fully operational after her miraculous three-day repair stint in Pearl Harbor's Dry Dock Number One, and together they would wait for the opportunity to ambush the Japanese fleet.

Nimitz had provided the strategy; the tactics he left in the hands of Spruance. Such was Nimitz's style of leadership: Rather than issuing overwrought operational plans and meddling in their execution from afar,

---

* Beginning in 1913, naval aviators were permitted to wear shiny brown shoes with their uniforms, while officers assigned to the surface fleet continued wearing their traditional black shoes; hence, the "brown shoe" and "black shoe" distinction. The "Gun Club" was a somewhat sardonic term used by aviators to refer to the "good old boy" network of battleship and cruiser officers. Interestingly, Japanese naval aviators also referred to their surface navy counterparts as members of the *teppo ya*—the Gun Club—in a similar manner.

he trusted his subordinate commanders on the scene to make the appropriate tactical decisions in the heat of battle.

"You will be governed by the principle of calculated risk," Nimitz wrote to Spruance in a letter of instruction, "which you shall interpret to mean the avoidance of exposure of your force to attack by superior enemy forces without good prospect of inflicting, as a result of such exposure, greater damage to the enemy."

On the morning of June 3, one of thirty PBY Catalina flying boats operating from Midway Island spotted the Japanese invasion force steaming east from the Marshalls at a distance of some 500 miles. Nine Army B-17 Flying Fortresses took off from Midway to attack the transports but failed to achieve any hits. At 5:30 a.m. the following day, another PBY spotted Nagumo's carriers, and a mixed force of US Marine Corps SBD Dauntless and SB2U Vindicator dive-bombers, navy TBF Avengers, army B-26 Marauders, and B-17 Flying Fortresses took off from Midway's airstrip to attack the Japanese armada.

The Japanese carriers had already launched an airstrike of their own. Zeroes violently swept aside the obsolete Marine Corps fighters that rose to Midway's defense, but as the Val and Kate bombers made their attack runs they encountered heavy and accurate antiaircraft fire from the Sixth Marine Defense Battalion dug in around the airstrip and were forced to withdraw without inflicting any serious damage. Losing eleven of his aircraft without putting the Midway airfield out of action, Lieutenant Joichi Tomonaga, the strike leader, radioed Admiral Nagumo: *There is a need for a second attack.*

For the next hour and a half, Nagumo's carrier force would be subjected to repeated and determined attacks from the Midway air group. The Americans, however, would lose eighteen planes to intense antiaircraft fire and patrolling Zero fighters without scoring a single hit on the Japanese carriers. In the midst of all of this, Admiral Nagumo would receive an ambiguous signal from a reconnaissance seaplane launched from the cruiser *Tone*, reporting the presence of an American aircraft carrier north of Midway.

The harried Nagumo, who had already ordered the Kate torpedo bombers on his flight decks rearmed with general-purpose bombs for the recommended second strike against Midway, countermanded the order and directed that the planes should once again be fitted with torpedoes for attacking the American fleet. Because of the delay this caused, worsened by the need to launch and recover Zero fighters for countering the persistent American attacks, the Japanese were unable to launch a second strike mission before the first one returned to their carriers, battle-damaged and low on fuel.

Then even more American planes attacked the Japanese fleet. This time it was three squadrons of TBD Devastator torpedo bombers from the *Enterprise*, *Hornet*, and *Yorktown*. The slow and lumbering TBDs were easy prey for the Zeroes of the combat air patrol and the antiaircraft guns of the Japanese screening vessels. The US Navy would never again use the Devastator in combat; of the forty that attacked Nagumo's carriers, only six would return. The *Hornet*'s Torpedo Squadron Eight was nearly massacred; all fifteen TBDs were shot down and only one man survived.

The sacrifice of the American torpedo squadrons, however, added further to the chaos occurring on the cluttered flight decks of the Japanese carriers. Aircraft spotting for the pending launch had been thrown into disarray and hoses charged with volatile aviation gasoline snaked across the decks in between parked aircraft and stacks of bombs and torpedoes. The Zero fighters that were supposed to be protecting the fleet were either drawn away to the southeast, chasing the surviving TBDs just above the waves, or were slowly circling the carriers, low on ammunition and fuel and needing recovery. It was at this moment, when the Japanese were most vulnerable, that American dive-bombers arrived high overhead to deliver their death blows to the First Carrier Strike Force.

Commander Wade McClusky, leading the *Enterprise* air group, had spotted the destroyer *Arashi* steaming at flank speed to catch up with the Japanese fleet after dueling with the American submarine *Nautilus*. Serving as an unwitting guide for the SBDs of Scouting Squadron Six and Bombing Squadron Six, the *Arashi* led the Americans directly to Nagumo's carriers. Thirty Dauntlesses pushed over into steep dives on *Kaga* and *Akagi*. The *Yorktown*'s Bombing Three, led by Commander Max Leslie and arriving at almost the same time as the *Enterprise* strike group, screamed downward toward the twisting, turning shape of the carrier *Soryu*.

A 1,000-pound bomb struck a mobile fuel tank beside the control island of the *Kaga* and killed everyone on the bridge, including the ship's captain. Three more bomb hits turned the rows of parked aircraft on the *Kaga*'s flight deck into a blazing pile of wreckage. Another bomb penetrated the *Akagi*'s flight deck and detonated among eighteen Kate bombers stored closely together on the hangar deck below, starting a fire that would be uncontrollable. A near-miss also took out the *Akagi*'s steering gear. His flagship doomed, Nagumo was forced to escape out a porthole and jump into a boat sent over from the destroyer *Nowaki*. In the meantime, three direct hits from Leslie's *Yorktown* dive-bombers turned the *Soryu* into a raging inferno.

While planes from the surviving Japanese carrier *Hiryu* would mount a successful strike that afternoon against the *Yorktown*, putting that American carrier out of action, the *Hiryu* would in turn be bombed by two dozen *Enterprise* and *Yorktown* Dauntlesses. At 9:00 a.m. the following morning, the *Hiryu* would join her sisters *Akagi*, *Kaga*, and *Soryu* on the bottom of the ocean. An attempt to salvage the *Yorktown* was abandoned on June 6 after she was struck by two torpedoes fired from the Japanese submarine *I-168*. A third torpedo meant for the *Yorktown* cleaved the destroyer *Hammann* in two as she kept station alongside the damaged carrier. Remaining afloat for several hours after her crew departed, the stubborn but tired *Yorktown* would finally roll over and sink, an oversized American flag still fluttering solemnly from her signal mast.

Despite the utter disaster that had befallen Nagumo's command, Yamamoto still doggedly attempted to engage the Americans in a surface action. On the evening of June 4, a detachment of screening cruisers and destroyers from the First Carrier Strike Force, with no carriers left to screen, was sent to bombard Midway and, if possible, to locate the American fleet. Their search would be in vain, for Spruance had chosen wisely to retire eastward for the night.

The mission of the Japanese cruisers also met with calamity after the *Mogami* and *Mikuma* collided in the darkness while attempting to avoid an American submarine. As she staggered westward in the light of the next morning, the damaged *Mikuma* was ravaged by Spruance's dive-bombers and sunk.

In the space of a few hours, the entire course of the war in the Pacific had radically shifted. The US Navy would seize the initiative and never let it go. The Imperial Japanese Navy, on the other hand, had tasted bitter defeat for the first time in its history. Over 3,000 Japanese sailors and airmen were dead. The Combined Fleet had lost two-thirds of its strength in fleet carriers, along with over 250 aircraft.

For the industrially weak Japan these kinds of losses were unsustainable, especially when one considers what they were up against in terms of war production. In 1942 the Japanese would complete the construction of 4 new aircraft carriers; in 1943, the keels of 2 more would be laid. American shipyards would produce 18 aircraft carriers in 1942 and *65* the following year. Over the same two-year period Japanese factories would produce 26,000 military aircraft, while the Americans would crank out 134,000.

Not only would the American aircraft industry outstrip the Japanese in sheer numbers, the quality and performance of American combat aircraft would soon exceed that of Japanese types. The Mitsubishi A6M Zero, for example, was clearly superior to the Grumman F4F Wildcat, the workhorse of US Navy and Marine fighter squadrons throughout 1942. The next year would see the deployment in great numbers of the vastly improved Grumman F6F Hellcat and the deadly Chance-Vought F4U Corsair, carrier-based fighters with self-sealing fuel tanks and armor plating (the Zero had neither), along with greater firepower and more-powerful engines.

The loss of so many trained pilots created a deficit from which the Japanese would never recover. Believing that the war would be quickly won by a relatively small force of hand-picked and superbly trained naval aviators, the Japanese Navy spent an average of three years training each of their pilots. Only the best of these were assigned to carrier duty, a number that appears to have been around one hundred per year.

The performance of Japanese naval aviators in the opening months of the war was certainly impressive, the result of a rigorous and inflexible training regimen which proved utterly incapable of replacing the losses sustained in the battles of Coral Sea, Midway, and Guadalcanal. By the end of the Solomons campaign, a significant portion of these highly trained personnel were dead. For that matter, so was Isoroku Yamamoto, his personal aircraft ambushed by American P-38 Lightning fighters over Bougainville after a radio message containing the schedule for his travel itinerary was decrypted by Station HYPO.

In their shortsightedness, or perhaps arrogance, the leaders of Japanese naval aviation had failed to develop the training infrastructure required to replace their combat losses. Japan lacked the adequate facilities, instructor cadre, training aircraft, spare parts, and fuel reserves necessary to train a sufficient number of pilots. The inevitable result, as the losses piled up, was a lowering of standards for recruitment and aviation cadets being rushed through training before they were flung out to operational squadrons.

The Americans, on the other hand, were able to train large numbers of naval aviation cadets drawn from what was known as the V-5 program, which was open to qualified high school graduates and college students. At numerous training airfields across the United States, cadets spent an average of twelve months in ground school and flight training before receiving a reserve commission and reporting for active duty as an aviator. Training aircraft such as the North American SNJ and Boeing NS were available in significant numbers. The Americans were also able to rotate many seasoned combat aviators to rear-area training bases to serve as instructors, something the Japanese could ill afford.

In time, these disparities would prove catastrophic for the Japanese. When the American and Japanese carrier fleets met in June 1944 at the Battle of the Philippine Sea, a horribly lopsided engagement that American fighter pilots would dub "The Great Marianas Turkey Shoot," nearly six hundred hastily schooled Japanese replacement pilots were blown out of the air by well-trained American reservists. By the time the two-day battle was over, there were barely enough planes and pilots left for the Japanese Navy to form a single carrier air group. Such horrific losses in aircraft and personnel, during the Marianas campaign and in the desperate battles still to come, were yet another disastrous consequence resulting from Yamamoto's failed gamble for a "short war."

On June 8, 1942, in the wake of the resounding American victory at the Battle of Midway, Admiral Nimitz sent the following radio message to Vice Admiral William Pye, commander of the reconstituted Battle Force, Pacific Fleet, which on April 4 had been redesignated as Task Force 1:

> For a period of four days operate in square about 300 miles each side southeast corner latitude 37-30 north longitude 142-30 west passing through designated point at 0300 zulu 13 June. No shipping known to be in assigned area. Within four days signal route for crossing traffic lanes southward.

Pye's task force, which had stood out from San Francisco Bay on June 5, was made up of the battleships *Colorado*, *Mississippi*, *Idaho*, *New Mexico*, and the repaired *Pennsylvania*, *Maryland*, and *Tennessee*, with air cover provided by the escort carrier *Long Island.* For the first six months of 1942 the battlewagons and their restless crews had for the most part remained on the West Coast, engaged in training evolutions as well as patrol and escort duty.

With the intelligence picture indicating a major engagement shaping up in the waters surrounding Midway, Pye's battleships stood ready as a tactical reserve and blocking force approximately 1,200 miles west of San Francisco. Had the Japanese defeated the American fleet and invaded Midway, or if they had attempted to make an end run around Spruance and Fletcher toward the West Coast, Task Force 1 would have been in a position to intervene. After the battle, even though air reconnaissance and signals intelligence indicated that the Japanese were giving up on Midway and retreating westward, Nimitz wanted the battleships to remain between the Japanese and the West Coast for at least the next four days.

Even if they had been available for service, the elderly battleships would certainly not have joined the carrier task forces for the hit-and-run raids of early 1942 or the battles of Coral Sea and Midway. Simply put, they were too heavy and slow and could not have kept up. Aircraft carriers like the *Enterprise* and her escorting cruisers were capable of speeds of up to 32 knots; their accompanying destroyers were even faster.

The heavily armored dreadnoughts, however, were rated to make only 21 knots of speed. Even that ponderously slow pace was questionable given their advanced age, along with the extra weight gained from modifications and the high fuel loads necessary for long-range missions. It was not until the new "fast battleships" of the *North Carolina*, *South Dakota*, and *Iowa* classes arrived in the Pacific that big-gunned vessels would be capable of operating with Fast Carrier Task Forces.

Even so, the necessary shift in American naval tactics and strategy that followed Pearl Harbor had resulted in the aircraft carrier permanently replacing the battlewagon as the US Navy's premier capital ship. Considering the advancements made in the speed, range, and deadly effectiveness of carrier-based aircraft, and the fact that the first two decisive battles of the Pacific War (Coral Sea and Midway) were fought outside visual range, the likelihood of opposing battle lines engaging in a daylight surface action was appearing more and more remote. The aged battleships, it seemed, not only represented obsolescent technology but also outmoded battle doctrine.

By midsummer of 1942 there were some senior American naval officers, including the Commander-in-Chief of the Pacific Fleet, who were beginning to wonder if recent events had forced the plodding old dreadnoughts out of a job.

CHAPTER 15
THE VIEW FROM THE SIDELINES

In late December 1941 the USS *Pennsylvania* eased into the dry dock at Hunter's Point in San Francisco Bay after an anxious eight-day journey from Pearl Harbor, a crossing remembered for its miserable weather, exceedingly long and dark nights, and frequent stands at General Quarters brought on by jittery lookouts after sighting Japanese submarines that may or may not have actually been there. Earlier that morning, the *Maryland* and *Tennessee* parted company with the *Pennsylvania* as the convoy of three battleships and four destroyers neared the West Coast.

"The weather was a picture of dreariness," was how Chief Boatswain's Mate Ed Swanson of the *Maryland* described the morning of December 29 in his memoirs. Their foghorns issuing an occasional long and mournful groan, the battered *Maryland* and *Tennessee* turned slowly onto a northern bearing and disappeared into the low-lying mists, bound for Bremerton, Washington, and the Puget Sound Navy Yard.

A modernization program for the US Navy's older battleships was already in the drafting stage, but for the *Maryland*, *Tennessee*, and *Pennsylvania*, there would be no time for complex reconstruction projects, at least not in the closing days of 1941. Compared to the battleships left behind at Pearl, the three had been only superficially damaged and would be hurried through a lightning round of repairs before being quickly returned to sea duty. After an astounding monthlong run of smashing enemy successes in the Pacific, the frightening possibility of a Japanese strike force appearing suddenly off the West Coast near Seattle, San Francisco, or Los Angeles seemed very real indeed. Americans on the home front, who had endured the Great Depression and the looming threat of war for the past two years, now had something more to fear than fear itself. The journeyman shipwrights living in Bremerton, Washington, believed their homes and families to be in grave danger, and for good reason. As one of only two naval facilities on the West Coast capable of performing major repairs to capital ships, it seemed likely that the Puget Sound Navy Yard would be targeted by the Japanese due to its military significance, just as Pearl Harbor had been.

"People were scared to death around here," recalled Delmer Shoemaker, who worked as a welder at Puget Sound throughout the war. Apprentice electrician Don Serry would remember the sense of urgency that pervaded the shipyard when the wounded *Maryland* and *Tennessee* first arrived. The Puget Sound Navy Yard was soon transformed into a beehive of activity, with work being performed around the clock at a feverish pace that would not slacken for the better part of the next four years. In those uncertain first months of 1942 the majority of Navy Yard personnel, Serry explained, "were really concerned and wanted to get those people back out there fighting."

The Royal Navy's experience in having to fend off intense air attacks by Axis forces in the Mediterranean, in Norwegian waters, and at Dunkirk had led to the establishment of the Navy Department Antiaircraft Defense Board, headed by the future Chief of Naval Operations, Ernest J. King. The King Board, as it became known, was convened for the purpose of studying the adequacy and effectiveness of antiaircraft weapons systems and countermeasures aboard the ships of the US Navy. King's final report to Admiral Stark, submitted in December 1940, stated: "The Navy Department Antiaircraft Defense Board considers that the lack of adequate close range antiaircraft gun defense of existing ships of the Fleet constitutes the most serious weakness in the readiness of the Navy for war."

The Bureau of Ordnance then set out to rectify the shortcomings of the US Navy's antiaircraft defenses. At the time most American naval vessels were fitted with the 5-inch / 25 caliber heavy antiaircraft gun and the 3-inch / 50 caliber multipurpose gun, while the Browning .50 caliber machine gun provided close-in point defense. BuOrd embarked upon a program to install the rapid-firing 1.1-inch antiaircraft gun in a quadruple mount on the navy's ships to increase their antiaircraft protection. Early combat operations in the Pacific, however, would reveal that the 1.1-incher was inadequate for defense against modern dive-bombers and low-flying torpedo planes. Not only was it being deployed in insufficient numbers, the problematic weapon's firepower did not compensate for the great weight of its mount, which often affected the stability of the ship itself.

To alleviate this problem, the more-reliable and -effective Swiss-designed 20-millimeter Oerlikon and Swedish-designed 40-millimeter Bofors guns were being procured and installed upon new American warships. Ships already serving with the fleet would have their 1.1-inch guns augmented by, or replaced with, the new Bofors and Oerlikon during their scheduled overhauls.

The *Pennsylvania* would emerge from the Hunter's Point dry dock after just twelve days. Splinter holes had been patched and buckled bulkheads, dished deck plating, and distorted stanchions replaced around the site of the explosion in the Number Nine Gun Casement. Protective shielding was added for the crews of her 5-inch / 25 caliber antiaircraft guns. On the boat deck, obsolete 3-inch / 50 caliber guns were replaced with quad-mounted 1.1-inch weapons. An additional sixteen new 20-millimeter Oerlikons were also installed. After a brief period of sea trials, the *Pennsylvania* would join Pye's Task Force 1 to perform training and patrols along the West Coast.

Captain Charles Cooke Jr. had remained in command of the *Pennsylvania* throughout her course of repairs and modifications at Pearl Harbor and in San Francisco. In March 1942, Navy Secretary Knox submitted to President Roosevelt a list of forty officers deemed by a panel of senior admirals to be the most competent in the navy. The creation of the list had been requested by the president himself, who had grown frustrated with the dismal performance of certain naval officers in the opening months of the war, men who were efficient peacetime administrators but had proven to be lackluster wartime commanders. Officers drawn from the list were not only installed into newly created positions within the naval hierarchy, they also replaced those who were judged as deficient in the performance of their duties. "Savvy" Cooke had made the list of Knox's elite and would soon be promoted to rear admiral, on his way to Washington to serve for the duration of the war as the principal planning officer on the staff of Admiral Ernest J. King. He was relieved by Captain Thomas S. King II—no relation—on April 3.

After the Battle of Midway, the *Pennsylvania* would return to San Francisco Bay where on the afternoon of July 3 Admirals King and Nimitz were piped aboard, the first time the two had met since their respective appointments as COMINCH and CINCPAC in December 1941. Nimitz was still smarting from contusions he had received in a plane crash three days earlier, when the Sikorsky XPBS-1 Flying Boat that had carried him from Pearl Harbor struck a submerged log during a water landing near NAS Alameda. One of the seaplane's officers, Lieutenant Thomas M. Roscoe, was killed in the accident. Nimitz managed to extricate himself from the wrecked fuselage to stand atop the broad upper wing, at first refusing evacuation and directing rescue operations until the flying boat began to sink beneath him. Shivering under a blanket, Nimitz was standing in the bow of the last boat to leave the crash site when the coxswain shouted angrily for his still-stunned passenger to sit down. As Nimitz wordlessly complied, the coxswain glimpsed the four silver stars pinned to the admiral's shirt collar. Greatly embarrassed, the young man offered an effusive apology to the Commander-in-Chief of the Pacific Fleet.

"Stick to your guns, sailor," Nimitz told him. "You were quite right."

During a series of conferences held over the next several days, King and Nimitz would discuss the state of current and future operations in the Pacific. They would meet, at intervals, with Richmond Kelly Turner, who had left his post in War Plans to assume command of Amphibious Force, South Pacific, and with William Pye to hear his recommendations regarding the future employment of the battleships of Task Force 1. But first, Admiral King would conduct an award ceremony on the quarterdeck of the *Pennsylvania.* Standing uncomfortably at attention in his dress blue uniform, Chester W. Nimitz received the Distinguished Service Medal for shepherding the Pacific Fleet through the first harrowing six months of 1942.

Up in Washington, work on the *Maryland* was completed by February 9, 1942. Like the *Pennsylvania*, she would leave the dry dock with few alterations made to her general appearance. Along with final repairs being made to her relatively light bomb damage, steel shielding was added to protect her bridge and pilothouse from shell fragments, and she received a significant boost to her antiaircraft defenses.

For the time being the *Maryland* would retain most of her 5-inch / 51 caliber broadside secondary batteries mounted in armored casements, the design of which harkened back to the coal-burning pre-dreadnoughts of the late nineteenth century and revealed Old Mary's true age. Two of these guns, however, were removed to save topside weight. Eight of the 5-inch / 25 caliber weapons were replaced with 5-inch / 38 caliber guns, essentially an improved version of the 5-inch antiaircraft gun that featured greater range, muzzle velocity, and accuracy, especially when paired with the new Mark 37 Fire Control System. The *Maryland* would receive both SC search radar and FC fire control radar, and her superstructure would bristle with sixteen new 20-millimeter cannons. Captain Donald C. Goodwin, who had been in command of the ship for less than three weeks before the attack on Pearl Harbor, would stay on as the *Maryland*'s skipper through the end of 1942.

The bomb that struck the *Tennessee*'s forward Turret Number Two, resulting in the blast that killed Captain Bennion of the *West Virginia*, had fractured the barrel of the center 14-inch gun and gouged the barrels of the guns on either side with steel splinters. The after Turret Number Three had also been hit, resulting in the wrecking of its left-hand 14-inch gun. The decision was made to replace all twelve of the *Tennessee*'s Mark Four 14-inch guns with new Mark Eleven weapons. The time required to re-gun the *Tennessee*'s entire main battery allowed for additional simultaneous modifications to be made to the ship.

Shortly after the attack on Pearl Harbor, Vice Admiral Walter Anderson, in his capacity as COMBATPAC—Commander Battleships Pacific Fleet—made the recommendation for the old battleships to have their main masts removed. Another design feature left over from the dreadnought era, the towering main masts and their "bird bath" platforms were used to house lookouts and direct the fire of the battleship's main and secondary batteries by visual observation of the "fall of shot." With the advent of search radar and radar-equipped fire control directors, the masts and their heavy platforms were rendered obsolete, becoming unnecessary topside weights that obstructed the sky arcs of the ship's antiaircraft guns.

While the *Tennessee*'s heavy guns were being replaced, so were several distorted and fire-blackened hull plates along with many miles of fried electrical wiring, the result of flames impinging on the ship's fantail after floating oil from the ruptured fuel bunkers of the *Arizona* had caught fire. Open portholes were covered with steel plates and a great number of teakwood planks on the main deck were replaced. The tall lattice-work main mast was replaced with a prefabricated steel "stump tower," upon which the after fire control director and a battery of searchlights was installed, a structure that had been fashioned by the workers of the Puget Sound Navy Yard while the *Tennessee* was still at Pearl. A similar stump tower had been ordered and constructed for the *Maryland*, but the need to get her back at sea and defending the West Coast was considered paramount; the tower would remain at the Navy Yard until it was finally installed in early 1944. Like the *Pennsylvania* and *Maryland*, the *Tennessee* would also receive sixteen 20-millimeter antiaircraft guns, as well as four 1.1-inch quad mounts.

Fifty-nine days after her arrival in Puget Sound, on February 26, 1942, Captain Charles E. Reordan ordered the *Tennessee* to raise steam and depart for San Francisco, once again in the company of the *Maryland*. There the two battlewagons would join the *Pennsylvania* and the three *New Mexicos* under Admiral Pye's command. The refitted *Colorado* would arrive a month later to round out a battleship task force which was, if a bit long in the tooth, capable of mounting a formidable challenge to any Japanese seaborne assault on the West Coast as long as it received air support from escort carriers or land-based aircraft.

It was a critically important mission to be sure, especially with the Japanese version of *blitzkrieg* rolling unabated across the Pacific in early 1942, but a relegated status nonetheless. Once the pride of the Pacific Fleet, the battleships along with their frustrated black shoe officers and bluejackets had been left to stand on the sidelines while Halsey and his flyboys were hitting back at the Japanese and getting all the press. Task Force 1 would range impatiently along the West Coast throughout that first spring and early summer of the war, engaged in patrols, convoy escorting, and relentless drill.

The training was sorely needed, not only to shake the bugs out of the new radar and fire control systems, zero-in the new antiaircraft weapons, and perform engineering tests, but also to make actual sailors of the many raw recruits who had joined the battleship crews, men who were scarcely more than boys and who had been enjoying their first taste of adult life in the civilian world just weeks before. The three refitted battleships that had been damaged at Pearl Harbor were at a particular disadvantage, due to the fact that many of their experienced enlisted personnel had been reassigned to combat duty aboard outbound cruisers and destroyers immediately following the attack. Replacing them were apprentice seamen fresh from their three-week boot camps in San Diego and Great Lakes.

All across America young men had crowded into armed forces recruiting stations on the morning after Pearl Harbor; by the end of December the navy alone accepted forty thousand new recruits. In the late summer and fall of 1942, the monthly total of new inductees was equivalent to what the entire peacetime strength of the navy had been. Fresh contingents of these wide-eyed youngsters, in spanking new crackerjack uniforms and nervously clutching their sea bags, were waiting to come aboard the big and imposing gray battlewagons whenever they pulled into San Francisco, San Pedro, or San Diego. The *Tennessee* would receive four hundred of these fledgling sailors in the first weeks of 1942.

On the morning of August 1, Task Force 1 would finally steam west in tactical column, accompanying the carrier *Hornet* and the rest of Task Force 17 on their way to Hawaii. After two weeks of joint exercises off the southern end of the Big Island, both task forces arrived at Pearl for "recreation, fuel, supplies and repair." Three days later, on August 17, the *Hornet* group stood out from Pearl Harbor bound for the Solomon Islands. The dreadnoughts, however, would not be joining them.

Hoping to capitalize on their victory at Midway, the Americans launched their offensive drive in the South Pacific beginning with Operation Watchtower on August 7, 1942. Richmond Kelly Turner's Amphibious Task Force 62, spearheaded by the First Marine Division under the command of Major General Alexander Vandegrift, invaded the Japanese-held islands of Tulagi and Guadalcanal in the eastern Solomons. Supporting the landings was Jack Fletcher's Task Force 61, made up of the carriers *Enterprise*, *Saratoga*, and *Wasp*, along with the new fast battleship *North Carolina*, eleven cruisers, and thirty destroyers.

The Japanese had already established a naval anchorage and seaplane base on Tulagi and were in the process of building an airfield on the much-larger island of Guadalcanal, still hoping to interdict the southern line of communications between the United States and Australia. The American capture of these islands would not only deny the area to Japan, it would also allow the Allies to establish advanced bases of their own for further operations against the Japanese in the Solomons, the Bismarck Archipelago, and the Admiralty Islands. Evicting the Japanese from this region would, in the words of a July 1942 CINCPAC strategic estimate, "reduce the threat of Australian invasion almost to the vanishing point," and "permit us to initiate strong attrition against enemy forces and positions in the Carolines and the Marshalls."

On Tulagi and on two smaller nearby islands, Gavutu and Tanambogo, the marines would meet with fierce resistance from Japanese naval troops. Tulagi would be secured by August 8, after the garrison of some 800 Japanese had been wiped out and 120 Americans were killed in action. For the marines that landed on Guadalcanal, the relative ease of the first day gave absolutely no indication that a bloody six-month fight for the island was to come. Encountering virtually no resistance, the Leathernecks were able to secure the airfield by the afternoon of August 8. Japanese troops and their conscripted Korean construction workers, taken completely by surprise, had fled into the surrounding jungle in the face of the naval bombardment that preceded the marine landings. The marines promptly named their new airstrip Henderson Field in honor of Major Lofton Henderson, a marine squadron commander killed at the Battle of Midway.

In response to the Tulagi–Guadalcanal landings, Japanese bombers and fighters based at Rabaul raided the American amphibious forces on August 7 and then again on August 8. The destroyer *Jarvis* was damaged and a stricken Kate crashed into the transport *George F. Elliott*, which would sink two days later. The raids cost the Japanese thirty-six planes, while the American carriers lost fourteen of their Wildcats in aerial combat. Fletcher, worried about aircraft losses and the threat to his carriers, decided to withdraw Task Force 61 from the area on the afternoon of the second day.

The short-fused Turner, a man whom Ed Layton would later describe as "the Navy's Patton," was predictably incensed. Fletcher was supposed to remain in the area to protect the cargo vessels, which had not yet finished unloading, until at least D-Day Plus Three. Now without air cover, Turner's amphibious group would be forced to withdraw as well. Several hours later the Japanese Navy displayed its prowess in night combat operations during a surprise surface attack against the Allied cruisers screening Turner's amphibious task force near Savo Island, off the northwestern tip of Guadalcanal. Three American cruisers, the *Vincennes*, *Astoria*, and *Quincy*, and the Australian cruiser *Canberra* were sent to the floor of the channel, which would soon be tagged with the eerie nickname of Ironbottom Sound.

While *Hornet* and her escorts steamed south to reinforce the thinly stretched naval units operating in the Solomons, a lack of tonnage in fleet oilers would contribute to Nimitz's decision to retain the battleships of Task Force 1 in Pearl Harbor. The First World War–era standard-type battleship, as one might expect, was not exactly designed with fuel economy in mind. The *Maryland*, for example, burned somewhere around 1,800 gallons of oil per hour while cruising at just 15 knots. At the onset of the war there were a dozen ships with the hull classification of AO—auxiliary oiler—assigned to the Pacific Fleet. In January the *Neches* was sunk by the submarine *I-72*, and the *Neosho*—which managed to steam away from Battleship Row on December 7 without sustaining any damage—was sunk by Japanese bombers in the Coral Sea in early May.

Before the year was out, American shipyards would launch eleven new fleet oilers and the navy would acquire four more by charter, but in August 1942 Nimitz was down to just ten, and three of those were needed to fuel the ships of Rear Admiral Robert Theobald's Task Force 8, holding the line against the Japanese in the Aleutians. The remaining seven vessels were not enough to support carrier task forces and a squadron of oil-guzzling dreadnoughts during combat operations in the South Pacific.

In a radio message sent to the Navy Department on August 12, Nimitz informed Admiral King that he was "unable [to] provide logistic support in SOPAC area for battleships of Task Force One with ships now available," and that he "doubted their usefulness" for the present operation. For these reasons, Nimitz stated, "I will not send any of the slow battleships south unless so directed by you."

Task Force 1 would stay behind "to counter any Japanese landings in the Hawaiian area" while making frequent sorties from Pearl Harbor for intensive gunnery practice, including exercises in shore bombardment. These extra weeks of training, which few commands in the Pacific Theater could then afford, would later pay rich dividends. Nevertheless, the battleship sailors grew increasingly restless in what was now the rear echelon, while their comrades in the South Pacific light forces were bearing the brunt of the war. They were reminded of this fact every time a war-weary cruiser or destroyer returned to Pearl Harbor with battle flags flying and her crew proudly manning the rails, or when they were forced to endure the ribbing, not all of it good-natured, of fellow sailors just returned from combat in the bars of downtown Honolulu.

On August 27, the *Tennessee* would once again depart Pearl Harbor for Puget Sound. Admiral Frederick J. Horne had been appointed to the newly created position of Vice Chief of Naval Operations, which oversaw training and logistics for the navy, including repairs and modifications to ships of the fleet. Just after assuming his new post, Horne issued orders for the modernization of the *California*, *West Virginia*, and *Tennessee.*

According to Horne's plan each battleship would receive an additional 3 inches of Special Treatment Steel (STS) over their ammunition magazines for protection against aerial bombs and plunging gunfire, in the hope of averting another *Arizona*-like disaster. All secondary batteries would be replaced with twin turrets of dual-purpose 5-inch / 38 caliber guns of the type being installed on the new fast battleships of the *North Carolina* and *South Dakota* classes, paired with radar-equipped Mark 37 fire control directors. Additional 20-millimeter Oerlikon and 40-millimeter Bofors guns would bolster the ships' antiaircraft capability.

In order to compensate for the loss of buoyancy these additions would cause (the new deck armor alone weighed 1,400 tons), steel blistering would be added to the hull of each battleship. In the *Tennessee*'s case, this would increase the beam by 16 feet, which also provided additional protection from enemy torpedoes. With the Allies now on the offensive in the South Pacific, it was felt that the threat of a Japanese attack against Hawaii or the West Coast had subsided to the point that the *Tennessee* could be safely detached from the battleship group and sent to Bremerton to begin her refit.

So began the gradual dissolution of Task Force 1. On September 20, 1942, Vice Admiral William Pye would be relieved of his command by Vice Admiral Herbert F. Leary. A week later, Leary would also relieve Vice Admiral Walter Anderson to become Commander Battleships, Pacific Fleet. When the newly organized British and American Combined Chiefs of Staff met in March 1942, they had agreed to divide the Pacific theater of operations into sectors of responsibility. In addition to his role as CINCPAC, Nimitz was designated commander of the Pacific Ocean Areas. Primarily, this command would be responsible for the westward thrust toward Tokyo across the Central Pacific. Initially headquartered in Australia, the Southwest Pacific Area became the domain of General Douglas MacArthur, who was poised to go on the offensive against Japanese forces in New Guinea and drive north toward the Philippines. Nimitz nominated Pye for command of the South Pacific Area, which would include Operation Watchtower and subsequent efforts to expel the Japanese from the Solomons.

Still angry with Pye over the decision to recall the Wake Island relief expedition, King flatly rejected the proposal. The South Pacific Area command was instead given to Vice Admiral Robert L. Ghormley, a personal favorite of President Roosevelt who would prove so ineffective in the job that by October, Nimitz would end up replacing him with Halsey. William Pye would return to the United States, serving for the remainder of the war as president of the Naval War College before announcing his retirement.

"There is no gainsaying that the Solomons are a hard-bitten bunch of islands," Jack London wrote in 1911. "On the other hand, there are worse places in the world. But to the new chum who has no constitutional understanding of men and life in the rough, the Solomons may indeed prove terrible."

Apart from those who may have read London's *South Sea Tales*, very few Americans had ever heard of the Solomon Islands, and even fewer could have located them on a map of the Pacific prior to 1942. Guadalcanal would be among the first of many obscure and far-flung islands with strange and exotic-sounding names where a generation of young Americans would go to fight and where many would go to die, names that would one day be as renowned and venerated in the annals of American history as those of Lexington and Concord, Antietam, Gettysburg, or the Meuse-Argonne.

The victory at Midway may have been the turning point of the war against Japan, but the fight for Guadalcanal—on land, on the sea, and in the air—was surely the acid test for the armed forces of the United States. It would measure whether or not the American fighting man possessed the courage, skill, and endurance necessary to stand toe-to-toe with his Japanese adversary and defeat him, over the course of a brutal and protracted campaign in which no quarter was given or expected. It would also determine whether or not his commanders had the strategic and tactical wisdom and logistical expertise to out-plan, outmaneuver, and ultimately outfight their vaunted Japanese counterparts.

A series of furious actions on the seas surrounding Guadalcanal would take place in the late summer and autumn of 1942, the bloody consequences of which would impel Admiral Nimitz to recall his aged dreadnoughts from the sidelines and begin to deploy them—albeit tentatively—to the South Pacific Area. On August 20, nineteen Marine Corps Wildcats and a dozen Dauntlesses took off from the escort carrier *Long Island* and landed at the newly completed Henderson Field. The "Cactus Air Force" was now in business, the name taken from the Allied code name for Guadalcanal. For the better part of the next three months, the Imperial Japanese Army would batter itself bloody against the stubbornly defended perimeter the marines had cast around Henderson Field in a series of ill-conceived and costly assaults. Efforts to reinforce and resupply their beleaguered troops on Guadalcanal during the daylight hours would become too dangerous to continue, with their slow-moving transport and supply vessels under the constant threat of attack by aggressive US Marine aviators flying from the very same airfield the Japanese sought to recapture.

Japanese destroyers would begin making runs down the New Georgia Sound from their advanced base in the Shortlands under the cover of darkness, delivering badly needed replacement troops and supplies to Guadalcanal and taking the opportunity to lob naval artillery shells into the marine positions. For the Americans, with their penchant for pithy nicknames, the long and narrow sound that transected the Solomon Islands would be known as "the Slot," while the nocturnal destroyer runs to Guadalcanal became the "Tokyo Express." While the opposing carrier groups slugged it out at the Battle of the Eastern Solomons on August 24 and the Battle of the Santa Cruz Islands on October 25, the US Navy's light forces were doing their utmost to derail the Tokyo Express.

Off Guadalcanal's Cape Esperance on the night of October 11–12, the Tokyo Express would run afoul of an American task force of four cruisers and five destroyers led by Rear Admiral Norman Scott, sent by Ghormley to cover the movement of the US Army's 164th Infantry Regiment to the island. Three cruisers and two destroyers under the command of Rear Admiral Aritomo Goto were planning to strike Henderson Field, while a convoy of two seaplane tenders and six destroyers landed ammunition and food for Imperial Army units on Guadalcanal.

As the Japanese force approached Savo Island, Scott's radar-equipped cruisers *San Francisco*, *Boise*, *Salt Lake City*, and *Helena* "crossed the T" of the enemy formation and opened fire at only 5,000 yards—point-blank range in terms of naval gunnery—sinking the heavy cruiser *Furutaka* and smashing the bridge of the flagship *Aoba*, killing Admiral Goto. The *Boise* would be damaged and the destroyer *Duncan* lost to enemy gunfire as she attempted a torpedo run. At sunrise the retreating Japanese force would also lose a destroyer after being attacked by land-based aircraft from Guadalcanal. Three nights later, on October 14, the battleships *Haruna* and *Kongo* steamed down the Slot to deliver a punishing bombardment of Henderson Field. Forty men were killed and half of the aircraft belonging to the Cactus Air Force, which by then had grown to a complement of ninety, were demolished by a barrage of nearly a thousand high-explosive 14-inch shells.

In the weekly conference held at CINCPAC headquarters in Pearl Harbor on October 30, Admiral Nimitz and his staff discussed the pros and cons of deploying at least two of the older battleships of Task Force 1 to the South Pacific. Three American cruisers had been lost at Savo Island and a fourth, *Chicago*, had been badly damaged and was headed to San Francisco for repairs. After being hit by two heavy shells at Cape Esperance, the *Boise* would also be laid up for an extended period of time in the Philadelphia Navy Yard.

These losses had greatly weakened the striking power of the US Navy's surface forces in the South Pacific Area, now under the command of Vice Admiral Bill Halsey, who had replaced the parochial and indecisive Ghormley. The fact that the heavy naval bombardment of Henderson Field on October 14 had gone unopposed was another compelling reason for moving battleships into the area. In early November, Nimitz would order Battleship Division Four—consisting of the sister ships *Maryland* and *Colorado*, under the command of Rear Admiral Harry W. Hill—to set sail from Pearl Harbor for the South Pacific. They would depart on November 8, 1942, with Hill flying his flag from the *Maryland*.

At the direction of Admirals Nimitz and Leary, during their prolonged stay in Pearl Harbor throughout the autumn of 1942 the crews of the *Colorado* and *Maryland* had performed many expedient, stopgap modifications to their ships with the help of the Navy Yard. The top section of their main masts were cut off and hoisted away, their height reduced by nearly two-thirds, creating a temporary and makeshift substitute for the prefabricated stump towers that were in storage awaiting the eventual return of the *Colorado*-class battleships to Puget Sound. This reduced topside weight, opened skyward fields of fire for antiaircraft guns and allowed for additional 20-millimeter weapons, antennae, and searchlights to be installed. Dark gray and black paint was applied to the hull and superstructure of both ships in the MS-31 "dazzle" camouflage pattern, designed to confuse the perception of a ship's range and speed and thereby hamper the enemy's ability to achieve a firing solution for naval gunfire or torpedoes.

Before the ships of BATDIV Four could arrive in the South Pacific Area, yet another major sea battle would take place in the hotly contested waters off Guadalcanal. When trade winds finally swept away the thick layer of gun smoke hanging low over Ironbottom Sound after three vicious days of combat, nearly two thousand Japanese and seventeen hundred Americans, including two admirals, would be dead. One of only two battleship-versus-battleship duels of the Pacific War would be fought, and the Japanese would find that they could no longer stomach the cost of holding on to Guadalcanal.

Just after midnight on Friday the thirteenth, a powerful bombardment force under the command of Vice Admiral Hiroaki Abe and centered around the battleships *Hiei* and *Kirishima* rounded Savo Island. A convoy of eleven transport ships was also steaming down the Slot, intending to land seven thousand Japanese troops on the shores of Guadalcanal at daybreak after Abe's battleships had finished pulverizing Henderson Field. Standing in their way were five American cruisers and eight destroyers led by Rear Admiral Daniel J. Callaghan.

In the utter darkness and foul weather, a wild and confused melee ensued at short range. Illumination rounds burst and flickered, casting their reflections across the surface of an ink-black sea and revealing the shadowy forms of enemy ships close at hand. Streams of fiery tracers crisscrossed one another in surreal, tangled patterns. Ships exploded and burned. Confounding and conflicting orders were given, and ships on the same side fired upon one another. The two forces would break contact after twenty-four murderous minutes, which Admiral King would describe as "one of the most furious sea battles ever fought." An American destroyer captain would compare the fight to "a bar room brawl after the lights had been shot out."

The light cruiser *Atlanta* was sunk after being torpedoed and shattered by heavy gunfire, taking Rear Admiral Norman Scott down with her. Halsey would later state that the death of his close friend Scott "was the greatest personal sorrow that beset me in the whole war." The *Atlanta*'s sister ship, *Juneau*, was heavily damaged but survived the battle, only to be torpedoed later in the morning by a Japanese submarine and sunk with a heavy loss of life among her crew, including five brothers belonging to the Sullivan family. The bridge of the *San Francisco* would sustain a direct hit which killed Admiral Callaghan and the cruiser's new captain, the intrepid Cassin Young.

The Japanese, well-versed in night combat operations and possessing superior low-light optics, had fared well in the battle but had not come through unscathed. Abe was wounded and his chief of staff killed when gunfire from the destroyer *Laffey* struck the bridge of his flagship *Hiei*. This appeared to have taken the fight out of the admiral, and he ordered his forces to withdraw without completing their mission. The *Hiei*'s steering gear was also wrecked by a shot from the *San Francisco*, and she would succumb to air attacks in the coming daylight, the first Japanese battleship to be sunk by American forces in the Pacific War.

The following night, a half-dozen Japanese cruisers bombarded Guadalcanal but failed to knock Henderson Field out of action. At dawn the seething and sleep-deprived pilots of the Cactus Air Force descended upon them with a vengeance, assisted by planes from the *Enterprise*. The cruiser *Kinugasa* was sent to the bottom along with five hundred of her crew. The American fliers then turned their attention to the inbound convoy of troopships and sank seven of them, drowning a good number of Japanese infantrymen. Anticipating that the tenacious Japanese would regroup and try again that night, Halsey ordered the fast battleships *Washington* and *South Dakota* and four destroyers, under the command of Rear Admiral Willis "Ching" Lee, to peel off from the *Enterprise* task force and steam into Ironbottom Sound.

"This plan flouted one of the firmest doctrines of the Naval War College," Halsey would admit. "The narrow, treacherous waters north of Guadalcanal are utterly unsuited to the maneuvering of capital ships, especially in darkness. The shade of Mahan must have turned even paler."

Just before 11:00 p.m. the Americans picked up a large formation of Japanese ships on their surface search radar. It was the *Kirishima* again, along with four cruisers and nine destroyers led by Rear Admiral Nobutake Kondo. Two of Lee's destroyers would be lost charging into a fusillade of heavy gunfire and torpedoes from the Japanese squadron; the other two were badly damaged and forced out of the fight. Searchlights then swept through the darkness to illuminate the *South Dakota*, which had suffered a major electrical failure at a most inopportune and critical moment, leaving her "deaf, dumb and blind" without power to her radio, radar, or fire control systems. While enemy gunfire concentrated on the near-helpless *South Dakota*, Admiral Lee ordered his flagship to close with the *Kirishima.*

No one aboard the Japanese ships saw the approach of the *Washington* until she let fly with a terrifying broadside from her 16-inch main guns at 8,500 yards. The *Kirishima* would be hammered by nearly twenty armor-piercing projectiles, her decks littered with two hundred dead. Holed three times below the waterline, *Kirishima* quickly took on a heavy list to starboard and the night sky above Ironbottom Sound was soon aglow from the intense fires that ran the length of the Japanese battleship. The *Washington* then turned her guns upon and promptly dispatched the destroyer *Ayanami.* At 1:00 a.m. Kondo ordered his battered forces to withdraw; two hours later the *Kirishima* would roll over and sink.

The following day the four remaining Japanese transports deliberately beached themselves and began to disgorge their cargoes on the northern shore of Guadalcanal, where they were sitting ducks for aircraft from Henderson Field and Marine Corps heavy artillery. Less than half of the Japanese reinforcements that were supposed to spearhead a new offensive on Guadalcanal actually made it ashore. Most of them were empty-handed, having lost their weapons, ammunition, food, and equipment.

As the Naval Battle of Guadalcanal was still raging on November 14, CINCPAC would signal Harry Hill to proceed to Viti Levu in the Fiji Islands. Operating from that newly established forward base, BATDIV Four would stand ready to supply Admiral Halsey with additional firepower if required. Despite the heavy losses to his cruiser forces and with a badly mauled *South Dakota* now shambling back to the Free French port of Nouméa, New Caledonia, for repairs, Halsey would still prove reluctant to utilize the *Maryland* and *Colorado.*

Only rudimentary modifications had been made to the two old battleships thus far. The upgrade to their antiaircraft batteries was still incomplete. On both vessels, the cutting down of the main mast for conversion to a temporary antiaircraft platform had required the removal of the aft main battery fire control director. Resembling a turret bristling with antennae rather than gun barrels, a naval gunfire director housed the equipment to measure the range and bearing of a target and transferred the information to an analogue ballistic computer, which calculated a firing solution after taking into account the speed and heading of the target, humidity, wind speed, and wind direction. The data was then transmitted directly to servomotors in the gun turrets, which elevated and rotated the guns to accurately track the target.

Maryland and *Colorado* were currently operating in the combat theater with only their forward main battery directors until their next scheduled round of modifications. If the single director should be damaged in battle or suffer a technical failure, the guns would have to be aimed "locally" by the turret crews themselves, a less-than-optimum method which was sure to result in fewer shots being placed on target. Halsey also questioned whether enough had been done to ensure the watertight integrity of the older battleships, especially after the lessons hard-learned from the *Nevada*, *Oklahoma*, and *California* at Pearl Harbor. Halsey ordered Harry Hill and BATDIV Four to continue operating out of Fiji, within a day's steaming of the Solomons, and tasked them with patrolling the vital sea lanes to Australia and New Zealand and escorting battle-damaged ships to rear area ports.

On November 30 there would be another brawl between Halsey's cruisers and the Tokyo Express, this time off Tassafaronga Point on Guadalcanal's northern shore. Surprised by the sudden appearance of an American cruiser force, the Japanese destroyers turned and fled up the Slot, but not before firing a deadly spread of their "Long Lance" torpedoes. The *Northampton* was sunk, the *Minneapolis*, *Pensacola*, and *New Orleans* seriously damaged. Worried that Halsey would not have enough strength to parry another Japanese thrust, Nimitz ordered the two battlewagons that constituted BATDIV Three, *Mississippi* and *New Mexico*, to join Hill's division in Fiji.

Ernest King would express many of the same reservations shared by Halsey about sending the old dreadnoughts into the breach before the necessary modernizations were performed to ensure their survivability. With the US Navy's hull classification for a battleship being the letters *BB*, in their message traffic King and Nimitz had begun to refer to the dreadnoughts as *OBBs*, meaning "Old Battleships." In a signal dated December 3, 1942, Nimitz explained his rationale for the deployment of two more OBBs to the South Pacific.

CINCPAC TO COMINCH

For Admiral King Only. Highest secrecy. Had given full consideration to disadvantages raised by your 011605 as to operating BATDIV 3 in SOPAC. Logistics can be met. I have had the AA batteries of BATDIV 3 increased by addition of 2 40mm quads and 46 20mm guns per ship making them comparable to that of BATDIV 4. These AA batteries will of course be improved when they receive their remaining 40mm guns and replace 5″-25s with 5″-38s but their underwater defense will not be satisfactory until third deck centerline compartments are made watertight. It was with all this in mind I decided in view of the military situation that these ships should go to SOPAC. It is probable that the enemy will make at least one more powerful move against CACTUS including more of his battleships than he used last time. The need for additional gun power to defeat this move has been accentuated by recent heavy losses in cruiser strength. I consider this situation more acute than in the past which led to suggestions for the use of OBB. I believe that decision should be made now whether we should lay up all OBB for lengthy modernization or whether we shall keep available and utilize some in situations where their hitting power may be the deciding factor. Will await your further advice before cancelling transfer of BATDIV 3 one ship at least of which will be required as part of escort for troop convoy departing December 6.

Later that day Nimitz would receive King's tacit approval for BATDIV Three's forward deployment:

> <u>COMINCH TO CINCPAC</u>
>
> Decode only for Admiral Nimitz. Ultra Secret. Last paragraph your 030521 think only sound course is to continue modernization and rehabilitation of OBBs as underway in TENNESSEE and CALIFORNIA which must be adjusted to Navy Yard capabilities after consideration new construction and battle damage repairs. However only acute needs such as now exist in SOPAC should cause us to unduly expose OBBs which have not been modernized.

On November 23, Halsey would reorganize the task forces of his South Pacific Area command, grouping the *Maryland* and *Colorado* together with the escort carriers *Nassau* and *Altamaha* and six destroyers to form Task Force 65. The *New Mexico* and *Mississippi* would become part of Task Force 69, commanded by Vice Admiral Herbert Leary. The dreadnoughts would spend the rest of 1942 patrolling the shipping lanes to Australia and escorting convoys, after Nimitz informed Halsey that he "desired that they not be unnecessarily exposed . . . unless they are required in an urgent situation." The *Maryland* and *Colorado* would continue to operate from Viti Levu until mid-February.

"Viti Levu was a very beautiful island, though during the middle of the day the heat was oppressive," wrote the authors of the *Maryland*'s wartime cruise book. "Wonderful sunrises and sunsets made the mountains a beautiful purple and the water in the bay a turquoise green." Sitting idle in this backwater of the Pacific War, the battleship sailors passed their off-duty hours by spearfishing from their ship's quarterdeck. On some days the catch was bountiful enough to supply an evening fish fry in the galley. Throughout the afternoon whaleboats shuttled the men back and forth to the small town of Lautoka, which offered little amusement as a liberty port.

"Little shops where natives sold lovely jewelry were filthy and smelly," the *Maryland*'s historian would write. "With the influx of American sailors the value of the American dollar soon went down. The Great Northern Hotel had the only restaurant, serving abominable food and warm drinks."

After the novelty of visiting Lautoka quickly wore off, some of the sailors contented themselves with touring the island on rented bicycles or hitching rides on the narrow-gauge sugar train into the nearby mountains.

Halsey would avail himself of the "hitting power" of the OBB Task Forces only once. In early February 1943, search planes from Guadalcanal spotted a force of two Japanese carriers, two battleships, four cruisers, and a dozen destroyers steaming south from Truk.

"It is believed that this force has been operating in this vicinity for the past two days and will be employed to cover a major push toward the Solomons sea area," a CINCPAC staff report opined. Halsey would sortie nearly all of the naval forces at his disposal, including the *Enterprise* and *Saratoga* carrier groups along with the two task forces of older battleships to counter this new threat to American troops on Guadalcanal. The Japanese ships closed to within 700 miles of the island before they apparently turned about and were "presumed to have withdrawn beyond the search limit . . . Our task forces in the South Pacific are cruising the same general areas as before, awaiting developments."

It had been a strategic feint. In early December 1942, the Imperial Japanese Navy had proposed that Guadalcanal be evacuated, having failed utterly in their efforts to sustain the army troops still fighting there with nightly runs of the Tokyo Express. Nearly twenty thousand Japanese soldiers had perished in the six-month-long campaign. Those that remained lacked the serviceable weapons and ammunition needed to effectively resist, were starving on one-third rations, and suffering from a myriad of tropical diseases such as malaria, dysentery, and beriberi. On December 31, an evacuation order had been issued by the Imperial General Staff and endorsed by Emperor Hirohito. The movement of the task force from Truk had been a diversion, part of Operation Ke, which evacuated the last surviving Japanese troops from Guadalcanal on the night of February 7, 1943.

"Guadalcanal is no longer merely a name of an island in Japanese military history," General Kiyotake Kawaguchi of the 35th Infantry Brigade would lament. "It is the name of the graveyard of the Japanese Army."

The first year of the Pacific War, which saw both humiliating defeats and incredible triumphs for the US Navy, had come and gone. The dreadnoughts of Pearl Harbor had yet to fire their main batteries in anger, their crews still awaiting the opportunity to exact vengeance against an enemy that had surprised and rained death upon them.

The year 1943 would be different, after the "OBBs" of the Pacific Fleet were tasked with a new mission and granted a new purpose.

Captain Alfred Thayer Mahan, the highly influential historian, author, and lecturer widely recognized for his progressive views on naval strategy. LIBRARY OF CONGRESS

The USS *Arizona* under way in Hawaiian waters, 1940. NATIONAL ARCHIVES

Ships of the Pacific Battle Force at anchor in Maui's Lahaina Roads, 1940. NAVAL HISTORY AND HERITAGE COMMAND

TOP LEFT: Admiral James O. Richardson, Commander-in-Chief of the United States Fleet, who was vehemently opposed to basing the Pacific Battle Force at Pearl Harbor. NAVAL HISTORY AND HERITAGE COMMAND

TOP RIGHT: Admiral Isoroku Yamamoto, commander of the Imperial Japanese Navy's Combined Fleet, the avid gambler who masterminded the surprise attack on Pearl Harbor. NAVAL HISTORY AND HERITAGE COMMAND

LEFT: Admiral Husband E. Kimmel, Commander-in-Chief of the Pacific Fleet at the time of the Japanese attack on Pearl Harbor. NAVAL HISTORY AND HERITAGE COMMAND

Japanese sailors lift their caps and cheer as a Kate torpedo bomber is launched from the carrier *Shokaku* on the morning of December 7, 1941. NAVAL HISTORY AND HERITAGE COMMAND

A Japanese combat photograph of Pearl Harbor's Battleship Row in the first moments of the attack, probably taken from the rear seat of a northbound torpedo plane. Left to right are the *Nevada*, the *Arizona* with the repair ship *Vestal* alongside, *West Virginia* outboard of the *Tennessee*, *Oklahoma* outboard of the *Maryland*, the oiler *Neosho* at the Ford Island gasoline dock, and the *California*. Upon close inspection one can see a deep cavitation and a tall column of water on the port side of the West Virginia rising as high as her masts, indicating that she has just sustained a torpedo hit. The tracks of converted Type 91 aerial torpedoes can be seen streaking toward the *West Virginia* and *Oklahoma*. Expanding concentric shock waves in the water are also present. In the background, smoke rises from the attack on Hickam Field. Note the presence of the large number of oil tanks, the destruction of which would have severely hampered the Pacific Fleet's ability to wage war in the coming months, but they were shortsightedly ignored by the Japanese, who chose instead to concentrate their efforts on disabling the battleships. NAVAL HISTORY AND HERITAGE COMMAND

The catastrophic explosion that destroyed the *Arizona*, when her forward magazines were detonated by a Japanese armor-piercing bomb. NATIONAL ARCHIVES

Battleship Row during the Japanese attack, taken from the vicinity of the Ten-Ten Dock. The damaged *Maryland* is at left. The *Oklahoma* has capsized; astern of her the *West Virginia* can be seen listing to port, on fire and sinking. The huge column of black smoke at right is coming from the destroyed *Arizona*. NATIONAL ARCHIVES

The tugboat *Hoga* fights fires aboard *Nevada* after the battleship was beached on Waipio Point. NATIONAL ARCHIVES

Sailors and Navy Yard personnel swarm over the hull of the capsized *Oklahoma* at the beginning of search-and-rescue operations. Thirty-two survivors trapped belowdecks would eventually be freed. NATIONAL ARCHIVES

What was left of the *Arizona* on December 10, 1941, after her fires were finally extinguished. NATIONAL ARCHIVES

LEFT: Admiral Chester W. Nimitz assumed command of the Pacific Fleet on December 31, 1941. He would serve as CINCPAC and Commander-in-Chief Pacific Ocean Areas until the end of the war. NATIONAL ARCHIVES

BELOW: Vice Admiral William F. Halsey Jr., who led US carrier forces on the early hit-and-run raids against Japanese bases in the Central Pacific and carried Doolittle's bombers to within striking distance of Tokyo. Halsey later commanded the South Pacific Area and the Third Fleet. NAVAL HISTORY AND HERITAGE COMMAND

Captain Homer Wallin (center) confers with salvage officers aboard the *California* in early 1942. NAVAL HISTORY AND HERITAGE COMMAND

The giant "window-frame" patch made by carpenters in the Pearl Harbor Navy Yard to cover torpedo holes in the *Nevada*'s hull. The overturned hull of *Nevada*'s sister ship *Oklahoma* was used as a template for its fabrication. NATIONAL ARCHIVES

One of the *California*'s massive 14-inch guns being removed prior to refloating operations. NAVAL HISTORY AND HERITAGE COMMAND

Raising the *California*. Note the presence of the wooden cofferdam around her port bow and the absence of her guns and mainmast. NAVAL HISTORY AND HERITAGE COMMAND

A team of navy divers in Pearl Harbor. These men performed all kinds of salvage work aboard the sunken battleships, from operating cutting torches, patching bomb and torpedo holes, and closing off watertight doors to the removal of paymaster safes, live ammunition, and human remains, all in complete and utter darkness. NAVAL HISTORY AND HERITAGE COMMAND

ABOVE: The *West Virginia* after being refloated, on her way to Dry Dock Number One with seawater still being pumped overboard. NATIONAL ARCHIVES

LEFT: The *West Virginia* in dry dock. The concrete-sealed patches are in the process of being removed, revealing the huge gashes made in her port side by Japanese torpedoes. NATIONAL ARCHIVES

The *Pennsylvania* bombards the Japanese-held Aleutian island of Attu with her 14-inch main guns, May 1943. NAVAL HISTORY AND HERITAGE COMMAND

The *Tennessee* performing sea trials off the coast of Washington State in May 1943, now looking more like a *South Dakota*–class battleship after her modernization. Extensive torpedo blistering has been added to the hull, her superstructure has been completely redesigned and rebuilt, and her boilers are trunked into one funnel instead of two. The secondary battery now consists of 5-inch / 38 caliber guns in twin turrets, and she is equipped with multiple 20mm and 40mm antiaircraft guns. A Mark 34 main battery fire control director equipped with Mark 8 FH radar can be seen on the forward aspect of the superstructure. NAVAL HISTORY AND HERITAGE COMMAND

The *Maryland* fires her 16-inch guns in support of the US Marine assault on Betio Island in the Tarawa Atoll, November 1943. Note the presence of the cut-down cage mainmast. Rear Admiral Harry Hill and his staff are on the portside bridge wing in the foreground. The muzzle blast from the *Maryland*'s 16-inch guns had the unfortunate effect of disrupting Hill's radio communications during the battle. NATIONAL ARCHIVES

The *Tennessee* bombarding Parry Island in the Eniwetok Atoll from point-blank range on February 22, 1944, just prior to an assault by the 22nd Marines. This photo shows just how close battleship captains were willing to approach Japanese-held islands in order to destroy enemy fortifications and minimize casualties among the landing forces. NATIONAL ARCHIVES

LEFT: Seaman Second Class John Henry Ashby of the *Maryland*. KIMBERLY THORN

RIGHT: Rear Admiral Richmond Kelly Turner, commander of the US Navy's amphibious forces during the westward thrust across the Central Pacific. NAVAL HISTORY AND HERITAGE COMMAND

The *Tennessee* (left) and *California* in Tanapag Harbor, Saipan, June 1944. NATIONAL ARCHIVES

The *Maryland* enters Dry Dock Number Two in the Pearl Harbor Navy Yard on July 10, 1944, after being torpedoed by a Japanese aircraft off the coast of Saipan. NATIONAL ARCHIVES

Chester Nimitz, Ernest King, and Ray Spruance in conference aboard the *Indianapolis* during the Marianas campaign. NATIONAL ARCHIVES

A "daisy chain" of American sailors passes 5-inch / 38 caliber full-service charge ammunition aboard the *Pennsylvania* just prior to the bombardment of Peleliu, September 1944. NATIONAL ARCHIVES

ABOVE: Two photos showing the radical transformation of the *West Virginia*. The first was taken in San Francisco Bay in the 1930s, with the battleship appearing as she did before the attack on Pearl Harbor. The second photo was taken in Puget Sound on July 2, 1944, after her reconstruction and modernization. NATIONAL ARCHIVES

Rear Admiral Jesse Oldendorf aboard his flagship *Louisville* during the bombardment of Leyte, October 1944. NAVAL HISTORY AND HERITAGE COMMAND

Sailors watch from the 40mm gun gallery of the *West Virginia* as a *Fletcher*-class destroyer lays a smoke screen in Leyte Gulf, October 1944.
NATIONAL ARCHIVES

"I have returned." General Douglas MacArthur wades ashore at Leyte, October 20, 1944.
NATIONAL ARCHIVES

The *West Virginia* firing a main battery salvo at the *Yamashiro* during the Battle of Surigao Strait.
NAVAL HISTORY AND HERITAGE COMMAND

After the battle, the crew of *PT-321* rescues an oil-drenched Japanese sailor from the waters of Surigao Strait, October 25, 1944. NAVAL HISTORY AND HERITAGE COMMAND

The *Pennsylvania* leads a column of battleships and cruisers through Philippine waters in late 1944. NATIONAL ARCHIVES

CHAPTER 16
"COMMENCE FIRING"

On March 15, 1943, Admiral Ernest J. King reorganized the naval forces of the United States into a system of numbered fleets, establishing an organizational structure for the future expansion of various combat commands. Units of the Atlantic Fleet were assigned even numbers, while odd numbers were given to commands in the Pacific. The ships assigned to Vice Admiral Bill Halsey's South Pacific Area became the Third Fleet. Central Pacific forces would eventually be designated Fifth Fleet, while naval units assigned to the Southwest Pacific Area were renamed Seventh Fleet. This clarified the designation of naval task forces, which were now numbered to reflect the fleet to which they were assigned. A task force of the Third Fleet, for example, would be numbered Task Force 31, while Task Force 51 would belong to Fifth Fleet.

Two weeks later, on March 28, the Joint Chiefs of Staff approved General Douglas MacArthur's final plan for Operation Cartwheel, a succession of leapfrogging assaults meant to dislodge the Japanese from the northern coast of New Guinea, seize the Admiralty Islands, and occupy positions on New Georgia while Halsey's South Pacific forces conducted a simultaneous drive up the Solomon Island chain, all in order to isolate the Japanese bastion of Rabaul on the island of New Britain.

Rear Admiral Francis Rockwell's North Pacific Force would launch Operation Landcrab in early May to sweep the Japanese from two remote Aleutian Islands, Attu and Kiska. In November, Ray Spruance along with Kelly Turner and US Marine Corps Major General Holland Smith would embark upon their conquest of the Central Pacific, beginning with assaults on Japanese advanced bases in the Gilbert and Marshall Islands.

From an American perspective, the war in general and the Pacific theater of operations in particular would consist of a series of amphibious landing operations, each one requiring the protection and support of warships. Lightly armed attack transports, landing ships, and cargo vessels needed to be escorted to their objectives and positive control of the surrounding sea needed to be maintained throughout the campaign. Naval gunfire support would prove to be an essential component of these amphibious operations. Kelly Turner, the man who would command the amphibious forces in their drive across the Pacific, believed that the super dreadnoughts, which were in essence floating platforms of heavy artillery, would prove ideally suited for the task.

As amphibious task groups converged upon Japanese-held islands, older battleships acted as powerful escorts for convoys of transport and supply vessels. This was a duty performed by the old dreadnoughts, according to one officer serving with the fleet, that was "quite generally overlooked, at least underrated. A dozen transports, each carrying several thousands of military personnel, constitute a valuable convoy. It is not enough to send a few destroyers along with them, and a couple of [escort] carriers for air cover. There is always the chance that the enemy will bring out a fast heavy cruiser, or a pocket battleship (which is the same thing), in the hope of making a killing."

Directed by their own catapult-launched seaplanes, the big guns of the battleships "softened up" invasion beaches, blasting Japanese gun emplacements, pillboxes, bunkers, vehicles, and ammunition and supply dumps. Once assault troops were landed, the battleships would remain offshore to deliver on-call fire support as required, coordinated by teams of radio-equipped forward observers accompanying the landing force. The modernized older battleships would also be tasked with providing protection for the amphibious fleet against enemy air and surface threats when they were most vulnerable, during the process of unloading and boating troops, ammunition, provisions, and supplies in the roadstead.

After receiving updated air and surface search radar, improved fire control systems, new antiaircraft weapons, increased splinter protection, deck armor, torpedo blistering, and an array of other refinements, the dreadnoughts would set sail across the vast expanse of the Pacific to stand watch over the amphibious forces that were steadily blazing a path toward Tokyo.

"*Nevada* from Shore Control, commence firing."

Off the southern coast of the bleak, treeless, and wind-scoured volcanic island of Attu in the western Aleutians, the 14-inch / 45 caliber main guns of the USS *Nevada* erupted with a deafening roar, illuminating the surrounding fog with great bursts of flaming powder and sending a salvo of 1,500-pound high-explosive shells hurtling into a network of defensive positions that the Japanese had carved into a barren hillside.

Thirty minutes later, at 6:45 p.m. on May 13, 1943, the Cheer Up Ship would send a query to the naval gunfire liaison officer embedded with the assault troops of the US Army's 7th Infantry Division.

"Shore Control from *Nevada*, for information, how are we doing over there?"

"*Nevada* from Shore Control, forward observer says there are a lot of yellow fellows over there and you are *not* wasting ammunition."

Paying little heed to the advice of Lord Nelson, who once counseled his junior officers that "a sailor's a fool to fight a fort," Captain Willard Kitts ordered the *Nevada* to approach the rocky southern shore of Attu as closely as he dared, well within range of any coastal artillery batteries that the Japanese might have placed there. Kitts wanted to provide the most effective fire support possible to the infantry units fighting their way inland from the beaches of Massacre Bay, an objective whose name must have sounded rather discomfiting to the young soldiers packed into landing craft and headed ashore for their first amphibious assault. Even while maneuvering slowly, with an officer maintaining a constant watch on the ship's fathometer, Kitts had to twice order the *Nevada*'s engines backed at full emergency power to avoid grounding the ship on uncharted shoals. After two hours of near-constant firing, the *Nevada* received a situation report from the shore control party of the landing force.

"*Nevada* from Shore Control, observer says all salvos but four have been very effective. You have hit machine guns, mortars, artillery positions, and entrenchments."

Willard Augustus Kitts III was from the city of Oswego in Upstate New York, a graduate of the Naval Academy Class of 1916, and the recipient of a master's degree in engineering from MIT. He had served with distinction aboard the battleships *Arkansas* and *Colorado*, along with tours of duty with the Bureau of Ordnance in Washington and CINCPAC Headquarters in Hawaii, where he had occupied the billet of fleet gunnery officer under Admiral Kimmel. Rather than the fictional Captain Victor "Pug" Henry in Herman Wouk's *The Winds of War*, it was actually Captain Willard Kitts who was given command of the heavy cruiser *Northampton* following the attack on Pearl Harbor.

On the night of November 30, 1942, the thin-skinned *Northampton* was severely damaged by a Japanese torpedo during the Battle of Tassafaronga. Kitts skillfully maneuvered his sinking ship clear of the enemy-held shoreline before ordering her abandoned, allowing most of the crew to be picked up by American destroyers. Though badly injured himself, Kitts swam to the rescue of a floundering mess steward who was unable to swim. For these actions he was awarded the Navy Cross, and in January 1943 Kitts arrived in Puget Sound to take command of the battleship USS *Nevada.*

Of the three standard-type dreadnoughts seriously damaged at Pearl Harbor, *Nevada* had been the first to return to active service following a seven-and-a-half-month refit. As the oldest battleship in the Pacific Fleet, she was expected to play only a limited role in future combat operations, and in early 1942 the Bureau of Ships made the recommendation for only minimal modifications to be made, essentially restoring the dreadnought to her prewar configuration. Admiral King demurred, favoring a more-extensive overhaul of the *Nevada.*

As they had for the *Tennessee*, the "yardbirds" at Puget Sound replaced *Nevada*'s main mast with a prefabricated stump tower. New Mark 37 directors controlled her secondary batteries, which consisted of eight new 5-inch / 38 caliber guns mounted in twin turrets. Jutting skyward were the barrels of eight new quadruple-mounted 40-millimeter Bofors along with forty-one 20-millimeter Oerlikon antiaircraft guns. To offset these increases in topside weight, the ship's conning tower, one of her seaplane catapults, and all boat cranes were removed.

As a further weight-trimming measure, the *Nevada* would go to sea with smaller quantities of main battery ammunition, fuel oil, and freshwater, relying upon the logistics train of the fleet for underway replenishment of these commodities. The conning tower's removal allowed for the superstructure to be thoroughly modernized, with a new open bridge leading aft to a network of enclosed spaces that served as the nerve center for fighting the ship, where officers and sailors manned stations for conning and steering, the radar plot, main battery fire control, and air defense.

Following her refit, the *Nevada* embarked upon a three-month course of sea trials and training, and on April 7, 1943, stood out from the port of San Pedro for Alaskan waters. On the final day of April she rendezvoused with the remainder of Rear Admiral Howard F. Kingman's Operation Landcrab Support Group in Cold Bay, Alaska. The shore bombardment and close air support unit consisted of seven destroyers, the escort carrier *Nassau*, and the battleships *Idaho* and *Pennsylvania*.

After the disbandment of Task Force 1 in Pearl Harbor, *Pennsylvania* had set sail for the Bethlehem Steel shipyard in San Francisco, arriving there on October 4, 1942. Like the *Nevada*, the *Pennsylvania*'s conning tower was removed and her bridge modernized. Two booms replaced the battleship's boat cranes and a new deckhouse was constructed where her tripod main mast had been. Mark 3 FC radar-equipped fire control directors were installed, along with two additional SG search radar sets. Significant upgrades to the *Pennsylvania*'s armament were also made: The 5-inch / 51 caliber casement-mounted broadside guns were gone, along with all 5-inch / 25 caliber and 1.1-inch antiaircraft guns. Replacing these weapons were eight twin-mounted 5-inch / 38 caliber dual-purpose guns in armored turrets, as well as ten quad-mounted 40-millimeter Bofors and fifty-one 20-millimeter Oerlikons.

On February 6, 1943, the refitted *Pennsylvania* steamed into the port of Long Beach, California, where Captain Thomas King was relieved by Captain William Anderson Corn of Ogden, Utah. Once described as a "square and practical" officer, reserved, stern, and thorough, Corn immediately set to work preparing his crew for the upcoming campaign in the Aleutians, which included several trips to the ship-to-shore live firing range on the California Channel Island of San Clemente.

"The crew naturally could not know what was in the wind, and there were loudly-voiced complaints that the *Pennsylvania* would serve as nothing more than a training ship throughout the war," wrote Lieutenant Clifton B. Cates Jr., a *Pennsylvania* officer who served as the ship's wartime historian.

The *Pennsylvania* departed Long Beach for Cold Bay on April 23. Upon their arrival at the remote anchorage, the officers and sailors of the Support Group were met with the kind of weather that typically graced the Alaskan peninsula in mid-spring: freezing rain accompanied by a howling wind.

"No one questioned the aptness of the name, Cold Bay," Cates recorded.

Along with the bombing of Dutch Harbor, the Japanese had seized the distant and sparsely inhabited Aleutian Islands of Attu and Kiska in a campaign that was conducted at the same time as their failed Midway operation in June 1942. There had been no American military presence on either island except for ten naval personnel manning a weather station on Kiska; two were killed by the invaders and the rest packed off to Japan as POWs. On Attu there were only forty-five native Aleuts and a married civilian couple in their sixties from Ohio, Charles and Etta Jones. After murdering Charles, the Japanese evacuated his wife and the Aleuts to mainland Japan.

"Until the end of the Pacific War no one can make a conclusive statement of the objectives of the Japanese attack on the Aleutian Islands in June 1942," read a summary by the Office of Naval Intelligence written in May 1945. "The enemy may have been planning the subsequent conquest of all the islands in order to obtain access to Canada and our northwestern states. He may even have aimed at an immediate invasion of Alaska, only to be deterred by our victory at Midway.

"It is well known that the Japanese had long coveted Alaska and the Aleutians, and that many of their military leaders considered these poorly-defended outposts the logical route for an invasion of North America. The enemy's intentions may have been less ambitious, however; he may merely have planned to protect his northern flank, to divide our forces, and to complicate our defense of Hawaii and the West Coast after the expected capture of Midway."

Lieutenant General Kiichiro Higuchi of the Fifth Area Army would later confirm that Japanese designs on the Aleutians were indeed "less ambitious" than the Americans had feared. The objective of Japan's Aleutian adventure, according to Higuchi, was to establish a network of defensive bases along the Americans' northern axis of advance toward the Japanese Home Islands. In the event that the Soviets should enter the Pacific War, Japanese forces stationed in the Aleutians would be in a position to impede air and sea communications between the United States and Siberia.

Glancing at the map with the benefit of hindsight, it seems appropriate to question whether or not the strategic importance of Attu and Kiska made them worth the cost of their recapture. The sound practice of bypassing and isolating heavily fortified or far-removed Japanese holdings—a strategy that the Americans employed with great success during their island-hopping campaign across the Pacific—might have easily been applied in the Aleutians. Any expedition sent to reclaim Attu and Kiska would have been forced to contend with not only the stubborn resistance of the Japanese, but with some of the most inhospitable weather, sea states, and terrain to be found on planet Earth.

"It was a theater of military frustration," Morison would write. "Both sides would have done well to have left the Aleutians to the Aleuts for the course of the war."

Regardless of Japan's motivation for stationing troops there, Nimitz and the Joint Chiefs wanted Attu and Kiska retaken. However outlying or militarily insignificant they may have been, the two bare and desolate islands were still American soil. The westernmost Attu, defended by some 2,500 Japanese troops, was invaded first in a two-pronged amphibious assault beginning in the small hours of May 11, 1943. The submarines *Nautilus* and *Narwhal* and the fast transport *Kane* successfully landed the US Army 7th Infantry Division's reconnaissance teams just after 3:00 a.m. Later that afternoon, they were joined by two rifle regiments making near-simultaneous assaults at Holtz Bay on the island's northern shore and at Massacre Bay to the south.

The invasion force would find Attu shrouded in a layer of dense fog, despite a weather forecast which had called for clear skies. Visibility was so poor, in fact, that the scheduled shore bombardment was called off for fear of hitting friendly troops. Later that day the *Pennsylvania*, accompanied by the *Idaho*, struck a Japanese stronghold near the sheltered harbor of Chichagof, where Attu's main settlement was located.

"No land was visible," Captain Corn would state in his after-action report. "Guns were controlled from navigational position obtained through radar ranges and bearings and checked by radar ranges to the beach in the line-of-fire. Salvo fire was used throughout. Air and ground bursts were used."

The *Pennsylvania* withdrew after firing 672 rounds from her new 5-inch / 38 caliber guns and would approach the foggy harbor of Chichagof again later that afternoon, this time employing her 14-inch main guns as well as her secondary battery, with fire adjusted by shore control parties.

The following day, as the *Pennsylvania* was steaming north of Attu, the alert crew of a PBY Catalina patrolling overhead made a startling call over the VHF radio frequency.

"Look out for torpedo! Torpedo headed for the ship!"

Making a full-over turn at flank speed, the *Pennsylvania* managed to evade the torpedo, which sliced through her wake. The offending submarine was then pounced upon by the escorting destroyers *Edwards*, *Farragut*, and *Frazier*. After ten hours of relentless depth-charge attacks, a periscope was spotted amid the churning waves. More than likely damaged and rising to periscope depth for a look-around before surfacing, the submarine *I-31* was forced to dive once more after the *Edwards* and *Frazier* opened fire with their 5-inch guns. Quickly obtaining a sonar bearing on the submarine, the *Frazier* attacked with a full pattern of depth charges, and the *I-31* was sunk with all hands.

On May 14 the skies over Attu were at least partially clear, and the *Pennsylvania* provided fire support for an infantry attack near Holtz Bay and Chichagof, using her own Kingfisher spotting planes. Five days later, while steaming in the company of the *Nassau* north of Attu, the *Pennsylvania* suffered an explosion in a forward aviation gasoline storage compartment. Fortunately no one was injured in the accident, though some structural damage was sustained. After a brief stop at the island of Adak, the *Pennsylvania* proceeded to Bremerton, Washington, for repairs.

On May 29 the commander of the Japanese forces trapped on Attu, Lieutenant General Yasuyo Yamasaki, led the six hundred remaining men of his command in a final *banzai* charge against the American lines. The desperate attack managed to break through to the rear echelon where the starving Japanese soldiers ran amok, with some of them stopping to "eat ravenously" at an American ration dump. Company clerks, medics, staff officers, and cooks were suddenly forced to pick up their seldom-used weapons and fight back, in some cases engaging in hand-to-hand combat. Nearly all of the attacking Japanese were killed, including Yamasaki himself, and that afternoon all organized resistance on Attu came to an end.

Her Aleutian mission complete, in early June the USS *Nevada* steamed for San Francisco, where she underwent maintenance at Mare Island Navy Yard. Later that month *Nevada* would transit the Panama Canal, headed for Norfolk, Virginia, and a transfer to the Atlantic Fleet, where she would eventually see action during the invasion of Normandy. The vacancy created by her departure would soon be filled by the USS *Tennessee.*

The *Tennessee* had cast off from the docks of the Puget Sound Navy Yard and steamed through the Strait of Juan de Fuca to begin sea trials on May 8, 1943, upon the completion of a comprehensive nine-month modernization that cost just over $20 million, an amount nearly equal to the purchase price of three *Fletcher*-class destroyers, or roughly 570 new Grumman F6F Hellcat fighter planes.

"The ship was garbed in a new blue battle dress," wrote Lawrence Bellatti, a specialist (X) first class serving aboard the *Tennessee*, "and even the crew was decked in colors, you might say, because they were as green as the grass that covered the hills along the straits."

Bearing little similarity to her former self, the profile of the *Tennessee* now more closely resembled that of a modern *South Dakota*–class battleship than a dreadnought commissioned in 1917. The configuration of *Tennessee*'s upper works had been drastically altered: After the removal of the original conning tower, a smaller and lighter armored structure of the type designed for light cruisers of the *Brooklyn* class took its place. Gone was the tall cage foremast, replaced by a steel tower which housed the bridge and two Mark 34 main battery fire control directors equipped with the latest Mark 8 FH radars. Sprouting from the new superstructure was a forest of antennae for SG surface search, SC air search, and IFF "identify friend or foe" radars. The *Tennessee* now had a single smokestack instead of two; the exhaust vents of all eight boilers had been redirected into the forward stack and the after funnel was removed.

This new compact superstructure opened clear arcs of fire for a new battery of antiaircraft weapons. The *Tennessee* now boasted ten quad-mounted 40-millimeter Bofors and forty-three 20-millimeter Oerlikons. Eight twin turrets of 5-inch / 38 caliber dual-purpose guns controlled by Mark 37 fire control directors made up the secondary battery, finally replacing the old 5-inch / 51 caliber broadside guns in casements. Her ammunition magazines were now protected by the promised three inches of STS deck armor, and the second deck and turret roofs were also reinforced with 2 more inches of steel plating. To compensate for the 8,000-ton addition to the *Tennessee*'s overall displacement caused by these modifications, capacious torpedo blisters were added, which increased her beam to 114 feet and inspired the crew to coin an unflattering new nickname for their ship: "Old Blisterbutt." Now too broad in the beam to pass through the locks of the Panama Canal, the *Tennessee* was destined to spend the remainder of her service life with the Pacific Fleet.

"Old hands who left the ship when she entered dry dock could not recognize the 'Rebel' when they returned a few months later," Bellatti wrote. To service and man the various new weapons, machinery, and systems aboard the modified *Tennessee*, many of the "old hands" were sent to navy specialist schools during the ship's refitting, and the size of the crew was increased to 114 officers and 2,129 enlisted personnel. Changes to interior living quarters were made to accommodate the new additions. To keep passageways clear, the crew's berthing spaces were reconfigured with each sailor assigned a "trice rack," or stowable bunk, rather than the traditional navy hammock. "No one is agitating for their return," a sailor would later write of the discarded hammocks.

The ship's galley space was also expanded to include an enlisted mess, a feature incorporated into the design of newer warships, and the practice of sailors eating on foldable tables in their division berthing areas was dispensed with.

Captain Robert Stevenson Haggart of Salem, New York, had been a "tin can sailor" for most of his naval career, having commanded the destroyers *Hull* and *William B. Preston*, as well as Destroyer Squadron 16. A recipient of the Navy Cross, Haggart had seen action during the landings at Vera Cruz and while commanding the *Hull* in the North Atlantic during the First World War. Now in command of the *Tennessee*, Haggart had just three weeks to perform engineering tests on the refurbished battleship and get his crew ready for combat. While the *Tennessee* steamed a zigzag course along the West Coast, Captain Haggart and his executive officer, Commander Cy Cutler, relentlessly drilled a crew that included many a novice seaman.

All throughout the month of May the pace of training and preparation never relaxed. A full power test conducted off the coast of Port Townsend, Washington, on May 12 revealed that the old battleship, despite her recent weight gain, was still capable of making 20.8 knots. Structural firing tests were performed on the new guns. Radar and range finders were calibrated, seaplanes were catapulted and recovered, and antiaircraft guns blasted away at aerological balloons and target sleeves towed by airplanes. There were engineering casualty drills, General Quarters drills, and air defense drills carried out in the early-morning hours and in the dead of night. Haggart and Cutler would find their greatest challenge in getting the officers and men who were manning the radar plot and fire control stations to work together seamlessly with the gun crews, something achieved only after many arduous hours of live fire practice.

Finally, on the sunny Southern California afternoon of May 31, 1943, the *Tennessee* arrived at the port of San Pedro. Those hoping for anything more than a Cinderella liberty on the waterfront were sorely disappointed. Just twenty-four hours later, restocked with ammunition, fuel, and provisions, the *Tennessee* sortied for Alaska.

From the new conning tower of the USS *Tennessee* the snowcapped peak of Qisxan Kamgii, the 4,000-foot-tall stratovolcano that dominates the rugged landscape of Kiska Island, hove into sight through the surface haze on the afternoon of July 29, 1943. Along with the faraway droning of radial aircraft engines, the *Tennessee*'s lookouts could hear the muffled rumble of explosions from across the cold gray waves of the Bering Sea. Eighteen B-24 Liberator heavy bombers of the army's Eleventh Air Force were giving Kiska what sounded like a thorough pounding before the navy's ships closed the distance to begin their shore bombardment. Hopefully the airedales would leave something for them to shoot at, a *Tennessee* sailor would remark to his shipmates.

Captain Robert Haggart's *Tennessee* was serving as the flagship of the task group, which included the battleship *Idaho* and four destroyers under the command of Rear Admiral Howard Kingman. While Kingman's force approached Kiska from the north, another task group was steaming along the southern coast of the island, made up of five cruisers and five destroyers. The bombardment of Kiska, which would be the first offensive action taken by the *Tennessee* in the Pacific War, was one of several air and surface operations meant to soften up the Japanese defenses on the island prior to an amphibious assault scheduled for August 15.

The *Tennessee* would fire just thirty rounds from her 14-inch main guns, while the 5-inch / 38 caliber secondary hurled 363 rounds of high explosive into Kiska's rocky shores. With the ceiling of clouds at only 1,000 feet, the pilot of the ship's Kingfisher observation plane had difficulty spotting the placement of the *Tennessee*'s fire.

"The pilot was required by circumstances to take a spotting position rather close to the trajectory of the projectiles," Haggart would write in his after-action report. "The unexpected passage of a main battery salvo rocked the plane severely and proved disconcerting to the observing spotter."

Captain Haggart believed (and his traumatized young aviator would have surely agreed) that communication and coordination between the fire control staff, radio operators, and spotter planes needed to be improved, but he was otherwise very pleased with the overall performance and discipline of the *Tennessee* crew on their first mission. After many tedious weeks of drill and patrols upon the foggy Bering Sea, this first introduction to combat provided a much-needed morale boost for the men, however brief it was. The *Tennessee* and her cohorts would retire after firing upon Kiska for only thirty-five minutes. Curiously, there had been no response from the Japanese shore batteries.

The *Tennessee* would return to Kiska as part of Kingman's Support Group for the landings on August 15, paired once again with the *Idaho*, along with two cruisers and a half-dozen destroyers. The *Pennsylvania*, having arrived from Puget Sound with her damage repaired and reconfigured as a command-and-control vessel, served as the flagship of Admiral Rockwell, the overall commander of the invasion force consisting of twenty-seven warships and twenty-five transport and cargo vessels.

Intelligence estimates placed about 4,000 troops of the Imperial Japanese Army on Kiska, along with an equal number of naval personnel. The Allied landing force, therefore, would be larger than the one that assaulted Attu. The US Army's 7th Infantry Division was once again tasked for the job, reinforced by a regiment of specially trained troopers from the 10th Mountain Division, the 13th Canadian Infantry Brigade, and the commandos of the American-Canadian First Special Service Force.

Following the preparatory shore bombardment, 34,400 Allied troops stormed the beaches of Kiska just after 6:00 a.m. They would find only a pair of rawboned and frightened mongrel dogs waiting for them, for the Japanese had slipped the noose and evacuated Kiska under the cover of a thick fog two weeks before. The Aleutian Campaign was over.

CHAPTER 17
"GIVE THE BASTARDS HELL"

"When the decision to open the central Pacific was made I was in the Aleutians," wrote Robert Sherrod. "The central Pacific sounded more exciting than anything I had seen in the war against Japan."

Thirty-four years old, possessing a head of wavy auburn hair, a pair of grimly serious dark eyes, and an oversized aquiline nose, Sherrod looked very much like a Hollywood casting director's impression of a war correspondent. After covering the anticlimactic invasion of Kiska and growing "sick of the Aleutians weather," the veteran *Time-Life* reporter headed south for sunnier climes, hoping find more-compelling material for his overseas dispatches. Hearing a rumor that preparations for the next great campaign of the Pacific War were under way, Sherrod caught a ride on an outbound ship, stopping in Pearl Harbor before making his way to New York City.

"The naval strength I saw—though it was puny compared to what I saw later—convinced me that the central Pacific was going to become the main news story in the Pacific War and, since nearly every reporter prefers to follow the main story, I wanted more than ever to see the curtain rise in the new theatre," Sherrod wrote. "I learned enough about the impending opening of the central Pacific to convince my editors—without telling them what would happen—that here was a story worth covering."

By late October 1943 Sherrod was back in Hawaii, where he joined a group of fellow correspondents in boarding the USS *Tennessee* just before she set sail from Pearl Harbor, bound for a secret rendezvous with the ships of Task Force 53 somewhere in the Pacific. Sherrod found the battleship to be "crowded, like most old ships which have been rearmed with many additional guns and gadgets. She carried more than two thousand officers and men—many hundreds more than she was built to carry. Her complement of officers was even more overcrowded than her complement of men, because old ships must train the officers who will run the new ships a-building."

As the *Tennessee* steamed into the lower latitudes, Sherrod would observe that "our wartime voyage might as well have been a peacetime cruise in the South Seas. The brilliant sunlight, the far-reaching, incredibly blue Pacific, the soft breezes at evening and the Southern Cross in the sky—all these were no different than they had always been." On the afternoon of November 5, 1943, the *Tennessee* stood into Havannah Harbor on the island of Efate in the New Hebrides, the staging base for Operation Galvanic.

The Allied strategic plan for the defeat of Japan, developed by the US Joint Chiefs of Staff and approved at the Anglo-American Trident Conference in Washington, DC, called for two concurrent offensive drives across the Pacific to be conducted in 1943–1944. Designed to place unrelenting pressure and inflict heavy losses on Japanese forces, the plan included the severing of the vital lifeline of oil and strategic resources between Japan and the East Indies, along with the seizure of advanced bases for the new long-range B-29 Superfortress and the opening of a strategic bombing campaign against the Japanese Home Islands.

General Douglas MacArthur's Southwest Pacific Forces were to complete the encirclement and isolation of the huge Japanese base complex at Rabaul, then advance northwest along the coast of New Guinea and through the intervening islands of the East Indies toward the Philippines. The Central Pacific Forces under Nimitz were to drive westward, seizing Japanese bases in the Marshalls, Carolines, and Marianas. These two lines of advance were to eventually converge in the western Pacific.

Once given the green light from the Joint Chiefs, Nimitz executed his plan for the Central Pacific Campaign drawn up by the CINCPAC staff, code-named "Granite." Under the heading of "Concept of Operations," Granite's listed objectives were to "Destroy the Japanese fleet at an early date. Inflict the maximum attrition on enemy air forces. Intensify air, submarine, and mining operations against enemy shipping and lines of communication. Enable us to launch shore-based and carrier-based air attack on Japan."

Following his brilliant victory at Midway, Ray Spruance had been recalled to Pearl Harbor to become Nimitz's chief of staff, and in September 1942 was also named Deputy Commander-in-Chief of the Pacific Fleet. On the subject of who was to lead the Central Pacific Force in late 1943, Spruance had told his boss that he "would like another crack at the Japs" but was not expecting to be released from his post for another combat command. After sleeping on it, Nimitz decided to promote Spruance to vice admiral and place him in command of the organization that would spearhead the drive across the Central Pacific.

"Spruance, you are lucky," Nimitz told him. "I decided that I am going to let you go after all."

The first of many tasks for the new commander was the selection of key players for the Central Pacific Force senior staff. Spruance wanted Richmond Kelly Turner as commander of Amphibious Forces and Major General Holland M. Smith of the Marine Corps to command the assault troops, appointments which were soon approved by Nimitz and King. Turner had attended the Naval War College in 1935 while Spruance was serving there as a staff member. Despite his waspish personality Turner possessed a truly brilliant mind, astonishing Spruance with his ability to keep track of hundreds of minute details.

"Our ideas on professional matters were thoroughly worked out together, and we usually thought alike," Spruance would say of his relationship with Turner.

Spruance had also been greatly impressed by Holland M. Smith's knowledge of amphibious operations, having witnessed Smith's training of the US Army's 7th Infantry Division for the Aleutian landings. A veteran of several expeditionary deployments and director of Operations and Training during the formative years of the Fleet Marine Force, Smith was already a revered patriarch of amphibious warfare. At sixty-one years old the Alabaman looked rather like a bespectacled Walter Cronkite in ill-fitting dungarees, which made his explosive temper all the more startling for the uninitiated.

An irascible character himself, Kelly Turner knew why the marines believed that Smith's first two initials stood for "Howlin' Mad," but he had nonetheless recommended the grizzled old campaigner to lead his landing forces. According to a biographer, Spruance knew that he would often be playing referee between Turner and Smith, and that "each was a strong personality, stubborn in support of his own views . . . [Spruance] foresaw that there would be conflicts of views between the two, but believed, correctly, that he could diplomatically reconcile any differences of opinion between them." The marines and amphibious-trained army units assigned to Spruance's Central Pacific Force were designated as Fifth Amphibious Corps, under Holland Smith's command.

Rather than launching the Granite Campaign with a direct attack on the Marshall Islands, Spruance was in favor of first capturing Japanese outposts in the Gilbert Islands, a British colony 400 miles southeast of the Marshalls and 2,400 miles southwest of Hawaii. Once secured, the Gilberts could provide bases for land-based photo aircraft and heavy bombers in preparation for an assault on the Marshalls. Air and submarine reconnaissance had discovered that the Japanese were busily constructing a 4,000-foot airstrip on the heavily defended island of Betio in the Gilberts' Tarawa Atoll. Not keen on the idea of such a base remaining on the southern flank of his axis of advance, Nimitz endorsed the plan to take the Gilberts first, which was duly approved by the Joint Chiefs. The launch date for the operation to seize the Tarawa, Makin, and Abemama atolls in the Gilbert Islands, code-named Galvanic, was set for November 20, 1943.

It was, to date, the most powerful seaborne invasion force ever assembled. The armada that converged upon the Gilbert Islands in late November 1943 was actually larger than the entire US Pacific Fleet had been at the time of the attack on Pearl Harbor. There were 140 warships, among them 6 fleet aircraft carriers, 6 light carriers, 3 escort carriers, 6 fast battleships, 7 older battleships, 9 heavy and 5 light cruisers, 66 destroyers, 22 troop transports, 8 landing ships, and 3 minesweepers. Embarked were 850 combat aircraft and 2 infantry divisions, 1 marine and 1 army, totaling

35,000 troops. They were joined by fleet oilers, tenders, cargo vessels, ammunition ships, and a myriad of other auxiliary units along with their escorting destroyers, swelling the number of ships under Spruance's command to some 200.

"If the Japanese naval staff could have seen the list," James Jones would write, "they would have shuddered. It was a far cry from Guadalcanal, and all I can think of is how insignificant and small a single infantry private must have felt, standing at the rail of one of those twenty-two transports." In reviewing the order of battle himself, Rear Admiral John Towers, commander of Naval Air Forces Pacific Fleet, would comment: "Spruance wants a sledgehammer to drive a tack."

Despite the impressive naval might now at his disposal, Spruance could not help but feel a bit apprehensive about the Galvanic plan. Steaming into battle aboard his flagship *Indianapolis*, he found himself in the disquieting position of a commander having to divide his forces in the face of the enemy. In order to retain the element of surprise, the three amphibious operations were to be carried off simultaneously. The two main targets, Tarawa and Makin, were separated by nearly 100 miles of ocean. The Galvanic fleet was therefore split into three separate task forces and multiple sub-unit task groups.

The Carrier Force (Task Force 50), commanded by Rear Admiral Charles Pownall, would maintain air supremacy over the Gilberts and provide close air support for the landings. Kelly Turner, flying his flag from the *Pennsylvania*, was the overall commander of Galvanic's amphibious ships and would also lead the Northern Attack Force (Task Force 52), charged with landing the army's 27th Infantry Division on Makin. Holland Smith, commanding the assault element, was accompanying Turner on the Makin operation. The Southern Attack Force (Task Force 53), led by Harry Hill aboard the *Maryland*, would support the Second Marine Division's assault on the island of Betio in the Tarawa Atoll and land a company of marine scouts on the lightly defended Abemama.

The possibility of the Japanese Combined Fleet attempting to challenge the Galvanic landings was looming large in Spruance's mind. It appeared as if the man who had succeeded the late Isoroku Yamamoto as its commander-in-chief, Mineichi Koga, was anticipating an American offensive in the Central Pacific. Koga was known to have staged at least seven carriers and ten battleships in the Truk anchorage, a fleet powerful enough to force the long-sought-after decisive battle.

"We must be prepared at all times during Galvanic for a fleet engagement," Spruance cautioned in a letter of instruction to his subordinate commanders. "If a major portion of the Japanese fleet were to attempt to interfere with Galvanic, it is obvious that the defeat of the enemy fleet would at once become paramount." If this opportunity presented itself, Spruance issued standing orders for the *Maryland*, *Tennessee*, and *Colorado* to split off from the Southern Attack Force at Tarawa and join with Turner's ten battleships to create a formidable battle line backed by Pownall's aircraft carriers.

Following a preliminary air and naval bombardment of Makin on the morning of November 20, the army met with little resistance on the landing beaches. The four hundred Japanese defenders chose instead to make their stand from inland fortifications, which were cleaned out by the troops of the 27th Infantry Division at a creeping pace, leaving Howlin' Mad Smith thoroughly exasperated. Nevertheless, Makin was declared secured by the morning of November 23 after the near-annihilation of the Japanese garrison.

Sixty-six American soldiers were killed in the battle, but in terms of casualties the navy would bear the brunt of the Makin operation. Forty-three sailors were killed in a tragic accident aboard the battleship *Mississippi* when an explosion occurred in her Number Two Turret during the initial shore bombardment. At dawn on November 24 the escort carrier *Liscome Bay* was struck by a torpedo from a Japanese submarine which detonated her aerial bomb magazine. Fifty-three officers and 591 enlisted sailors were killed when the ship blew up and sank, including Cook First Class Doris Miller, who had returned to sea duty after receiving the Navy Cross and performing a war bond tour across the United States.

The Abemama operation was quickly wrapped up by a reinforced company of marines from the Amphibious Recon Battalion landed by the submarine *Nautilus.* Upon learning that the Americans had arrived, the lone Japanese officer on Abemama assembled the twenty-five troops under his command and began delivering an impassioned speech, all the while gesturing wildly with a loaded sidearm. The pistol went off accidentally, the officer dropped dead, and his disheartened men committed ritual suicide. Rather than meeting enemy fire, the marines waded ashore to be greeted by young, half-nude Gilbertese girls, offering fruit and serenading the Americans with songs learned from Catholic missionaries. The strangely Michener-esque scene was a world away from what was happening on Tarawa, just 75 miles to the northwest.

Completely flat and featureless, Tarawa's Betio Island is a narrow strand of coral only 2 miles long and 800 yards wide. Measured in square acres, it is about half the size of New York City's Central Park. The garrison commander was Rear Admiral Keiji Shibazaki, a veteran of the war in China who looked much younger than his forty-nine years. Shibazaki was in command of 2,500 well-trained troops of the Special Naval Landing Force, all of whom were prepared to die for their emperor, along with 1,400 Korean laborers brought to the island to construct the airstrip and defensive positions.

Over a year's time, the Japanese had transformed the tiny island into a veritable fortress. Betio was honeycombed with over five hundred concrete pillboxes and bunkers reinforced with layers of coconut logs and sand, positioned to allow for interlocking fields of fire and connected by an extensive network of trenches. Four Vickers 8-inch guns brought from the captured British base at Singapore, along with a dozen other heavy coastal defense guns and forty field artillery pieces, were hidden within concrete emplacements, some with roofs of up to 12 feet thick. Fourteen light tanks were stationed about the island to fill any gaps in the defenses. To his men Shibazaki had declared that Betio "could not be taken by a million men in a hundred years."

As if nature itself were aiding in Betio's defense, a huge coral reef completely encircled the island, in some places extending nearly 1,000 yards from shore. The plan called for an assault by three infantry battalions, two from the Second Marines and one from the Eighth, landing abreast on three designated invasion beaches on the north, or lagoon side, of Betio on the morning of November 20. This was during a period of "neap tide," when the sun, Earth, and moon are at right angles to one another. In planning the invasion, the marines enlisted the help of several British subjects familiar with the complex hydrography of the Gilbert Islands. One member of this "foreign legion," as the Second Marine Division staff came to call the group, was Major Frank Holland of the Fiji Regiment, a New Zealander who had once served as His Majesty's Director of Education for the Gilbert Islands.

Holland warned the Americans that the waters off Betio were prone to "dodging tides" during the neap tide phase, which could recede quickly and unexpectedly, leaving less than a foot of water over the reef and the marines stranded perilously in their landing craft. The decision was made to utilize 125 amphibious tractors to carry the first wave of marines ashore. Known as "amphtracks" or "alligators," these buoyant, lightly armored and tracked vehicles were capable of crawling over the coral reef and onto the beaches. The remaining troops of the landing force, however, would have to follow in shallow-draft Higgins boats. Admiral Turner made sure that a cautionary note about the possibility of dodging tides was included in his operations order, but the consensus of the foreign legion was that the water over Betio's reef would be about 5 feet deep at H-Hour.

The Japanese on Betio were in a state of high alert, having been bombed by B-24 Liberators and carrier-based aircraft every day since November 14, and after aerial reconnaissance confirmed the presence of the Central Pacific Force in the area on November 17. Three days later, as the ships of Hill's Southern Attack Force approached the atoll in the predawn darkness, the insomnolent Japanese sent up a red star shell and opened fire with their long-range artillery.

Amid towering splashes from Japanese shells, the attack transports chugged into position to the northwest of Betio, while Rear Admiral Howard Kingman's Task Group 53.4—the Fire Support Group, which included the dreadnoughts *Maryland*, *Tennessee*, and *Colorado*, four cruisers, and nine destroyers—formed an arch which extended from the south of Betio to the waters off the northwestern shore. The *Maryland*, firing her main battery in anger for the first time in her twenty-two years of service, began to answer the thumping Japanese shore batteries with 16-inch high explosive. Her fifth salvo landed in what only could have been an ammunition dump, resulting in a tremendous secondary explosion.

The *Maryland* was pulling double duty as a fire support vessel and flagship of the Southern Attack Force. Embarked were Rear Admiral Harry Hill and Major General Julian C. Smith, commander of the Second Marine Division. During a five-week-long overhaul at the Pearl Harbor Navy Yard, the Old Mary had been converted to serve as a floating command post. Hill's radio operators were now located on a wing of the *Maryland*'s flag bridge, a cramped arrangement that resulted in a host of technical difficulties that would hamper the admiral's ability to communicate with his ships and aircraft throughout the battle. When installed side by side in confined spaces, the radio sets of the day had a tendency to interfere with one another, a problem made worse by the fact that the flag bridge was close to the muzzle blast of the *Maryland*'s 16-inch guns.

The dawn featured what would have otherwise been a serene and picturesque tropical sunrise, the eastern sky becoming an artist's palette of bright blues, yellows, and pinks. The sky slowly lightened to a hue that was many times paler than the deep azure of the surrounding sea, and a low-lying strip of gleaming white sand and coconut palms soon appeared, barely discernible on the horizon amid the smoke and coral dust. As several chroniclers of the battle have already pointed out, it would be the last sunrise that many hundreds of young men would ever witness.

Hill had already ordered his ships to cease fire in anticipation of an airstrike by carrier-based planes scheduled to begin at daybreak. The navy fliers, however, were late, and Hill's radio operators were unable to raise them. Shibazaki apparently used the brief respite to his advantage, shifting the bulk of his troops from the southern shore to the lagoon side of the island where the transports and their landing craft could be seen assembling. The planes of Task Force 50 finally arrived a few minutes after six o'clock, bombing and strafing Betio for just seven minutes before Hill ordered Kingman to begin the general shore bombardment. The week before, during a planning session at the Efate staging base, Kingman had grandly announced: "Gentlemen, we will not neutralize Betio. We will not destroy it. We will obliterate it!"

"At 0620, commence scheduled bombardment. Give the bastards hell!" Captain Carl Jones of the *Maryland* told his crew in the orders of the day.

Over the next two hours the Fire Support Group pounded Betio with 3,000 tons of explosives. For the heavily laden marines streaming over the gunwales of transport ships and down dangling cargo nets into their pitching landing craft, the sustained roar of the cannonade sounded very reassuring, with the thunder of the old battleships' main guns offering the most comfort of all. No one could live through such a massive barrage, or so it was thought, and more than one marine wondered aloud if they would find anything other than mangled Japanese corpses on the sands of Betio.

Robert Sherrod, packed into a half-swamped Higgins boat with a squad of marines, would later write: "Once I tried to count the number of salvos—not shells, salvos—the battleships, cruisers, and destroyers were pouring on the island. A Marine who had a waterproof watch offered to count off the seconds up to one minute. Long before the minute had ended I had counted over one hundred, but then a dozen more ships opened up and I abandoned the project."

The bombardment paused again just after 8:00 a.m. to allow fighters from the escort carriers *Barnes* and *Nassau* to strafe the landing beaches. At 8:54 a.m., with the island completely concealed in smoke, Admiral Hill ordered another cease-fire to avoid hitting the marines in their landing craft. Circling high above Betio in one of the *Maryland*'s Kingfishers was Lieutenant Commander Robert MacPherson, providing Admiral Hill with frequent reports on the progress of the landings. Looking down upon the waters of Betio's lagoon, MacPherson discovered to his great horror that Major Holland's dire prediction about dodging tides had proven correct. The mean depth of the water over the reef was only about 3 feet; the Higgins boats needed at least 4 feet. MacPherson quickly alerted Admiral Hill's flag bridge, but by then it was too late. The amphtracks had already crossed the line of departure and were churning toward the beaches, with the Higgins boats not far behind.

As the initial assault waves approached the island the Japanese defenses once again sprang into life, sweeping the amphtracks with machine-gun, mortar, and artillery fire. Despite Admiral Kingman's assurances, airstrikes and shore bombardment had failed to neutralize, destroy, or obliterate Betio. The first rifle companies to reach the shore were quickly pinned down by machine guns and snipers firing from well-concealed positions and began to take heavy casualties. With their Higgins boats unable to make it over the reef, subsequent waves of marines were forced to wade ashore in waist-deep water—for hundreds of yards—into a horrible deluge of gunfire from the entrenched Japanese.

"It was painfully slow, wading in such deep water," Robert Sherrod described. "And we had seven hundred yards to walk slowly into that machine gun fire, looming into larger targets as we rose onto higher ground. I was scared, as I had never been scared before . . . I could have sworn that I could have reached out and touched a hundred bullets."

Electrician's Mate First Class Floyd Welch watched the marines struggling ashore from the decks of the *Maryland*. "Many were easy targets, and were slaughtered in withering enemy fire. Nothing could be done to help them. After what seemed an eternity, we managed to silence the skillfully hidden enemy guns ashore. By then, an enormous number of our men were floating dead in the water. This carnage imprinted itself on my mind more than anything I had witnessed during the remainder of the war."

John Henry Ashby was an eighteen-year-old seaman second class from Centertown, Kentucky, one of several newcomers who had reported aboard the *Maryland* during her recent overhaul period in Pearl Harbor. The youngster had obviously made a good first impression, for Ashby was quickly made a shell handler on the crew of the Number Three Turret. The crews that served the main batteries of battleships in World War II tended to be highly selective when taking on new members and maintained high standards of performance; any sailor unwilling or unable to function as part of the tightly knit team soon found himself peeling potatoes in the galley. The fight for Tarawa was the first of eight Pacific campaigns Ashby would experience while serving aboard Old Mary.

"Tarawa was a really terrible battle," Ashby remembered. "There were a lot of dead bodies in the water and they floated out to us. One of them was a Jap officer. Some of the boys got a hook and tried to snag him; I think they were trying to get the gun that he had on him. Then one of our officers came along and told them to knock it off."

The sight of so many marines being killed while crossing the reef proved too much for another of the *Maryland*'s Kingfisher pilots, Lieutenant (j.g.) F. C. Whaley. With the battleships now having to hold their fire, and having managed to procure a supply of hand grenades, the spirited Texan decided to provide the hard-pressed marines with some additional close air support.

"He went right down on the deck, strafing and dropping hand grenades on the Jap machine gun nests," Ashby described. "We counted over thirty bullet holes in that plane when they got back to the ship." One of those bullets passed through the Kingfisher's pontoon and lodged into the thigh of Whaley's radioman, Robert Houle.

The situation ashore had become truly precarious, to the point that Julian Smith, when asking for the Sixth Marines to be committed to the battle, ended his message with the ominous statement: "Issue in doubt." Displaying tremendous courage, small groups of marines managed to fight their way over the seawall and began destroying the Japanese positions one by one with grenades and flamethrowers. The use of these "corkscrew and blowtorch" tactics gradually expanded their tenuous toehold into a usable beachhead; infantry reinforcements and tanks were then landed, and shore control parties began directing naval gunfire onto Japanese strongholds. By 4:00 p.m. on November 21, with his Second Marines advancing steadily across Betio, Colonel David Shoup was able to report to the *Maryland*'s flag bridge: "We are winning."

In order to avoid lurking Japanese submarines, the dreadnoughts and their cohorts withdrew for the night to the waters southwest of Betio and returned to their assigned fire support sectors at first light. On the morning of November 22, the *Tennessee* received a request to deliver gunfire onto "targets of opportunity" on the eastern tip of the island. During a fire mission that lasted just over seventeen minutes, the *Tennessee* sent 70 rounds of 14-inch and 322 rounds of 5-inch ammunition into the Japanese positions.

Just before 6:00 p.m., as a fiery sunset colored the western horizon, the escorting destroyers *Meade* and *Frazier* obtained a sonar contact and began dropping depth charges. Minutes later the damaged *I-35* sprang to the surface 11,000 yards to the west of the *Tennessee*, and a half-dozen white-garbed figures were seen scrambling from the conning tower to man the doomed submarine's 5.5-inch deck cannon. The *Tennessee*'s secondary battery director quickly acquired the enemy boat and unleashed a booming volley of twenty-one rounds from her 5-inch guns. After ringing up flank speed the skipper of the *Frazier*, Lieutenant Commander Elliot Brown, raised the *Tennessee* on the Talk-Between-Ships frequency and requested that the battlewagon hold her fire. The lionhearted little *Frazier*, with two Japanese submarines already to her credit, then rammed and sank the *I-35*.

After seventy-six hours of some of the most savage combat to occur in an already brutal Pacific War, Betio was at last declared secure. The Second Marine Division had suffered an astounding 25 percent casualty rate; in all, over 1,000 Americans had been killed, with twice that many wounded. Only 17 Japanese and 129 of their Korean laborers survived to be taken prisoner. The body of Admiral Shibazaki was never found.

"Tarawa taught us the necessity for more naval gunfire and more air bombing before we undertook a landing," a very bitter Holland Smith would record in his memoirs. "What was considered by the Navy a paralyzing amount of fire was directed at Betio, in our first wedding of naval guns and airplane bombs in the reduction of a fortified atoll, but until after Tarawa we could not calculate accurately the result of this type of attack on concentrated fortifications such as the Japanese had constructed. Moreover, the Navy was inclined to exaggerate the destructive effect of gunfire, and this failing really amounted to a job imperfectly done. The Marines discovered this fact only when they tried to land. Air assistance was no better gauged than naval support, and the strikes were poorly coordinated. The planes were not there when needed. The secret of amphibious warfare is concentration of your forces and meticulous coordination of all elements, plus as much naval gunfire and air bombardment as you can pour into enemy positions."

On November 25, a transport aircraft carrying Admiral Nimitz and his entourage landed on Betio just after the Seabees had finished bulldozing debris and filling shell holes on the coral airstrip. Waiting to accompany the Commander-in-Chief of the Pacific Fleet on a tour of the devastated island were Ray Spruance and Julian Smith. Already a compassionate leader of men, the experience would leave Chester Nimitz thoroughly shaken.

Smoke drifting from hundreds of blackened pillboxes carried with it the nauseating stench of burned human flesh. Burial parties were still collecting the bodies of dead marines scattered across the blood-soaked sand or floating at the water's edge, drifting slowly with the lapping rhythm of the surf. Ragged, filthy survivors of the onslaught trudged wearily past the admiral, their eyes fixed in the hollow-eyed gaze known to veterans as "the Thousand Yard Stare."

The detritus of combat was everywhere: wrecked landing craft, burned-out tanks, tangled strands of barbed wire, battered helmets, broken weapons, ammunition cans, empty plasma bottles, cartridge belts, shell casings, and even more bodies, or parts of bodies, both American and Japanese. While nearly every tree on the island had been blasted into a splintered stump, most of the deadly fortifications the navy had promised to destroy were still intact. Rather than being pulverized by the big guns of the battleships, the Japanese defenders had to be burned or blasted from their concrete warrens by marines wielding flamethrowers and satchel charges of TNT.

When news of the Tarawa battle and its horrific number of casualties reached the home front, the American people were shocked to the core. Angry recriminations against the leadership of the US Navy and Marine Corps were made in the editorial pages of major newspapers and in the halls of Congress, and soon a wave of hate mail began to flood the mailroom of CINCPAC headquarters. "You killed my son at Tarawa," the distressed mother of a fallen marine wrote to Admiral Nimitz.

"The facts were cruel, but inescapable," Robert Sherrod would write. "Probably no amount of shelling and bombing could obviate the necessity of sending in foot soldiers to finish the job. The corollary was this: there is no easy way to win the war; there is no panacea which will prevent men from getting killed. To me it seemed that to deprecate the Tarawa victory was almost to defame the memory of the gallant men who lost their lives achieving it."

Even so, Nimitz, Spruance, Turner, and Holland Smith were all determined that the mistakes made at Tarawa would not be made again. While still en route to Hawaii aboard his flagship *Pennsylvania*, Turner had a white paper entitled "Lessons Learned at Tarawa" flown to Pearl Harbor for analysis by Nimitz and his staff. Among the many newfound truths that Turner listed was the need for targeted islands to be pounded into dust before the marines ever set foot on them, with sustained bombing and shelling from land-based heavy bombers, carrier aircraft, and warships.

Shore bombardment by battleships needed to be conducted over a period of days, not hours, Turner insisted. The now-indomitable strength of the United States Navy (which was only continuing to grow daily on a massive scale) and its ability to exercise control of the air and sea in a given battlespace was quickly making the element of surprise an unnecessary concern. The old battleships could now afford to remain on-station close to their objective for many days, receiving strong air cover from Fast Carrier Task Forces, to deliver the necessary volume of destructive firepower against enemy defenses and ensure a successful amphibious assault with fewer casualties.

Koga's anemic response to Operation Galvanic had underlined this point: While the Central Pacific Force did have to contend with an aggressive submarine threat, Japanese air forces had offered only weak and sporadic counterattacks. Despite Spruance's forebodings, the ships of the Combined Fleet had not budged from their Truk anchorage, mostly due to a lack of air cover. Stripped of its air squadrons, which had been sent south to Rabaul to replace the heavy losses being inflicted by Halsey and MacArthur's forces, the once-feared Japanese carrier fleet had become a toothless tiger.

The naval gunfire support plan for Tarawa had been drafted in keeping with the principles outlined in *Fleet Training Publication 167*, the doctrine for amphibious warfare developed by the US Navy and Marine Corps in the 1930s. The subsequent training of naval officers in accordance with this doctrine stressed Lord Nelson's famous dictum with regard to "fighting a fort," and cited the painful lessons learned by the Royal Navy during the disastrous Gallipoli landings in World War I.

"This meant that a ship could not stand within range of shore batteries and effectively engage without encountering the risk of being sunk or seriously damaged," wrote Major General Donald Weller, a Marine Corps artillery expert who would eventually serve Holland Smith as Naval Gunfire Officer, Fleet Marine Force Pacific. "The maximum that could be achieved was short-term neutralization [of enemy defenses] by ships firing at long range while maneuvering at high speeds."

This point was illustrated by the navy's failure to destroy the heavy Japanese defenses of Betio by firing from such stand-off distances. Captain Robert Haggart, for example, had ordered the *Tennessee* to open fire on Betio from 10,870 yards—a distance of over 6 miles—apparently to little effect. The 1,800-pound high explosive shells of the *Maryland* had been able to smash a concrete revetment that housed one of the 8-inch Vickers guns, but only after Captain Carl Jones ordered the distance closed to 5,000 yards.

Despite the impressive array of heavy guns the Japanese had amassed on Betio, by all indications the perceived danger posed by coastal artillery had been overstated. The only fire support vessel to be hit by Betio's shore batteries had been the *Ringgold*, and that was after her skipper, Commander Thomas Conley, ordered the *Fletcher*-class destroyer to enter the lagoon and engage the enemy at point-blank range. The kind of "good luck ship" that sailors long to serve aboard, *Ringgold* had been struck by two 5-inch shells, both of which failed to explode.

"It was now apparent that something more than neutralization of enemy defenses was required to effectively pave the way for a landing against serious opposition at the waterline," General Weller would write in a widely read treatise on the development of naval gunfire support. "Actual destruction of individual defensive installations that could bear on the ship-to-shore movement and the landing of assault troops became, as the result of this bloody operation, a requirement in future bombardment. In effect, this amounted to an entirely new concept: one of destruction as opposed to neutralization. This destruction could only be realized by medium and heavy calibers from short ranges. As a result of the Tarawa assault, all future operations in the Central Pacific were to be preceded by several days of pre-D-Day bombardment designed to ensure destruction of beach defenses."

In planning the Tarawa bombardment, Hill's staff had remained wary of the possibility of a fleet action, a concern that had been instilled by their training and study of *Fleet Training Publication 167* and reinforced by Spruance's letter of instruction. In order to conserve an adequate supply of ammunition in case the Combined Fleet sortied from Truk, they felt obligated to limit the length of the preparatory shore bombardment. Operations plans for the Marshalls campaign would take this into account, making sure that more than enough ammunition was available for use against Japanese shore defenses.

It was also discovered that the Fire Support Group had been using the *wrong type* of ammunition. When martial law was declared in the Hawaiian Islands after the attack on Pearl Harbor, the small island of Kahoʻolawe in the shadow of Maui's Haleakala volcano was acquired by the navy for use as a shore bombardment range. Upon his return from Tarawa, Nimitz had the Seabees build concrete bunkers and pillboxes on Kahoʻolawe, replicas of the ones found on Betio Island. Subsequent experiments revealed that the High Explosive ammunition of the type used by the dreadnought battleships was ineffective against these hardened targets. The thin-skinned 5-inch / 38 caliber "AA Common" shells fired by the secondary batteries of the old battlewagons, while deadly effective against troops and vehicles in the open, proved capable of penetrating only about 2 feet of concrete. Rather than saturating the target island with high explosive bombardment shells from a distance, the battleships would now move in much closer, targeting heavy fortifications for precision strikes with 2,200-pound Armor Piercing High Capacity projectiles from their main batteries. More extensive and detailed photographic reconnaissance and analysis of the objective was therefore required, in order to identify enemy strongpoints and target them for destruction.

The doctrinal changes in naval gunfire support that resulted from the Tarawa experience called for the future shore bombardment of Japanese-held islands to be conducted in three distinct phases. The preliminary bombardment, which took place for several days before the invasion, began the "softening up" process. In this phase, enemy airfields, anti-aircraft emplacements, supply and ammunition dumps, shore batteries, and fortifications were targeted for multiple strikes. These fires were also intended to kill or wound a significant portion of the enemy garrison, leaving the survivors shell-shocked and exhausted.

The pre-landing bombardment on D-Day targeted the pillboxes, machine-gun nests, rifle pits, and trenches that made up the beach defenses. At Tarawa, the delay that occurred between the lifting of the final naval bombardment and the arrival of the first wave of amphtrack-borne marines allowed the Japanese to shake off the effects of the shelling and man their weapons. Future pre-landing bombardments were meticulously timed with the launching of assault waves, a "rolling barrage" to keep the surviving enemy troops hunkered down in their prepared positions and reluctant to raise their heads to engage the landing force.

The opening of the third phase coincided with the actual landing of assault troops. The old battleships along with their accompanying cruisers and destroyers were to remain close to the landing beaches in an "on-call" posture, ready to receive requests from shore control parties for naval gunfire support. Generally speaking, these strikes were directed against enemy positions that stood in the way of the infantry's advance. Along with close air support and, once ashore, the field artillery of the landing force, naval gunfire completed a triad of fire support available for use by shore control parties.

After Tarawa, efforts were made to improve the efficiency of the shore control organization by the formation of Joint Assault Signal Companies, or JASCOs. Twelve-man JASCO detachments were assigned to both marine and army infantry battalions during amphibious operations, composed of a naval gunfire liaison officer with a five-man communications team and a marine artillery officer with a team of five forward observers. Field telephones connected the observers with the communications team, while man-portable TBX and jeep-mounted TCS radio sets linked the JASCO detachment with Combat Information Centers (CICs) aboard fire support ships at sea. The legendary Navajo Code Talkers, Native Americans who spoke an unwritten language completely unintelligible to the Japanese, served as marine radio operators in these very same JASCO units. Senior naval gunfire liaison officers—known colloquially as "No-Glows"—were also made available to infantry units at the regiment and division levels to assist with the operational planning of naval gunfire and close air support.

The next objective of the Central Pacific drive, the capture of Kwajalein Atoll in the Marshall Islands, was scheduled for late January 1944. The *Pennsylvania*, *Tennessee*, *Maryland*, and *Colorado* departed from the Gilberts in early December, bound for points east to refit and prepare for the upcoming campaign. After delivering Kelly Turner and Holland Smith to Pearl Harbor, the *Pennsylvania* would remain in Hawaiian waters to perform gunnery practice on the Kaho'olawe range, while the *Colorado*, *Maryland*, and *Tennessee* steamed for San Francisco. During the month of December 1943, scheduled maintenance and minor repairs were performed and daily Cinderella liberties were granted by section. Sailors that lived within a day's journey of the Bay Area were allowed the rare opportunity to go home for Christmas on a seventy-two-hour leave.

The *Maryland* would receive a new skipper, Captain Herbert James Ray of Milwaukee, Wisconsin. At the beginning of the war, Ray had been chief of staff to Rear Admiral Frank Rockwell, then commander of the Sixteenth Naval District at the Cavite Navy Yard in the Philippines. When Japanese bombers devastated Cavite on December 10, 1941, Ray directed the hopeless firefighting effort there before leading the evacuation of base personnel to Corregidor. Moving to Mariveles Bay at the tip of the Bataan Peninsula, Ray helped to facilitate the operations of Motor Torpedo Boat Squadron Three, one of the US Navy's few viable combat units left in the islands. It was Ray who organized the departure of Douglas MacArthur and his party by PT boat after President Roosevelt ordered the general to relocate to Australia. Ray had served MacArthur's Southwest Pacific Area as a naval advisor until January 1943, when he was recalled to Washington by Admiral King.

After spending nearly a year at Main Navy, Ray's efficiency and perseverance was rewarded with the command of the *Maryland*. He has been described as a man who "loves to have his own way, and gets just a bit peeved when anyone crosses him in his ideas, plans and assertions," and also as one who tended to display "marked skill and coolness" in the face of danger. Ray had already been awarded the Silver Star, Legion of Merit, and Army Distinguished Service Medal by the time he arrived in San Francisco on December 15, 1943, to relieve Captain Carl Jones, and he was anxious to finally have a go at the Japanese on near-even terms. His son James, an officer serving aboard the destroyer *Jarvis*, had been killed during an air attack off the shores of Guadalcanal in August 1942.

Captain Ray ordered the *Maryland* to stand out from San Francisco Bay on December 29, 1943. She was joined by the *Colorado* and Robert Haggart's *Tennessee*, now repainted with the dizzying Ocean Gray, Deck Blue, and Dull Black Measure 32/16D camouflage pattern. The three battlewagons set a course for the ship-to-shore range on San Clemente Island to prepare for the upcoming Kwajalein operation, code-named Flintlock.

"The main and secondary batteries blasted pseudo targets and the crew kept an eye on the clock, hoping that practice would be over early enough to make a dash back to San Pedro," wrote the *Tennessee*'s Lawrence Bellatti. "By the time the ship rounded the breakwater, liberty parties were decked out in blues and were ready to make the break for Pecos Street landing and their favorite spots in Long Beach and Los Angeles."

Departing San Pedro on January 13, 1944, the *Tennessee*, *Maryland*, and *Colorado* steamed for Hawaii and a rendezvous with Task Force 53 in Lahaina Roads, arriving on the morning of January 21. Anchored upon the crystal blue channel between the leeward shores of Maui and the deep purple, cloud-veiled silhouette of Lanai rising from the sea to the west, the battlewagons took on ammunition and provisions and had their fuel bunkers topped off by fleet oilers. That afternoon, Undersecretary of the Navy James Forrestal was piped aboard the *Tennessee* along with a delegation of admirals representing the various bureaus of the Navy Department. As the man in charge of procurement for the navy, Forrestal wanted to observe the upcoming Flintlock operation for himself. On January 23, 1944, the ships of Task Force 53 were once again under way and steaming west to do battle, this time bound for Kwajalein Atoll in the Marshall Islands.

Considered by the Japanese to be part of the outer ring of their Home Islands' perimeter defense, the Marshalls were among the many German possessions in the Pacific seized by the Empire of Japan during the First World War, and thereafter retained under a mandate from the League of Nations. Over the following two decades, Japanese administration of the Marshalls was conducted under a shroud of secrecy and travel to the area by foreigners severely restricted, leading the Americans to suspect that the Japanese were illegally militarizing the islands. Several intelligence operatives of Western nations wishing to reconnoiter the region—Ed Layton among them—had been frustrated in their attempts to book passage to the Marshalls by the Japanese government. Signal intelligence, and now photographic reconnaissance conducted by aircraft flying from newly acquired airfields in the Gilberts, confirmed that the Japanese had established airfields and a submarine base in Kwajalein Atoll.

Made up of ninety-seven different islands and islets, Kwajalein is the largest atoll in the world, encompassing 839 square miles. The largest of the islands was Kwajalein itself, twice the size of Betio and located at the atoll's southern end, where the Japanese had stationed five thousand army and navy troops and were constructing an airfield for medium bombers. On the northern end of the atoll were the two small islands of Roi and Namur, linked by both a natural sand spit and a concrete causeway, the home to a completed naval air station and submarine base and defended by three thousand Japanese. Severely beaten down by their attempts to defend Rabaul and the Gilberts, the Japanese naval air force had but thirty-five aircraft of various types to station at Roi-Namur, and only ten thus far at Kwajalein. Airfields were also located on the nearby atolls of Maloelap, Mili, Wotje, and Eniwetok, the last being a base of significant size with over one hundred combat aircraft.

Spruance's forces would once again be executing three near-simultaneous amphibious operations. Kelly Turner, his flag now flying from the new purpose-built amphibious command ship *Rocky Mount*, would lead the Joint Expeditionary Task Force of 297 ships, a third larger than the fleet that had conquered the Gilberts. Turner, accompanied by Holland Smith, would also command the Southern Attack Force and land the army's 7th Infantry Division on Kwajalein Island. Rear Admiral Richard L. Conolly, a veteran surface warrior who had participated in Halsey's early carrier raids and the amphibious landings at Sicily and Salerno, commanded the Northern Attack Force, landing the 4th Marine Division on Roi-Namur. Harry Hill's task group was assigned to grab the undefended Majuro Atoll, 280 miles southeast of Kwajalein, with the marines of the Amphibious Recon Battalion and a regiment of the 27th Infantry Division. The Fast Carrier Task Forces, now under the command of Vice Admiral Marc Mitscher, were tasked with dominating the skies over the Marshall Islands.

And dominate they did. Already ravaged by repeated airstrikes from planes of the Army Air Forces now based in the Gilberts, the Japanese airfields on Kwajalein, Wotje, and Maloelap were hit by over seven hundred aircraft from Mitscher's twelve aircraft carriers on January 29, 1944. Land-based Dauntlesses, B-24s, and B-25s were also busy pounding the airfields on Jaluit and Mili and keeping them out of the fight. That evening, Task Force 58's eight fast battleships, six cruisers, and their screening destroyers blasted Eniwetok, destroying the remaining Japanese planes parked along the airstrip and rendering the crushed coral runways unusable. The following morning, with enemy air opposition in the Marshall Islands nearly wiped out, the ships of the Northern and Southern Attack Forces closed in on Kwajalein.

"That's reveille, you slant-eyed sons of bitches!" A sailor shouted from the decks of the *Pennsylvania* as her first main battery salvo rocketed toward Kwajalein Island just before dawn on January 30. Over the next three days, the navy would use four times the number of aerial bombs and naval artillery shells dumped on Betio to reduce Roi, Namur, and Kwajalein to barren moonscapes. On the morning of the first day, the *Pennsylvania* would close to within 2,000 yards of shore in order to demolish a blockhouse that had been built into Kwajalein's seawall, firing armor-piercing projectiles from her 14-inch guns.

"The first one fired hit the blockhouse, penetrated the thick concrete wall, leaving a hole some three feet in diameter, and burst inside," wrote the *Pennsylvania*'s Clifton Cates. "It seemed reasonable to assume that everything and everyone inside the blockhouse had been destroyed, but for good measure one more AP was fired. That, too, burst inside the blockhouse after passing through the hole left by the other projectile!"

On the opposite end of the 60-mile-wide lagoon, the *Tennessee*, *Maryland*, and *Colorado* approached Roi and Namur at a speed of 12 knots, guided by the flickering light of multiple fires still burning on the islands, the handiwork of Mitscher's carrier pilots. At dawn the battlewagons catapulted their Kingfishers, and at 6:50 a.m. the crew of the *Tennessee*'s main battery, having already been at General Quarters for two and a half hours, received the order to commence fire on a blockhouse located on the sand spit between the two islands.

For hours the three old battleships, the cruisers *Mobile* and *Louisville*, and their destroyers relentlessly pounded the two islands, stopping occasionally to allow the swooping dive-bombers of Task Force 58 to deliver their deadly payloads. Roi and Namur were not as heavily fortified as Betio had been, and the few Japanese guns that offered sporadic counter-battery or antiaircraft fire were quickly silenced. Dick Conolly, however, was taking no chances. Like Spruance, Turner, and Smith, the admiral was fearful of another "Bloody Tarawa." Broadcasting on the TBS frequency from the bridge of the new command ship *Appalachian*, he encouraged the ships of his task force to inch ever closer to the conjoined islands—close enough to use their 40mm guns under director control—endearing him to the 4th Marine Division and earning the nickname "Close-In Conolly."

"The navigator told the captain of mine fields, and warned that we shouldn't go in closer," recalled Gunner's Mate First Class Charles Peay of the *Maryland*. "The captain said *take her in!* We went in to 1,000 yards. Small arms fire began ricocheting off our bulkheads and [the] superstructure of the ship."

Around midday the battleships withdrew from the fire support area to recover their seaplanes, while coffee and sandwiches were hustled from the galley to the sailors still at their battle stations. Once the Kingfishers were refueled and aloft, the warships continued their bombardment until 5:00 p.m., when they finally retired for the night.

"Weary crew members, begrimed with sweat, grease and powder crawled from battle stations and lined up for supper," Lawrence Bellatti described. "There was a rush for the showers and into the sack, as GQ would come early when the bombardment was resumed."

With so many ships operating in the Kwajalein lagoon, the volume of fire and the inherently flat trajectory of naval gunfire made for some harrowing moments over the next two days. On at least two occasions, while the *Maryland* and *Tennessee* were operating on opposite sides of Roi-Namur, heavy-caliber shells skipped off the island like flat stones off a pond and ricocheted wildly into the roadstead.

"I remember those strange sounds going by us," Photographer's Mate First Class William Chase of the *Maryland* recorded in his memoirs. "*Whomp whomp*. Several times. I was on the open bridge photographing the action when I heard a radio transmission telling the *Tennessee* to cease firing, as her armor piercing shells were actually ricocheting off the island and going off all around us."

"Shells that looked like freight cars" exploded 500 yards off the *Tennessee*'s port quarter, while another barely missed the battleship's starboard bow. The fantail of the heavy cruiser *Louisville* was peppered with nineteen shell fragments from another near-miss but fortunately there were no casualties.

"It was learned later that the fire was coming from the USS *Maryland*," Lawrence Bellatti wrote. "A request to change the line of fire disposed of any more unpleasant near misses."

After nearly seventy-two hours of intense aerial and naval bombardment, the distinct features of the three target islands were barely visible from the decks of the battlewagons. Billowing columns of smoke from blasted fuel and ammunition dumps rose into the pale sky. From the air the islands appeared to be scrubbed bare, nearly denuded of all vegetation.

"The island is a mass of thick black smoke," one of the *Tennessee*'s Kingfisher pilots radioed to his ship's CIC while surveying Roi-Namur. "Can't see how any living thing can be left on the island."

Under covering fire from the *Pennsylvania*, combat swimmers from Underwater Demolition Team One determined the depth of Kwajalein's reef, checked for underwater obstacles, marked routes for the amphtracks, and plotted the positions of Japanese fortifications. Drawn from members of the Seabees' Naval Combat Demolition Units under the direction of Admiral Turner, the Marshalls campaign would be the first deployment in the Pacific War for these daring forerunners of the modern-day Navy SEALs. Nine small islets close to Roi-Namur and Kwajalein Island were quickly seized and field artillery was emplaced to cover the landings, which took place at first light on February 1, 1944.

On Roi-Namur, the marines went ashore standing up. With the fortifications covering the landing beaches on Kwajalein Island likewise obliterated, the soldiers of the 7th Infantry Division also landed to light resistance. One soldier would state that Kwajalein "looked as if it had been lifted up to 20,000 feet and then dropped." Though it would take some sharp fighting to root the remaining Japanese from their hideouts, Major General Harry Schmidt of the 4th Marine Division was able to declare Roi-Namur secure by D-Day-Plus-Two. On the afternoon of February 4, 1944, Kelly Turner announced over the TBS frequency: "Commander Task Force 52 has the pleasure to announce that our troops of the 7th Army Division completed capture of Kwajalein Island at 1525 today." American casualties had been a third of those suffered at Tarawa, while the Japanese that survived the pre-invasion bombardment, bound by their warrior code of *bushido*, once again fought to the death. Of the 8,000 defenders of Kwajalein Atoll, only 253 would be taken prisoner.

Chief Petty Officer William Francis McGraw was a thirty-year navy man who had reported aboard the *Maryland* in April 1942. Like everyone serving aboard the old dreadnoughts, the gun captain of the Number Three Turret was dedicated to the task of providing effective fire support for the marines landing on Roi-Namur and avoiding another hellish bloodbath like Tarawa. With the turret operating under local control, McGraw made sure that every bunker and pillbox that came before his guns received his full attention and went down in a cloud of flaming smoke and concrete dust. After the island was declared secure, the old salt asked for permission to take one of the *Maryland*'s boats ashore. He wanted to survey the results of the work for himself.

Peering into the smoking, crumbled ruins of several Japanese fortifications, the chief was satisfied that he and his gunners had done their job well, and had saved the lives of countless young marines. Turning to a friend, and with an audible tremor in his voice, the fifty-two-year-old sailor remarked, "If I die tomorrow, I'll die happy."

They found Chief McGraw in his bunk aboard the *Maryland* early the next morning, after he had failed to rise for reveille. Evidently he died a happy man.

CHAPTER 18

CATCHPOLE, HAILSTONE, AND FORAGER

"WITH A NAVY MUCH SUPERIOR TO THAT OF THE ENEMY, AFTER ALLOWance made for the length of the line of operations which has to be secured, it is permissible to strike at once for the coveted objective; the sooner the better."

This pearl of wisdom from Alfred Thayer Mahan, first issued in the lecture halls of the Naval War College near the turn of the twentieth century, must have seemed truly prophetic to the principal strategists of the Central Pacific Campaign in early February 1944. For Chester Nimitz, Ray Spruance, Kelly Turner, and Holland Smith, the ability to sustain the forward momentum of their offensive was of critical importance. In order to keep the enemy off balance, they needed to exploit the shining success of the Kwajalein operation and move on to their next objective quickly—the sooner the better—before it could be significantly reinforced and fortified.

Consisting of some forty-odd islands and a vast lagoon capable of accommodating over five hundred ships, Eniwetok Atoll was expected to provide an excellent forward operating base and fleet anchorage for future operations aimed at capturing Japanese possessions in the Marianas. Even before his task forces sortied for Operation Flintlock, Spruance had approached Nimitz with the idea of taking Eniwetok as soon as possible after Kwajalein was secured. On February 3, with nothing but good news flowing in from the Battle of Kwajalein, Nimitz radioed Spruance to ask if an early start to the Eniwetok operation was still in the cards. Spruance, Turner, and Smith all agreed that it was. Two fresh rifle regiments, the 22nd Marines and the army's 106th Infantry, had been held in floating reserve and were not utilized for the Kwajalein operation. A navy salvage diver, inspecting a sunken Japanese ship in the Kwajalein lagoon, had recovered a treasure trove of top-secret navigational charts of the mandate islands, including Eniwetok and Truk, which would help expedite planning.

The Japanese had been using Eniwetok only as a stopover point during their travels, much like the Micronesian sailors who first visited around 1000 BC and gave the atoll its name, which means "the land between sunrise and sunset." Another grouping of tiny coral islands in the Marshalls chain acquired by the Japanese under their South Seas Mandate, Eniwetok was home to a lonely airstrip built for the purpose of refueling aircraft flying between Truk and the Gilberts. That is, until the Americans seized the Gilberts, at which time the Imperial Japanese Army rushed 2,500 garrison troops from Manchuria to Eniwetok along with additional aviation personnel to begin fortifying the atoll and expanding the airfield's capabilities.

The massive four-engined Coronado flying boat assigned to the headquarters of Commander-in-Chief Pacific Fleet touched down in the turquoise waters of Kwajalein's lagoon around midday on February 6. After surveying the destruction wrought by the fire support ships and carrier planes, Nimitz met with his commanders to discuss the plans for the Eniwetok operation, code-named Catchpole. Harry Hill had been tapped to lead the invasion force, landing assault troops on the three main islands of Engebi, Eniwetok, and Parry. The *Pennsylvania*, *Tennessee*, and *Colorado* would once again be tasked with providing naval gunfire support. The *Maryland*, however, would be heading home.

The "Fighting Mary," as her crew now called her, remained in Kwajalein lagoon for nearly two weeks after the battle, acting in the capacity of a floating gas station and general store, distributing provisions, freshwater, clothing, canteen supplies, ammunition, and fuel oil to ships of the fleet that were remaining behind in the combat zone. Now flying Admiral Conolly's flag, *Maryland* weighed anchor on the afternoon of February 17 and steamed for Pearl Harbor, arriving on the morning of February 24 and tying up to quay Fox Three, where the *California* had been moored on December 7, 1941.

The following afternoon she was under way once again, screened by the destroyers *Helm* and *Mugford*. Rounding the lighthouse at Makapu'u Point, the *Maryland* settled into a standard cruising speed of 17 knots and steered a course for Bremerton, Washington, and the Puget Sound Navy Yard, where she would remain until May 5, 1944. Along with an overhaul of her engineering plant and the bolstering of her radar and antiaircraft suite, the *Maryland* would finally receive her aft superstructure tower with an additional main battery fire control director, and forever lose her cut-down mainmast.

The *Pennsylvania*, *Tennessee*, and *Colorado* had already stood out from Kwajalein on February 6, bound for the newly captured Majuro Atoll and a rendezvous with the ammunition ship *Mauna Loa*. On the afternoon of February 9, the *Mauna Loa* tied up alongside the *Pennsylvania* in the Majuro lagoon and began transferring over one hundred containers of smokeless gunpowder to the battleship's forecastle. Before the containers could be struck below to the ship's magazines, one of them suddenly exploded and caught fire. An alert boatswain's mate aboard the *Mauna Loa* quickly turned a fire hose onto the flames and prevented the other containers from exploding, while *Pennsylvania* sailors shoved the remains of the burning powder can overboard.

Three members of the *Pennsylvania*'s crew were seriously hurt in the event, but what happened two days later would be even worse. Another of the powder cans exploded while it was being manhandled through the doorway of the Number One Turret's ready service magazine. Four sailors were killed and seven others injured in the blast, which by some miracle did not detonate the remainder of the magazine's powder stores. Convinced that the ammunition ship had been loaded with a bad batch of unstable gunpowder, Captain Corn ordered the entire lot to be discarded.

"With the necessity after each of the powder explosions of condemning all of that lot of powder already received on board and of transferring it off the ship and then receiving another load, it looked very much as though the *Pennsylvania* would not complete loading ammunition in time to take part in the next operation," Clifton Cates wrote. "But, by the afternoon of the twelfth, after more than seventy-nine hours of almost continuous work, the job was finished." Forty-five minutes later, with her frustrated and downcast crew now spoiling for a fight, the *Pennsylvania* got under way for Kwajalein and a rendezvous with Task Force 51.

To ensure the safety of the Eniwetok invasion force, Admiral Spruance ordered an intensive aerial bombardment of the huge Japanese naval base at Truk by Mitscher's Fast Carrier Task Forces to begin on February 16, an operation aptly named Hailstone. Knowing that he could do little to stop Mitscher, Mineichi Koga had already ordered an evacuation of major fleet units from Truk to bases in the nearby Palaus. Helldiver and Avenger pilots from the *Enterprise*, *Essex*, *Bunker Hill*, and the new *Yorktown* still managed to catch ten Japanese warships and over thirty auxiliary and merchant vessels in the open, quickly transforming Truk lagoon into a world-class shipwreck exploration venue for future generations of scuba diving enthusiasts.

Upon hearing that Japanese ships were attempting to escape through Truk's northern passage, Admiral Spruance, flying his flag from the new fast battleship *New Jersey*, personally assumed tactical command of Task Force 50.9 and led the battleship *Iowa*, the heavy cruisers *Minneapolis* and *New Orleans*, and four destroyers on a counterclockwise sweep around Truk Atoll. The indulgence caused some furrowed brows and shaking heads among the admiral's staff as well as the brown shoe clan, especially after a stern radio announcement was issued for the carrier pilots to back off and let Spruance's battle line close with the enemy.

The normally prudent and decorous Ray Spruance, whose promotion to four-star rank had been confirmed by the Senate that very morning, was not about to let the opportunity to command battleships and cruisers in a daylight surface action slip away. It was, after all, an event for which he had trained his entire adult life. The big guns of Task Force 50.9 made short work of the fleeing Japanese ships, picking off the light cruiser *Katori*, the destroyer *Maikaze*, a minesweeper and an armed merchant vessel as they emerged from Truk lagoon. The *Nowaki*, the same destroyer that had rescued Nagumo from his burning flagship at Midway, somehow managed to escape.

Along with wreaking havoc in the anchorage, the American carrier-based planes pummeled Truk's airfields and destroyed some 250 Japanese aircraft on the ground and in the air. Unlike Nagumo's pilots at Pearl

Harbor, Mitscher's fliers did not ignore Truk's shore establishment, and set ablaze over 5 million gallons of the Combined Fleet's precious fuel oil. After two days of airstrikes, which sank 200,000 tons of shipping and killed nearly 4,500 Japanese, the so-called "Gibraltar of the Pacific" was a shattered mess covered by a dense pall of black smoke.

The ships of Harry Hill's Catchpole task force were then able to go about their deadly business free from the worry of Japanese air attacks. Just after 9:00 a.m. on February 17, 1944, the *Pennsylvania* and *Tennessee* steamed through the Deep Entrance of Eniwetok lagoon, with the *Pennsy*'s 20- and 40-millimeter guns blazing away at the Japanese-held islands on either side. Led by minesweepers and accompanied by the destroyers *McCord* and *Heermann*, the two battlewagons launched their spotter planes and moved into their firing positions just off the shores of Engebi, the location of Eniwetok's airfield.

At 11:25 a.m. the main batteries of the *Pennsylvania* and *Tennessee* opened fire with a thunderous roar, the beginning of an intense shore bombardment that would continue for the next eight hours. Late in the afternoon the main and secondary batteries of the battleships provided covering fire for the boats of UDT One as the frogmen slid into the shallow water and marked coral heads along the reef. As at Kwajalein, small undefended islets near the objectives were seized for the placement of Marine Corps field artillery to aid in the pre-landing bombardment. The battleships finally ceased fire at 7:00 p.m. and anchored in Eniwetok lagoon for the night. When dawn broke over the atoll at 6:55 a.m., they closed to within 4,900 yards and resumed their systematic pounding of Engebi.

"Coconut logs, immense chunks of concrete fortifications and Japanese soldiers were tossed high in the air," Lawrence Bellatti reported, as witnessed from the decks of *Tennessee*. "Great clouds of smoke and dust furnished a perfect screen for the invasion forces. Dive bombers swarmed over the scene."

Two hours later the first and second battalions of the 22nd Marines stormed ashore to feeble resistance, and by 3:00 p.m., Engebi was declared secure. At the same time the Engebi landings occurred, two battalions from the 106th Infantry assaulted Eniwetok Island itself. Eniwetok would prove to be a tougher nut to crack; though the island's eight hundred defenders did not have enough time to complete their fortifications, dense jungle undergrowth and numerous camouflaged one-man fighting positions—dubbed "spider holes" by the soldiers and marines—slowed the advance. Eniwetok was finally taken on February 21.

Japanese documents found on Eniwetok Island contradicted earlier intelligence estimates. While Parry was first thought to be a seaplane base where a handful of naval aviation personnel were stationed, it turned out that the 2-mile-long island was the actual location of the Japanese headquarters for the atoll, and more heavily defended than either Engebi or Eniwetok. On February 22 the *Pennsylvania* and *Tennessee* along with the cruisers *Indianapolis* and *Louisville* clobbered the island with nearly 1,000 tons of explosives, while marine artillery batteries stationed on nearby islets threw in 245 more. One of the *Pennsylvania*'s spotter pilots reported that "the Japanese on Parry Island appeared to have become hysterical and were running frantically up and down the trail on Eastern Beach, into the bushes and out into the water during the bombardment."

As the landing force assembled for the assault, one of the many LCI (Landing Craft, Infantry) in the lagoon received a direct hit from a Japanese 5-inch shell and exploded, "throwing smoke and debris over a wide area of the churning water." *LCI(G)-440* had been carrying a party of forward observers, including a handful of officers from the *Colorado*. The helmsman then steered his stricken craft toward the nearest large ship, which happened to be the *Pennsylvania*. "When the LCI came along the starboard quarter of the battleship, her decks were literally running with blood," Clifton Cates wrote.

The *Pennsylvania*'s guns continued to blast Parry Island even as the casualties were brought aboard and hustled below to sick bay. After receiving emergency treatment from the *Pennsylvania*'s doctors and corpsmen, the wounded were then transferred by landing craft to the hospital ship *Solace*.

The first amphtracks rattled ashore just before noon, and after six hours of vicious fighting, Parry was in the hands of the 22nd Marines. "Finally we killed them all," a marine platoon commander wrote in a dispatch published by the *Atlantic Monthly*. "There was not much jubilation."

Nearly nine hundred Americans had been wounded and three hundred killed in the taking of Eniwetok Atoll, while nearly ten times that number of Japanese perished in trying to defend it. Examinations of captured communiqués and interrogations of the very few Japanese survivors revealed that the commander of the Imperial Army forces on Eniwetok, Major General Yoshimi Nishida, had challenged his men to "die gloriously for the Emperor." Even the wounded had been ordered to commit suicide rather than be captured alive.

"The capture and consolidation of Kwajalein, Majuro, and Eniwetok, together with the successful fleet operations against Truk and the Marianas, have created changes in the strategic situation which permits advancing the timing of operations contemplated by the Granite plan," Nimitz wrote in a letter to King in early March. The next phase of the plan was Operation Roadmaker, which called for the seizure of Truk itself.

Admiral King was now adamantly opposed to the move. Even after the thorough pasting Truk had received from the Fast Carrier Task Forces during Hailstone, the base was still heavily manned and fortified. The seizure of Truk would require a significant expenditure of American lives when, like Rabaul, it could be easily bypassed and isolated, and its garrison left to starve. The rest of the Joint Chiefs agreed, and on March 12 Nimitz received orders to skip Roadmaker and proceed to the next operation on the list, Forager, the capture of Saipan, Tinian, and Guam in the lower Marianas. Advanced bases established on these islands would bring mainland Japan within range of Army Air Forces B-29s; support further advances into the Philippines, Formosa, or China; and allow the Americans to cut Japan's lifeline to the oil fields of the East Indies. The beginning phase of Operation Forager, the conquest of Saipan, was set for June 1944.

While legions of Seabees, army engineers, and garrison troops were busily unloading the heavy equipment, construction materials, and supplies needed to transform Eniwetok into a major air and fleet base, the *Tennessee*, *Pennsylvania*, and *Colorado* weighed anchor and steamed for Majuro and a rendezvous with the ships of Service Squadron 10. On the first of March, fully stocked with provisions, fuel oil, and ammunition, *Tennessee* and *Pennsylvania* stood out from Majuro along with the *New Mexico*, *Mississippi*, *Idaho*, and a half-dozen destroyers for the New Hebrides. A week later, after performing tactical exercises near the Gilbert Islands, the battleships arrived in Havannah Harbor, Efate, having passed south of the equator and into the operational control of Admiral Halsey's South Pacific Area.

On March 15 the *Tennessee* sortied from Efate as the flagship of Task Force 37 under the command of Rear Admiral Robert Griffin, along with the *New Mexico*, *Mississippi*, *Idaho*, two escort carriers, and fifteen destroyers. Their objective was the bombardment of the Japanese naval base at Kavieng on the island of New Ireland, while MacArthur's forces made an unopposed landing on nearby Emirau, one of the final strategic movements in the effort to encircle and isolate Rabaul.

Long overdue for a rest, the crew of the *Pennsylvania* would sit the mission out. The *Pennsy* would spend the remainder of March and most of April in Havannah Harbor, where there was little recreation other than the daily "swim call" and the sipping of canned beer on a designated liberty beach. On April 23, the crew would don their dress whites and stand for a change-of-command ceremony. Captain William Corn was relieved by Captain Charles Martin of Augusta, Georgia, a former battleship officer who had also commanded submarines. Martin was known as a congenial Southern gentleman who, like Charles Cooke before him, had also been nicknamed "Savvy" by his fellow officers.

"Shortly before this time scuttlebutt had begun to circulate that the ship would make a visit to Sydney, Australia, and for once the scuttlebutt was right," Clifton Cates wrote. Along with the *New Mexico* and *Idaho*, the *Pennsylvania* stood into Sydney harbor on April 29, 1944.

"To their crews, Sydney turned out to be just about what Paris was to our troops in France during World War I," Cates continued. "The sailors had a little difficulty in dealing in pounds and shillings and in understanding certain Aussie expressions, but they had no difficulty at all with the girls. The *Pennsylvania* gave two dances, one for each watch, at the Sydney Town Hall. Half the female population of the city must have been present." A week later and none the worse for wear, the crew of the

Pennsylvania would bid a reluctant farewell to the women of Sydney and depart for Efate. They would spend most of May 1944 steaming through the hallowed waters that surrounded Guadalcanal, performing gunnery practice and participating in a series of amphibious exercises at Cape Esperance, the dress rehearsals for the upcoming Operation Forager. On June 2, 1944, the *Pennsylvania* got under way for Kwajalein to join Kelly Turner's Joint Expeditionary Task Force.

The *Tennessee*, in the meantime, set sail for Pearl Harbor after completing her bombardment mission to New Ireland, where she fired 252 rounds of 14-inch and 1,891 rounds of 5-inch ammunition into the Japanese installations. As she cruised north by northeast and withdrew from the South Pacific Area, the *Tennessee*'s radio room received a short message from Admiral Halsey, which Captain Haggart read to the crew over the ship's 1MC: "Congratulations on your effective plastering of Kavieng."

The deep green mountains of Oahu finally hove into sight on the morning of April 16, 1944. Her battle ensign fluttering in the trade winds and crew manning the rails, the *Tennessee* passed through the Pearl Harbor channel to once again make berth along Battleship Row. The ship's liberty boats began their hourly runs to Merry Point, and Captain Robert Haggart said his good-byes. Going ashore for the final time was the skipper who had overseen the *Tennessee*'s extensive modernization, transformed a herd of unfledged landlubbers into a well-drilled crew of seafaring professionals, and led them through a string of combat actions stretching from Alaska to the Solomons. Haggart was to report to San Diego and assume command of the Naval Training Center, a post he would occupy until he retired in 1948 at the rank of commodore. Haggart was replaced by Captain Andrew de Graff Mayer of Maple Lake, Minnesota. A graduate of the Annapolis class of 1916 and classmate of the *Nevada*'s Willard Kitts, Mayer had served as a battleship gunnery officer and commander of Minesweeping Division One of the Pacific Fleet.

On the afternoon of April 29, the *Tennessee* was guided through the caisson of Dry Dock Number Two. She would spend the next week perched upon keel blocks having her hull scraped free of rust and barnacles and repainted while her four huge bronze propellers were removed and re-coned by the Navy Yard. On May 7, the battleship was reported as "in all respects ready for sea," and the following day she began three weeks of tactical maneuvers in Hawaiian waters, engaging in live antiaircraft firing practice and training exercises with Underwater Demolition Teams. On the final day of May 1944, the *Tennessee* stood out from Pearl Harbor as the flagship of Task Group 52.17 on a course for Kwajalein. Following behind in Cruising Disposition 5-RB, making 16 knots from her turboelectric engines and with a wave of white foam cresting alongside her clipper bow, was the *Tennessee*'s sister ship, *California.*

As the two battleships steamed together in formation, it was difficult to tell them apart. The repair and modernization of the Prune Barge had taken the Puget Sound Navy Yard a full fifteen months, during which time her main battery turrets were removed and the entire superstructure razed down to the level of the second deck. Bristling with radar antennae, the new superstructure was almost identical to that of the *Tennessee,* including the *Brooklyn*-class cruiser conning tower, the placement of the Mark 34 main battery fire control directors, the single funnel, and the after stump tower. New blistering widened the beam to provide greater stability and torpedo protection.

The main battery was then reinstalled, and 3 extra inches of STS covered the magazines, while 2 inches were added to protect the remainder of the ship's vitals. Sixteen 5-inch / 38 caliber guns in eight armored turrets had been added, and eleven quadruple-mounted and six twin-mounted 40-millimeter Bofors provided antiaircraft protection along with forty-three 20-millimeter Oerlikons. Like the *Tennessee,* the *California*'s hull and upper works were painted in dazzle camouflage, and her crew roster was the exact same length as that of her sister, at 114 officers and 2,129 enlisted men.

Back in January the *California* had set forth from Elliott Bay, Washington, to begin sea trials, with Captain Henry "Bobby" Burnett of Shelbyville, Kentucky, in command. Burnett had come aboard the previous November, just as the finishing touches to the refit were being applied in the Navy Yard. A Class of 1915 alumnus, Burnett wore the gold dolphins of a submariner on his chest, his first seagoing command being an *O*-class boat during the early 1920s. He had also served as a destroyerman and had skippered the USS *Wickes,* one of the elderly "four pipers" handed off to the Royal Navy in the destroyers-for-bases deal between the United States and Great Britain in 1940.

The *California* had spent the blustery late winter and spring of 1944 in coastal waters performing engineering economy trials, where fuel consumption rates were correlated with the horsepower delivered to her propeller shafts, along with standardization tests and turning trials under the watchful eyes of officers from the Bureau of Inspection and Survey. This was followed by a rigorous twelve-week shakedown training period using the port of San Pedro as a base. Many hundreds of 14-inch and 5-inch shells were expended in gunnery exercises in and around the island of San Clemente, which included radar-controlled and local-controlled firings, night exercises using star shell illumination, and shore bombardment.

Thousands of 20- and 40-millimeter shells were fired at towed target sleeves and radio-controlled drones acted as stand-ins for Japanese dive-bombers and torpedo planes. Radar and radio operators performed communication and coordination exercises with naval aircraft, vectoring fighter pilots to intercept simulated flights of inbound hostile aircraft. That the *California* could be hit by enemy fire was accepted as a likely and sobering possibility, and drills on the grim but necessary topics of firefighting, triage, and first aid were conducted almost daily. When under way on the open sea in wartime battleships could not stop for replenishment or to evacuate casualties, so the sailors of the deck division practiced rigging for underway refueling from fleet oilers and for the passing of litter patients, supplies, and mail between ships.

While the *California*'s crew was being put through their paces, destroyers patrolled nearby like vigilant sheepdogs, watching and listening for the presence of prowling Japanese submarines. A frequent companion of the *California* during her shakedown training was the *Cassin Young*, a new *Fletcher*-class destroyer named for the late hero of Pearl Harbor. In early May, after being away from the fleet for over a year and a half, the *California* stood out of San Francisco Bay and set a course for the Hawaiian Islands to take part in Operation Forager.

The flag officer who would command the dreadnoughts of Pearl Harbor throughout the campaign to seize the Marianas, and then later during the bloody assault on Peleliu and at the epic Battle of Leyte Gulf, was Rear Admiral Jesse Barrett Oldendorf.

Oldendorf had been born and raised along with his two sisters in his parents' farmhouse amid the rolling citrus groves of Riverside, California. Jesse's grandfather had emigrated from Hesse-Darmstadt in Germany and began farming in Illinois sometime during the 1850s. In the 1880s Jesse's father had made his way west and had likewise become a farmer, and Jesse probably would have become a farmer as well had he not been accepted for entry into the United States Naval Academy in the autumn of 1905.

His classmates called him "Oley" for short, remembering the baby-faced midshipman as "a confirmed fusser," or a ladies' man who cut a fine figure in uniform and was apparently well-liked by his peers. After graduating in 1909, Oldendorf would spend the first decade of a colorful career serving aboard a mixed bag of different ship types, including the armored cruiser *California*, the cruiser *Denver*, and the destroyer *Whipple*. In May 1918 Oldendorf was the gunnery officer aboard the troopship *President Lincoln* when it was torpedoed and sunk by a German U-boat off the coast of Ireland, and with a dozen other survivors spent several hours huddled in a drifting lifeboat until rescued by a destroyer. Like Chester Nimitz, Oldendorf's first command would be one of the five vessels named for the naval hero Stephen Decatur, this particular ship being a destroyer of the *Clemson* class launched in 1921.

Professionally speaking, Oldendorf's forte was mathematics and the science of celestial navigation. By the 1930s he was widely regarded by his fellow officers as something of a guru when it came to this most essential of nautical disciplines. He was so good at it, in fact, that he would twice be called to serve as a professor of navigation—at the Naval Academy, and later, at the Naval War College—between tours of sea duty.

In October 1939, after a stint as executive officer of the battleship *West Virginia*, Oldendorf assumed command of the heavy cruiser *Houston*, a proud ship for which Franklin Roosevelt held a special affection and used as his official conveyance on four separate occasions. Captain

Oldendorf would skipper the *Houston* until September 1941 before leaving to serve on the staff of the Naval War College; six months later the *Houston* would be sunk in the Battle of Sunda Strait, and less than a third of Oldendorf's former shipmates would survive.

Oldendorf's time in Newport would be brief, for he had made Secretary Knox's secret list of the forty most competent officers in the navy, and in March 1942 was promoted to rear admiral and assigned to the Caribbean Sea Frontier. By early 1944, Oldendorf had managed to make it to the Central Pacific where all the action was taking place and was given command of the cruiser division of "Close-in" Conolly's Task Force 53 just in time to participate in the Kwajalein operation. For his flagship Oldendorf selected the *Louisville*, a sister of the *Houston*.

At fifty-seven years of age Oldendorf was stocky, broad-shouldered, silver-haired, and no longer smooth-cheeked. He now possessed the rugged, weather-beaten, and distinctly working-class face of a man one might expect to see presiding over a meeting of union pipefitters or sitting behind the front desk of a busy precinct house. As a flag officer, Oldendorf was straightforward and pragmatic, and his approach to operations and planning would be that of the mathematician: coldly realistic, calculated, and precise. This methodology would fail Oldendorf in the first of two battles for which he is famous, Peleliu, where certain intangibles, such as the cunning and tenacity of the enemy, were not included in his calculus. It would serve him well for the second, Surigao Strait, where a complex scheme of maneuver on an exacting timetable was brilliantly executed.

It was June 10, 1944. Wearing a set of faded working khakis, his eyes shaded by the long bill of an olive drab fatigue cap, Admiral Oldendorf stepped onto the bridge wing of the *Louisville* and gazed to the southeast. Spread across the deep blue waters between the wake of his flagship and the fading smudge of Kwajalein on the horizon, an impressive array of camouflage-painted warships cruised on a zigzag course, west by northwest at 15 knots, rising and falling gently upon the morning swells. The formation of battleships, cruisers, and destroyers belonged to Oldendorf's Task Group 52.17, listed on the plans for Operation Forager as Fire Support Group One.

Along with the *Louisville*, Oldendorf's task group was made up of the battleships *Tennessee*, *California*, *Maryland*, and *Colorado*, the heavy cruiser *Indianapolis*, and the light cruisers *Birmingham*, *Portland*, *Montpelier*, and *Cleveland*. The heavy ships were being screened by sixteen destroyers, all but one of the fast and functional *Fletcher* class that had become the workhorses of the fleet. Oldendorf's force was accompanied by Rear Admiral Walden Ainsworth's Task Group 52.10, with the *Pennsylvania* serving as flagship, along with the *Idaho*, *New Mexico*, six cruisers, and nine destroyers. Above the sustained roar of all that steel colliding with salt water could be heard the steady thrumming of 1,200-horsepower aircraft engines, coming from Wildcat fighters of the escort carriers *Gambier Bay* and *Kitkun Bay* as they provided air cover for the invasion fleet.

Unlike the tiny spits of coral in the Gilberts and Marshalls, the southern Marianas were much larger and more densely populated. A Japanese colony since 1914 and the first objective of Operation Forager, Saipan is 12 miles long and 5.5 miles wide, standing at just over 1,450 miles from Tokyo. For the first time in the Pacific War, the Americans would have to contend with a large enemy civilian population; in 1944 the island was home to nearly thirty thousand Japanese immigrants, with a like number of military personnel stationed there. The invasion of the southern Marianas would be the most ambitious undertaking yet attempted by American forces in the Pacific, and once again the OBBs would have the job of softening up Japanese defenses prior to the landings.

In the darkness before the dawn of June 14, 1944, 10 miles north of Saipan's Marpi Point, the ships of Oldendorf's first bombardment unit formed a single column and steamed a southwesterly course toward their designated fire support area. Leading the formation was the veteran *Tennessee*, followed by the *Birmingham* and *California*. Nerves were a bit on edge for the novice crew of the Prune Barge, even as well-drilled as they were. Following a directive from the ship's chief surgeon, the *California*'s officers and bluejackets were all showered, shaved, and wearing fresh uniforms, a measure intended to help prevent the infection of wounds. There had been little of the usual morning horseplay and joshing among the young sailors as they queued up for breakfast, and when the eastern sky finally began to lighten to reveal an overcast sky and calm sea, the call to General Quarters shattered an eerie silence that had settled over the ship.

"The planes were launched as the horizon became discernible at the first light of dawn," Captain Andrew Mayer of the *Tennessee* would write. The *California* also launched a pair of Kingfishers, and just before 6:00 a.m. both battleships opened fire on the west coast of Saipan with their main batteries from 15,000 yards. Most of the shore bombardment was concentrated against Japanese trenches and fortifications on the beaches south of Saipan's main village of Garapan, where the leathernecks of the Second and Fourth Marine Divisions were to land the following morning, as well as the enemy airstrip situated near Afetna Point.

Steaming on a track north to south at 15 knots, the ships made multiple simultaneous turns, reversing course, gradually closing the distance to Saipan's reef and firing continually as they went. The huge shells ripped through the air in great arcs over a unit of minesweepers that were motoring slowly along the coral shelf to clear a path for the marines, after reporting to Admiral Oldendorf that a swath of ocean extending 2 miles out from Saipan's reef was free of enemy mines. From over the horizon came the *Indianapolis*, with Admiral Spruance's new four-star flag flapping from her foremast in the morning breeze. Sliding into the column between the *Tennessee* and *Birmingham*, the cruiser added to the already deafening rumble of the bombardment with the heavy report of her 8-inch guns.

The beaches of Saipan were soon obscured by low-lying clouds of dust and the smoke of bursting shells and blazing shore installations. Near the village of Chalan Kanoa just inland from the designated landing beaches, a column of black smoke rose high in the air from a burning sugarcane refinery, and bursts of flak began to dot the sky around the circling Kingfishers. One of the *California*'s pilots spotted the antiaircraft battery at the edge of the Afetna airstrip, and just moments later it was taken under fire and destroyed by the battleship's 14-inch guns.

A Japanese shore battery situated near Garapan then challenged the *California*, only to be quickly silenced by another deadly salvo from her main battery. Two hours into the bombardment, the rubber boats of three Underwater Demolition Teams were launched from high-speed destroyer transports and closed upon the reef, while the battleships laid down suppressive fire with their secondary batteries.

"At this time the ship was sufficiently close to the city of Garapan to distinguish buildings," Captain Burnett of the *California* wrote in his after-action report. "Heavy clouds of smoke hung over the beach, oil storage tanks were burning fiercely and this ship and others north and south of us continuously firing at enemy installations at and near the water's edge."

"The enemy, however, began to unlimber their shore batteries," the *Tennessee*'s Lawrence Bellatti wrote. "Japanese shells dropped in the immediate vicinity of the *Birmingham* and *Indianapolis*. Machine guns, set up in beached Japanese small boats, raked the demolition team and for a while it was impossible to watch the proceedings on the beach due to smoke. Heavy mortar fire from the beach endangered the courageous demolition team making reconnaissance under the very guns of the enemy. The *Tennessee* dropped a smoke screen about 100 yards inland to screen the activities of the team from the enemy. The battery which had been harassing the team near the reef was located by *Tennessee* observers and a barrage from the 'Big T' destroyed the battery, throwing dirt and machinery high in the air. With hardly a pause, the main battery switched to nearby Tinian, silencing a battery which had been firing on the American task force with great regularity."

Another Japanese 10-centimeter gun, however, its angry snout jutting from the entrance of a cave on Tinian just 5 nautical miles southwest of Saipan, was quickly finding the range to the American column. Shells plunged into the water around the *Birmingham* and *Tennessee*, the geysers reaching high into the air with each impact, stunning white against the blue backdrop of the sea. Suddenly, a burst of fire erupted from the new superstructure of the *California* as she was rocked by a direct hit.

"The shot appeared to come off the port quarter and fell nearly vertically, with the explosion venting upward and downward from the 09 to 07 deck," Burnett wrote. The howitzer shell crashed into the *California* just aft of the main battery director platform, buckling the after bulkhead, main deck, and STS shield and spraying the area with steel fragments. The blast took out one of the battleship's fire control radars and two search radars and did significant damage to the ship's radio and internal communications systems.

Killed instantly was Harry Kelekian, a water tender third class from the Bronx who was just one month short of his twenty-first birthday, while eight other men standing nearby were cut down by flying shrapnel. Even as corpsmen evacuated the casualties and damage control parties moved in to extinguish the resulting electrical fire, the crew of the *California*'s secondary battery never stopped loading and shooting. The swimmers of the Underwater Demolition Teams were still paddling along the reef, stretching fishing wire and dropping buoys to mark lanes of travel for the amphtracks coming the next day, and were in desperate need of cover fire. Control for the 14-inch turrets was quickly shifted to the main battery plot and soon the battleship's big guns were back in action, resuming their relentless pounding of Saipan.

The *Maryland* and her sister *Colorado*, operating with the *Portland*, *Louisville*, and three destroyers, were also taken under fire by coastal defense guns as they bombarded Japanese positions in and around the town of Tanapan a few miles to the north. The Japanese had stationed at least two pieces of heavy artillery on the small islet of Maniagassa, just north of Tanapan Harbor. After observing splashes in the water off the *Maryland*'s port beam and muzzle flashes coming from deep within the islet's dense jungle growth, Captain Herbert Ray had the *Maryland*'s engines brought to all-ahead standard speed and ordered the secondary and antiaircraft weapons to engage the shore battery while the Fighting Mary's main guns were brought to bear upon the target. The Japanese guns were quickly destroyed by a salvo of 16-inch shells.

Oldendorf's battlewagons continued to pound Saipan until just after 6:00 p.m., when they recovered their seaplanes and withdrew to the waters west of the island for the night. Twelve hours later they were back in their assigned fire support sectors to deliver phase two of the bombardment, while carrier-based aircraft bombed and strafed the beaches and the amphtracks and amphibious tanks loaded with over eight thousand marines, so far the largest landing force of the Pacific War, rolled down the ramps of the landing ships and waddled slowly toward the line of departure.

"I have at last come to the place where I will die," a Japanese soldier on Saipan would write in his diary. "I am pleased to think that I will die calmly in true samurai style. Naval gunfire supported this attack which was too terrible for words."

Despite the terror unleashed upon the garrison of Saipan by the battleships and their cohorts, and the good number of Japanese coastal defense and antiaircraft batteries thus destroyed, there were still plenty of well-camouflaged and shielded defensive positions remaining to enfilade the invasion beaches with deadly machine-gun and mortar fire. Several concealed artillery positions on the reverse slopes of hills overlooking the landing beaches had also been missed by the ships' observation planes. Due to the sheer mass of Saipan, the concentration of pre-invasion air and naval bombardment of the type seen in the Marshalls campaign had not been achieved. The aggressiveness of the Japanese shore batteries on Saipan would also play a role in the bombardment's shortcomings.

"This operation marked the first time that counter-battery fire has been encountered to any extent," Captain Mayer of the *Tennessee* wrote. "In general it did not appear as if the Japanese had very good control of their gunfire. Many splashes were observed landing close to this ship as well as other ships of Fire Support Unit One and some of these ships were hit. This does not prove that the Japanese had excellent control, however, as it must be remembered that all these ships were operating at extremely low speeds close to the beach presenting a splendid and easily hit target."

As a result, the Second and Fourth Marine Divisions hit the beaches of Saipan under a torrent of enemy fire. Though the marines were able to establish a beachhead 6 miles wide and extending a half-mile inland on D-Day, the landing force sustained some two thousand casualties. Just after 9:00 a.m., after blasting away at the well-entrenched Japanese on Afetna Point and a group of light tanks moving in to attack the beachhead, the *Tennessee* was also hit.

A salvo of three 6-inch shells fired by a Japanese battery on Tinian struck the battleship on her starboard side. The first shell smashed into the Number Seven 5-inch turret; a second punched a hole in the outer blister before being stopped by the ship's armor belt; while a third direct hit blew a 2-by-3-foot hole in the main deck directly above the officers' wardroom. Eight enlisted men were killed, most of them members of the Number Seven gun crew, while one officer, sixteen sailors, and six marines were wounded. Even while her 40-millimeters continued to engage enemy targets on Saipan, the *Tennessee* unleashed the fury of her remaining secondary guns upon Tinian, raining down 382 rounds of 5-inch AA Common on the offending Japanese shore battery, detonating the ammunition dump and wiping out the four 6-inch guns along with their crews.

The *California*, in the meantime, had closed to within 5,800 yards of the landing area designated Red Beach One with her guns blazing. "Large explosions were observed on the shore at this time and heavy machine gun fire from enemy on Red Beaches," Captain Burnett wrote. "During this period immediately prior to the landings, both main and secondary battery delivered continuous fire on the beach ahead of the advancing boat waves, lifting the fire at about 0835 to points further inland."

While the *California* continued to fire upon Japanese positions that could be observed by her spotter planes, the radio operators in the ship's Combat Information Center were attempting to establish contact with the naval gunfire liaison officer that had been assigned to the ship. By 9:40 a.m. the *California*'s two Kingfishers were running low on fuel and departed the fire support area for a rendezvous with the *New Mexico*, which was lying several miles offshore and assigned the duty of servicing the seaplanes of the battleships and cruisers. Minutes later Admiral Turner signaled the fire support ships that Japanese tanks were spotted leaving the town of Garapan, headed south toward the beachhead.

The tanks could be seen clearly from the decks of the *California* as they clanked along the coastal road and were taken under fire by her 5-inch guns. After two of the vehicles were obliterated, the surviving tanks scurried for cover. Just before noon the *California* was able to make contact with one of the No-Glows, who believed that the members of the shore control party assigned to the ship were among the casualties scattered across the beach. Without seaplanes or forward observers to guide her shots, the Prune Barge continued to strike carefully at targets of opportunity beyond the known phase line and managed to break up another Japanese tank attack in the early afternoon.

Shortly thereafter the speakers in the CIC crackled with the first static-laden radio contact from Shore Control Party 62, to the sighs of relief from the officers and men standing the watch, and for the remainder of the day the *California* remained offshore to answer their requests for fire support. As dusk approached, the ships of the task group were recovering their Kingfishers and preparing to depart westward for the night, when the signal "Flash Red" was received from Turner's flagship *Rocky Mount.* The *Maryland* and *Tennessee* had already been tracking the inbound bogies while the *California*, now lacking her air search radar, had to take the admiral's word for it.

Four Kate torpedo bombers zoomed over the ships of Task Group 52.17, one of them releasing a bomb which narrowly missed one of the American destroyers. For the first time the *Tennessee* and *California* made use of their new antiaircraft guns, but the Japanese planes were gone as quickly as they had appeared and no hits were scored. As another group of aircraft approached both the *California* and *Maryland* opened up with their Bofors mounts, but the fire was quickly checked when it was realized that the planes racing past were American fighters in hot pursuit of the fleeing Kates.

Oldendorf's ships returned to deliver phase three on-call fire support over the next several days. On June 16, shore control parties requested the battleships to fire "full salvoes as rapidly as possible" to disperse a Japanese counterattack supported by more light tanks. The following morning the Japanese air forces continued their sporadic, piecemeal harassment raids against the American fleet. At first light a "Betty" medium bomber made an unsuccessful attack run on the battleships; moments later a single-engined Kawasaki Ki-61 "Tony" dove upon the *Maryland*, dropping a bomb which plopped harmlessly into the sea. Forty-millimeters aboard the *Maryland* and *California* opened fire and splashed the enemy fighter, the first antiaircraft kill for the American dreadnoughts. On June 19, while the battleships were cruising offshore and delivering fire support to the marines fighting their way inland, their radio operators began to overhear a flood of reports being transmitted to CINCPAC, telling of a major carrier battle taking place just a few hundred miles to the west.

Admiral Soemu Toyoda, who had succeeded Mineichi Koga as Commander-in-Chief of the Combined Fleet after the latter's death in a seaplane crash, had decided that the time was ripe to challenge the forces of Ray Spruance on the high seas. Toyoda ordered the Mobile Fleet, led by Vice Admiral Jisaburo Ozawa, to sortie from bases in the Philippines and seek a long-awaited decisive battle in the waters of the Philippine Sea west of the Marianas. Ozawa's carrier-based planes, along with aircraft based on Guam, Yap, and other nearby island bases, launched a series of attacks against Marc Mitscher's Fast Carrier Task Forces on the morning of June 19.

While Mitscher's Hellcat pilots were slaughtering what was left of Japanese naval aviation in their "Great Marianas Turkey Shoot," American fleet submarines were busy hunting down the Japanese aircraft carriers. The *Shokaku*, one of the last two surviving carriers of the Pearl Harbor raid, blew apart and sank when three torpedo hits from the USS *Albacore* pierced her aviation gasoline storage tanks. After being hit just once by the submarine *Cavalla*, Ozawa's brand-new flagship *Taiho* would also be wracked by internal explosions and sink. American dive-bombers and torpedo planes also destroyed the *Hiyo* and heavily damaged three other Japanese carriers.

After two days of this, Ozawa's punch-drunk force staggered away on a northwesterly course for Formosa and the Ryukyus, having lost three fleet carriers and nearly six hundred aircraft along with their irreplaceable pilots. Now without any hope of relief, Lieutenant General Yoshitsugu Saito's besieged troops on Saipan would resolve to fight to the last man.

The evening of June 22, 1944, would find the *Maryland*, *Tennessee*, *California*, and *Pennsylvania* swinging at anchor in 17 fathoms of water, just off the western coast of Saipan near the village of Garapan. Except for several troublesome snipers left behind, the Japanese had been forced out of Saipan's coastal region and were making their stand in the mountainous center of the island where the marines, now reinforced by the army's 27th Infantry Division, were working hard to dislodge them from a defensive line that threaded through a series of volcanic caves. As the sailors of the battleships loafed on the weather decks in the twilight, the occasional burst of star shell could be seen flickering over the hills beyond the now-flattened town, followed by the faraway, eerie crump of heavy mortars. At 6:00 p.m. the *California* and *Tennessee*, both in need of repair and replenishment, weighed anchor and got under way for the fleet base at Eniwetok.

"It was a heavy, humid evening," wrote Fire Controlman Third Class Fred Vreeken of the *Maryland*. "The enclosures of steel walls below decks were filled with stale, humid air. Crowded quarters added to the discomfort. Most of us went topside to enjoy the cool of the evening. The decks topside were filled with sailors, spread out on blankets, chatting and swapping yarns. I pulled off my shoes and laid on my stomach. The teakwood deck was my bed, a seaman's hat was my pillow. I closed my eyes and listened to the chatter of the crew, gathered in small groups playing cards, and laughing and jokes. It was pleasant and peaceful."

Among the many sailors relaxing on the bow of the *Maryland* was Houston Smith, a young Alabaman whose Southern accent and vernacular were so thick that, predictably, his shipmates had nicknamed him "Snuffy" after the hillbilly comic strip character. When the whine of aircraft motors was heard in the darkened sky over the roadstead, Snuffy Smith jumped to his feet, grabbed up his GI blanket, and began scurrying aft.

"Where you going, Snuffy?" one of the men asked.

"I'm gettin' the hell out of here," the astute Smith answered, pointing in the direction of the quickly approaching airplane. "That's a Betty!"

"Without so much as turning around," Vreeken wrote, "he quickened his pace, as all eyes looked into the direction that Snuffy's finger pointed."

John Ashby and his buddies from the *Maryland*'s third division were also stretched out on the main deck and enjoying the cool night.

"You could tell the Japanese planes from the American planes by the sound of their engines," Ashby explained. "The Jap engines had a much higher-pitched sound. I thought it was a Jap, someone else said it was American. We were just lying there, arguing over whose plane it was, when we got hit by a torpedo."

"At dusk, a Betty slipped around a large hill on Saipan and was over our force before it had been sighted or picked up by radar," Clifton Cates recorded. "It dropped its torpedo almost on top of the *Pennsylvania* and was gone before any ship fired a shot."

Less than a mile away, American PBM Mariner seaplanes had been running up their engines and preparing to take off for a night patrol. "Two lookouts, who had been especially stationed on the forecastle, in anticipation of small boats trying to reach the ship, saw the plane as it headed for the ship and thought it was a PBM until it banked," read the *Maryland*'s war diary. "At that time it was identified as an enemy plane, but by that time the torpedo was in the water."

Seconds later came the shuddering impact, a fiery explosion, and the ear-rending sound of tearing metal. Striking between frames 8 and 11, the torpedo killed two sailors and nearly succeeded in blowing the bow off the *Maryland.*

"You could have driven a car through that hole in the bow and come out the other side," John Ashby remembered, a description that one could hardly call an exaggeration after observing official navy photographs of the damage. Fortunately the bulkheads and doors just abaft the torpedo strike had held and the *Maryland* was able to maintain watertight integrity. At 11:35 p.m., after several small leaks were secured by the ship's divers, the Fighting Mary was under way for Eniwetok "at best practical speed," shielded by the destroyers *Mertz* and *Norman Scott.*

The *Maryland* was able to make 10 knots even with her bow open to the sea, while repair parties kept a constant watch on the shored bulkheads to watch for structural failures and leaks. The following evening a burial-at-sea ceremony was held for the two sailors killed by the torpedo attack and on June 25, aircraft from Eniwetok appeared overhead to escort the crippled battleship and her destroyers.

Two days later the *Maryland* steamed into Eniwetok lagoon and dropped only her starboard anchor, the power to her portside windlass having failed. The technicians of Service Squadron 10 then went to work making the temporary repairs necessary for the *Maryland* to make the journey to Pearl Harbor, which she began on the morning of July 1 at a ponderous 9.5 knots, accompanied by the destroyers *Braine* and *Pruitt.*

After an agonizingly slow ten-day voyage the *Maryland* slid into Dry Dock Number Two of the Pearl Harbor Navy Yard, where everything forward of the ship's fourteenth frame was cut away and an entirely new bow, stretching from the keel to the main deck, was fabricated and installed.

In a month's time, the battleship that Radio Tokyo had declared sunk off the coast of Saipan was under way for the South Pacific to rejoin the fleet.

The Battle of Saipan, in the meantime, would come to its final bitter, bloody, and tragic conclusion. Howlin' Mad Smith had once again become frustrated with what he considered to be the slow progress and dismal fighting spirit of the army's 27th Infantry Division, and on June 23 he sacked the unit's commander, Major General Ralph C. Smith. As head of the Fifth Amphibious Corps, Holland Smith had the authority to do so and had obtained the permission of Turner and Spruance beforehand. Nonetheless, the highly contentious decision would add to the already strained relationship between US Army forces in the Pacific and the Marine Corps.

On July 7, with his mountain hideouts outflanked and surrounded, General Saito ordered a final banzai charge of some four thousand Japanese troops—the largest of the Pacific War—which even included the bandaged and limping wounded. Though they managed to overwhelm several American positions and inflict heavy casualties, after fifteen hours of fighting the frenzied attackers were nearly annihilated.

Wounded himself during the desperate effort, Saito would retreat into the cave that had been serving as his headquarters, where he was shot to death by his chief of staff after committing ritual *seppuku.* Frightened by the lies of Japanese propagandists, which included a claim that American marines were rapists and cannibals, Japanese residents of the island gathered to commit mass suicide by throwing themselves off the 600-foot cliff at Saipan's Marpi Point. In one of the more horrifying events yet to occur in the Pacific War, many Japanese mothers hurled their young children over the edge before jumping themselves. The sad total of civilians that died in this manner is unknown but is believed to be in the thousands. Bested by Raymond Spruance yet again, the admiral in command of Japanese naval forces on Saipan, Chuichi Nagumo, shot himself in the head.

On July 9, 1944, Kelly Turner declared Saipan secured. Humiliated by the loss of Japanese sovereign territory, the embattled Prime Minister Hideki Tojo and his cabinet were compelled to resign.

After a month's delay caused by the Battle of the Philippine Sea and the stubborn resistance encountered on Saipan, the Japanese-occupied United States territory of Guam was invaded by Major General Roy Geiger's Third Amphibious Corps on July 21, followed by an assault on Tinian by the Second and Fourth Marine Divisions three days later, on July 24. After providing preliminary shore bombardment, Oldendorf and Conolly's bombardment task groups—centered upon the dreadnoughts *Tennessee*, *California*, *Pennsylvania*, *Colorado*, *Idaho*, and *New Mexico*—shuttled back and forth between the two islands, providing on-call fire support, illumination, and harassing fire, while making frequent stops at Saipan harbor for replenishment of fuel and ammunition.

The tiny isle of Tinian was secured on August 1 and would be transformed into a major air base for the B-29s of General Curtis LeMay's 21st Bombardment Command, from which a devastating strategic bombing campaign against the industrial cities of the Japan would soon be launched. After three weeks of heavy fighting, Guam was back in American hands and buzzing with Seabees and army engineering battalions, with construction on additional bomber fields and a new fleet base well under way before the echoes of the final gunshots had even faded.

The southern Marianas had been conquered, at the cost of five thousand American lives. Nearly sixty thousand Japanese had died in their futile effort to hold them.

CHAPTER 19

"A THOROUGH WORKING OVER"

"Douglas, where do we go from here?" the President of the United States asked.

Dressed in a crisp white linen shirt with signature bow tie and a pair of pressed khaki trousers, Franklin Delano Roosevelt was seated comfortably in a padded rattan chair before a huge map of the Pacific Ocean, erected in the main room of a lavish three-story house overlooking Waikiki. The sprawling beachfront property, complete with lush ornamental gardens and swaying palms, belonged to the estate of the recently departed Christian Holmes II, a local businessman and heir to the Fleischmann's Yeast fortune. Leased by the navy for the purpose of resting and recuperating its aviators between combat operations, the house had been selected by the Secret Service to serve as Roosevelt's personal accommodations during his brief stay on Oahu.

Occupying the chair on the president's left was his longtime friend and trusted confidant Admiral William Leahy, a former Chief of Naval Operations, Ambassador to France, and Governor of Puerto Rico who was now—in effect, if not in actual title—the first chairman of the Joint Chiefs of Staff. Seated to the president's right was a national hero and potential political rival, the son of a Medal of Honor recipient and a recipient of the award himself, a man whose intelligence, personal courage, brilliance as a military strategist, and gift for stirring oratory were rivaled only by his boundless ambition and tremendous ego. Of the many biographies that would be written about him in the coming decades, the most celebrated would also be the most appropriately titled: *American Caesar*.

General Douglas MacArthur rose from his chair and accepted the long bamboo pointer offered by Admiral Chester Nimitz. MacArthur had initially declined the invitation to attend the Pacific strategy conference on the grounds that he was "too busy," before being ordered to do so by his boss, Army Chief-of-Staff George C. Marshall. The order did not stop the imperious MacArthur from grumbling about the inconvenience to the staff of his Southwest Pacific Area GHQ, stating that during the First World War he had "never for a moment left my division, even when wounded by gas and ordered to the hospital. I've never before had to turn my back on my assignment." In Brisbane on July 25, 1944, MacArthur boarded a plane for Hawaii to participate in what he at first believed to be nothing more than a "picture-taking junket" with Roosevelt and Nimitz. In the end he would be glad to have made the journey.

MacArthur rested the tip of the pointer on an oddly shaped land mass in the central Philippines.

"Leyte, Mr. President," the general said, "and then Luzon."

The declaration came as a surprise to no one, of course. During his long and storied career, MacArthur had developed a great personal affection for the lands and peoples of Southeast Asia in general and the Philippines in particular—to the point that some of his fellow officers believed the general to have "gone Asiatic." Upon his retirement from the army in 1937, MacArthur took up residence in Manila and assumed the post of military advisor to the commonwealth government of the Philippines—though he much preferred the self-styled title of "Field Marshal of the Philippine Army"—and in 1941 was recalled to active duty and made commander of United States Forces of the Far East.

In the dark days of February 1942, with America's position in the Philippines becoming more precarious by the day, President Roosevelt ordered the evacuation of MacArthur and his staff to Australia, not wanting his most experienced field commander to fall into the hands of the Japanese. Upon his arrival in Melbourne, MacArthur concluded his remarks to reporters with "I came through and I shall return," a now-iconic statement which gained considerable traction in the popular press at the time and, for many, came to epitomize American steadfastness and determination.

MacArthur, warming to his subject in singularly grandiloquent style, then began to list the many reasons that justified a triumphant return to the Philippines, which included the far-reaching geopolitical as well as strategic. The archipelago had been a territory of the United States since the turn of the century, MacArthur reminded his audience, and the Filipino people had suffered greatly under Japanese occupation. The preservation of American honor, and of America's reputation in the Far East for many years to come, demanded that the Filipinos be liberated along with the nearly four thousand starving and brutalized American prisoners of war who were still languishing in Japanese prison camps in the islands. Once taken, Luzon could be transformed into an enormous staging base for the eventual invasion of Japan itself, as England had been for the invasion of Fortress Europe, with the added benefit of isolating all Japanese forces remaining in the southwest Pacific and completely cutting off the flow of strategic resources from Japan's southern conquests.

Nimitz was carrying the ball for the absent Admiral King, who believed that Luzon should be bypassed in favor of an invasion of Formosa, the capture of which would place American forces in a better position to launch an invasion of mainland Japan and facilitate close cooperation with the Nationalist Chinese. Securing Luzon would not be possible without capturing the city of Manila, an undesirable urban warfare scenario which could cost a significant number of American lives.

On the contrary, MacArthur would argue, once on the shores of Luzon he would quickly gain control of the island with the help of Filipino partisans and take Manila within five weeks. Formosa was likely to be much more heavily fortified than Luzon (it was), with a civilian population loyal to the Japanese. Leapfrogging over Luzon would also leave thousands of Japanese troops uncontained in the rear.

Several members of the CINCPAC staff and a handful of senior commanders, including Bill Halsey and Ray Spruance, had also expressed to Nimitz and King their belief that taking Formosa would be a more difficult and costly operation than Luzon. Spruance viewed Luzon, along with Iwo Jima in the Volcano Islands and Okinawa in the Ryukyus, as the next three logical steps on the path leading to Japan. Nimitz himself wasn't sold on the Formosa idea, something MacArthur had easily sensed during the conference.

"Admiral Nimitz put forth the Navy plan, but I was sure it was King's and not his own," the general would later state. To be fair, King had made his preference for an invasion of Formosa known to Nimitz, but had not issued any ironclad directives. Instead, the CNO had asked Nimitz to think the matter over carefully and to use his best judgment. By the time the conference was over, MacArthur had managed to convince both Nimitz and Roosevelt that his "Leyte then Luzon" strategy was the smarter play.

The president would pass the recommendation along to the Joint Chiefs, who nevertheless remained at an impasse largely due to the stubborn resistance of Ernest King, and agreed only to table the decision for the time being. The following month, at a meeting of the Combined Chiefs of Staff in Quebec, orders were drawn up for MacArthur's Southwest Pacific Forces to land at Morotai in the East Indies and then Mindanao in the Philippines, while Nimitz's Central Pacific Forces were to seize Peleliu, Anguar, Yap, and Ulithi in the western Carolines.

These operations were for the purpose of neutralizing Japanese resistance against, and establishing bases to support, the subsequent invasion of Leyte scheduled for December 1944. Air and naval forces based on Leyte would then support a possible invasion of Luzon, or neutralize Japanese airfields on Luzon while American forces invaded Formosa, depending on which fork in the road the Joint Chiefs eventually decided to take. The ink had barely dried on this new schedule of operations before a top-secret message from Admiral Halsey was forwarded to the still-ongoing Quebec conference by Admiral Nimitz.

In June 1944 Halsey had been ordered to relinquish command of the South Pacific Area and report to Pearl Harbor for a new assignment. Nimitz had decided to implement a new rotational command system in order to utilize the full potential and talents of his top two admirals. While Ray Spruance was at sea commanding the Central Pacific Force, Halsey and his staff would be planning the next operation to take place. Halsey's group would then relieve Spruance and his staff, who would retire to Pearl Harbor and begin planning the following operation. While Halsey was in command, the Central Pacific Force would be named Third Fleet, and would become Fifth Fleet when Spruance took over.

"Instead of the stagecoach system of keeping the drivers and changing the horses, we changed drivers and kept the horses," Halsey would explain. "It was hard on the horses, but it was effective. Moreover, it consistently misled the Japs into an exaggerated conception of our seagoing strength."

Using the *New Jersey* as his flagship, Halsey relieved Spruance on August 26 and rendezvoused with Marc Mitscher's carriers in the Philippine Sea on September 11. Commander Third Fleet then ordered a series of airstrikes against Japanese installations in the Philippines by the Fast Carrier Task Forces.

"We opened our attack on the central Philippines on September 12, from a position within sight of the mountains of Samar," Halsey wrote. "That day we flew 1,200 sorties; on the thirteenth, another 1,200; and when the last plane had returned aboard on the fourteenth, our Air Combat Intelligence officers showed me a box score that made me whistle. We had shot down 173 planes, destroyed 305 more on the ground, sunk 59 ships, and probably sunk another 58, besides tremendous damage to installations. Our losses? Eight planes in combat, one operationally, and ten men!"

Halsey then contemplated sending a message to Nimitz, recommending that the landings in the western Carolines be canceled and the timetable for invading the Philippines accelerated. "We had just dealt a crippling blow to Jap air power, and we had found the central Philippines a hollow shell with weak defenses and skimpy facilities. In my opinion, this was the vulnerable belly of the Imperial dragon."

After consulting his staff, Halsey recalled that he "sat in a corner of the bridge and thought it over. Such a recommendation, in addition to being none of my business, would upset a great many applecarts, possibly all the way up to Mr. Roosevelt and Mr. Churchill. On the other hand, it looked sound, it ought to save thousands of lives, and it might cut months off the war by hurrying the Nips and keeping them off-balance." This was reason enough to convince Halsey to compose and transmit the message, which concluded with the statement: "Believe that Leyte fleet base site can be seized immediately and cheaply without any intermediate operations if initial landings were covered by Task Force 30 until land based air can be installed."

A new operational timetable was then devised, and MacArthur's invasion of Leyte was advanced to October 1944. In what would be perhaps his most controversial decision of the entire war, Nimitz agreed to cancel all "intermediate operations" with the exception of the two-phased Operation Stalemate—the landings at Anguar and Peleliu in the Palaus in mid-September. Japanese aircraft based in the Palaus were likely to be a thorn in the right flank of MacArthur's northward advance, Nimitz reasoned, while the seizure and subsequent utilization of their airfields would provide a means of supporting it. As soon as practicable after the Palau operation was under way, Jesse Oldendorf's fire support ships were to detach from Third Fleet and report to Vice Admiral Thomas Kinkaid's Seventh Fleet to take part in MacArthur's assault on Leyte.

The decision to proceed with Operation Stalemate would send the veteran First Marine Division walking into a firestorm.

With the conclusion of Operation Forager, the ships of Oldendorf's task group steamed for the fleet anchorage at Eniwetok, where they remained for a week conducting routine maintenance, taking on fuel oil, and replenishing their depleted ammunition stocks. On August 19, with the *Pennsylvania* acting as guide, the battleships *Tennessee* and *California*, the heavy cruiser *Minneapolis*, and six destroyers set sail for Espiritu Santo in the New Hebrides. There the crews were to receive a brief period of rest before they were scheduled to rendezvous with Admiral Theodore "Ping" Wilkinson's Joint Expeditionary Task Force at Florida Island in the Solomons and begin preparing for the upcoming Operation Stalemate.

The passage was rather uneventful until just after the beginning of the morning watch of August 23, 1944, when Captain Andrew Mayer was summoned to the bridge of the *Tennessee*. The battleship had suffered a failure of its main steering motor, causing her to swing out of formation in the predawn darkness as the ships of the task group zigzagged their way south. Within three minutes control was switched to the auxiliary pneumatic steering gear and the *Tennessee* was slowly brought back on course while repairs were made—too hastily, as it would turn out—to the primary steering system. A sheared pin was located and replaced but the main gear it held was reconnected backwards, 180 degrees out of alignment.

Control was then switched back to the main steering motor, which immediately overloaded and failed. Mayer then ordered the engines brought to "back full emergency" and the ship's running lights illuminated, but by that time the *Tennessee* was already bearing down upon her sister ship, *California*. The announcement that the *Tennessee* had fallen victim to a steering casualty was made over the TBS frequency mere seconds before the two ships collided with a calamitous crash.

The starboard bow of the *Tennessee* ripped through a portside berthing compartment of the *California*, killing seven men as they lay sleeping in their bunks. An eighth sailor was tossed into the sea, never to be found; another eight men were injured; and a gaping hole "the size of a two-story house" was gouged into the *California*'s upper hull. The affected compartments were sealed off, with the bodies of five men still grotesquely pinned in the tangled wreckage, while the *California* continued on to the New Hebrides. The following day she entered the floating dry dock *ABSD-1* in Pallikulo Bay, where she would remain under repair until September 11 and therefore unavailable for the Palau operation.

Aboard the *Tennessee* the only casualties were the careers of Captain Mayer and the ship's navigator, Commander Bruce Ware, after a Board of Investigation headed by Rear Admiral Oscar Badger, Commander Service Squadrons South Pacific, recommended their relief at the earliest practicable date. In early October Mayer was replaced by Captain John B. Heffernan, the commander of destroyers at the Naval Battle of Casablanca, who had also led a flotilla of transports during the invasion of Guam. Heffernan would serve as the *Tennessee*'s commanding officer for the remainder of the war.

"The location and destruction of all enemy coast defense guns, antiaircraft and field artillery batteries in the combat area is desired, as well as thorough bombardment of beach defenses, and the destruction of enemy fuel, ammunition and supply dumps," read Rear Admiral Jesse Oldendorf's Operation Plan 1-44. "A thorough 'working over' of the areas assigned with the ammunition available should accomplish these aims. Ships should initially take under fire targets listed in their assigned areas and then locate and destroy any targets not listed."

Beginning at 5:30 a.m. on September 12, 1944, the guns of Oldendorf's Task Group 32.5 opened fire on the 5-square-mile chunk of jagged coral and dense rainforest that was Peleliu. The *Maryland* and *Pennsylvania*, the cruisers *Indianapolis* and *Honolulu*, and four destroyers made up Fire Support Unit Able, commanded by Rear Admiral Walden Ainsworth. Oldendorf, in overall command of the fire support ships for Operation Stalemate, was also leading Fire Support Unit Baker from the *Louisville*, accompanied by the *Idaho*, *Mississippi*, *Portland*, and five destroyers. The *Tennessee* was serving as the flagship of Rear Admiral Kingman's Fire Support Unit One along with the cruisers *Minneapolis* and *Cleveland* and three destroyers, assigned to strike the nearby island of Anguar.

Oldendorf's ships gave Peleliu a "thorough working over" until dusk, stopping only to allow carrier-based planes to drop half-ton bombs and canisters of napalm onto the soon-to-be-infamous Umurbrogol ridge, the high ground which offered a commanding view of the landing beaches. That night the admiral and his staff pored over a stack of reconnaissance photographs snapped by low-flying seaplanes and compared them to pictures taken before the bombardment. Peleliu's 6,000-foot runway was a cratered ruin, littered with the skeletal remains of wrecked Betties and Zeroes. Every building, pillbox, bunker, and blockhouse visible had been reduced to smoking piles of broken concrete, and what had once been dense jungle foliage and coconut groves was now blackened wasteland.

"This growth had been systematically destroyed and only charred tree stumps and scarred rocks remained. Numerous caves were then visible on the slopes of the high land," read Oldendorf's after-action report. Conspicuously absent from the photographs taken after the bombardment was any evidence of the heavy guns known to be on the island, and Japanese counter-battery fire had been virtually nonexistent.

"Bombardment of this nature was becoming almost routine," an officer on the *Maryland* would write of the Peleliu mission. As they had on every amphibious operation since Kwajalein, the fire support ships laid down a blistering cover fire for the Underwater Demolition Teams as they performed hydrographic reconnaissance, worked to clear submerged obstacles, blasted channels, and smoothed the lip of the reef to permit the passage of marine amphtracks.

The second day of the shore bombardment was a repeat of the first, with the four battleships, four cruisers, and nine destroyers of Oldendorf's task group delivering their sustained and systematic punishment of the landing beaches. Every target on the list was struck, not once but multiple times, by naval gunfire and carrier-borne aircraft.

After viewing the reconnaissance photos taken in the twilight of D-Day-Minus-Two, Oldendorf would send a message to Ping Wilkinson aboard the command ship *Mount McKinley*, claiming that Task Group 32.5.1 had "run out of targets." Whether Oldendorf intended the message to sound as cavalier as it did, or if the admiral simply meant to convey that he had already hit everything he could see, remains a matter of speculation. In any event, it would be a statement that Oldendorf would soon regret.

"Boy, it must cost a fortune to fire them 16-inch babies," a member of the Third Battalion / Fifth Marines remarked to his buddies as their amphtrack plowed through the waters of Peleliu's lagoon and main battery fire from the battleships shrieked overhead.

"Screw the expense," one of his fellow marines snarled in response.

In another of the amphtracks was Private First Class Robert Leckie of the Second Battalion / First Marines. "Naval shells hissed shoreward in the air above us," Leckie wrote. "Those of us who had been on Guadalcanal, remembering our own ordeal with naval bombardment, could spare a pang of pity for the foe—thankful nevertheless for the new direction the war had taken."

All three regiments of the First Marine Division were closing in on the southern shore of Peleliu in a line abreast, within a stone's throw of the decimated airfield. The Fifth Marines were in the center, headed for the landing beaches designated Orange One and Two. On their right, the Seventh Marines were landing on Orange Beach Three. To their left were the First Marines, under the command of Colonel Lewis B. Puller, making an assault on the two White Beaches, which were flanked by a

30-foot-tall coral outcropping known to those who fought on Peleliu as "the Point."

A "mustang" who had enlisted as a private and later earned an officer's commission, the recipient of four Navy Crosses for bravery (he would eventually be awarded five), a veteran of the Banana Wars in Haiti and Nicaragua and the Pacific War battles of Guadalcanal and Cape Gloucester, "Chesty" Puller was already a legendary figure in the Marine Corps. After viewing aerial photographs of Peleliu, Puller found it difficult to share the optimism of his division commander, Major General William H. Rupertus, who predicted that Peleliu would be "rough but fast" and taken within three days, perhaps even two. Puller knew that if *he* were in charge of defending Peleliu, he would have turned the Point into a stronghold capable of pouring enfilading fire onto the invasion beaches. A request was forwarded through the chain of command to have the outcropping singled out for special attention by the fire support ships, but the Point had somehow failed to make the target list.

A part of the Japanese South Seas Mandate since the First World War, Peleliu had been the site of an extensive phosphate mining operation. In preparing their defense of the island, Colonel Kunio Nakagawa and his eleven thousand Imperial Army troops made the best use of the existing caverns, mine shafts, and tunnels within the Umurbrogol hills for the placement of their artillery and mortars, even to the point of installing sliding steel doors to conceal the cave entrances and make them fairly impervious to naval gunfire and airstrikes.

Rather than oppose the marines at the water's edge, Nakagawa left a single battalion on the landing beaches to fight a delaying action, while keeping the bulk of his troops inland and underground. There the defenders were under strict orders to maintain fire discipline so as not to reveal their positions; as a result the Japanese suffered few casualties from the pre-invasion bombardment. Nakagawa had also issued orders forbidding the use of the futile and wasteful *banzai* charge, and instead had his men remain in their concealed positions to fight a battle of attrition against the Americans. This change in tactics would prove to be deadly effective.

"My surprise and chagrin when concealed batteries opened up on the assault craft can be imagined," Jesse Oldendorf would later admit.

Heavy mortars, registered to strike upon the landing areas from positions of defilade within Umurbrogol ridge, began to rain fire upon the reef as the first waves of amphtracks approached the beach. Concealed 47-millimeter and 20-millimeter cannons then opened up, set up at right angles to catch the marines in a deadly cross fire. Soon nearly sixty landing craft were wrecked and burning upon the reef and the beaches. Then the Point exploded with the chattering of Japanese machine guns and automatic cannon, firing from within recessed positions.

"That big promontory on my left hadn't been touched by the ships' guns and planes, and we got a whirlwind of fire," Chesty Puller recalled.

"We were pinned down, but not by mortars alone," Robert Leckie described. "Machine gun fire came from an invincible outpost the Japanese had blasted out of a coral promontory jutting into the bay. We had found an opening in it, and even then were filling it with all manner of small arms fire; grenades, sticks of dynamite hurled by men who had crept up to it, or billowing fire from the flame throwers who also had gained the hole—but the answering fire continued to rake our deadly picnic ground."

The marines would manage to claw their way ashore to establish a 2-mile-long beachhead, all the while receiving heavy incoming fire from mortars and artillery placed on the high ground. After the Fifth Marines had pushed through to the edge of the airfield, Nakagawa launched a counterattack of light tanks supported by infantry, which was quickly wiped out by a combination of marine armor and pack howitzers along with on-call naval gunfire and airstrikes.

After neutralizing the Point, the First Marines would encounter two large and well-camouflaged concrete blockhouses overlooking the White beaches which were "not even nicked" by the naval bombardment. Their inhabitants had to be killed the hard way—by marine infantrymen using flamethrowers and explosives.

On that first day of the Battle of Peleliu, the First Marine Division would lose 200 killed in action and 900 wounded. On the morning of the second day the airfield was taken, allowing the marines to push on into the forbidding Umurbrogol—which they quickly renamed "Bloody Nose Ridge"—to begin blasting and burning the Japanese from their entrenchments. Peleliu would not be conquered within two or three days; rather, the marines would fight on for another five weeks before being relieved by the army's 81st Infantry Division. The struggle for the blood-drenched island would not end until November 27, with only 300 members of the 11,000-man Japanese garrison surviving the battle to be taken prisoner, while 1,800 Americans were killed in what many of the participants—and many historians since—have considered an unnecessary campaign and a needless waste of lives.

Some marine officers, including the deputy commander of the First Division, Brigadier General Oliver P. Smith, would acknowledge that there was only so much the navy could have done to prevent the high number of casualties, given the nature of Peleliu's complicated terrain and the enemy's ability to exploit it. "The bulk of the defensive installations and the ones which caused most of the casualties among the troops were not capable of neutralization by naval gunfire," Smith would report. Still other marines would remain rancorous over the navy's shortcomings at Peleliu, placing much of the blame for the carnage squarely on the shoulders of Jesse Oldendorf.

Some years later, in response to such criticism, the admiral would remark: "If military leaders—and that includes Navy brass—were gifted with the same accuracy of foresight that they are with hindsight, then the assault of Peleliu should never have been attempted."

Oldendorf's flagship *Louisville* and the battleships *Tennessee*, *Pennsylvania*, and *Maryland* would remain in the waters surrounding Palau until September 25, when they set sail for the isle of Manus in the Admiralties. A largely undeveloped volcanic island thick with rainforest and mangroves, Manus had been seized by MacArthur's Southwest Pacific Forces in March 1944 primarily for its strategic location, at 200 miles northeast of New Guinea and 350 miles northwest of Rabaul, and for the huge 120-square-mile sheltered bay on the island's northeast coast, Seeadler Harbor.

Halsey's Seabees had since transformed Seeadler Harbor into a major fleet hub, with adjoining airfields and facilities that rivaled that of Pearl Harbor. Waiting there for Oldendorf's task group to arrive was the

California, her collision damage repaired and ready to rejoin the battle fleet, along with the service squadrons of the Seventh Fleet to replenish their fuel, ammunition, provisions, and general stores. While the time and place of their next combat operation would remain a closely guarded secret, it soon became apparent to the rank-and-file battleship sailors that, whatever it was, it was to be no minor affair.

"We knew it was going to be big," said Fred Vreeken of the *Maryland*. "It could be gauged by the very heavy traffic of vessels of all descriptions which began to pour into the area. There were supply ships, ammunition ships, all types of men-of-war and transports. It was obvious that something big was in the wind." In the coming days over 340 ships would gather in Seeadler Harbor, and on October 5, 1944, the four veteran dreadnoughts of Pearl Harbor would be joined by a long-lost sister, the USS *West Virginia*.

Officers lifted binoculars to incredulous eyes as the battleship stood into the harbor, while many a disbelieving sailor looked to his shipmates for confirmation, jutting a finger in her direction and asking the question: *What ship is that?* For those who had been in Pearl Harbor in the days and weeks following the surprise attack and had borne witness to her tragic plight, the transformation of the *West Virginia* was truly astonishing. More than one naval historian has since compared her resurrection to that of the mythical phoenix, rising anew from the ashes of destruction.

The towering hyperboloid cage masts, armored conning tower, and broadside gun casements of a World War I–era dreadnought were gone. The *West Virginia*'s upper works had been stripped away and a completely new superstructure stood in its place, giving her a streamlined appearance similar to the battleships of the *Tennessee* class. The ship was now being conned from a light cruiser–type tower just aft of her Number Two Turret, and a new tower mast, topped with antennae for SG and SK search radars, now housed the bridge and Mark 8 FH-radar-equipped main battery director. Mark 12 radars were located within her sky directors, and experimental Mark 27 radars extended like ears from either side of the Number Three Turret.

The *West Virginia*'s eight Babcock and Wilcox boilers were now trunked into a single enlarged funnel, and where the after funnel and main mast had once been a stump tower now stood, serving as an elevated platform for her after main battery director equipped with Mark 8 FH fire control radar. Four Mark 37 directors controlled the new secondary battery of sixteen 5-inch / 38 caliber guns in twin turrets, and the *West Virginia* was now studded with a deadly array of antiaircraft cannons, including ten quad-mounted Bofors and forty-three Oerlikons. Three inches of armor had been added over her magazines and 2 inches over the machinery spaces, and like the *Tennessee* and *California*, new torpedo blistering broadened her beam to 114 feet. The *West Virginia* now sported the Measure 32/7D dazzle camouflage paint scheme, which seemed to add even further to her modern and aggressive appearance.

The yard workers of Puget Sound had celebrated Independence Day of 1944 by watching the *West Virginia* cast off her mooring lines and get under way for a first round of sea trials. While her muster rolls contained many new inductees who had never been to sea, there were many old salts aboard to teach them the ropes, including several dozen enlisted men who had survived the sinking of the carrier *Yorktown* at Midway. Of the *West Virginia*'s officers who were present at Pearl Harbor, only Lieutenant Commander William White still remained aboard, now serving as first lieutenant. White had become the acting commanding officer after the death of Captain Bennion, and had seen the *West Virginia* through her first grueling year of salvage and repair.

The new skipper of the *West Virginia* was Captain Herbert Victor Wiley of Chillicothe, Missouri, a graduate of the Naval Academy class of 1915. After spending a decade aboard battleships and destroyers, "Doc" Wiley received the designation of lighter-than-air naval aviator and began serving with the navy's ill-fated rigid airship program. In September 1925 Wiley would survive the crash of the *Shenandoah* when the dirigible broke up in the skies over rural Ohio; seven years later he would be one of three men out of a crew of seventy-six, and the only officer, to live through the crash of the *Akron* when she went down in a thunderstorm off the coast of New Jersey.

Wiley subsequently became commanding officer of the *Akron*'s sister ship *Macon*, a "flying aircraft carrier" rigged to launch and recover a pair of Waco biplanes and one of the largest dirigibles ever built. During a patrol over the Pacific in June 1934, Wiley managed to locate the heavy cruiser *Houston* as it carried Franklin Roosevelt on a voyage from Hawaii to Washington, even going so far as to launch the *Macon*'s biplanes so they could drop the current issues of several major newspapers onto the *Houston*'s quarterdeck for the president's consumption. This admirable feat of navigation and airmanship greatly impressed both President Roosevelt and the chief of naval aeronautics at the time, Ernest J. King, who quickly promoted Wiley to the rank of commander. Two years later, Wiley would survive yet another crash of an airship when the *Macon* went down off Point Sur, California, and received the Navy and Marine Corps Medal for rescuing a member of his crew.

At the outbreak of the Pacific War, Doc Wiley commanded the elderly four-pipers of Destroyer Squadron 29 of the Asiatic Fleet during their gallant but futile effort to deny the Dutch East Indies to the Japanese. In early December 1943, while serving on the staff of the Naval Academy, Wiley received orders to report to the commandant of the Thirteenth Naval District in Seattle and take command of the *West Virginia*. Upon meeting their new captain, many aboard the *West Virginia* assumed Wiley to be much older than his fifty-three years, with a head of wavy hair turned completely white and a body wracked by injuries suffered from three airship crashes. One former *West Virginia* bluejacket recalled that the skipper "walked like it hurt him," and at its loudest, Captain Wiley's voice was scarcely more than a whisper, the result of an injury to his throat sustained during the crash of the *Shenandoah*. Though he was remembered as being "a man that was all business," Wiley apparently saw the wry humor in the nickname that the *West Virginia* sailors soon bestowed upon him: "High Velocity."

At 6:50 a.m. on the morning of October 12, 1944, the *West Virginia*, *Maryland*, *Tennessee*, *California*, *Pennsylvania*, and *Mississippi* weighed anchor and sortied from Seeadler Harbor. Six dreadnoughts, all but one the battle-scarred survivors of the surprise attack on Pearl Harbor, together with eight cruisers and twenty-one destroyers comprised Task Group 77.2, Rear Admiral Jesse Oldendorf commanding. His flagship

Louisville was in the center of the cruising disposition acting as fleet guide, on a course of 313 degrees true at a speed of 15 knots. The destination was Leyte Gulf.

CHAPTER 20
SHO-GO

The general stood on the beach, waterlogged shoes and trouser legs coated with sand, while nervous infantrymen probed the nearby jungle thickets for the presence of snipers and the muffled, rhythmic timpani beat of naval gunfire rolled across the waters of San Pedro Bay. As he gripped the microphone of a portable radio set and drew a deep breath, the low clouds of a tropical squall that had been lingering over the eastern shores of Leyte decided to open, darkening the general's braided cap and the khaki that covered his shoulders with fat drops of tepid rain. Undeterred, he began to speak.

"This is the voice of freedom: General MacArthur speaking . . . People of the Philippines: *I have returned!* By the grace of Almighty God our forces stand again on Philippine soil—soil consecrated in the blood of our two peoples. We have come, dedicated and committed, to the task of destroying every vestige of enemy control over your daily lives, and of restoring, upon a foundation of indestructible strength, the liberties of your people . . .

"The hour of your redemption is here. Your patriots have demonstrated an unswerving and resolute devotion to the principles of freedom that challenges the best that is written on the pages of human history. I now call upon your supreme effort, that the enemy may know from the temper of an aroused and outraged people within, that he has a force there to contend with no less violent than is the force committed from without.

"Rally to me! Let the indomitable spirit of Bataan and Corregidor lead on! As the lines of battle roll forward to bring you within the zone of operations, rise and strike! Strike at every favorable opportunity. For your homes and hearths, strike! For future generations of your sons and daughters, strike! In the name of your sacred dead, strike! Let no heart be faint. Let every arm be steeled. The guidance of divine God points the way. Follow in His Name to the Holy Grail of righteous victory!"

On the fire support ships out in Leyte Gulf, gunner's mates in rolled-up dungarees sweated fiercely in the hot, humid air of the monsoon, while continuing their repetitive, laborious cycle of loading and firing. Officers and men in the cramped and airless gun directors, the bustling plotting rooms, and the dimly lit Combat Information Centers exchanged the data and corrections needed to keep the guns on target. In the pilot-houses, conning officers sang out crisp orders calling for adjustments to heading and speed in a nautical language few members of the bridge watch would have comprehended just a year or two ago. Captains and their XOs stood on the open navigation bridges in their haze gray helmets and kapok jackets, scanning the distant shore with powerful binoculars, while radar operators and antiaircraft gunners maintained their constant vigil for the approach of Japanese planes. In the engineering spaces below, the "black gangs" kept the boilers fired and the turbines running, with the clock being their only reference as to the presence of daylight or darkness topside.

Those whose battle stations were within earshot of a radio speaker were also listening to MacArthur's broadcast. Reaction to the speech was mixed. Some of the younger and less-jaded felt their chests swell with patriotic pride or were actually moved to tears, while the more salty and cynical dismissed it as melodramatic rhetoric that borrowed a little too heavily from Shakespeare's *Henry V*. On one thing they could all agree: General Douglas MacArthur was keenly aware that he had arrived at his defining moment in history. As he was delivering his rousing address, the 200,000 troops of Lieutenant General Walter Krueger's Sixth Army were storming across the flat, sandy beaches just south of the city of Tacloban.

"It didn't even look like the same army," James Jones would write. "Compared to the thinly-armed soldiers with their soup-plate helmets and wrap leggings who had fought here and lost in 1942, this army seemed like aliens from Mars. Even compared to their immediate ancestors, like us on Guadalcanal, they were a different army. New fatigue uniforms had been designed for them, new and better boots served their feet. New and better packs rode their backs. All sorts of new technologically improved arms and small arms accompanied them or were carried in their hands. Food and fuel and supplies followed them in such richness that it was unbelievable. Here were truly totally 'new' Americans, come to reestablish and reconfirm their old association with these islands."

It didn't look like the same navy, either. In terms of manpower, the number of American sailors that would fight in the campaign to liberate the Philippines was greater than the entire strength of the United States Navy *and* Marine Corps in 1939. The naval forces arrayed to support MacArthur's invasion of Leyte were enormous, among the mightiest the world had ever seen or will likely ever see again. Vice Admiral Thomas Kinkaid's Seventh Fleet included the 6 dreadnought battleships along with 5 amphibious command ships, 5 heavy cruisers, 4 light cruisers, 34 destroyers, 17 of the new destroyer escorts and numerous submarine chasers, Patrol Torpedo (PT) boats, and other light combatant craft. Flying from the decks of 18 escort aircraft carriers were 280 fighter planes and 190 torpedo bombers. Nearly 300 attack transports, amphibious landing ships, Liberty cargo ships, and support vessels had been required to conduct the sealift of Krueger's two army corps along with their vehicles, weapons, ammunition, equipment, food, and supplies. There were oilers, tenders, ammunition ships, minesweepers, fleet tugs, hospital ships, even a floating dry dock; in all, some 110 fleet auxiliaries of various types.

On-station in the Philippine Sea was Admiral Bill Halsey's Third Fleet of 9 fleet aircraft carriers, 8 light carriers, 6 fast battleships, 4 heavy cruisers, 10 light cruisers, 58 destroyers, and 26 destroyer escorts, followed by a train of 11 escort carriers carrying replacement aircraft and pilots, some 30 fleet oilers, 10 seagoing tugs, and a half-dozen ammunition ships. In addition to sweeping the skies above the main Philippine island of Luzon, the 560 fighters, 250 dive-bombers, and 220 torpedo bombers of Third Fleet's Task Force 38 were to perform long-range reconnaissance, attack Japanese shipping, and assist Kinkaid's fliers with conducting airstrikes against targets on Leyte. There were 29 submarines of the Pacific Fleet patrolling Leyte Gulf and the surrounding seas, keeping a sharp eye for the approach of the Japanese Navy. In all, the combined

Seventh and Third Fleets in Philippine waters numbered over 700 ships and some 144,000 naval personnel.

Halsey's four Fast Carrier Task Groups had spent the first days of October 1944 conducting a reign of terror over the anchorages and airfields of Luzon, Formosa, and the Ryukyus, steadily diminishing the Japanese air and sea power that might pose a challenge to MacArthur's invasion. In three days of devastating airstrikes against the naval facilities of Formosa, Task Force 38 destroyed 500 Japanese aircraft and sank scores of enemy ships. So ineffective were his defending fighter pilots against American Hellcats conducting fighter sweeps over Formosa that the Japanese air commander compared them to eggs being hurled against a stone wall.

Convinced that Halsey's carrier raids were a precursor to an Allied invasion of Formosa, the Imperial General Staff then committed the bulk of their available air forces to a maximum effort aimed at destroying the powerful Task Force 38. Ozawa's remaining carriers, still tucked into mainland Japan's Inland Sea taking on replacement aircraft and training new pilots after the thrashing they had received off the Marianas, were ordered to transfer their air groups to Formosa, ready or not. Air units from the Japanese Home Islands and the thinly stretched squadrons based on Luzon were also directed to take part in the operation.

In two twilight raids conducted on October 13 and 14, the Imperial Army and Naval air forces would lose 91 more planes in attacking Halsey's fleet, while managing to put torpedoes only into the *Canberra* and *Houston*, two new heavy cruisers named after ships previously lost in combat. The Japanese pilots that survived the mission, however, would return to their aerodromes making wild exaggerations of their success, claiming to have sunk or heavily damaged "a total of 57 enemy warships including 19 aircraft carriers and four battleships."

While some members of the Japanese admiralty viewed these incredible reports as abject fantasy, the Japanese press, including the infamous English-language radio propagandist known as Tokyo Rose, would declare the American fleet to have been utterly decimated, with its remnants in full retreat to the east. Upon hearing these illusionary reports,

Adolf Hitler would send a message of congratulations to Emperor Hirohito, whose subjects all received a ration of "celebration sake," courtesy of the Japanese finance ministry. Admiral Soemu Toyoda, apparently, had chosen to accept the fantastic claims of his aviators at face value, and on the evening of October 14 messaged his land-based air squadrons that the "enemy striking force has received our stinging attack and is retreating" and to "carry out annihilation operations as directed."

Admiral Halsey would respond to the Japanese claims with a signal to Chester Nimitz which ruthlessly mocked Radio Tokyo:

> The Third Fleet's sunken and damaged ships have been salvaged and are retiring at high speed toward the enemy.

What the inexperienced Japanese pilots had actually seen, Halsey believed, was the glow cast upon the American ships from the scattered, burning debris of numerous Japanese airplanes floating upon the water. Viewed from the air in the half-light, the ships themselves must have appeared to be on fire. Halsey then discussed the possibility of exploiting the Japanese illusions with his chief of staff, Rear Admiral Robert Carney, and his operations officer, Captain Ralph Wilson.

"Our basic orders, they pointed out, stated that 'in case opportunity for the destruction of a major portion of the enemy fleet offers or can be created, such destruction will become the primary task,' " Halsey later wrote. "Here was that opportunity, right in our laps. The enemy already believed that he had cut our fleet to pieces, and had announced that he was pursuing its remnants. Why not hide our real strength, lure him into attacking the task group around the cripples, in the supposition that these were the remnants, and then spring the trap and blow him out of the water?"

The damaged *Canberra* and *Houston* were then taken under tow at the creeping pace of three and a half knots and, much to the discomfiture of their crews, were promptly christened "BAITDIV One" by the sailors of the Third Fleet. Halsey ordered two of his carrier task groups to shadow the towing operation, over the horizon and out of sight. On

October 15, Hellcat pilots would swat down fifty more Japanese planes sent after the crippled warships. The poor *Houston* was torpedoed yet again, but remained afloat due to excellent damage control. That same day, CINCPAC headquarters transmitted the following message:

> Suspicion exists enemy surface force may have departed EMPIRE area to mop up on Blue cripples withdrawing FORMOSA strikes.

This was the Second Striking Force, consisting of three heavy cruisers, a light cruiser, and a destroyer squadron under Vice Admiral Kiyohide Shima which, sure enough, had sortied from the Inland Sea with orders to locate and destroy the "remnants" of the American fleet. Shima must have accepted the assignment with a healthy measure of presentiment, for after being attacked by American planes that were obviously carrier-based, he chose wisely to retire. Soon the ships of BAITDIV One were towed beyond the range of Japanese land-based aircraft to make safe harbor at Ulithi.

Halsey may not have provoked the fleet action that he had hoped for, but his Fast Carrier Task Forces were able to deliver yet another stunning blow to Toyoda's air fleet, which now had far fewer combat aircraft available to counter the next Allied move in the western Pacific. Imperial Army squadrons based on Luzon had also been severely beaten down, losing nearly half their strength.

"Giant waves swept over our quivering bow as it rose high out of the rough sea, only to come crashing forcibly down again under the depths," wrote Fred Vreeken of the *Maryland.* "Each time it surfaced against hundreds of tons of raging sea with shuddering force. All hands were ordered below as we plowed on to our fateful destination."

"There was no dodging the storm and for the next three days the 'Big T' pitched and rolled in heavy seas," said Lawrence Bellatti of the *Tennessee.* "The wind screamed through the halyards on the signal bridge, gusts of 45 knots being recorded by the anemometer."

After braving cyclonic gales, driving rain, and angry seas on their passage from Manus, the tempest-tossed vanguard of the United States Seventh Fleet arrived at the eastern approaches to Leyte Gulf on the morning of October 17, 1944. Enemy observation posts established at Desolation Point on the northern tip of Dinagat Island and on the outlying islands of Homonhon and Suluan were attacked and quickly neutralized by elements of the Sixth Ranger Battalion, but not before the Japanese sailors manning the Suluan lighthouse were able to transmit a warning to the headquarters of the Combined Fleet.

The Minesweeping and Hydrography group then led the way into Leyte Gulf itself, their already daunting task made all the more difficult by another storm system which swirled into the area. So as not to delay the landings that were scheduled to commence in just two days, Admiral Oldendorf decided to enter the gulf before being given the all-clear, with the *Louisville* leading the fire support ships in column behind a trio of minesweepers. The battleships themselves deployed their streaming paravanes—tethered underwater kites designed to snare floating mines. The paravanes of the *California* surfaced one Japanese mine as the battleship entered the channel, which was exploded by the rifle fire of her marines. While 229 Japanese mines were located and destroyed at the entrances to Leyte Gulf, few if any were encountered inside the gulf itself. Just after 2:00 p.m. on October 18, the bombardment of the invasion beaches began.

"As usual, fire was directed at predetermined targets and targets of opportunity, the object being destruction whenever possible," wrote the *Pennsylvania*'s Clifton Cates. "Chief emphasis, however, was placed on covering beach reconnaissance and underwater demolition teams and minesweeping units operating in Leyte Gulf and San Pedro Harbor." Phase One bombardment continued for the remainder of the day, and at 8:30 the following morning the fire support ships steamed into San Pedro Bay, their guns pounding steadily in support of UDT combat swimmers as they reconnoitered the landing beaches.

"The work of the Underwater Demolition Teams in amphibious warfare is deserving of the highest recognition," Admiral Oldendorf's war diary would claim. "These brave officers and men gamble their lives in order to clear enemy-made and natural obstacles from the beaches selected for landing craft, and are an example of Americanism which is never published—their reward is seeing landing craft hit the beach with its ramp down and machines and men move forward which is possible only through their devotion to country."

"All morning long the ships blasted Japanese installations, the *Tennessee* paying particular attention to Catman Hill, a strong point covering the beaches," Lawrence Bellatti reported. "Hundreds of rounds blasted the hillsides and the beaches, but there was no return fire. There were reports, from time to time during the day, of Japanese planes in the vicinity, but none came in to attack. In the afternoon a high-altitude enemy bomber was knocked from the air by antiaircraft fire." The firing would last until sunset when the battleships, following the detailed set of orders contained within the thick sheaf of mimeographed papers that was the fire support plan, withdrew from coastal waters for the night.

Aboard the many warships steaming through the dark waters of Leyte Gulf, "no one talked much, for there was not much to say, but all hands had plenty to think about," according to Morison. "Few episodes in war were more vivid in the minds of American sailors than the story of heroism and death on Bataan. Yet if any of these men felt like avenging angels or crusaders they kept it very much to themselves. More important to them was the fact that this was a big step along the road to Tokyo and the end of the war."

At 1:07 a.m. the *Louisville*'s radar detected the attack transports and landing ships of MacArthur's invasion force steaming through the entrance channel of Leyte Gulf, guided by the white beams of navigation lights placed upon the barrier islands by Army Rangers. The dawn of October 20 would bring brutally oppressive heat and miserable humidity, but the sea was at least calm, and except for a few clouds lingering on the horizon the skies had cleared. At 5:45 a.m. an "Oscar" fighter of the Japanese Army Air Force appeared over the bay and was driven off by antiaircraft fire from the *West Virginia*; a half-hour later a handful of Japanese naval aircraft buzzed the transport group and were fired upon by the *West Virginia*, *California*, and *Maryland*.

At 7:00 a.m. the battleships closed to within 9,000 yards of Leyte's shores and began the second phase of the pre-invasion bombardment, with their main and secondary batteries methodically pummeling the beach defenses. They would lift their fire just after 10:00 a.m., as many hundreds of landing craft carrying four full army divisions surged forth from the line of departure to hit the beaches. This began Phase Three of the naval bombardment, the delivery of on-call fire support as directed by JASCO detachments ashore. The expertly planned and coordinated landings were executed flawlessly, for the amphibious forces of the Seventh Fleet had amassed a great deal of practical experience over the past two years, having performed many such operations throughout the Solomons, the Bismarcks, New Guinea, and the Admiralties.

Compared to what the battleship sailors had witnessed during the Central Pacific Campaign, the initial Japanese response to the invasion was astonishingly weak. There were more sporadic air attacks throughout the morning, one of which caused minor damage to the escort carrier *Sangamon.* Three LSTs were struck by Japanese mortar fire, causing a temporary shift in the landing schedule until the enemy positions could be located and silenced. By noon, the US Army had established two 4-mile-long beachheads on Leyte, at a loss of just 49 killed and fewer than 200 wounded. An hour later, a landing craft would be brought alongside the cruiser *Nashville* to whisk General MacArthur and his party to the edge of Red Beach for their dramatic march through the surf.

Soemu Toyoda was surveying the damage done to Formosa's naval facilities and inspecting that island's preparations for a possible Allied invasion when he received the text of the final message transmitted from Suluan lighthouse. With the true fate and disposition of Halsey's carriers still unclear, the Commander-in-Chief of the Combined Fleet decided not to rush back to his Tokyo headquarters, lest he suffer the same fate as Yamamoto. For the time being, at least, he preferred to stay put and take his chances with the Army Air Forces B-29s that were frequently raiding the island from bases in mainland China, and sent a radio message directing his chief of staff to execute the first of a series of war plans known as *Sho-Go.*

The Combined Fleet had already warned its area commanders that another assault by American amphibious forces could be expected within the final ten days of October. For Toyoda, it was now a matter of assessing the available intelligence and reconnaissance information, trying to distinguish the enemy's true intent from his diversion and deception, and deciding which of the *Sho-Go* plans to implement. Roughly translated, *Sho-Go* means "Operation Victory" in Japanese. *Sho-1* outlined the response of Japanese forces to an Allied invasion of the Philippines. The aerial component of *Sho-2*, the plan for the defense of Formosa and the Ryukyus, had already been initiated and most of its assets brutally sacrificed. *Sho-3* and *Sho-4* directed the defense of the northernmost Japanese Home Island of Hokkaido and the Kuriles, respectively. In activating *Sho-1*, Toyoda would prove to be as daring a gambler as his late predecessor, as if to announce "all in" while pushing his stacked chips into the center of the Pacific poker table.

"The Imperial Navy will endeavor to maintain and make advantageous use of the strategic status quo; make plans to smash the enemy's strength; take the initiative in creating favorable tactical opportunities, or seize the opportunity as it presents itself, to crush the enemy fleet and attacking forces," the *Sho-1* plan optimistically declared. "In close conjunction with the Army, the Navy will maintain the security of sectors vital to national defense and prepare for future eventualities. It will also cooperate closely with related forces to maintain the security of surface routes between Japan and vital southern sources of materials."

The authors of *Sho-1* were quite correct in their prediction that "enemy forces will advance on the Philippines either directly from the New Guinea area or Saipan, or after capturing intermediate bases. The initial landing will probably be made in the central or southern Philippines, somewhere between (and including) Leyte and Mindanao."

"If the enemy attack occurs after the end of August, the Second Striking Force will be incorporated under the command of the Task Force Main Body as a vanguard force," *Sho-1* directed. "The Main Body will then assume the mission of diverting the enemy task forces to the northeast in order to facilitate the attack of the First Striking Force, and will also carry out an attack against the flank of the enemy task forces."

"Main Body" referred to Jisaburo Ozawa's motley collection of nearly empty aircraft carriers, which no longer had the ability to mount such an attack after its air groups had been tragically squandered in the vain attempt to destroy the US Third Fleet off Formosa. They could, however, serve as an enticing bait to lure the American carrier forces away from the Philippines, a strategy designed to take advantage of the natural aggressiveness of American fleet commanders like Bill Halsey.

Ozawa's flagship was the *Zuikaku*, the sole surviving fleet carrier of the Pearl Harbor Strike Force, which was accompanied by three light carriers and two odd battleship-carrier hybrids. A pitifully understrength combined air group of 116 planes, consisting of only 36 strike aircraft and 80 of the now-obsolete Zero fighters, had been scraped together and embarked, while 3 light cruisers and 8 destroyers provided the screen. The Main Body got under way from Bungo Suido on the evening of October 20. This time the Japanese were actually hoping to be spotted by American search planes.

Vice Admiral Shima's Second Striking Force, after its abortive attempt to engage the "remnants" of Halsey's fleet, had steamed for the Japanese isle of Amami Oshima before proceeding to the Mako Naval Base on Formosa to take on fuel. When Shima's unit stood out for Manila Bay on the afternoon of October 21, his final assignment was still uncertain. He was no longer in a position to serve as the vanguard for Ozawa's Main Body, as *Sho-1* had previously suggested, and the question of whether or not his ships would be escorting infantry reinforcements to the western shores of Leyte or join in a surface attack on MacArthur's invasion force was still being tossed back and forth between Manila and Tokyo.

The most serious naval threat to Allied forces in the region was the brawny First Striking Force under Vice Admiral Takeo Kurita, currently stationed 132 miles southwest of Singapore at Lingga Roads. Kurita's force was made up of three sections: the first composed of the super battleships *Yamato* and *Musashi*, the battleship *Nagato*, seven cruisers, and nine destroyers. The second section included battleships *Kongo* and *Haruna*, five cruisers, and a half-dozen destroyers. The Third Section, under the command of Vice Admiral Shoji Nishimura, was made up of the dreadnoughts *Yamashiro* and *Fuso*, the heavy cruiser *Mogami*, and four destroyers. That such a powerful surface fleet had to be based at Lingga Roads is a testament to the deadly efficiency of the US Navy's submarine campaign, which sank 4.7 million tons of Japanese merchant shipping during the Pacific War. By October 1944, American submarine attacks had reduced to a trickle the flow of oil reaching Japan from the Dutch East Indies, requiring the First Striking Force to be positioned at its source.

Kurita's ships put to sea from Lingga Roads at 1:00 a.m. on October 18, and, in accordance with the *Sho-1* operations plan, stood into Brunei harbor on Borneo two days later. As oil barges chugged into position to top off the immense fuel bunkers of the great ships, signal flags were hoisted from Kurita's flagship, the heavy cruiser *Atago*, directing the senior officers of First Striking Force to gather for a briefing.

Ozawa's Main Body was headed south with the objective of luring the American Fast Carrier Task Forces to the northeast, Kurita informed his commanders, thus clearing the way for First Striking Force to attack the Allied invasion fleet in Leyte Gulf. The great gamble was on whether or not Halsey rose to the bait; if he chose to stay in position, with the huge number of carrier-based planes at his disposal maintaining air supremacy over the Philippines, the chances of success were low. As long as Task Force 38 remained in the area, little help could be expected from the Imperial Army and Navy land-based air forces; between the two services there were hardly more than 200 flyable aircraft left in the Philippines.

Headquarters Combined Fleet had proposed that First Striking Force be divided into two groups, performing a double envelopment of the Allied invasion fleet. Generally speaking, a battle fleet sailing west to east through the Philippine archipelago had the choice of two routes into Leyte Gulf. The first was through San Bernardino Strait, the channel that separated the two large islands of Luzon and Samar. Passing through the strait and emerging into the Philippine Sea, the attacking force could then descend upon Leyte Gulf from the north. The second route was through Surigao Strait, skirting the coast of Mindanao and steaming north through the channel between Panaon and Dinagat Islands to approach the gulf from the south.

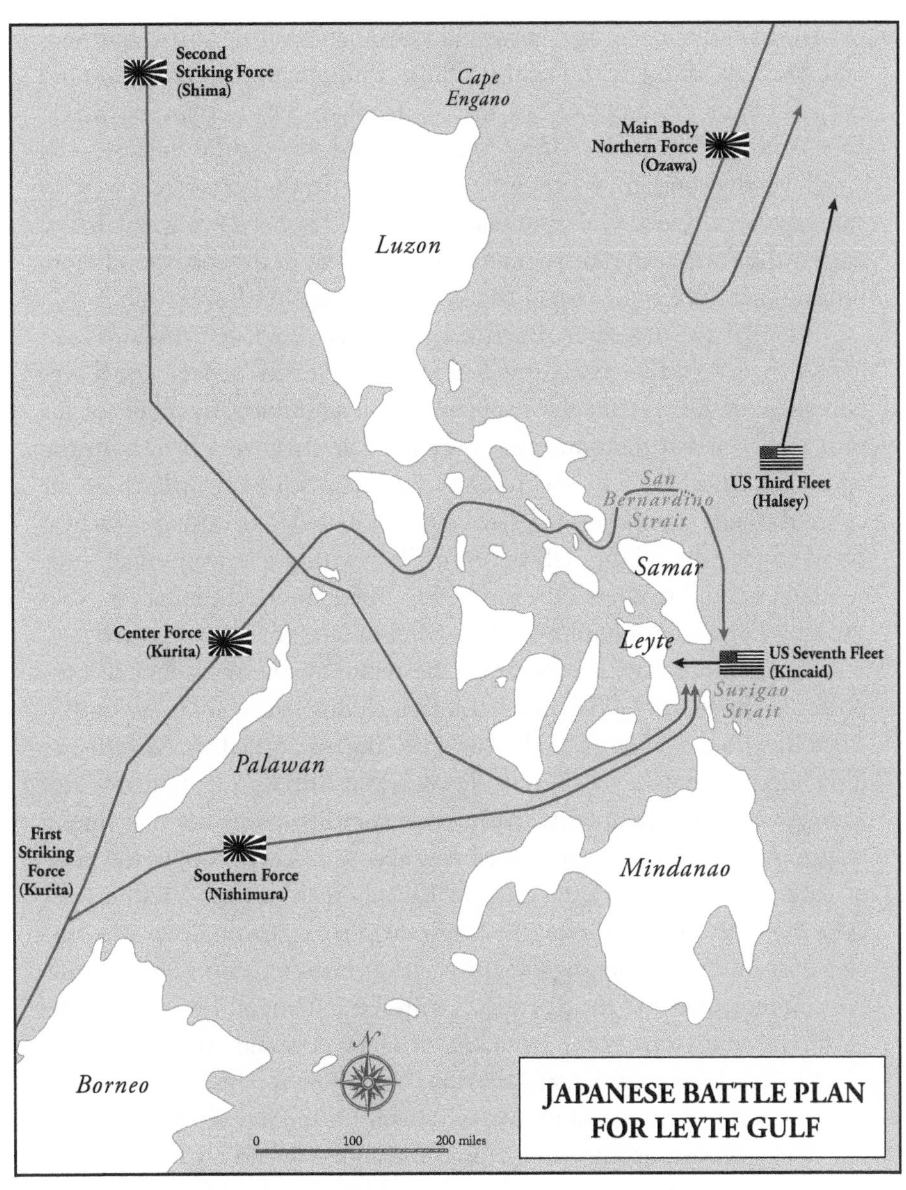
Second
Striking Force
(Shima)
Cape
Engano
Main Body
Northern Force
(Ozawa)
Luzon
US Third Fleet
(Halsey)
San
Bernardino
Strait
Samar
Center Force
(Kurita)
Leyte
US Seventh Fleet
(Kincaid)
Surigao
Strait
Palawan
First
Striking
Force
(Kurita)
Southern Force
(Nishimura)
Mindanao
N
Borneo
0
100
200 miles
JAPANESE BATTLE PLAN
FOR LEYTE GULF

Kurita announced that he would personally lead the First and Second Sections through the center of the Philippines, threading around the islands of the Sibuyan Sea to pass through San Bernardino Strait. Vice Admiral Nishimura's Third Section would traverse the Sulu Sea and attack via the southern route through Surigao Strait. Both forces were to converge upon Leyte Gulf on the morning of October 25 to wreak havoc among the American transport and supply vessels in the roadstead before turning their heavy guns upon MacArthur's troops on Leyte itself.

Shoji Nishimura, often described as a gentle, kind, and studious man with a cheerful disposition, is said to have received his orders with a certain stoic fatalism. After the conference was adjourned, members of his staff made known their anxieties over the role they were to play in the operation. Third Section was to cross the Sulu Sea with little to no air cover through submarine-infested waters, then steam through Surigao Strait to face the mighty US Seventh Fleet with a relatively small force centered around two aged dreadnoughts. The news that Shima's Second Striking Force might reinforce Third Section brought little comfort.

In the meantime, Kurita would be retaining the considerable firepower of the First and Second sections, including the giant sister battleships *Yamato* and *Musashi*, for his own use. The plan called for Nishimura's force to penetrate Leyte Gulf at dawn, while Kurita's was to arrive *two hours later*. Rather than participating in a coordinated pincer movement, it appeared as if Third Section was being sent into Leyte Gulf in the hope of reducing enemy strength prior to Kurita's main attack. Viewed with even the most objective eyes, the assignment smacked of a one-way suicide mission. After listening patiently to the grave concerns of his officers, Nishimura would end the discussion with the statement: "We will do our best." The admiral had been issued his orders and would do his duty.

Kurita's First and Second Sections, hereafter referred to as Center Force, stood out from Brunei two days later on the morning of October 22, 1944, and steamed northeast on a course that would take them along the western shores of Palawan Island. Nishimura's Third Section, or the Southern Force, weighed anchor and got under way that same afternoon. Once clear of Borneo's ragged coastline, Southern Force turned eastward into the Sulu Sea, bound for Surigao Strait. Having finally received his orders from Manila, Kiyohide Shima and his Second Striking Force were also headed for Surigao Strait, where they were to "cooperate" with Nishimura's southern thrust while remaining an independent command. Unfortunately for the Japanese, it would be Kurita's Center Force and not Ozawa's Main Body, or Northern Force, that was first spotted by the Americans.

Just after midnight on October 23, the submarine USS *Darter* was patrolling the Palawan Passage when her radar detected what could only have been a large enemy task force. There appeared to be two columns of heavy ships flanked by several destroyers, zigzagging north by northeast at a speed of 15 knots. It was Center Force, being led by Kurita's flagship *Atago*. At the time of the radar contact, *Darter* was surfaced alongside the submarine *Dace*, with their skippers in conference. The more senior of the two, Commander David McClintock of the *Darter*, ordered the *Dace* to lie ahead of the approaching formation and strike the easternmost column when it came within range. After dashing off a contact report to Commander Submarines Southwest Pacific, the *Darter* raced to the western flank of the Japanese formation and submerged for the attack.

"Heard five torpedo explosions. *Darter* must be getting in," Commander Bladen Claggett of the *Dace* would describe in a patrol report written in more of a jocular play-by-play fashion than in a militarily formal style using the past tense. Two minutes later, the crew of the *Dace* would hear "Four more torpedo hits. *Darter* is really having a field day. Can see great pall of smoke completely enveloping spot where ship was at last look. Do not know whether he has sunk but it looks good."

McClintock had put four torpedoes into the *Atago*, which quickly broke up and sank, leaving the paddling Admiral Kurita to be plucked from the churning sea by a destroyer. The *Darter*'s attack also severely damaged the next heavy cruiser in the column, *Takao*, which was forced to stagger back to Singapore. The *Darter* entered a deep dive to escape the depth charges being flung at random by scrambling Japanese destroyers; then it was *Dace*'s turn.

"This is really the submariner's dream, sitting right in front of a task force," Claggett wrote. At 5:54 a.m. the *Dace* fired a spread of five torpedoes from 7,000 yards. Four of them struck the heavy cruiser *Maya*, which exploded and immediately began to sink. "These explosions were apparently magazines as I have never heard anything like it," Claggett described. Within five minutes, the *Maya* was gone, along with 336 members of her crew.

Hours later, while still stalking the wounded *Takao*, the *Darter* ran hard aground on the treacherous Bombay Shoal within Palawan Passage. This would end her fourth and final war patrol; McClintock and his crew were then taken off by the *Dace* for the long journey back to Australia. By then, the shaken Kurita had transferred his flag to the *Yamato* and ordered his Center Force, now down three heavy cruisers, to continue at best speed for the Sibuyan Sea.

Three of the four carrier groups that made up Task Force 38 were at sea some 250 miles east of Luzon when Admiral Halsey received *Darter*'s contact report on October 23. Within minutes, Halsey ordered all three task groups to close with the Philippine coast "on a broad front," and to wait until dawn before launching long-range search-and-strike missions.

"Experience had taught us that if we interfered with a Jap plan before it matured, we stood a good chance of disrupting it," Halsey wrote.

Midway through the forenoon watch of October 24, with search flights already aloft and on their way to scout the Sibuyan, Visayan, and Sulu Seas surrounding the Philippine Islands, the screening vessels of Rear Admiral Frederick Sherman's Task Group 38.3 picked up three inbound waves of approximately fifty aircraft on their air search radar. They were what remained of the Japanese Navy's First Air Fleet, based on Luzon.

Hellcats of the Combat Air Patrol were vectored in to intercept and soon began taking a heavy toll among the enemy raiders. Commander David McCampbell of the *Essex* air group, who would end the war as the navy's top-scoring fighter ace, personally splashed an astonishing nine Japanese planes in the engagement. Most of the others were either shot down or chased off by McCampbell's fellow Hellcat pilots and the intense antiaircraft fire of the screen, but one "Judy" dive-bomber managed to get through to score a fatal hit on the carrier *Princeton* with an armor-piercing bomb. After the light cruiser *Birmingham* was brought alongside to assist with firefighting efforts, the *Princeton* was rocked by a secondary explosion which ravaged the *Birmingham*'s topside and killed 233 of her crew. Another 108 men were killed aboard the *Princeton*, which had to be abandoned and scuttled.

In the meantime, search planes from Rear Admiral Gerald Bogan's Task Group 38.2 located Kurita's Center Force as it rounded the island of Mindoro and steamed northeast into the Sibuyan Sea. Halsey ordered all three carrier groups to launch strike missions of Hellcats, Helldivers, and Avengers, and sent word for Vice Admiral John McCain's Task Group 38.1, which was en route to Ulithi for fuel and provisions, to reverse course and return to Philippine waters.

Center Force was first hit at 10:30 a.m. and would be fighting for its life well into the afternoon. In all there were 259 sorties flown by the carriers *Enterprise*, *Franklin*, *Essex*, *Intrepid*, *Cabot*, and the new *Lexington* against Kurita's ships, which were relentlessly bombed and strafed while receiving virtually no assistance from the Japanese air forces. The battleships *Nagato* and *Yamato* were damaged by bombs; at nightfall the *Musashi* would roll over and sink after being demolished by an estimated 17 bombs and 19 torpedoes. Nearly half of *Musashi*'s 2,300-man crew went down with the ship, including her captain. Another of Kurita's heavy cruisers, the *Myoko*, was knocked out of the fight and forced to retire to Borneo.

By midafternoon it appeared as if Kurita, even in the face of these punishing air attacks, might still attempt to force San Bernardino Strait. Halsey and his staff prepared a contingency plan in the event Kurita continued on his current course, informing the unit commanders of Third Fleet that the fast battleships "will be formed as Task Force 34 under Vice Admiral Lee Commander Battle Line. Task Force 34 [will] engage decisively at long ranges." While Nimitz and King were both secondary addressees of the message, Thomas Kinkaid was not. However, radio operators aboard the Seventh Fleet command ship *Wasatch* heard the transmission, which was decoded and delivered to Kinkaid.

The confusion caused by Halsey's communication would eventually cause a great deal of trouble for the Americans and nearly cost them the Battle of Leyte Gulf, as would the lack of a unified naval command structure, something that had been curiously left out of the planning for the Philippine operation. At 4:00 p.m., Kurita advised his commander-in-chief that he was, in fact, reversing course in order to put some distance between himself and Halsey's carriers.

Nishimura would also become a target of Bill Halsey's wrath. A search-and-strike group of twenty-seven aircraft from the *Enterprise*, including Hellcats armed with rockets, attacked the Southern Force around 9:10 a.m., some 50 miles southwest of the island of Negros. Rocket fire and strafing would kill twenty sailors aboard the flagship *Yamashiro*. Two bombs landing close aboard ruptured the seams of hull plates, causing the battleship to begin taking on water.

The *Fuso* received two direct hits. One bomb landed alongside the Number Two Turret and wiped out the crew of a secondary battery; the other struck the quarterdeck, setting afire two seaplanes sitting in their catapults. The explosions opened seams aboard the elderly *Fuso* as well and she began taking on a slight list to starboard. Her commanding officer, Rear Admiral Masami Ban, ordered a turn into the wind to clear the smoke away from the battleship's superstructure, resuming his original course once the burning floatplanes were shoved overboard. The fires and flooding aboard both battleships were quickly brought under control, and Southern Force continued with its steady eastward march across the Sulu Sea toward Leyte Gulf.

At 12:15 p.m. on October 24, 1944, Rear Admiral Jesse Oldendorf received a signal transmitted from Admiral Kinkaid's *Wasatch*, addressed to all task group commanders in the Seventh Fleet, with advisory copies sent to Halsey, Nimitz, MacArthur, and King.

> Prepare for night engagement. Enemy force estimated 2 BB, 4 CA, 4 CL, 10 DD reported under attack by our carrier planes in eastern SULU SEA at 0910 I (-9) 24 Oct. Enemy can arrive LEYTE GULF tonight. Make all preparations for

night engagement. TG 77.3 assigned to CTG 77.2 as reinforcement. CTG 70.1 station maximum number PT's lower SURIGAO STRAIT to remain south of 10-10 north during darkness.*

"It was obvious that the objective of the Japanese forces was the destruction of our transports and that my mission was to protect them at all costs," Oldendorf later wrote. "In order to accomplish my mission, the force under my command must be interposed between the enemy and the transports. I realized that I must not lose sight of my mission no matter how much I might be tempted to engage in a gunnery duel with him."

There was little time to spare. The Seventh Fleet's PT Boats were sent roaring south down Surigao Strait. Together with his chief of staff, Captain Richard Bates, Oldendorf began drafting battle plans and issuing warning orders. A message was flashed to the light cruiser *Phoenix*, summoning Rear Admiral Russell "Count" Berkey of Task Group 77.3, the Close Covering Group that had been assigned as reinforcements. Oldendorf also sent for Rear Admiral George Weyler, who had been commanding one of the two fire support units in Leyte Gulf.

In an afternoon conference aboard the *Louisville*, Oldendorf laid out his plan for Weyler and Berkey. Thirty-nine PT boats would be deployed in three-boat sections along the southern end of Surigao Strait to act as scouts and, if the opportunity presented itself, to make high-speed torpedo runs on the enemy column. Oldendorf would have three destroyer squadrons at his disposal. Two of them, DESRON 24 and DESRON 56, would steam south into the strait, hugging the coastlines of either side before making flanking attacks on the Japanese ships with torpedoes and gunfire. If the Japanese column continued to press northward, they would meet with the main battery fire of cruisers and battleships.

---

* A possible explanation for this overestimate of the strength of Southern Force is offered by a Naval War College analysis of the Battle of Surigao Strait: A radio operator aboard a Navy PB4Y search plane, overhearing the contact reports of Halsey's fliers as they attacked both Southern Force and Center Force, became confused as to the location and number of enemy ships sighted while relaying the reports to his base. The report made by the commander of the *Enterprise* strike mission that attacked Southern Force was actually very accurate: 2 BB (battleships), 1 CA (heavy cruiser), and 4 DD (destroyers).

An opportunity to seize the long sought-after Holy Grail of naval tactics, the "crossing of the T," was at hand. Arrayed east to west across the northern end of Surigao Strait would be two flanking groups of cruisers. The right flank, under Berkey, would consist of the *Phoenix* and *Boise* along with the Australian heavy cruiser HMAS *Shropshire*. In the event the Japanese might try to slip into Leyte Gulf through the channel that ran between Hibuson and Dinagat Islands, Oldendorf was assigning five cruisers to his left flank. The *Louisville*, *Portland*, *Minneapolis*, *Denver*, and *Columbia* would comprise this force, which Oldendorf himself would command. Weyler's two battleship divisions were to lie north of the cruiser forces, steaming in a line-of-battle formation from east to west. Leading the column would be Rear Admiral Theodore Ruddock's BATDIV Four, made up of the *West Virginia* and *Maryland* along with the *Mississippi*, from which Weyler would fly his flag. They would be followed by BATDIV Two, under Rear Admiral Theodore Chandler, consisting of the *Tennessee*, *California*, and *Pennsylvania*. A third squadron of six destroyers, designated DESRON X-Ray, would screen the battleships.

Weyler informed Oldendorf that the battleships were running low on armor-piercing ammunition and that "there was likewise a shortage of ammunition of all types throughout the force. It was therefore essential that the battleships fire at ranges where their percentage of hits and their fire effect would both be high. This was settled on as between 17,000 and 20,000 yards."

The briefing and discussion concluded, Oldendorf dismissed Weyler and Berkey to return to their flagships and prepare their respective commands for the coming battle. The operations plan had "met with their unqualified approval," Oldendorf recalled. "I then turned the plan over to my staff to be put into despatch form to be sent out by visual signal, as there was insufficient time to code and decode if sent by radio." It was at this time that Oldendorf received the welcome news that Ping Wilkinson was sending a fourth destroyer squadron, DESRON 54 under Captain Jesse Coward, to reinforce Task Group 77.2.

The battle plan was flashed to the ships of the fleet:

> The enemy forces to the westward of Leyte appear to be threatening us tonight with 2 BB 4 CA CL and 10 DD X Plan destroy by gunfire and torpedoes any enemy attempting to enter Surigao Strait X Battle line of 6 BB plus assigned DD destroy or repel Japanese battle line with guns quickly gaining moderate ranges around 20,000 yards X Left flank five cruisers and DD assigned protect own battleships and attack enemy battleships X Right flank three cruisers and DD defend own big ships and sink enemy battleships X Use disposition similar 10-A operating east and west X Bear in mind own and enemy destroyer attacks, etc.

At long last, the dreadnoughts would be engaging an enemy fleet in a surface action, finally performing the task for which they had been designed and engineered, and the scenario for which their senior officers and petty officers had trained for much of their long careers. As for the ninety-day wonders and recent inductees, it was what they had signed up for, what they had envisioned themselves doing upon joining the navy after Pearl Harbor.

They were no longer loosely joined collectives of officers and men, regulars and reservists, shellbacks and wogs. They were *crews*. Their ships, for which they had developed a deep affection and intense pride, had united them in cause and purpose. Countless hours of training and mentoring had honed their skills, tempered by the fires of combat and the rigors of life at sea. Together they had endured frigid arctic winds and tropical cyclones, backbreaking labor and seemingly endless midwatches, the tedium of escort duty and the horrors of modern war. They had killed, or had supported directly those who had. They had bandaged their comrades' bleeding wounds and salved their burns, and had stood to render honors while their dead were buried at sea. Many would not hesitate to lay down their life for a shipmate; most had already formed friendships that would last a lifetime. Now they were to sail beyond the darkness together to do battle. The fact that they were going up against a clever and resourceful enemy skilled in the art of night combat, and who had often come out on top in such engagements, was not lost on any of them.

Darkness falls quickly in the tropics. At six o'clock, as the sun was sinking behind the jagged crests of Leyte's deep green mountains and setting the sky ablaze with a dozen iridescent shades of yellow and orange, the battleships in Leyte Gulf sent their seaplanes ashore for the night, lest they become kindling for shipboard fires. The six dreadnoughts of Task Force 77.2 then formed a battle line and began steaming south for Surigao Strait. Leading the column was the USS *West Virginia* with the Stars and Stripes on her foremast snapping in the breeze, the very same national ensign she had flown on the morning of December 7, 1941.

CHAPTER 21

REVENGE OF THE DREADNOUGHTS

DUCKING IN AND OUT OF WHIPPING RAIN SQUALLS, THE THREE MOTOR torpedo boats pounded across the rolling groundswells of the Bohol Sea. Since sundown they had been patrolling the dark and stormy passage between the islands of Bohol and Camiguin, 50 nautical miles southwest of the entrance to Surigao Strait. At 10:36 p.m., two large blips had appeared on the *PT-131*'s search radar, making 18 knots' speed on a northeasterly heading of 065 degrees.

Leading the formation was Lieutenant (j.g.) Joseph Eddins's *PT-152*. One of 326 PT boats built by the Elco Boat Company of Bayonne, New Jersey, the *152* was 80 feet long while displacing just 56 tons. The US Navy's PT boats were designed for all-out speed, in order to deliver lightning-fast torpedo attacks and disappear into the darkness before the enemy knew what had hit him. Built of layered mahogany, the boats carried no armor to speak of other than what their crews might have scrounged from wrecked airplanes, and installed themselves, to protect the more-vulnerable topside positions. Powered by three monstrous 1,500-horsepower Packard V12 engines, they screamed across the water at over 40 knots.

The PT boats were not only fast, they were also armed to the teeth. Their complement of weapons was often highly customized and varied somewhat depending on the needs of the mission, but the *PT-152*'s loadout was fairly typical: On the foredeck were swivel-mounted M4 37-millimeter and 20-millimeter Oerlikon autocannons; flanking either side of the cockpit amidships were turrets of twin Browning .50 caliber machine guns; facing aft was a 40-millimeter Bofors. The boat also carried four 21-inch Mark 13 torpedoes and eight Mark 6 depth charges.

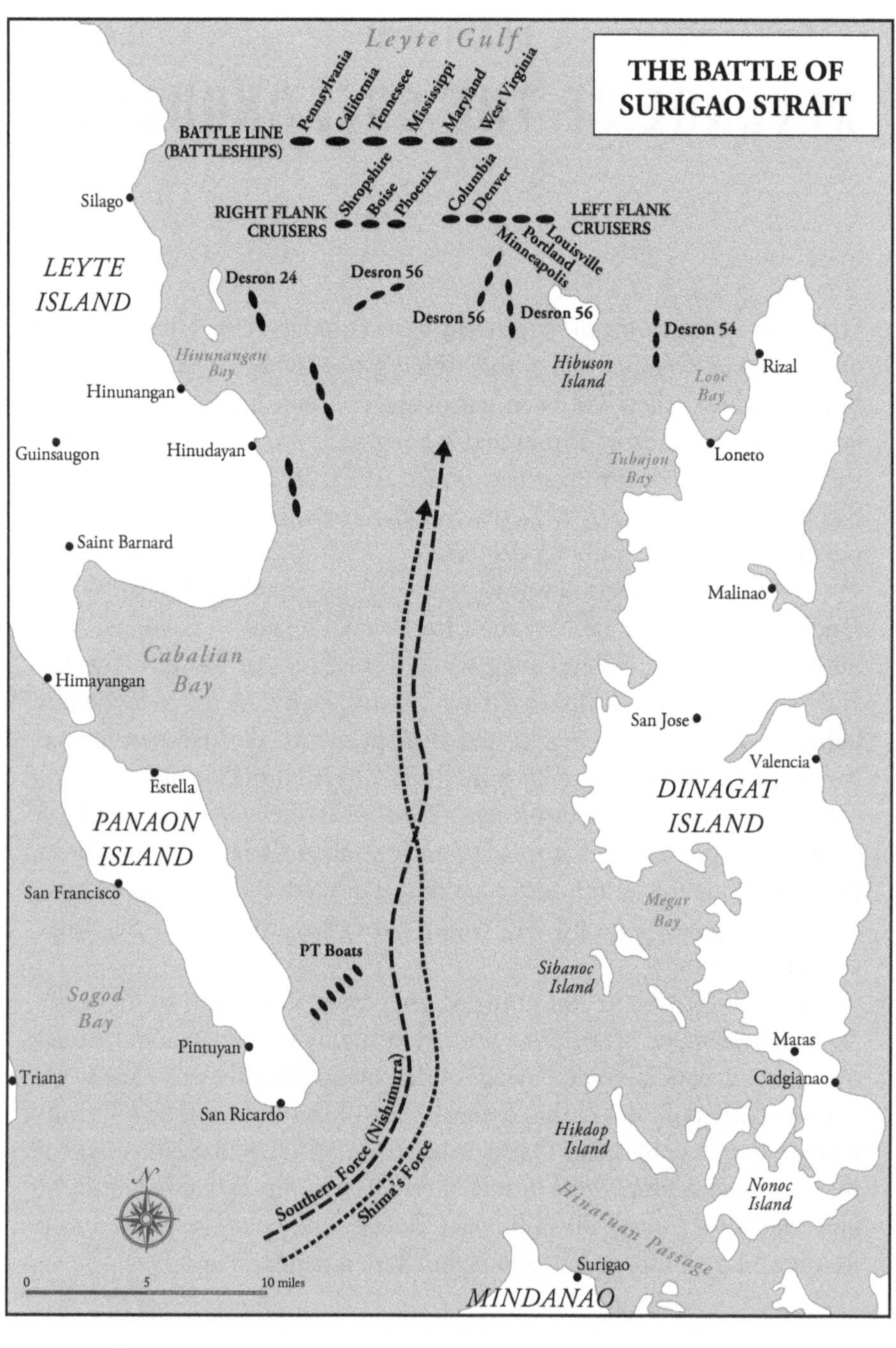

THE BATTLE OF SURIGAO STRAIT
Leyte Gulf
Pennsylvania
California
Tennessee
Mississippi
Maryland
West Virginia
BATTLE LINE (BATTLESHIPS)
Shropshire
Boise
Phoenix
Columbia
Denver
RIGHT FLANK CRUISERS
LEFT FLANK CRUISERS
Louisville
Portland
Minneapolis
Silago
LEYTE ISLAND
Desron 24
Desron 56
Desron 56
Desron 56
Desron 54
Hinunangan Bay
Hinunangan
Hibuson Island
Rizal
Looc Bay
Guinsaugon
Hinudayan
Loneto
Tubajon Bay
Saint Barnard
Malinao
Cabalian Bay
Himayangan
San Jose
Valencia
Estella
DINAGAT ISLAND
PANAON ISLAND
San Francisco
Megar Bay
PT Boats
Sibanoc Island
Sogod Bay
Pintuyan
Matas
Triana
Cadgianao
San Ricardo
Southern Force (Nishimura)
Shima's Force
Hikdop Island
Nonoc Island
Hinatuan Passage
Surigao
0
5
10 miles
MINDANAO

Duty aboard the PT boats was often reserved for the spirited, the aggressive, and the very young. Crouched alongside Eddins in the cockpit of the *152* boat was the skipper of Motor Torpedo Boat Squadron Twelve, a naval reserve lieutenant named Weston Pullen Jr. from Norwich, Connecticut, who at twenty-seven years of age was considered the "old man" of the outfit. Along with the Underwater Demolition Teams, today's Naval Special Warfare community traces their lineage directly to these swashbuckling PT crews, who often carried out commando-style raids on the shores of remote Japanese-held islands and performed many daring rescues of downed aviators under fire. This night, however, they were on a scouting mission to the southern approaches of Surigao Strait, where they were to "remain south of a line of latitude 10 degrees 10 minutes, to report enemy progress, and to attack if opportunity presented."

Youthful exuberance and excitement may have been to blame, or if Lieutenant Pullen is to be given the benefit of the doubt, he may have decided to investigate the radar contact before transmitting a report to the *Wachapreague*, a motor torpedo boat tender anchored in Liloan Bay on the northern end of Panaon Island and charged with relaying messages from the scouting PTs to Commander Task Group 77.2. Either way, obedience to Admiral Oldendorf's strict instruction was thrown out of order as the three PTs swung into their attack run without making a contact report. Over the PT Common frequency, Ensign Peter Gadd of the *131* boat announced that there now appeared to be *five* blips on their radar. The three skippers pushed their throttles forward to achieve a breakneck speed, the boats tossing clouds of spray in their wake.

"*Three enemy motor torpedo boats sighted, bearing 030 degrees!*"

The startling announcement had come from *Shigure* over the radiotelephone. From the bridge of the *Yamashiro*, Admiral Nishimura watched as the destroyer's 12.7-centimeter guns fired two illumination rounds into the night sky. The flickering red light soon revealed a trio of enemy PT boats at a distance of 3 miles and closing fast. The cry of the *Shigure*'s lookouts would prove that bursts of youthful excitability were not unique to Americans, for the true bearing of the incoming boats was 130 degrees, not 030 degrees. Nishimura's Southern Force had been spotted.

At noon that day, one of the *Mogami*'s seaplane pilots had circled low over the flagship to drop a message canister containing a report of his reconnaissance mission to Surigao Strait and Leyte Gulf. As of 6:50 a.m., four American battleships, two heavy cruisers, and two destroyers could be seen in the gulf, 8 miles east of the city of Dulag. Between the warships and the coast were at least eighty transports, with two more destroyers just off the landing beaches. No aircraft carriers were observed, but the pilot had been forced to avoid four US Navy fighters patrolling the skies over the gulf. Four destroyers and at least ten small craft were also spotted in Surigao Strait near Panaon Island.

Seven hours later, as many in the Southern Force were observing what would be their final sunset, a coded message was received from Commander-in-Chief, Combined Fleet. In what appeared to be a response to Kurita's announcement that he was reversing course, Admiral Toyoda had issued the order:

```
All forces to the attack, trusting in divine aid.
```

This was a reflection of Toyoda's belief, shared by Togo, Yamamoto, and others before him, in the concept of *shosu seiei shugi*—small numbers in a high state of readiness—together with the spiritual element that still remained prevalent in the battle doctrine and planning of the Imperial Japanese Navy. This was an implicit faith in the warrior ethos of the Japanese sailor, in the superiority of his fighting ability and of the Japanese-designed weapons he wielded, along with the assurance that his divine Emperor and the Seven Lucky Gods would guide and protect him. These articles of faith were at the core of a belief system that compelled Japanese soldiers and sailors, like Shoji Nishimura, to sally forth into battle in the face of insurmountable odds and almost certain death.

Nishimura would respond with a message stating his intention of engaging enemy forces off the coast of Dulag around 4:00 a.m., a departure from his earlier plan of arriving off Tacloban twenty to thirty minutes later. In order to keep to this schedule and avoid Allied submarines and air searches, Nishimura had made two course deviations during the voyage, rather than sailing on a direct route across the Sulu Sea. At 9:55 p.m., he received a change of orders from Kurita. Because of the delay caused by the temporary retirement of Center Force in the face of Halsey's unrelenting air attacks, they would not be making the 6:00 a.m. rendezvous with Southern Force. Nishimura was to attack Leyte Gulf as scheduled, then rejoin Center Force 10 miles northeast of Suluan Island for a second attack on the American fleet. That is, if Nishimura and his men were still alive.

Based on the floatplane's reconnaissance report, Nishimura had already ordered the *Mogami*, along with the destroyers *Michishio*, *Asagumo*, and *Yamagumo* to steam 20 kilometers ahead of the formation and sweep the route of advance for the "four destroyers and at least ten small craft" spotted earlier. Now here were three of the "devil boats" coming straight for him.

The *Shigure*, however, would soon remind everyone of the reason why destroyers are called "destroyers": The original purpose of the fast and nimble warships was to destroy the torpedo boats that attacked battleships. Making a sharp turn to starboard at flank speed in order to meet the inbound threat, *Shigure* opened fire with every gun that could be brought to bear. The *Yamashiro* and *Fuso* turned as well in order to present narrower targets, while contributing to the *Shigure*'s barrage with fire from their secondary batteries. The three PT boats, still too far away to launch their torpedoes and now bracketed by shell splashes, cranked into fast evasive turns and began laying down smoke.

The *PT-152* was soon caught in the blinding glare of the *Shigure*'s powerful searchlight. A 5-inch shell struck the boat's 37-millimeter mount, killing the gunner and knocking the loader unconscious. Putting the stern of the *PT-152* toward the pursuing destroyer, Eddins screamed for the crew of the after 40-millimeter gun to concentrate on the searchlight, while also ordering two depth charges to be set for 100 feet and dropped over the side.

The desperate countermeasures worked. The *Shigure* veered wildly off course after receiving the shock of two underwater explosions, and the rapid-fire Bofors "made the enemy reluctant to continue use of the searchlight." Another enemy shell struck the nose of a torpedo on the *PT-130*'s port side with a horrifying clang before angling downward to smash through the deck and punch a hole through the wooden hull above the waterline. Miraculously, neither the Japanese shell nor the warhead of the torpedo ever detonated. After twenty minutes, the *Shigure* gave up the chase and returned to her station alongside the battleships.

The shock and vibration of the gun action rendered the temperamental VHF radio sets of all three boats inoperable, leaving Pullen's section unable to transmit a contact report. After losing track of the *PT-152* in the darkness and smoke, the skipper of the *130* boat, Lieutenant (j.g.) Ian Malcom, signaled for the *PT-131* to follow and raced southward into the adjoining patrol sector off Camiguin Island. Finding the *PT-127* idling in the darkness, Malcolm clambered aboard and used that boat's radio to transmit a message to the *Wachapreague*, which was received at 12:15 a.m.

The three PT boats of Lieutenant (j.g.) Dwight Owens's section, *151*, *146*, and *190*, were lying-to and drifting with the current about 9 miles south of Limasawa Island, approximately 25 miles due west of the entrance to Surigao Strait. "Off to the southwest over the horizon we saw distant flashes of gunfire, star shells bursting and the far-off sweep of searchlights," Owens would write. Their attempts to report the sighting to the *Wachapreague* would be frustrated by the electronic jamming of the radio net by the Japanese.

"The display continued about fifteen minutes, then blacked out," Owens continued. "Squalls came and went. One moment the moon shone bright as day and the next you couldn't make out the bow of your boat. Then the radar developed the sort of pips you read about."

It was the *Mogami* and her three accompanying destroyers, which Owens incorrectly identified as a battleship, a cruiser, and three destroyers. Detecting the high-pitched whine of boat propellers on her hydrophones, the *Mogami* began sweeping the surrounding sea with a searchlight just as the *151* and *146* boats closed to within 1,800 yards of the heavy cruiser's port quarter and launched torpedoes, both of which missed. When the PTs wheeled around for another pass, a searchlight beam from the *Yamagumo* found them and gunfire soon ripped through the water close aboard. The boats responded with their 40-millimeter guns, sending blazing tracer rounds streaking into the black silhouette of the destroyer's superstructure and dousing the light. At 12:26 a.m., a volley of star shells suddenly exploded in the sky, casting their eerie red glow upon the scattered rain clouds, and the *Mogami* turned abruptly to the north, trailed by the three destroyers. The *PT-190* sped off in pursuit but for some reason was unable to close the distance, finally breaking off the chase without ever firing her torpedoes.

Thirty-eight miles to the southwest, lookouts aboard the *Nachi* saw the star shells as well. Second Striking Force was steaming to the northeast on a zigzag course at 22 knots, and had thus far managed to remain undetected by the outer cordon of American torpedo boats. Shima's force now consisted of his flagship *Nachi*, another heavy cruiser, *Ashigara*, and the light cruiser *Abekuma*. His fourth cruiser, *Aoba*, had been torpedoed the day before by the submarine USS *Bream* in the South China Sea west of Luzon and was forced to put into Manila.

Shima was also missing three destroyers from his original complement of seven, which had been detached for the purposes of transporting aviation mechanics and spare parts from Formosa to Manila. Rushing to rejoin Second Striking Force after completing their errand, they were caught off the coast of Mindoro by strike aircraft from the carrier *Franklin*. The *Wakaba* was sunk, and after collecting her survivors the remaining two destroyers returned to Manila Bay instead of continuing on to their rendezvous. Incredibly, they neglected to inform Admiral Shima of the decision, which he surely would have vetoed.

As for coordinating his movements with Nishimura's Southern Force, Shima had been given a free hand. He intended to enter Surigao Strait around 3:00 a.m. and arrive in Leyte Gulf after Nishimura, engaging enemy shipping in a clockwise sweep before retiring *south*, back down the strait. This plan offered little in the way of "cooperation" with Nishimura, leaving the analysts of the US Naval War College to later speculate that Shima may have wished to avoid a rendezvous with Kurita and risk having his independent command absorbed into the First Striking Force. Shima was still drafting a dispatch to inform the principal Japanese commanders of his intentions when illumination rounds were seen bursting over the horizon.

The star shells were coming from both sections of Nishimura's divided Southern Force. Nerves were jangled after the two whirlwind torpedo boat attacks, and Captain Ryo Toma of the *Mogami* had nearly opened fire on his own flagship as the two groups merged in the darkness. Once the friend-or-foe issue was sorted out, Nishimura's ships began assuming a Number Two Approach Formation. The destroyers *Michishio* and *Asagumo* steamed ahead to take the lead, 4 kilometers ahead of the battleship *Yamashiro*, followed at 2-kilometer intervals by the *Fuso* and *Mogami*. The two remaining destroyers, *Yamagumo* and *Shigure*, began moving to either side to protect the flanks of the capital ships. Southern Force then steered onto a course of 090 degrees due east at a speed of 18 knots, while Nishimura's radio operators tapped out a message addressed to Admirals Kurita and Shima.

> Will pass through southern entrance of Surigao Strait at 0130 and penetrate into Leyte Gulf. Several torpedo boats sighted but enemy situation otherwise unknown. Weather: Some squalls but visibility gradually improving.

"Where *are* they?"

Jesse Oldendorf stared at the straight penciled lines and scrawled calculations on the *Louisville*'s flag plot. It had been just over fifteen hours since "four Japanese battleships, eight cruisers, and ten destroyers" were sighted by Halsey's pilots steaming on an eastward course across the Sulu Sea, obviously bound for Surigao Strait. Nine hours had elapsed since Kinkaid had issued the order to "prepare for night engagement."

It was now becoming clear that the Imperial Japanese Navy was attempting a three-pronged assault on Leyte Gulf. In addition to the southern group, another more powerful surface force had been found in the Sibuyan Sea headed in the direction of San Bernardino Strait and had been badly beaten up by the planes of Task Force 38. Now the long-absent Japanese carrier fleet had appeared northeast of Luzon. Just after 8:00 p.m. Halsey sent a message to Kinkaid, Nimitz, and King which read:

> Enemy force SIBUYAN SEA 1925 I (-9) position Latitude 12-45N Longitude 122-40E course 120 speed 12. Strike reports indicate enemy heavily damaged. Am proceeding north with three groups to attack enemy carrier force at dawn.

The Japanese Northern and Center Forces were, for the time being at least, Bill Halsey's problem. Oldendorf's job was to protect MacArthur's invasion forces in Leyte Gulf, which meant stopping the Southern Force from entering the gulf through Surigao Strait. The best estimates of the admiral and his staff had the Southern Force arriving at the entrance to the strait around 7:00 p.m. It was now after midnight. There had been no word from Halsey's search aircraft, nothing from Fleet Air Wing One or the army's Thirteenth Air Force. There had been no reports from the submarines of the Seventh Fleet, and nothing from the motor torpedo boats deployed along the southern end of the strait . . . *nothing!*

So where was the Southern Force? Had its major units been significantly damaged by the *Enterprise* air strike and forced to retire? Was the southern movement a diversion, meant to lure Oldendorf's battleships away from Leyte Gulf, leaving MacArthur's troops and transports vulnerable to an attack coming from another direction? Perhaps the Southern Force did not intend to give battle at all, as Kinkaid had theorized, and was actually a new incarnation of the Tokyo Express, tasked with running reinforcements and supplies to the west coast of Leyte.

Fourteen thousand yards to the north of Oldendorf's line of cruisers were the battleships, which for the past five hours had been steaming in column on the same east-to-west oval track, due east of Leyte's Hinunangan Point. Oldendorf had placed the battle line at this location "because it gave me the maximum sea room available and restricted the enemy's movements. This position also permitted me to swing my battle line to cover the eastern entrance to the Gulf should the Center Force under Admiral Kurita arrive ahead of the Southern Force." Maintaining this position at just 5 knots of speed was difficult, and not only because of the strong currents to be found at the northern end of Surigao Strait. Ever since Operation Galvanic, the battleship crews had been concentrating on mastering the art of shore bombardment, and little training had been done in the way of traditional line-of-battle station keeping.

At 11:26 p.m., Oldendorf ordered all ships to set Condition One Easy, a more relaxed alert status where battle stations were still constantly manned and watertight integrity was maintained, but certain ventilation shafts and doors were allowed to remain open as long as someone stood ready to secure them at a moment's notice. Condition One Easy also allowed for some crew members to sleep at their stations, but hardly anyone did. It was too hot, stifling, and unpleasant to sleep, especially inside the gun turrets and belowdecks, where the smell of machinery, lubricants, and sweating bodies hung thickly in the stale air and the steel overheads dripped with condensation. The younger sailors were too keyed up, fueled by strong navy coffee, tobacco, and adrenaline. The more senior were too heavily burdened with the weight of responsibility and the gnawing instinct in their guts that told them: *This is it—it's the real thing this time.*

Lawrence Bellatti's battle station was on a platform abaft the *Tennessee*'s stump tower with the crew of a Mark 37 director, some 50 feet above the quarterdeck.

"We stood quietly in the darkness," the young sailor wrote. "All eyes strained over the dark waters toward the strait. The pitch black night was broken only by flashes of lightning in the distant mountains. It was very, very quiet."

Hurry up and wait—the common annoyance shared by every man in uniform since the inception of armies and navies. Hurry up, we're getting under way. It's going to be a long night, so hurry up and grab some chow. Hurry up, secure that gear, and report when your station is ready in all respects. Hurry up, get ready, then wait. Many a sailor has said that the long hours spent waiting anxiously for something to happen was the worst part; once the shooting started, there was little time to think about how scared you were.

Then at 12:26 a.m., the message from *PT-127* made it into the hands of Admiral Oldendorf:

> `Contact 10 miles southeast of Bohol, 3 DD, 2 large unidentified, bearing 310 degrees and closing.`

The *PT-134* roared out of the darkness and haze with automatic cannons blazing, loosing three torpedoes toward the center of the Japanese formation before zooming into a violent heeling turn, a giant "rooster tail" sprouting from her stern. Searchlight beams and tracer rounds chased the *134* boat through the glistening spray as she sped off to the west. Due to intense enemy fire coming at him from several directions, Lieutenant (j.g.) Ed Wakelin had been forced to launch his torpedoes from a distant 2,500 yards. Knifing through the water at 33.5 knots, all three of them passed harmlessly through the wake of the battleship *Fuso*.

Southern Force was fending off yet another attack by American torpedo boats as it entered the mouth of Surigao Strait, just minutes after a "friendly fire" incident had claimed the lives of three Japanese sailors. Nishimura's ships were still maneuvering to achieve their desired approach formation when lookouts aboard *Fuso* reported an unidentified ship lurking just 3,000 yards off the port bow. The *Fuso* opened up with her 6-inch guns; seconds later an urgent call came over the radio-telephone pleading for the battleship to cease fire. The strange, darkened ship had been the *Mogami*. One of the *Fuso*'s shots had torn through the heavy cruiser's sick bay, killing three luckless men who had been previously wounded in the morning's air attacks. There had been little time to reproach or extend apologies. Shortly after the *Mogami* had steered into *Fuso*'s wake, the *Yamagumo* reported another enemy contact. Minutes later the destroyer was dodging the torpedoes fired by PT boats *137* and *132*.

As the *134* boat shadowed the enemy formation along the eastern coast of Panaon Island, Lieutenant Commander Robert Leeson was able to raise the *Wachapreague* on the PT Common frequency, reporting that a "very large ship" had been attacked by his section off Binit Point, near the southern end of Surigao Strait. The time was 2:06 a.m. To the north, the three torpedo boats commanded by Lieutenant (j.g.) John McElfresh had been lying-to in the center of Surigao Strait when four targets appeared on the SO radar scope of the *PT-490,* just off the coast of Panaon Island at a distance of 8 miles.

McElfresh plotted a course to intercept and started motoring south, with the *491* and *493* boats following in echelon at 200-yard intervals. More rain squalls clouded the strait and made visual acquisition of the targets difficult, a problem that was solved by the Japanese themselves as they attempted to illuminate Leeson's boats with their searchlights. The steady hum of powerful engines crescendoed into a deafening rumble as the three boats began their attack run on the head of the Japanese column.

The *PT-490* closed to within a harrowing 700 yards before sending two of her steel "fish" barreling toward the *Michishio*, while the *491* launched another pair at the *Asagumo*. The *493* boat also attempted to launch one of her starboard torpedoes but the weapon stalled frustratingly in its rack. Steering clear of the inbound torpedo tracks, the two leading destroyers turned their searchlights upon McElfresh's boats and began laying down a fearsome barrage, while every gun aboard the darting PTs hammered away in return. The *PT-490* launched her two remaining fish from just 500 yards, which also missed, before the three boats "commenced retiring at high speed, making smoke."

Japanese gunners soon found the range, causing damage to the *490* and peppering one of her torpedo men with shell fragments. The unfortunate *493* boat received three direct hits as she fled to the west under the smoke screen. One shell punched a hole completely through the hull above the waterline; a second tore through the engine compartment and went out the other side, taking with it the auxiliary generator that powered the boat's radio and radar. A third 5-inch round struck the boat's chart room and killed two enlisted sailors, including the boat's corpsman. The same shell also wounded the skipper, Lieutenant (j.g.) Richard Brown, the XO Ensign Robert Carter, and three other men. Fortunately Carter was able to get to his feet, shake off the effects, and stand to the helm.

Machinist's Mate Second Class Albert Brunelle, a slight and gentle young man from whom no one aboard the *493* ever expected an act of heroism, let alone one that would save the boat and their lives, had been at his station in the engine room when the armor-piercing shell smashed through the wooden hull and nearly killed him. As seawater gushed in, Brunelle quickly doffed his kapok life jacket and stuffed it into the splintered hole to partially stanch the flood. Brunelle then remained in the still-leaking compartment to keep the engines running, knowing that the very survival of his crew depended on it. By the time Ensign Carter was able to safely beach the stricken *PT-493* on the eastern coast of Panaon Island, Brunelle and his engines were nearly underwater. For his actions Albert Brunelle would be awarded the Navy Cross.

As McElfresh's section was making good their escape, the PTs *523*, *524*, and *526* closed in from their designated staging point off Sumilon Island. Their officer in tactical command also failed to transmit a contact report before taking action, and their four torpedoes launched from over 2,000 yards failed to strike any Japanese ships. At 2:35 a.m. the skipper of the *327* boat, lying off Kanihaan Island just 20 nautical miles south of Oldendorf's left flank cruisers, advised over the PT Common that he had a radar contact on the enemy column at a distance of 10 miles, on a course of 000 degrees true north at 20 knots. The report was quickly answered by a stern order for the motor torpedo boats to stand down and stay clear. Destroyer Squadron 54 was steaming south down Surigao Strait.

Jesse Coward's seven destroyers had been patrolling the southern end of Leyte Gulf and Surigao Strait since the dawn of October 20, watching and listening for Japanese submarines attempting to sneak into the roadstead. By 7:50 p.m. on October 24 the DESRON 54 flagship, the *Fletcher*-class destroyer *Remey*, had closed to within TBS range of Admiral Oldendorf's forces arrayed across the northern end of Surigao Strait, and Captain Coward hailed the *Louisville*.

"In case of surface contact to the southward, I plan to make an immediate attack with fish, then retire to clear you," Coward boldly informed Oldendorf. "If you approve this, I will submit my plan shortly."

The captain wanted his squadron to have a piece of the action, rather than be relegated to screening duty. His plan called for two destroyers to remain on antisubmarine patrol in the channel that separated Dinagat and Homonhon Islands, the southeastern entrance into Leyte Gulf. His remaining ships would then steam south down Surigao Strait, divided into two attack groups. Coward would lead the first group of three destroyers, *Remey*, *McGowan*, and *Melvin*, down the eastern side of the strait. The second division of two ships, *McDermut* and *Monssen*, would steam south along the strait's western side.

"Will use individual target plan, intermediate speed setting," Coward told the admiral. "After delivery of fish, retire normal to the axis to clear area for Commander Task Group 77.2 and then north near coast line."

A former "tin can" skipper himself, Oldendorf had to admire Coward's pluck. Rather than allowing himself to be put off by the captain's assertive style, Oldendorf readily approved the plan, which was in sound keeping with well-established destroyer doctrine.

At 2:36 a.m., after piecing together the various fragmentary reports and determining that Southern Force had indeed arrived in Surigao Strait, Admiral Oldendorf ordered the battleships and cruisers brought to General Quarters. By that time DESRON 54 was already headed south in attack formation.

"This is going to be good," Oldendorf told his staff.

Two minutes later, the *McGowan* raised Captain Coward, reporting a radar contact bearing 184 degrees south at a range of 22.5 miles. Soon the *Remey* and *Melvin* had the contact as well, estimating the enemy ships to be on a northerly course of 007 degrees and making 18 knots. Coward released control of the western attack group into the hands of Commander Richard Phillips aboard the *McDermut*. Then *McGowan* and *Melvin* began following *Remey* into a series of eastward maneuvers, as Coward sought to achieve the appropriate angle of attack.

The *Louisville* then called *Remey* on TBS: "As soon as you have targets on screen let me know, include number, over."

"Five targets," Coward replied, "two large and three small, attacking now, four miles west of Kanihaan Island, over."

At 2:59 a.m., Captain Coward ordered the destroyers of the eastern attack group to increase speed to 30 knots on a heading of 120 degrees southeast. Seconds later, eight Mark 15 torpedoes leapt from the *Remey*'s starboard tubes, leaving gleaming wakes of phosphorescence as they ran "hot, straight and normal" through the dark waters. Two of the *Remey*'s fish had misfired and failed to launch, while the *McGowan* fired a full spread of ten torpedoes and the *Melvin* got off nine. Dense black smoke pumped from the funnels of all three destroyers as they turned sharply to port and began steaming north at flank speed. Star shells burst overhead, followed by the hair-raising shriek of incoming 14-inch shells.

"We are being straddled now," Captain Coward reported to Oldendorf. "Fish are in the water and we are retiring northward."

A rolling fireball ascended from the middle of the Japanese column. Then another. At least one of the *Melvin*'s torpedoes had hit the *Fuso*, which began to slow down and shear out of the column while listing to starboard. At 3:10 a.m. on the western side of the channel, Commander Phillips ordered the *McDermut* and *Monssen* to fire full salvoes of ten torpedoes each before making swift turns to starboard and fleeing to the west at 33 knots. Searchlight beams cut through the darkness, the crack of gunfire echoed across the water, and then the *McDermut* and *Monssen* were also being straddled.

Dead ahead lay three American motor torpedo boats, and as the lead destroyer *McDermut* maneuvered to clear them, radio operators in the CIC heard one of the boat captains over the PT Common frequency asking his section leader for permission to launch torpedoes. The *McDermut* quickly responded that the destroyers were "friendlies" and ordered the PT boats, which were further north than they ought to have been, to hold their fire.

"Lookouts report explosion on starboard beam," the *Maryland*'s log stated in an entry made at 3:20 a.m. Men aboard the cruisers *Minneapolis* and *Columbia* saw the blast, too; they actually felt the shock wave in the plotting room of the *Denver*. Of the twenty torpedoes fired by the *McDermut* and *Monssen*, six had found their targets. The *Yamagumo* was slammed by three of them in her port side amidships, which most likely detonated her own stock of torpedoes. The destroyer exploded spectacularly, jackknifed, and immediately sank, killing all but two of the 230 men on board. The two destroyers in the van, *Michishio* and *Asagumo*, were also hit. The flagship *Yamashiro* was struck by a torpedo in her port quarter, causing an oil fire to break out which was seen and reported by Captain Coward.

The sharpshooting *McDermut* and *Monssen* continued their flight to the west, so as to hug the coastlines of Panaon and Leyte before proceeding north. This was done to confuse Japanese radar, which was believed to be much less sophisticated than that of the Americans, making it difficult for its operators to distinguish land masses from ships. The Japanese reliance on star shells and searchlights during night combat had borne this theory out, indicating a lack of confidence in their own radar technology.

Phillips also wanted to move as far west as possible to clear the way for DESRON 24, which was now southbound and accelerating to attack speed. These six destroyers under the command of Captain Ken McManes were assigned to Admiral Berkey on the right flank. At 3:02 a.m., Berkey's flagship *Phoenix* raised McManes on TBS: "Lighthead from Compound, proceed to attack. Follow down west shore line. Follow other groups in, then retire to northward making smoke, over."

Captain McManes, who rather than stationing himself on the bridge of his flagship *Hutchins* had taken the extraordinary step of taking command from the CIC, had organized his destroyers into two parallel columns. The *Hutchins* led the westernmost column, followed by the *Daly* and *Bache*, while the eastern column was headed by the Australian destroyer *Arunta*, trailed by the American *Fletcher*-class ships *Killen* and *Beale*.

At 3:23 a.m., just as the bright flare of the explosion that destroyed the *Yamagumo* began to fade, the eastern column launched a total of nineteen torpedoes before making a starboard turn and retiring north, while the *Hutchins*, *Daly*, and *Bache* turned hard aport and sent fifteen fish streaming toward the enemy column. A pair of Japanese Long Lance torpedoes then cut between the *Hutchins* and *Daly*; shortly afterward the western column engaged the damaged *Michishio* and *Asagumo* and the cruiser *Mogami* with fire from their 5-inch guns. Their task complete, the destroyers completed their turn to the north and retired under a heavy smoke screen.

Shoji Nishimura pressed stubbornly northward, still determined to penetrate Leyte Gulf even as Allied torpedo attacks were steadily whittling away the strength of his Southern Force. At 3:20 a.m., just as the *Yamagumo* was meeting her demise, lookouts sighted the second squadron of enemy destroyers closing in for the attack. Nishimura then ordered a change in course from due north to 315 degrees northwest in order to point the bows of his ships toward the next fusillade of torpedoes that was sure to come.

The *Yamashiro* soon passed the *Michishio*, which had taken a torpedo in her engine room and was now drifting on the south-running current without power. Also laying to starboard was the stricken *Asagumo*, her bow blown off by a torpedo fired by the *McDermut*. After seven minutes Nishimura ordered another turn to the northeast, then at 3:30 a.m. the Japanese ships resumed a northerly course, at which time he transmitted a message to Kurita and Shima:

> Enemy destroyers and torpedo boats present on both sides of the northern entrance to Surigao Strait. Two of our destroyers torpedoed and drifting. YAMASHIRO sustained one torpedo hit but no impediment to battle cruising.

The text of this dispatch underscores the great deal of mayhem and confusion created by the relentless attacks of Allied light forces, between which the Japanese scarcely had time to catch their breath and assess the situation. It suggests that Nishimura was probably unaware of the fate of the *Yamagumo*, or the fact that *Fuso* had also been torpedoed and was no longer in formation, having made a slow turn to the south. The *Yamashiro*'s radiomen had barely finished transmitting the admiral's message before the flagship was hit again, this time by a torpedo launched from the destroyer *Killen*, which slammed into her port side. The *Yamashiro* then veered left and slowed to 5 knots.

Just a few minutes later, at around 3:40 a.m., the *Fuso* went down. Many eyewitness accounts, both Japanese and American, claim that she blew in half from an obvious magazine explosion, with the two flaming sections drifting upon the surface of Surigao Strait for quite some time before sinking. Other evidence suggests that the great, pagoda-masted dreadnought may have actually succumbed to flooding, capsized, and sank, with the appearance of an explosion created by the oil flowing from her fuel bunkers being ignited by onboard fires, even as she slipped beneath the waves. In either case the *Fuso* was gone, leaving behind just 10 survivors from a crew of 1,620.

Of this Admiral Nishimura appears to have remained ignorant, for he continued to issue commands instructing the *Fuso* to conform to his tactical movements. By 3:48 a.m. the *Yamashiro* was back to making 15 knots and steering north by northeast while firing upon the retiring American destroyers. According to Commander Richard Visser of the *Daly*, Nishimura's flagship seemed to be "frantically throwing steel through 360 degrees and initiating a general gun action between both forces." Bringing up the rear, having difficulty distinguishing friend from foe and holding her fire, was the still-undamaged *Mogami*, followed by *Shigure*, the one Japanese destroyer of Southern Force that remained combat-effective.

"Dummy from Bushwhacker, general consensus of opinion is two battleships, one or two cruisers and one destroyer," Jesse Coward responded to a query from Admiral Oldendorf as to the strength of the Japanese force. "Some targets definitely hit. We saw large burst of fire, couldn't tell what type of ship, over."

Over the TBS speaker, Oldendorf could hear George Weyler ordering the battleships to increase their speed to 15 knots. As the Japanese drew nearer, Weyler may have feared that the heavy dreadnoughts might soon find themselves in torpedo water and would need the extra speed to make evasive maneuvers. The single column of six American battleships, still being led by the *West Virginia*, was now steaming on an eastward course across the northern end of Surigao Strait, and though still in a position to cap the Japanese "T," would soon need to reverse course and countermarch to the west.

"My one anxiety during the early stages of the battle was that the enemy would not keep coming toward me," Oldendorf later wrote. "If his radar located the position of my battle line, he might reverse course before coming within gun range. If he did so, I knew that I would be strongly tempted to go after him. By doing so, I would give up the advantage of my position and might uncover the strait for one or more of his ships to slip through."

The admiral needn't have worried. The *Yamashiro*, despite having been struck by two Mark 15 torpedoes, was still steaming north by northeast at 18 knots while firing her main and secondary batteries. The *Mogami* was also closing fast and maneuvering to bring her portside guns to bear. Trailing behind the cruiser was *Shigure*, just 700 yards astern. The remaining Japanese ships, according to Oldendorf's flag plot, appeared to be "maneuvering radically." At 3:35 a.m., Oldendorf raised Captain Roland Smoot of DESRON 56.

"Bantam Six, launch attack," Oldendorf ordered. "Get the big boys."

Smoot's nine destroyers turned south and began steaming down the middle of Surigao Strait in three columns. The center column was led by Smoot's flagship, *Newcomb*, followed by the *Richard P. Leary* and *Albert W. Grant*. To the east were the *Bryant*, *Halford*, and *Robinson*, while the *Edwards*, *Leutze*, and *Bennion* made up the western column. The *Bennion* was a new *Fletcher* class named in honor of Captain Mervyn S. Bennion, the commanding officer of the *West Virginia* killed at Pearl Harbor. On the Fourth of July, 1943, the *Bennion* had been christened by the captain's widow, Louise, in the Boston Navy Yard.

At his battle station in the *Bennion*'s main battery director was twenty-two-year-old Lieutenant (j.g.) James L. Holloway III, a graduate of the Annapolis Class of 1942 who would one day become Chief of Naval Operations. The young officer was standing in the director's hatchway scanning the sea and sky with binoculars, observing the flashes of distant gunfire and the glow of burning ships. Feeling an insistent tug at his trouser leg, he turned to find an enlisted sailor gesturing to the viewfinder for the director's magnifying optics. Holloway took his seat and settled into the eyepiece. The clarity of the sight picture was startling. The director's crosshairs were centered upon the base of the *Yamashiro*'s towering pagoda mast, her entire length illuminated by the bright orange flares of main battery salvoes and the near-constant firing of her secondary guns.

Holloway gasped. "It looks just like a picture of a Japanese battleship," he exclaimed.

"Lieutenant," the sailor replied, "that *is* a Japanese battleship."

Consulting the flag plot once again, Jesse Oldendorf became worried that the destroyers of DESRON 56 would meet with the deadly fire of Japanese capital ships before they were able to close to within torpedo range. "To cover Smoot's attack, I gave the order to commence firing," Oldendorf recalled. "The gunnery officers must have been riding the triggers of their guns, because hardly had the words left my lips to be repeated over the telephone by my flag lieutenant, than the *Louisville* let fly with her first salvo without waiting to give the usual warning buzzer."

Darkness turned to daylight as the five left flank cruisers opened fire, their bright muzzle flashes momentarily blinding Admiral Oldendorf as he watched from the starboard bridge wing of the *Louisville*. Seconds later Berkey's three cruisers on the right flank began engaging the enemy ships; then at 3:53 a.m., Captain Herbert Wiley announced over TBS that the main battery director of the *West Virginia* had locked onto a target and his ship was about to open fire. Then all eight of the Wee Vee's 16-inch / 45 caliber guns fired as one with a frightening roar that rose above the already deafening din of battle.

"By increasing speed to fifteen knots the leading battleship, *West Virginia*, had reached a position so that her first salvo passed directly over the *Louisville*," Oldendorf remembered. "It sounded like a train of boxcars passing over a high trestle. Following this salvo with my binoculars, I had the satisfaction of seeing it land squarely on the forecastle of the leading ship of the enemy's column."

At that very moment on the flag bridge of the *West Virginia*, Admiral Ruddock heard a chuckle over the battleship's command circuit.

"Hey, Doc," Ruddock asked Captain Wiley over the net. "What's the glee?"

"Boy, did we hit him the first time," Wiley responded in his quiet voice.

From his perch on the forward superstructure of the *Bennion*, James Holloway watched in awe as one by one the American dreadnoughts joined the fight. After the *West Virginia*'s first salvo screamed overhead to explode aboard the *Yamashiro*, the *California*'s main battery began thundering away, followed in rapid succession by the big guns of *Tennessee* and *Maryland*. Though he had no way of knowing it at the time, Holloway was occupying a front-row seat to what would be world history's final clash between battleships.

"All along the northern horizon, enormous billows of flame from their 16- and 14-inch main battery guns lit up the battle line," Holloway described. "Directly over our destroyers stretched a procession of tracers as the battleship shells converged on the Japanese column. The apparent slowness of the projectiles was surprising, taking fifteen to twenty seconds in their trajectory before reaching the target. They seemed to hang in the sky. Through the director optics I could clearly see the explosions of these shells bursting on the Japanese ships, sending up cascades of flame as they ripped away topside gun mounts and erupted in fiery sheets of molten steel."

High above the quarterdeck of the *Tennessee*, Lawrence Bellatti also had a panoramic view of the action. "When a ship fired there would be a terrific whirling sheet of golden flame bolting across the sea followed by a massive thunder, and then three red balls would go into the sky—up, arch over, and then down. When the salvoes found the target there would be a huge shower of sparks, and after a moment a dull orange glow would appear. This glow would increase, brighten, and then slowly dull.

"The noise of firing became like the roll of continuous thunder, as salvo after salvo rolled out along the line, and the sky was practically continuously streaked with red projectiles," Bellatti continued. "The fire was very accurate; indeed, so accurate that a veritable hail of heavy projectiles was raining down on the leading group of enemy ships."

Standing on the platform alongside Petty Officer Bellatti was Captain Henry Coleman, commander of the *Tennessee*'s marine detachment. Lowering his binoculars and shaking his head in amazement, Coleman said aloud what the men around him were certainly thinking.

"It is unbelievable that a single Jap could live through that."

Even as late as 3:52 a.m., Vice Admiral Shoji Nishimura was attempting to raise *Fuso* by radio-telephone, still oblivious to the fact that his second battleship was now resting on the bottom of the Surigao Strait along with most of her crew. One minute later came the stunning realization that the Southern Force was not only being engaged by destroyers and torpedo boats, but had sailed directly into an ambush of battleships and cruisers. Dead ahead, the flat expanse of obsidian sea seemed to burst open with the fires of hell itself, and the wrenching explosions of armor-piercing shells began ripping the *Yamashiro* apart.

By 3:56 a.m., when Nishimura ordered a turn to the west, the flagship was wrapped from stem to stern in flames that reached masthead height, her decks and passageways cluttered with the dead and the dying. Despite the murderous volume of fire being hurled upon her, the *Yamashiro*'s remaining gun batteries kept pounding away in defiance, firing upon the attacking destroyers and walking shell splashes toward the cruiser *Phoenix* on the Allied right flank. Soon the *Minneapolis*, *Denver*, and *Columbia* on the left would report that they too were being straddled by enemy fire.

The *Mogami* hastily turned south while making smoke, a useless countermeasure against radar-directed naval gunfire. She soon found herself caught in a crossfire between the American battle line and the destroyers of DESRON 24, which were charging north in pursuit of the Japanese heavies after finishing off the drifting *Michishio* with a torpedo shot. The battleships and cruisers soon found the range to *Mogami*, as did the destroyers *Hutchins*, *Daly*, and *Bache*, and soon the heavy cruiser was shuddering from multiple direct hits and set ablaze.

At 4:02 a.m., just after Captain Toma ordered a spread of four torpedoes fired in the general direction of the American battleships, a shell struck the *Mogami*'s bridge and killed every officer there, including Toma, his XO, and the navigator. A chief quartermaster (whose surname, coincidentally, was Yamamoto) managed to pick himself up from the deck and take control of the conn. He then sent someone to locate the next senior surviving officer to assume command of the ship.

At about the same time as the deadly explosion on the bridge of the *Mogami*, Rear Admiral Weyler ordered his eastbound battle line to reverse course by making simultaneous starboard turns of 150 degrees, to achieve a course of 270 degrees due west. Each ship checked their fire before complying with the order. By that time the *West Virginia* had fired ninety-one rounds of 16-inch armor-piercing ammunition; the *California* had spent forty-three 14-inch shells; while *Tennessee* fired sixty-three rounds from her main battery, and the *Maryland*, forty. The *Maryland*, *Pennsylvania*, and *Mississippi*, with their older Mark 3 FC radar, had been frustrated in their attempts to acquire targets. The Fighting Mary's gunnery officers had solved the dilemma by zeroing in on the cascading splashes of shells fired by the *West Virginia*, which were surrounding the *Yamashiro*. The *Pennsylvania* and *Mississippi*, however, had yet to fire their guns.

As the *Tennessee* came about to obtain the proper westward heading, the darkened silhouette of a battleship suddenly loomed startlingly close to starboard. It was the *California*, which had been directly behind *Tennessee* in the column, now on a course that would carry her across the *Tennessee*'s bow.

Seeing what was about to happen, Rear Admiral Chandler grabbed the TBS handset.

"Aberdeen from Banker Two, did you receive the signal to turn? Acknowledge, over," Chandler asked the *California*.

"Wilco," came the reply.

Admiral Weyler's signal had, in fact, been misheard. The commanding officer of the *California*, Captain Henry Burnett, had ordered a turn of 15 degrees to starboard, rather than 150 degrees, and instead of turning west, the Prune Barge was now headed southeast. The two sister ships *Tennessee* and *California* were, once again, on a collision course. Only through the quick thinking and skillful ship handling of Captain John Heffernan was the *Tennessee* able to steer clear of the *California* and avert the impending catastrophe. The line-of-battle formation was thrown into disarray for several minutes while the errant *California* sought to turn about and regain her position in the column. By then the *Tennessee* had resumed firing, hurling another six-gun salvo of 14-inch shells at the blazing *Yamashiro*.

"I pushed the fire button on the torpedo control console and stood up to see our five fish shoot out of their tubes," Holloway remembered. "I could hear them slap the water, and they were running hot and straight. Our destroyer formation had become ragged; the ships were maneuvering independently to avoid enemy gunfire. As *Bennion* retired to the north at thirty knots, the scene of action was one of growing confusion. The Japanese formation had disintegrated. Some of their ships had circled out of control, others were dead in the water. Many were on fire and they shuddered from internal explosions. Still others were unrecognizable with bows gone, sterns blown away and topsides mangled."

After launching their torpedoes, all nine destroyers of DESRON 56 turned away at flank speed and began producing smoke, seeking cover along the coastlines of Leyte, Dinagat, or Hibuson Island, where their radar signatures would fade into the land clutter. At 4:05 a.m. the *Yamashiro* was slammed by yet another torpedo, one of the fish triggered by Lieutenant Holloway aboard the *Bennion*. Like a wounded beast the blazing dreadnought staggered away, making an agonizingly slow turn to the south while continuing to fire every gun she had left. The "tail end Charlie" of Smoot's center column of destroyers, *Albert W. Grant*, was hit by fire from the *Yamashiro* and possibly *Mogami* and *Shigure*. Then a volley of 6-inch shells, most likely from the cruiser *Denver*, screamed down upon the *Grant*.

"You're firing on Bantam Six gang!" Smoot exclaimed. "We're in the middle of the channel! You're firing on us!"

"All ships cease fire! All ships cease fire!" the *Louisville* ordered.

In less than two minutes' time, the *Grant* had been hit twenty times by shells fired from both sides. Nearly half of the crew were casualties—thirty-two were killed and ninety-four wounded—and the *Grant* herself was dead in the water. The Allied guns quickly fell silent, and Captain Smoot directed the *Newcomb* to close with the drifting *Grant* and pass her a towline.

The crew of the burning and listing *Yamashiro* would have little time to enjoy the respite. A torpedo fired a few minutes earlier by the *Newcomb* came whining in from the northeast to explode against her starboard side, finally stopping the Japanese battleship in her tracks. As she began a slow death roll to port, the order was given—much too late—to abandon ship. The *Yamashiro* capsized and began to sink, emitting a great cloud of steam and an otherworldly hiss as her raging fires were extinguished. At 4:19 a.m. she disappeared from Allied radar screens. Nearly all of the 1,636 officers and men aboard the *Yamashiro* would perish; like the crew of the *Fuso*, only 10 would live to see Japan. As fate would have it, Shoji Nishimura would die that morning in the very same waters where his son Teiji, a naval aviator, had been lost in December 1941.

Oldendorf's call to cease fire was an immense relief to Commander Shigeru Nishino and the crew of *Shigure*. The destroyer had been racing south for its very life, through a forest of shell splashes so dense that visibility was cut down to a few scant yards. She had already been hit by an 8-inch projectile which penetrated an oil storage tank but failed to explode, and a near-miss had damaged her rudder control cables. Rather than stand by his stricken flagship or attack the American battle line with torpedoes, Nishino had chosen to flee. From a tactical standpoint this made perfect sense, for rather than attacking against overwhelming odds, losing his ship and condemning his men to certain death, Nishino's retreat would save *Shigure* and her crew to fight another day. In the eyes of the samurai warrior, however, the act flew in the face of the code of *bushido*, which demanded a courageous sacrifice.

"When I saw *Mogami*, as far as I can recall, she was dead in the water," Nishino would tell a US Navy interrogator in November 1945. "When I started on a southerly course I was making thirty knots, so I saw her for a very short time. She was dead in the water, on fire amidships."

The *Mogami* was, in fact, still retiring south under her own power but at a painfully slow speed. Only one of her four geared impulse turbine engines was still operating unattended, after heavy smoke and fumes forced the black gang to evacuate the engine room. Her steering mechanisms had also been knocked out, causing her to be steered by hand and with great difficulty by Chief Quartermaster Yamamoto, who still remained at the conn. The tracks of her four northbound torpedoes had been spotted by the destroyer *Leary*, causing the American battleships to break formation. Upon hearing the *Leary*'s warning, the *Mississippi*, *Maryland*, and *West Virginia* executed a northward turn to increase the range. The *Mogami*'s torpedoes then ran out their course and sank.

While the *Mississippi* had been able to throw a single 12-gun salvo toward the *Yamashiro* before the order to cease fire was issued, the *Pennsylvania*'s guns had been forced to remain silent throughout the battle. Her Mark 3 FC radar-equipped main battery directors had been unable to acquire a target or generate a firing solution.

"A fact which will be forever galling to the men who were aboard the *Pennsylvania* that night is that the ship never opened fire," Clifton Cates wrote. "General Quarters was sounded at 0130 when the first contact report came through, and battle stations were manned in record time. Gun crews stood by for two hours, feverishly waiting for the word to commence firing. It never came. There was a good reason, but it could do little to relieve the disappointment of not having had a hand in the sinking of two Jap battlewagons when the chance finally came."

By the time Second Striking Force arrived in Surigao Strait, Vice Admiral Kiyohide Shima was attempting to shake off a strong sense of foreboding. With the approach of Japanese forces having been detected by the Americans, there was no longer a need to maintain radio silence. Shima had been in voice communication with Vice Admiral Nishimura for the past three hours, and knew that Southern Force had been running a gauntlet of enemy torpedo boats and destroyers. Nishimura, however, was no longer responding to Shima's hailing calls.

As Second Striking Force rounded Panaon Island and entered the strait, it was spotted by Lieutenant Mike Kovar of *PT-137*, who initiated an attack against the Japanese column even though his boat's auxiliary generator was out of commission, leaving him without a working radio transmitter or radar. *PT-137* launched a single fish toward one of Shima's destroyers before being driven off by gunfire, which missed the intended target but continued on to strike the *Abukuma* on her port side, killing thirty Japanese sailors and causing the light cruiser to slow and drop from the formation, down by the bow.

Continuing north, Shima's force ran across two large fires in the middle of the strait, most likely burning fuel oil and debris left over from the wreck of the *Fuso*. The admiral, however, believed that he had sighted the remains of both *Fuso* and *Yamashiro*. The assumption was false, of course, but that mattered little, for Southern Force had indeed been decimated. Ten minutes later another ship was spotted 10,000 yards ahead and to starboard, which was correctly identified as the *Mogami*, well involved in fire and appearing dead in the water.

His dread deepening, Shima sent his four destroyers ahead to close with the enemy surface forces that were surely concentrated at the northern end of Surigao Strait and ordered the cruisers to prepare to deliver a torpedo attack. At 4:18 a.m., a blip appeared on the *Nachi*'s radar, which was interpreted as two unknown ships bearing 025 degrees northeast at a distance of just over 7 miles. The *Nachi* and *Ashigara* then turned due east and launched eight Long Lance torpedoes which had little effect, since the target was more than likely Hibuson Island, and at a much greater distance than the primitive Japanese radar had indicated.

The luck of the Second Striking Force would only worsen, for Admiral Shima and the skipper of *Nachi*, Captain Enpei Kanooka, would soon realize to their horror that the *Mogami* was, in fact, under way at a slow speed and not dead in the water as they had originally thought. The course they had chosen for their rather impotent torpedo attack was carrying them across her southward path. The struggling *Mogami*, with her damaged steering gear, could do little to avoid the oncoming *Nachi*. Despite Kanooka ordering the *Nachi*'s rudder put hard right, the two ships collided at the bows with a shuddering crash. The *Nachi*'s stem was severely mangled, with seawater pouring into the anchor windlass and steerage rooms.

As damage control teams rushed to contain the flooding, Shima ordered *Nachi* and *Ashigara* to turn due south on a heading of 180 degrees at 5 knots, and for *Mogami* to follow along as best she could. The destroyer *Asagumo*, heading south down the strait and making 15 knots despite having had her bow removed by a Mark 15 torpedo, slowed and fell into the column behind the *Mogami*. Shima then signaled for his four destroyers to "reverse course to the south and rejoin," and at 4:35 a.m. the admiral sent a radio message to Tokyo and Manila:

```
This force has completed its attack and is tem-
porarily retiring from the battle area in order
to plan subsequent action.
```

Five minutes later, a signal lamp flashed in the darkness, issuing a challenge in Japanese.

"I am *Nachi*," the flagship's light blinked in response.

"I am *Shigure*," came the reply.

"Follow behind *Nachi*," Shima ordered.

After an elongated pause, *Shigure*'s light answered: "I am having steering problems."

The dawn of October 25, 1944, would reveal a thin layer of acrid smoke hanging low over Surigao Strait, the clear sapphire waters now marred by shining slicks of oil and scattered with flotsam and debris. The *Louisville* was leading a column of American cruisers down the strait, while scouting ahead were the destroyers of DESRON X-Ray.

"We just passed a large group of survivors," the destroyer *Claxton* announced. "There are several hundred survivors in this area, most do not accept lines."

Despite severe dehydration, injuries, and burns, many of the Japanese sailors who had survived the night's ordeal and were clinging to floating wreckage refused to be rescued by the passing American ships, a factor that contributed to the very low number of survivors among the Southern Force. Many would die of their wounds, drown after succumbing to exhaustion, or be taken by sharks. Others would strike out for the shores of nearby islands, only to be met on the beach and hacked to death by roving bands of machete-wielding Filipinos who had answered General MacArthur's call to "rise and strike."

"Open fire as targets bear," Admiral Oldendorf ordered at 5:29 a.m. The *Louisville*, *Portland*, *Minneapolis*, *Denver*, and *Columbia* would achieve several more direct hits on the slow-moving *Asagumo* and *Mogami* before Oldendorf ordered the column's retirement, not wanting his cruisers exposed to air or submarine attack in the narrow confines of Surigao

Strait in the coming daylight. At 6:44 a.m., however, just after the sun rose over the mountains of Dinagat, Oldendorf decided to detach the *Denver* and *Columbia* and two destroyers to finish the job.

The *Asagumo* was once again tracked down and this time sunk by gunfire, while the stubborn and still-burning *Mogami*, after fighting off two more assaults by PT boats, would make it as far as the Bohol Sea before being attacked by Avenger torpedo bombers from the Seventh Fleet's escort carriers and rendered drifting and powerless. After being abandoned by her surviving crew, *Mogami* was finally consigned to the deep by a torpedo from the Second Striking Force destroyer *Akebono*.

Just after 10:00 a.m., Commander Nishino would signal Toyoda and Kurita that "All ships of Third Section except *Shigure* went down under gunfire and torpedo attack." On the morning of October 27, the sole surviving warship of Southern Force stood into Brunei Bay.

"It is difficult to see what consolation the enemy could have derived from this battle," Samuel Eliot Morison would write. "His torpedo technique fell short of 1943 standards, his gunfire was ineffective; even his seamanship, as judged by the collision of *Nachi* with *Mogami*, was faulty. The most intelligent act of any Japanese commander in the entire battle was Admiral Shima's retirement."

Japanese appraisals of Shima's performance in the battle would be less favorable. In an interview with US Navy investigators, one surviving officer from the *Mogami* would describe Admiral Shima's failure to press the attack on the American battle line as "most deplorable," and that "considerable dissatisfaction on this score was felt among the personnel of both the *Akebono* and of the flagship *Nachi*." The same officer would find fault with Nishimura's headlong rush into Surigao Strait, claiming that overconfidence and "the virtually blind reliance placed upon the night fighting ability of the Japanese fleet" contributed greatly to the defeat of the Southern Force.

"I think the tactics used were wrong for the type of place we were going to fight in," said Commander Nishino of the *Shigure*, who believed Nishimura's decision to proceed in a straight column, rather than a staggered, zigzagging formation with destroyers in the van and heavy ships far to the rear, had led to disaster. Furthermore, it had been "foolish to have two independent forces engaged in the same operation.

"There are some people who think Nishimura was very fortunate not to have returned from this battle," Nishino would claim.

<u>CTG 77.2 to CTF 77, COM3RDFLT Info ALL TGC'S 7TH FLT, COMINCH, CINCPAC, CINCSOWESPAC:</u>

Met enemy force last night according to plan. Enemy stood UE SURIGAO STRAIT South in 2 groups. The 1st group consisted as reported by the MAC-GOWAN (DD678) of 2 battleships, 1 or 2 heavy cruisers, and 1 destroyer. The 2nd group consisted of 2 large and about 5 smaller craft. All craft were sunk or repelled. Number sunk not known but believed to be at least 8 of all sizes. Upon arrival this morning in lower end SURIGAO STRAIT found 8 units burning, 7 of which sank as we approached. Others had been sunk as we either sank them ourselves or picked up survivors. No opportunity yet for interrogating Japanese survivors. Own casualties not known. Damaged ship ALBERT W GRANT (DD 649).

At 6:53 a.m. on October 25, 1944, the six American battleships resumed their patrol of Leyte Gulf, their now-silent gun turrets, towering upper works, and teakwood weather decks awash in the warm light of a tropical sunrise. Wakes of perfect white flowed from their bows as they carved through the crystalline waters; colorful signal flags and battle ensigns streamed from their foremasts. Along with the smooth churning of their great screws and the rush of seawater upon their steel hulls could be heard the clear whistle of bosun's pipes and booming calls of *Now hear this: All hands, secure from General Quarters.*

The Battle of Surigao Strait was over. The mission to protect General MacArthur's beachhead and the amphibious forces of the Seventh Fleet in Leyte Gulf had been fulfilled. The dreadnoughts of Pearl Harbor had had their vengeance, though few of the proud men who sailed them could have imagined that their resounding victory had also signaled the end of an era.

The following day, Rear Admiral Jesse Oldendorf would conclude a somber message of gratitude to the officers and men of Task Group 77.2 by telling them: "How well we succeeded is now a matter of history."

CHAPTER 22
EPILOGUE

The fast battleship USS *Missouri* had been at anchor at berth F71 in Tokyo Bay since the morning of August 29, 1945, her complement of 1,900 officers and men busily preparing the ship to receive a legion of American general and flag officers, 170 reporters and cameramen, the dignitaries of nine Allied nations, and representatives from the Empire of Japan. The ceremony that would see the formal surrender of Japanese forces and bring an end to the Second World War was to occur aboard the *Missouri* on September 2, six years and one day after the German invasion of Poland and three years, eight months, and twenty-six days after the Japanese attack on Pearl Harbor.

The choice of the *Missouri* to host the surrender ceremony had not been made at random. The namesake of the *Iowa*-class battleship just happened to be the home state of President of the United States Harry S. Truman, and she had been christened by then-senator Truman's daughter Margaret before a crowd of 30,000 spectators in the Brooklyn Navy Yard on January 29, 1944. The Pacific War may have seen the battleship supplanted by the aircraft carrier as Queen of the Seas, but the battleship had nevertheless maintained its prestige and was still looked upon as a powerful symbol of United States naval might, and therefore a fitting platform upon which to hold such a solemn and historic ceremony.

The *Missouri* was certainly not alone in Tokyo Bay. The "Mighty Mo," as her bluejackets had nicknamed her, was accompanied by a fleet of over 250 Allied ships, not counting the Fast Carrier Task Forces of Raymond Spruance's Fifth Fleet lying off the eastern shores of Honshu, which were prepared to intervene against any last-minute, rogue acts of treachery. At anchor among all the light aircraft carriers, cruisers, destroyers, fleet submarines, command ships, minecraft, attack transports, landing ships, and auxiliaries were two British and eight American battleships, one of which had been present at Pearl Harbor on December 7, 1941. Lying serenely at anchor just a few hundred yards from *Missouri* was the USS *West Virginia.*

The night surface action in Surigao Strait was only one of four major and several minor engagements that comprised what came to be known as the Battle of Leyte Gulf. In the early-morning hours of October 25, at the same time Shoji Nishimura was attempting to fight off Jesse Oldendorf's destroyers, Takeo Kurita's Center Force was steaming unopposed through San Bernardino Strait. Having taken Ozawa's bait, Bill Halsey was racing northward to attack the Japanese carriers, taking with him the entire strength of the Third Fleet, including the fast battleships.

As the battle in Surigao Strait raged, Thomas Kinkaid transmitted a message to Halsey:

> `Our surface forces now engaged enemy surface forces SURIGAO STRAIT entrance to LEYTE GULF. Enemy force sighted in STRAIT by PT Boats about 0200 1 (-9) arrived entrance GULF about 0300 1 (-9) consists of 2 battleships 3 cruisers and destroyers. Question: Is TF 34 guarding SAN BERNARDINO STRAIT.`

Admiral Halsey, believing that Center Force had been so badly mauled by his carrier pilots on October 24 that it no longer posed a serious threat, had chosen to take Ching Lee's battleship task force with him and had left no one to stand watch over San Bernardino Strait. At 8:00 a.m. on October 25, just as the planes of Task Force 38 were starting their attack on Ozawa's carriers, desperate calls for help began pouring in from the Seventh Fleet.

Kurita's Center Force of four battleships—including the giant *Yamato*—six cruisers, and eleven destroyers had suddenly appeared off the east coast of Samar. The only American naval forces standing between them and Leyte Gulf were the small escort carriers, destroyers, and destroyer escorts of the Seventh Fleet, the closest being Rear Admiral Clifton Sprague's Task Group 77.4.3.

While Sprague's ungainly escort carriers turned and fled with all the speed they could coax from their reciprocal steam engines, their daring aviators made repeated, tenacious bombing and strafing attacks against Kurita's force. The much faster ships of the Japanese battle line, however, soon began to overtake the slow-moving carriers. Sprague's screening destroyers *Johnston*, *Hoel*, and *Heermann* and the destroyer escort *Samuel B. Roberts* then made a valiant charge directly into the teeth of the Japanese force, pounding away with their 5-inch guns and flinging torpedoes. The *Johnston*, *Hoel*, and *Roberts* were sunk, and the *Heermann* heavily damaged by the overwhelming volume of enemy fire.

The Japanese ships then began concentrating their long-range gunfire on Sprague's retreating escort carriers, damaging four of them and sinking the *Gambier Bay*. Kurita's force was lacking air cover, however, and had been scattered by the American counterattacks. Unsure of Halsey's whereabouts and convinced that Nishimura's force had been wiped out, at 9:20 a.m. Kurita suddenly and quite unexpectedly gave the order for Center Force to withdraw.

"Damn it, boys, they're getting away," a sailor aboard one of the escort carriers complained to his shipmates. Halsey would arrive too late to intercept Kurita before the Center Force reentered San Bernardino Strait and slipped away. The naval aviators of Third Fleet, however, had flown over five hundred sorties against Ozawa's Northern Force, sinking three of the four Japanese aircraft carriers.

Despite the near-disaster off Samar, the Battle of Leyte Gulf would result in a decisive victory for the Pacific Fleet and another major blow to the Imperial Japanese Navy. "Our invasion of the Philippines was not even slowed down," Admiral Nimitz would remark, "and the losses sustained by the Japanese reduced their fleet from what had been at least a potential menace to the mere nuisance level."

In desperation, the Japanese would resort to the use of *kamikaze* tactics, where pilots were ordered to make deliberate, suicidal crashes into

American ships. The *kamikaze*—or "divine wind" in Japanese—were used in significant numbers for the first time in the Philippine campaign. On November 29 while on patrol in Leyte Gulf, the *Maryland* was struck by a *kamikaze* between her forward 16-inch turrets. Although thirty-one of her crew were killed, the *Maryland* continued with her patrol duties until December 2, when she departed the Philippines to begin a lengthy course of repairs in Pearl Harbor.

The *Maryland* would return to the western Pacific in March 1945, providing naval gunfire support for the invasion of Okinawa. On April 7 she joined Task Force 54 in the effort to intercept the *Yamato* and her escorts, which were steaming south from mainland Japan toward Okinawa on a one-way suicide mission of their own. Before Task Force 54 could come within range, the Japanese flotilla was clobbered by planes of the Fast Carrier Task Forces and the *Yamato* was destroyed.

Later that afternoon the *Maryland* would be struck by another *kamikaze*, which crashed into the Number Three Turret only a few feet above the head of John Ashby. The life of the young sailor was spared, but ten others were killed and thirty-seven wounded. Nevertheless, the *Maryland* remained off the coast of Okinawa, providing on-call gunfire support until April 12, when she set sail for Puget Sound and an overhaul, and was in the midst of sea trials following her refit when the Japanese surrendered.

The *Maryland* would then participate in Operation Magic Carpet, transporting nine thousand servicemen home to the United States from the Pacific Theater. The Fighting Mary entered reserve status at Puget Sound in April 1946 and was decommissioned a year later. In 1957, she was sold to an Oakland steel firm for scrap.

The *California* would stay in Philippine waters until November 20, 1944, when she would depart for Seeadler Harbor to receive maintenance and replenishment. On January 6, flying the three-star flag of the newly promoted Vice Admiral Jesse Oldendorf, *California* steamed into Lingayen Gulf, her guns firing in support of General MacArthur's invasion of Luzon. Late that afternoon she was attacked by two Zero fighters of the *kamikaze* corps. The *California*'s antiaircraft guns sent one of the Zeroes down in flames, but the other crashed into her port side, killing 57 of the ship's company and wounding 155 more.

At the conclusion of the Luzon operation, *California* steamed for Puget Sound, arriving on St. Valentine's Day, 1945, where she would remain under repair until the end of April. Following a period of sea trials the Prune Barge headed for the Ryukyus on May 10, to participate in the final phase of the battle for Okinawa, and she would later watch over the troops of the Sixth Army as they landed on the shores of southern Honshu to begin occupation duties.

In mid-October, *California* departed the former Japanese naval base at Yokosuka, and after a port of call in Singapore proceeded into the Indian Ocean, tasked with a most unusual Magic Carpet mission. Stopping at the isle of Ceylon, she embarked a battalion of South African troops, which she spirited home to Capetown before setting a course for the mainland United States. *California* stood into the Philadelphia Navy Yard on December 7, four years to the day after her ordeal at Pearl Harbor. There her crew began preparing the ship to be laid up in reserve status, and as the work progressed they gradually became fewer in number as men were transferred or discharged from the navy. The USS *California* would remain in Philadelphia until she was finally stricken from the naval register in 1959 and sold to Bethlehem Steel.

The *Tennessee* departed the Philippines at the end of October 1944, also bound for Puget Sound. There her engines received a thorough overhaul and she received an upgrade to her fire control radar. February 1945 would find the *Tennessee* off the shores of Iwo Jima, providing naval gunfire support for the marine landings, and in April she would join Rear Admiral Morton Deyo's Task Force 54 for the Okinawa campaign. On April 12 the Japanese launched a major *kamikaze* attack against the invasion fleet, and the *Tennessee* was struck by a Val dive-bomber in her signal bridge, which killed 22 men while wounding 107. Despite having suffered significant damage, the *Tennessee* remained off the coast of Okinawa providing fire support for two more weeks before putting into Ulithi for repairs.

In June, while flying the flag of Vice Admiral Oldendorf, *Tennessee* began a series of patrols in the East China Sea and was there when the war ended. Along with the *California*, the Rebel would cover the landing of occupation troops on the Japanese Home Islands and call on Singapore before steaming for home. The USS *Tennessee* would remain alongside her sister in Philadelphia for the next fourteen years, until she too was sold to Bethlehem Steel and broken up for scrap.

Following the Battle of Surigao Strait, the *Pennsylvania* remained in Leyte Gulf to defend MacArthur's transports against attacks from the air. On October 25 her guns assisted those of other warships in splashing four Japanese aircraft; on October 28 her antiaircraft battery sent an attacking Kate torpedo plane spiraling into the waters of the gulf. *Pennsylvania* also took part in the Lingayen Gulf landings in January 1945, before heading to San Francisco for a scheduled refit. In late July *Pennsylvania* got under way for Okinawa and stood into Buckner Bay on August 12, where Vice Admiral Oldendorf was piped aboard. As commander of the newly formed Task Force 95, he had chosen *Pennsylvania* for his flagship. The honor would be short-lived, for that evening a Japanese Val zoomed over the bay and sent a torpedo crashing into the *Pennsylvania*'s stern, killing twenty of her crew. Another ten would earn their Purple Hearts that night, including the fifty-eight-year-old admiral.

Damage control teams managed to contain the flooding, and *Pennsylvania* was then taken under tow by seagoing tugs and brought to the fleet base at Guam. During the voyage Captain William Moses and his crew would receive word of the Japanese surrender. In 1946 the thirty-year-old former flagship of the Pacific Fleet would be designated as a target vessel for the atomic bomb tests at Bikini Atoll, and after enduring two nuclear blasts she would be towed to Kwajalein, where she was scuttled in February 1948.

After having participated in the Normandy invasion and the landings in Southern France, the USS *Nevada* returned to the Pacific Fleet after an overhaul at the Brooklyn Navy Yard, where she received three 14-inch / 45 caliber guns salvaged from the wreck of the *Arizona* as a replacement for the worn-out rifles of her Number One Turret. In February 1945, *Nevada* participated in the Iwo Jima operation and arrived off the shores of Okinawa in mid-March. There the Cheer Up Ship would also fall victim to the *kamikaze* scourge. On March 25 she found herself fighting off seven suicidal attackers, one of which crashed into *Nevada*'s Number Three Turret after being hit multiple times by antiaircraft fire, killing eleven sailors and wounding fifty.

After the close of hostilities *Nevada* would perform occupation duty in Japan, and then like the *Pennsylvania* would be chosen as a target ship for Operation Crossroads at Bikini, where the effect of nuclear weapons on naval vessels was being examined. Painted entirely in bright orange paint, the *Nevada* served as the aiming point for an Air Force B-29 Superfortress carrying an atomic bomb. The bombardier actually missed the *Nevada*, though his poor marksmanship was scarcely noticed. Two atomic bomb blasts would fail to sink the stubborn old dreadnought; two years later she was towed to a point 65 miles off the coast of Oahu and made the target of a gunnery exercise led by the fast battleship *Iowa*. After sustaining several direct hits the "Ship Too Tough to Die" still refused to sink, and *Nevada* finally had to be scuttled by an aerial torpedo.

Her sister *Oklahoma*, though deemed beyond repair after the attack on Pearl Harbor, became the subject of an extensive "parbuckling" operation by the Navy Yard beginning in the summer of 1942, the wreck having become a hazard to navigation and taking up valuable berthing space in the anchorage. Compressed air was pumped into the hull to force seawater from the open torpedo holes, and dredged coral was deposited around her bow to prevent the ship from sliding. Righting the *Oklahoma* commenced on March 8, 1943, using a series of steel cables attached to massive hydraulic winches on the shores of Ford Island. The ship was successfully rotated 180 degrees into an upright position, cofferdammed, and refloated, and in December 1943 was eased into Dry Dock Number Two. After being stripped of all that was useful, the *Oklahoma* was decommissioned and stricken from the naval register.

In 1946 the hulk was put up for auction and purchased for scrap by the Moore Dry Dock Company of Oakland, California. The following May, two civilian tugboats took the vessel under tow and departed for San Francisco Bay. A fierce storm was encountered during the journey and the hulk quickly took on water and sank, nearly dragging the tugs with it to the bottom of the Pacific before the towlines were disconnected.

The wreck of the *Arizona* had also been salvaged for anything of military value during the war, including her guns and ammunition stores. Efforts to remove the human remains still aboard proved too difficult and disturbing to carry out, and after the ship's superstructure was cut off below the water's surface, the hull was left at rest on the bottom of Pearl Harbor to serve as a tomb for 1,102 members of the *Arizona*'s crew killed in action on December 7, 1941.

In 1950 the Commander-in-Chief of the Pacific Fleet, Admiral Arthur Radford, ordered a flagstaff attached to the stump of the *Arizona*'s mainmast. Radford then directed that a national ensign be raised from the staff each morning and brought down at dusk, and for the ships of the fleet to render honors as they pass. This was the impetus for the USS *Arizona* Memorial, which was completed in 1962 and receives over two million visitors every year. As of this writing, forty-four former crew members of the USS *Arizona* who survived the attack on Pearl Harbor have had canisters containing their ashes placed aboard the ship by divers from the National Park Service, and have joined their shipmates in their final resting place.

The *West Virginia* went on to take part in the operations to recapture Mindoro and Luzon, performing shore bombardment and protecting amphibious forces from the growing *kamikaze* threat. In February her guns were heard off the coast of Iwo Jima as she provided fire support for the hard-pressed US Marines in their struggle against the island's deeply entrenched and stubborn Japanese defenders. They would be heard again off Okinawa in March, where she served as part of Task Force 54. A Japanese bomber would fall before her antiaircraft guns on March 26 and another on the morning of April 1. Later that same day a *kamikaze* would crash into the *West Virginia*'s superstructure, killing four and wounding seven.

Like many of the Japanese suicide planes this one had been carrying a bomb, which broke loose and tore through the galley and laundry compartment before coming to rest without detonating. For the second time in her service life, the Wee Vee had to contend with an unexploded Japanese bomb buried in debris on her second deck. The ship's bomb disposal officer defused the device, and the *West Virginia* continued on with her fire support duties. She would see the long and brutal campaign to secure Okinawa through to its bitter end, and was at anchor in Buckner Bay when word was received that the Japanese had surrendered.

Like her fellow dreadnoughts, the *West Virginia* would perform occupation duties and several Magic Carpet runs before making her final voyage to Seattle, where despite having earned five battle stars she would also be placed in reserve status and eventually decommissioned and sold to be "turned into razor blades." Before any of that would occur, however, the *West Virginia* would accompany *Missouri* on her mission to Tokyo Bay.

The sun rose over the Home Islands of Japan on the morning of September 2, 1945, to reveal a gloomy, overcast sky reflected upon the flat and calm waters of Tokyo Bay. At 8:00 a.m., Fleet Admiral Chester W. Nimitz was piped aboard the USS *Missouri.* Forty-three minutes later General of the Army Douglas MacArthur would arrive, there to fulfill his newly assigned duties as Supreme Commander of Allied Powers and receive the formal surrender of Japanese forces. MacArthur's five-star flag was broken alongside that of Nimitz on the *Missouri*'s main mast.

Just before the nine o'clock hour, a motor whaleboat carrying the Japanese delegation eased alongside the *Missouri.* Despite having lost his right leg to a partisan bomb in Shanghai several years earlier, Foreign Minister Mamoru Shigemitsu swiftly mounted the accommodation ladder and shuffled past the rows of saluting sideboys, carrying a polished wooden cane and dressed in a morning coat and top hat. With him were three officials of the foreign office in formal dress along with six military officers led by the grim Yoshijiro Umezu, Chief of the Imperial Army General Staff.

The group came to a halt on the *Missouri*'s quarterdeck before a table containing the surrender documents, which was backed by a sea of khaki uniforms. Gathered in loose formation several ranks deep was a collection of now-famous American naval officers who played prominent roles in the Pacific War victory, men with names like Nimitz, Halsey, Turner, Sherman, Lockwood, Kingman, Towers, and McCain. Watching intently from the *Missouri*'s upper works and the flat roofs of her enormous gun turrets were hundreds of enlisted men of the ship's company, clad in their dress whites. At 9:02 a.m., General MacArthur emerged from the crowd to stand before a microphone wearing his familiar custom-made dress cap, a circle of five gleaming stars pinned to his shirt collar.

The members of the Japanese delegation came stiffly to attention with all the dignity they could muster, a posture which belied their tremendous fear and humiliation. They had endured four long years of unsparing and vicious conflict, which saw the razing of Japan by a relentless strategic bombing campaign that had taken hundreds of thousands of lives, culminating in the destruction of two Japanese cities by atomic weapons. On August 15, Hirohito had broken the news of his capitulation to the Japanese public in a nationwide radio address. For most, it was the first time they had heard their emperor's voice.

"The enemy has begun to employ a new and most cruel bomb," Hirohito told his subjects, "the power of which to do damage is, indeed, incalculable, taking the toll of many innocent lives. Should we continue to fight, not only would it result in an ultimate collapse and obliteration of the Japanese nation, but also it would lead to the total extinction of human civilization . . . This is the reason why we have ordered the acceptance of the provisions of the Joint Declaration of the Powers. The hardships and sufferings to which our nation is to be subjected hereafter will be certainly great."

All had been lost, and from their conquerors the Japanese could expect only an unforgiving and oppressive subjugation. Among the delegates at the ceremony of surrender was Toshikazu Kase, a career diplomat who spoke perfect English, and who listened to General MacArthur begin his opening remarks with a great deal of trepidation.

"It is my earnest hope," the general said in an august and somber voice, "and indeed the hope of all mankind, that from this solemn occasion a better world shall emerge out of the blood and carnage of the past—a world dedicated to the dignity of man and the fulfillment of his most cherished wish for freedom, tolerance, and justice."

"MacArthur's words sailed on wings," Kase would later say. "The narrow quarterdeck was now transformed into an altar of peace."

General MacArthur would keep his remarks brief; in fact, the entire affair would last just thirty-four minutes. Signatures were affixed to the instrument of surrender by Foreign Minister Shigemitsu and General Umezu, by representatives from the Allied nations, and by MacArthur in his role as Supreme Commander. The honor of signing on behalf of the United States was bestowed upon Admiral Nimitz.

As the ceremony concluded, the gray clouds over Tokyo Bay began to part, allowing a shaft of sunlight to spill onto the decks of the *Missouri*.

General MacArthur once again stepped to the microphone.

"Let us pray that peace be now restored to the world, and that God will preserve it always," he said. "These proceedings are closed."

ACKNOWLEDGMENTS

As always, I am indebted to the talented writer and editor Tom McCarthy for his continued advocacy and inspiration; without him I would still be an unpublished dreamer. I would like to thank Melissa Baker for the magnificent and timely work she did in creating the maps shown in the book. My close friend and aficionado of naval technology, Lee Barnes, served as a sounding board for ideas and was a great source of information, advice, and support.

I am very thankful for the ninety-five-year-old veteran of the USS *Maryland*, John Henry Ashby, his remarkable memory, and his daughter, Kimberly Thorn, who put us in touch.

I would be remiss if I did not also thank my wife Kathleen, who on a daily basis continues to offer her encouragement and exercise the tremendous patience that being married to an author requires.

SOURCES

BOOKS

Agawa, Hiroyuki. *The Reluctant Admiral: Yamamoto and the Imperial Navy.* Tokyo: Kodansha International Ltd., 1979.

Asada, Sadao. *From Mahan to Pearl Harbor: The Imperial Japanese Navy and the United States.* Annapolis, MD: Naval Institute Press, 2006.

Bartholomew, C. A. *Mud, Muscle and Miracles: Marine Salvage in the United States Navy.* Washington, DC: Naval Historical Center and Naval Sea Systems Command, 1990.

Beach, Edward L. *Salt and Steel: Reflections of a Submariner.* Annapolis, MD: Naval Institute Press, 1999.

Brands, H. W. *TR: The Last Romantic.* New York: Perseus Books Group, 1997.

Bulkley, Robert J. *At Close Quarters: PT Boats in the United States Navy.* Washington, DC: US Government Printing Office Naval History Division, 1962.

Cannon, M. Hamlin. *The United States Army in World War II: The War in the Pacific—Leyte: The Return to the Philippines.* Washington, DC: Department of the Army, Center for Military History, 1993.

Cheser, S. Matthew, and Nicholas Roland. *Galvanic: Beyond the Reef. Tarawa and the Gilberts, November 1943.* Washington, DC: Department of the Navy, Naval History and Heritage Command, 2020.

Crowl, Philip A. *The United States Army in World War II: The War in the Pacific, Campaign in the Marianas.* Washington, DC: Department of the Army, Center for Military History, 1959.

Doyle, David. *USS* Tennessee *(BB-43): From Pearl Harbor to Okinawa in World War II.* Atglen, PA: Schiffer Publishing Limited, 2019.

Dyer, George C. *The Amphibians Came to Conquer: The Story of Admiral Richmond Kelly Turner.* Washington DC: US Government Printing Office Naval History Division, 1969.

———. *On the Treadmill to Pearl Harbor: The Memoirs of Admiral James O. Richardson.* Washington, DC: US Government Printing Office Naval History Division, 1973.

Evans, David C., and Mark R. Peattie. *Kaigun: Strategy, Tactics and Technology in the Imperial Japanese Navy 1887–1941.* Annapolis, MD: Naval Institute Press, 1997.

Forrestel, Emmet P. *Admiral Raymond A. Spruance, USN.* Washington, DC: US Government Printing Office Naval History Division, 1966.

Frank, Richard B. *Guadalcanal: The Definitive Account of the Landmark Battle.* New York: Random House, 1990.

Friedman, Kenneth I. *Afternoon of the Rising Sun: The Battle of Leyte Gulf.* Novato, CA: Presidio Press, 2001.

Friedman, Norman. *U.S. Battleships: An Illustrated Design History.* Annapolis, MD: Naval Institute Press, 1985.

Gunston, Bill. *Combat Aircraft of World War II.* London: Salamander House, 1978.

Halsey, William Frederick. *Admiral Halsey's Story.* New York: Whittlesea House, 1947.

Hastings, Max. *Retribution: The Battle for Japan 1944–45.* New York: Alfred A. Knopf, 2008.

Hipperson, Carol Edgemon. *Radioman: An Eyewitness Account of Pearl Harbor and World War II in the Pacific.* New York: Thomas Dunne Books, 2008.

Hornfischer, James D. *Neptune's Inferno: The US Navy at Guadalcanal.* New York: Bantam Books, 2011.

———. *The Fleet at Flood Tide: America at Total War in the Pacific 1944–1945.* New York: Bantam Books, 2016.

Jones, James. *WWII.* New York: Grosset and Dunlap, 1975.

Joy, Waldron Jasper, James P. Delgado, and Jim Adams. *The USS* Arizona. New York: St. Martin's Press, 2001.

Konoe, Fumimaro. *Memoirs of Prince Ayamaro Konoe.* Osaka: Asahi Shimbun, 1946.

Kimmel, Husband E. *Admiral Kimmel's Story.* Chicago: Henry Regnery Company, 1955.

Layton, Edwin T. *And I Was There: Pearl Harbor and Midway—Breaking the Secrets.* Annapolis, MD: Naval Institute Press, 1985.

Leckie, Robert. *Helmet for My Pillow: From Parris Island to the Pacific.* New York: Random House, 1957.

London, Jack. *South Sea Tales.* New York: Macmillan, 1911.

Lord, Walter. *Day of Infamy: The Bombing of Pearl Harbor.* New York: Henry Holt and Company, 1957.

———. *Midway: The Incredible Victory.* New York: Harper & Row, 1967.

Madsen, Daniel. *Resurrection: Salvaging the Battle Fleet at Pearl Harbor.* Annapolis, MD: Naval Institute Press, 2003.

Mahan, Alfred Thayer. *The Influence of Sea Power upon History: 1660–1783.* Boston: Little, Brown and Company, 1890.

———. *Retrospect and Prospect: Studies in International Relations, Naval and Political.* Boston: Little, Brown and Company, 1902.

———. *Naval Strategy Compared and Contrasted with the Principles and Practice of Military Operations on Land.* Boston: Little, Brown and Company, 1911.

Manchester, William. *American Caesar: Douglas MacArthur 1880–1964.* New York: Little, Brown and Company, 1978.

Marshall, M. Ernest. *Rear Admiral Herbert V. Wiley: A Career in Airships and Battleships.* Annapolis, MD: Naval Institute Press, 2019.

Mason, Theodore C. *Battleship Sailor.* Annapolis, MD: Naval Institute Press, 1982.

McCullough, David. *The Path Between the Seas: The Creation of the Panama Canal 1870–1914.* New York: Simon & Schuster, 1977.

Miller, John Jr. *The United States Army in World War Two, The War in the Pacific, Cartwheel: The Reduction of Rabaul.* Washington, DC: Office of the Chief of Military History, Department of the Army, 1959.

Miller, Nathan. *The US Navy: An Illustrated History.* New York: American Heritage Publishing, 1977.

Mitchell, Robert J., Sewell Tappan Tyng, Nelson L. Drummond Jr., and Gregory J. W. Urwin. *The Capture of Attu: A World War II Battle as Told by the Men Who Fought There.* Lincoln: University of Nebraska Press, 2000.

Morison, Samuel Eliot. *History of United States Naval Operations in World War II, Volume 12: Leyte June 1944–January 1945.* Boston: Little, Brown and Company, 1962.

———. *The Two Ocean War: A Short History of the United States Navy in the Second World War.* Boston: Little, Brown and Company, 1963.

Nofi, Albert A. *To Train the Fleet for War: The U.S. Navy Fleet Problems, 1923–1940.* Newport, RI: Naval War College Press, 2010.

Pleshakov, Constantine. *The Tsar's Last Armada: The Epic Voyage to the Battle of Tsushima.* New York: Perseus Books Group, 2002.

Potter, E. B. *Nimitz.* Annapolis, MD: Naval Institute Press, 1976.

Prange, Gordon W. *At Dawn We Slept: The Untold Story of Pearl Harbor.* New York: McGraw-Hill Book Company, 1981.

Raymer, Edward C. *Descent into Darkness: Pearl Harbor, 1941—A Navy Diver's Memoir.* Annapolis, MD: Naval Institute Press, 1996.

Rose, Lisle A. *Power at Sea, Volume 1: The Age of Navalism, 1890–1918.* Columbia: University of Missouri Press, 2006.

———. *Power at Sea, Volume 2: The Breaking Storm, 1919–1945.* Columbia: University of Missouri Press, 2006.

Rottman, Gordon L. *The Marshall Islands 1944: Operation Flintlock, the Capture of Kwajalein and Eniwetok.* Oxford: Osprey Publishing, 2004.

Russ, Martin. *Line of Departure: Tarawa.* New York: Doubleday and Company, 1975.

Seager, Robert (II). *Alfred Thayer Mahan: The Man and His Letters.* Annapolis, MD: Naval Institute Press, 2017.

Sherrod, Robert. *Tarawa: The Story of a Battle.* New York: Duell, Sloan and Pearce Inc., 1944.

Sledge, Eugene B. *With the Old Breed at Peleliu and Okinawa.* Novato, CA: Presidio Press, 1981.

Sloan, Bill. *Brotherhood of Heroes: The Marines at Peleliu, 1944—The Bloodiest Battle of the Pacific War.* New York: Simon & Schuster, 2005.

Smith, Holland M., and Percy Finch. *Coral and Brass.* New York: Charles Scribner's Sons, 1949.

Smith, Myron J. Jr. *Mountaineer Battlewagon: USS* West Virginia *(BB-48).* Charleston, WV: Pictorial Histories Publishing Company, 1982.

Toland, John. *But Not in Shame: The Six Months After Pearl Harbor.* New York: Random House, 1961.

Toll, Ian W. *Pacific Crucible: War at Sea in the Pacific 1941–1942.* New York: W. W. Norton and Company, 2012.

Tuchman, Barbara W. *The Guns of August.* New York: Random House, 1962.

Turk, Richard W. *The Ambiguous Relationship: Theodore Roosevelt and Alfred Thayer Mahan.* New York: Greenwood Press, 1987.

Utley, Jonathon G. *An American Battleship at Peace and War: The USS* Tennessee. Lawrence: University Press of Kansas, 1991.

Wallin, Homer N. *Pearl Harbor: Why, How, Fleet Salvage and Final Appraisal.* Washington, DC: US Government Printing Office Naval History Division, 1968.

Young, Steven Bower. *Trapped at Pearl Harbor: Escape from Battleship Oklahoma.* Annapolis, MD: Naval Institute Press, 1991.

PERIODICALS

Alexander, Joseph H. "Surprise and Chagrin: The Navy's Battle for Peleliu." *Proceedings, United States Naval Institute*, November 2004, Vol. 130/11/1221.

Ballendorf, Dirk Anthony. "Earl Hancock Ellis: The Man and His Mission." *Proceedings, United States Naval Institute,* November 1983, Vol. 109/11/969.

Barron, Chris. "Repairing America." *Kitsap Sun*, December 8, 2002.

Fioravanzo, Giuseppe. "The Japanese Military Mission to Italy in 1941." *Proceedings, United States Naval Institute*, January 1956, Vol. 82/1/635.

Frank, Richard B. "Picking Winners." *Naval History Magazine*, May 2011, Vol. 25/3.

Fuchida, Mitsuo. "I Led the Air Attack on Pearl Harbor." *Proceedings, United States Naval Institute*, September 1952, Vol. 78/9/595.

Gregory, Eric. "16 Days to Die at Pearl Harbor." *Seattle Times*, December 7, 1995.

Heinl, Robert D. Jr. "Naval Gunfire: Scourge of the Beaches." *Proceedings, United States Naval Institute*, November 1945, Vol. 71/11/513.

Hessler, William H. "The Battleship Paid Dividends." *Proceedings, United States Naval Institute,* September 1946, Vol. 72/9/523.

Hone, Thomas C. "The Destruction of the Battle Line at Pearl Harbor." *Proceedings, United States Naval Institute*, December 1977, Vol. 103/12/898.

Hone, Trent. "US Navy Surface Battle Doctrine and Victory in the Pacific." *Naval War College Review,* Winter 2009, Vol. 62/1, Article 7.

Layton, Edwin T., Captain USN. "Rendezvous in Reverse." *Proceedings, United States Naval Institute*, May 1953, Vol. 79/5/603.

"Lebbeus Curtis, 83, Navy Rear Admiral." *New York Times*, February 8, 1964, 23.

Meyer, Cord Jr. "On the Beaches." *Atlantic Monthly*, October 1944, 42–46.

"The Navy: *Life* Goes into Action with the US Fleet." *Life*, October 28, 1940, 23–40.

"News of West Coast Ships and Shipping Men." *The Log*, published by the American Society of Marine Engineers, July 1933 edition, 24.

Nimitz, Chester W., Fleet Admiral USN. "The Navy: My Way of Life." *Boys' Life*, December 1966, 16, 56–57.

———, Fleet Admiral USN. "Pearl Harbor Postscript." *Proceedings, United States Naval Institute*, December 1966, Vol. 92/12/766.

O'Connor, Christopher P. "A Taranto–Pearl Harbor Connection." *Naval History Magazine*, December 2016, Vol. 30/6.

Oldendorf, Jesse B., Admiral USN (Ret). "Comment and Discussion." *Proceedings, United States Naval Institute*, April 1959, Vol. 85/4/674.

Ruddock, Theodore D. Jr., Vice Admiral USN (Ret). "Comment and Discussion." *Proceedings, United States Naval Institute*, November 1959, Vol. 85/11/681.

Shapiro, Laura. "The First Kitchen: Eleanor Roosevelt's Austerity Drive." *The New Yorker*, November 15, 2010.

Stillwell, Paul. "Plenty of Blame to Go Around." *Proceedings, United States Naval Institute,* September 2016, Vol. 142/12/1,366.

Taussig, Joseph K. Jr., Captain USN (Ret). "I Remember Pearl Harbor." *Proceedings, United States Naval Institute,* December 1972, Vol. 98/12/838.

Wallin, Homer N. "Rejuvenation at Pearl Harbor." *Proceedings, United States Naval Institute,* December 1946, Vol. 72/12/526.

Weller, Donald M. "Salvo—Splash! The Development of Naval Gunfire Support in World War II." *Proceedings, United States Naval Institute,* August 1954, Vol. 80/8/618.

Woodward, Steve. "Navy Hero Francis J. Thomas Dies at 100." *The Oregonian,* January 24, 2005.

WEBSITES

"Battleship Photo Archive." NavSource Naval History: Photographic History of the US Navy. http://www.navsource.org/archives/01idx.htm. Accessed August–December 2020.

"Campaign Plan Granite." Defense Technical Information Center. https://apps.dtic.mil/dtic/tr/fulltext/u2/a606368.pdf. Accessed October 31, 2020.

Chernin, Ted. "My Experiences in the Honolulu Chinatown Red-Light District." University of Hawaii. https://evols.library.manoa.hawaii.edu/bitstream/10524/228/2/JL34209.pdf. Accessed September 13, 2019.

Czarnecki, Joseph. "Turboelectric Drive in American Capital Ships." NavWeaps. http://www.navweaps.com/index_tech/tech-038.php. Accessed July 15, 2020.

"Dictionary of American Naval Fighting Ships." Naval History and Heritage Command. https://www.history.navy.mil/content/history/nhhc/research/histories/ship-histories/danfs.html. Accessed April–June 2020.

Hamilton, Mark W. "Winston Churchill and the New Navalism." International Churchill Society. https://winstonchurchill.org/publications/finest-hour/finest-hour-177/winston-churchill-new-navalism-2/. Accessed February 6, 2020.

Hanes, Don. "USS West Virginia Sank In Pearl Harbor Attack With Trapped Sailors." Warfare History Network. https://warfarehistorynetwork.com/2017/04/26/uss-west-virginia-sank-in-pearl-harbor-attack-with-trapped-sailors/. Accessed July 27, 2020.

"Hyman G. Rickover." Naval History and Heritage Command. https://www.history.navy.mil/content/history/nhhc/research/library/research-guides/modern-biographical-files-ndl/modern-bios-r/rickover-hyman-g.html. Accessed July 11, 2020.

HyperWar US Navy in World War II. https://www.ibiblio.org/hyperwar/USN/. Accessed April–December 2020.

"Japan War Scare of 1906–1907." GlobalSecurity.Org. https://www.globalsecurity.org/military/ops/japan1906.htm. Accessed February 7, 2020.

Kronberger, Robert. "Porthole View of Hawaii." Pearl Harbor Survivors Association. http://www.pearlharborsurvivorsonline.org/html/Porthole20View20o20fHawaii.htm. Accessed September 13, 2019.

"The Lucky Bag: The Annual of the Regiment of Midshipmen, United States Naval Academy." Internet Archive. https://archive.org. Accessed October 2020–March 2021.

"Nimitz Gray Book: War Plans and Files of the Commander-in-Chief, Pacific Fleet." American Naval Records Society. http://www.ibiblio.org/anrs/graybook.html. Accessed March–December 2020.

Oral History Interviews, Pearl Harbor National Memorial, US National Park Service. https://www.nps.gov/valr/learn/historyculture/oral-history-interviews.htm. Accessed March 6–May 24, 2020.

Pearl Harbor History and Information, Pearl Harbor Visitor's Bureau. https://visitpearlharbor.org/pearl-harbor-history/. Accessed October 17–20, 2019.

PT Boat World. https://www.ptboatworld.com. Accessed February 23, 2021.

Pyne, Max E. "My View from the Bridge." USS West Virginia Reunion Association. https://www.usswestvirginia.org/stories/story.php?id=27. Accessed January 27, 2021.

Sobocinski, Andre B. "Navy Medicine at Pearl Harbor (December 7, 1941)." Navy Medicine Live. https://navymedicine.navylive.dodlive.mil/archives/3809. Accessed May 26, 2020.

Toppan, Andrew. "World Battleship Lists and Photo Gallery From 1860 to 2001." Haze Gray & Underway. http://www.hazegray.org/navhist/battleships/. Accessed August 23, 2020.

US Court of Appeals for the Fourth Circuit. *Pacific-Atlantic Steamship Company v. United States*. 175 F.2d 632, filed June 9, 1949. https://www.courtlistener.com/opinion/1474322/pacific-atlantic-ss-co-v-united-states/. Accessed August 3, 2020.

USS *West Virginia* Reunion Association. https://www.usswestvirginia.org. Accessed January 26, 2021.

"Wallin, Homer N." Naval History and Heritage Command. https://www.history.navy.mil/content/history/nhhc/our-collections/photography/us-people/w/wallin-homer-n.html. Accessed May 27, 2020.

"Why Japan Really Lost the War." Imperial Japanese Navy Page. http://www.combinedfleet.com/economic.htm. Accessed August 16, 2020.

"William M. Hobby (DE-236)." Naval History and Heritage Command. https://www.history.navy.mil/content/history/nhhc/research/histories/ship-histories/danfs/w/william-m-hobby.html. Accessed May 29, 2020.

"WWII Pearl Harbor Attack." Naval History and Heritage Command. https://www.history.navy.mil/research/archives/digitized-collections/action-reports/wwii-pearl-harbor-attack.html. Accessed November 20, 2019.

VIDEO

"Admiral Hyman Rickover, *60 Minutes* Interview by Diane Sawyer." Virginia Commonwealth University. Accessed July 11, 2020.

"The Battle of Surigao Strait—James L. Holloway III, Admiral USN (Ret)." Naval Historical Foundation. Accessed March 2, 2021.

"The Day Japan Surrendered, Ending World War II." NBC News, September 2, 2016. Accessed March 13, 2021.

"Hyland, Everett: Life Aboard the USS *Pennsylvania* (BB-38)." Digital Collections of the National World War II Museum. Accessed October 20, 2020.

"With the Marines at Tarawa." Documentary film by Louis Hayward, produced by the US Marine Corps, 1944. US National Archives. Accessed November 7, 2020.

ADDITIONAL SOURCES

"The Aleutians Campaign, June 1942–August 1943." Office of Naval Intelligence Combat Narrative Series, 1945. Department of the Navy, Naval History and Heritage Command.

Ashby, John Henry, Seaman First Class, USS *Maryland*, 1943–1945. Interviewed by the author, September 13, 2020, and November 29, 2020.

"The Attack on Lae and Salamaua, March 10, 1942." *Early Raids in the Pacific Ocean*. Office of Naval Intelligence Combat Narrative Series, 1943. Department of the Navy, Naval History and Heritage Command.

Bates, Richard W. *The Battle for Leyte Gulf, October 1944. Strategic and Tactical Analysis, Volume V, Battle of Surigao Strait, October 24–25*. Newport, RI: Naval War College, 1958.

"Building the Navy's Bases in World War II: History of the Bureau of Yards and Docks and the Civil Engineer Corps, 1940–1946." Washington, DC: US Government Printing Office, 1947.

"Campaign Plan Granite, United States Pacific Fleet and Pacific Ocean Areas, Office of the Commander-in-Chief." WWII Declassified Records, Department of Defense, Defense Technical Information Center.

Cates, Clifton B. Jr. *War History of the USS* Pennsylvania *BB-38*. Published by the USS *Pennsylvania* Ship's Welfare Fund and Metropolitan Press, Seattle, WA, 1946. Dean Mawdsley World War II Collection, J. Porter Shaw Library, San Francisco Maritime National Historic Park.

"Command History—Pearl Harbor Naval Shipyard." Compiled by Management Engineering Division–Management Planning and Review Department, Pearl Harbor Naval Shipyard, July 1959.

Cressman, Robert J. *The Official Chronology of the U.S. Navy in World War II*. Department of the Navy, Naval History and Heritage Command, 1999.

"Engagement off Balikpapan, January 23–24." *The Java Sea Campaign*. Office of Naval Intelligence Combat Narrative Series, 1943. Department of the Navy, Naval History and Heritage Command.

Hough, Frank O. *The Seizure of Peleliu*. Historical Branch, G-3 Division, Headquarters, US Marine Corps, 1950.

Hough, Frank O., Verle E. Ludwig, and Henry I. Shaw Jr. *Pearl Harbor to Guadalcanal: History of US Marine Corps Operations in World War II*. Historical Branch, G-3 Division, Headquarters, US Marine Corps, 1958.

National Archives Record Group 38: *GALVANIC Operation—General Instructions for, Commander Central Pacific Force, U.S. Pacific Fleet, 29 October 1943.*

———. *Records of the Office of Chief of Naval Operations 1875–2006, Papers of Vice Admiral Homer N. Wallin, 1941–1974.*

———. *World War II War Diaries, Other Operational Records and Histories, compiled 01/01/1942–06/01/1946, documenting the period 09/01/1939–05/30/1946.*

King, Ernest J. *United States Navy at War 1941–1945: First Official Report to the Secretary of the Navy Covering Combat Operations December 7, 1941 to April 30, 1944 by Fleet Admiral Ernest J. King*. Department of the Navy, Naval History and Heritage Command, 1944.

———. *United States Navy at War 1941–1945: Second Official Report to the Secretary of the Navy Covering Combat Operations March 1, 1944 to March 1, 1945 by Fleet Admiral Ernest J. King*. Department of the Navy, Naval History and Heritage Command, 1945.

"Peace and War, United States Foreign Policy 1931–1941." Department of State. Washington, DC: US Government Printing Office, 1943.

"The Raids on the Marshall and Gilbert Islands, February 1, 1942." *Early Raids in the Pacific Ocean*. Office of Naval Intelligence Combat Narrative Series, 1943. Department of the Navy, Naval History and Heritage Command.

"The Raids on Wake and Marcus Islands, February 24 and March 4, 1942." *Early Raids in the Pacific Ocean*. Office of Naval Intelligence Combat Narrative Series, 1943. Department of the Navy, Naval History and Heritage Command.

"Report by the Secretary of the Navy to the President." US Congress Joint Committee on Pearl Harbor Attack; Hearings, Part 24, 1749–56.

"Reports of General MacArthur, Japanese Operations in the Southwest Pacific Area, Volume 2, Part 1, Compiled from Japanese Demobilization Bureau Records." Department of the Army, Center for Military History, 1966.

"Salvage Diary, 1 March 1942 through 15 November 1943." National Archives and Records Administration / USS *Arizona* Memorial—National Park Service Industrial Department War Diary Collection.

"Summary of War Damage to U.S. Battleships, Carriers, Cruisers and Destroyers: 17 October 1941 to 7 December 1941 by Preliminary Design Section, Bureau of Ships, Navy Department." Submitted 15 September 1943. Department of the Navy, Naval History and Heritage Command.

"USS *California*: Report of Raid, 7 December 1941." Submitted 13 December 1941. Department of the Navy, Naval History and Heritage Command.

"USS *California* Torpedo and Bomb Damage, December 7, 1941 Pearl Harbor. War Damage Report Number 21, Bureau of Ships." Submitted 28 November 1942. Department of the Navy, Naval History and Heritage Command.

"USS *Maryland*: Report of Damage Sustained in Action, 7 December 1941." Submitted 19 December 1941. Department of the Navy, Naval History and Heritage Command.

USS Maryland *1941–1945 World War II Cruise Book*. Baton Rouge, LA: Army & Navy Pictorial Publishers, 1946. Department of the Navy, Naval History and Heritage Command.

"USS *Nevada* Torpedo and Bomb Damage, December 7, 1941, Pearl Harbor. War Damage Report Number 17, Bureau of Ships." Submitted 18 September 1942. Department of the Navy, Naval History and Heritage Command.

"USS *Oklahoma*: Report of Damage Sustained during Action at Pearl Harbor," with enclosures. Submitted 20 December 1941. Department of the Navy, Naval History and Heritage Command.

"USS *Pennsylvania:* Report of Action during Enemy Air Attack Morning of Sunday, 7 December, 1941," with enclosures. Submitted 16 December 1941. Department of the Navy, Naval History and Heritage Command.

"USS *Tennessee*: Action Report—Japanese Attack on Pearl Harbor, 7 December 1941," with enclosures. Submitted 11 December 1941. Department of the Navy, Naval History and Heritage Command.

USS Tennessee *7 December 1941–7 December 1945 World War II Cruise Book*. Philadelphia, PA: Clark Publishing House, 1946. Department of the Navy, Naval History and Heritage Command.

"USS *West Virginia*: Action of December 7, 1941, Report of," with enclosures. Submitted 11 December 1941. Department of the Navy, Naval History and Heritage Command.

"USS *West Virginia* Crosses the Equator Again—October 1944." *World War II Cruise Book*. San Francisco, CA: The Trade Pressroom, 1945. Department of the Navy, Naval History and Heritage Command.

"USS *West Virginia*: Report of Salvage of." Submitted 15 June 1942. Department of the Navy, Naval History and Heritage Command.

Weller, Donald M. "Naval Gunfire Support of Amphibious Operations Past, Present and Future." Naval Sea Systems Command and Headquarters, US Marine Corps, 1978. Department of Defense, Defense Technical Information Center.

INDEX

Abe, Hiroaki, 54, 155, 156
Abemama, 179, 180, 181
aircraft carriers
  development of, 28
  hit-and-run raids, 139–40
  in prewar Fleet Problems, 124
  training under Kimmel, 42
  See also specific carriers
Akagi, 17, 53, 79, 131, 135, 136
Akebono, 293
Akiyama, Saneyuki, 26–27
Albacore, 222
Aleutian Islands
  Attu and, 130, 163, 165, 168–71, 175
  Dutch Harbor and, 168
  Japanese attack and, 168
  Japanese design on, 168–69
  Japanese motivation for troops and, 169
  Kiska and, 130, 168–69, 173–75, 176
  mission conclusion, 175
  Nevada and, 165
  Pennsylvania and, 168, 169–70
  Tennessee and, 173–75
  US invasion force, 169
Anderson, 81
Anderson, John, 66
Anderson, Walter (Admiral), 82–83,
    145, 151
Anglo-Japanese Alliance, 276
Argonne, 76
Argus, 28
Arizona
  abandon ship order, 66
  artillery shells and, 59
  in Battleship Row, 3
  casualties, 75
  crew aboard the *Nevada*, 69
  damage assessment, 90
  destruction of, 59
  early morning December 7th, 50
  explosions, 59–60, 67
  fires, 82–83
  first moments on, 51–52
  as floating inferno, 61
  salvage of, 100, 302–3
  survivors, 60–61, 68
  as tomb, 303
  See also Pearl Harbor attack
Arizona Memorial, 303
Arkansas, 41, 166
Ashby, John Henry, 186, 223, 224
Ashigara, 291
Atago, 257
Atlanta, 155
Atlantic Fleet, 43, 171, 301
Attu, 130, 163, 165, 168–71, 175
Augusta, 96
Australia, 128–29
Avocet, 72

BAITDIV One, 247–48
Ban, Masami, 260
Battleship Row
  confusion, 51
  early morning December 7th, 50
  as hellish nightmare, 68
  moorings, 3
  Secretary of the Navy sight of, 92
battleships
  "all big gun," 22
  anti-torpedo protections, 58
  "dreadnoughts," 22–24, 27, 99, 123
  "fast," 140
  Pearl Harbor, classes of, 2–3
  in prewar Fleet Problems, 124
  as pride of Pacific Fleet, 146
  purpose of, 2
  serving aboard as honor, 3
  shore bombardment by, 190
  weather decks, 4

See also specific battleships; *specific classes of battleships*
Beach, Edward, 115, 116
Bellatti, Lawrence, 274, 285
Bennion, 283, 285
Bennion, Meryn, 51, 58, 62–63
Berkey, Russell "Count" (Admiral), 261, 262
Betio Island
about, 182
aftermath on, 189
assault plan, 182–83
assault waves, 185–86
bombing of, 183, 184–85
declared as secure, 188
Higgins boats and, 183, 185–86
as Japanese fortress, 182
Japanese guns on, 191
landing force, 183, 185
Maryland and, 183–84, 186–87
Nimitz on, 189
Sherrod and, 185, 186
Tennessee and, 188
waters around, 182–83
See also Tarawa
Billingsley, Garnett, 58–59
Birmingham, 216, 217, 259
Bobolink, 83
Bofors guns, 143, 150, 166–67, 172, 211, 240, 265
Bogan, Gerald (Admiral), 259
Boise, 153–54, 262
Bothne, Adolph, 81–82
Boulton, Robert, 4–5
Brooks, Roman, 50–51
Brunelle, Albert, 277
Buehl, Herbert, 60–61
Bunkley, Joel, 108, 109
Burnett, Henry "Bobby," 211–12, 217

Cactus Air Force, 152, 153
Calhoun, William, 87, 109
California
after-action report, 108
background, 3
in battleship queue, 57
in Battleship Row, 3
design of, 109
drills (1944), 212
Eniwetok repairs and, 223
fires, 75, 108
first moments on, 51
General Quarters, 107
kamikazi attacks and, 299
Leyte Gulf and, 249, 250–51
listing, 68
Magic Carpet mission, 300
modernization of, 150
at Philadelphia Naval Yard, 300
Philippines and, 241, 300
as "Prune Barge," 3, 110, 112, 114, 116, 211, 220
at Puget Sound Navy Yard, 211
Saipan battle and, 215–17, 220–21, 222–23
sea trials (1944), 211–12
in Seeadler Harbor, 239
sinking, 75, 107
Surigao Strait and, 287
Tennessee striking, 233
torpedo attacks and, 57, 107
California salvage
clearing debris, 112
cofferdams and, 109–10, 111, 113
damage assessment/analysis, 89, 108–9
departure for Puget Sound and, 116
dewatering, 110
dry dock, 114
explosion and, 114
fallen crewman remains and, 113
navy divers and, 110, 113
oil drainage, 113
Operation K and, 112
Rickover and, 114–16
technical problems, 100
test runs, 116
turboelectric propulsion and, 115–16
Canberra, 247
Carney, Robert (Admiral), 247
Cartwheel, Operation, 163
Cassin, 73, 74, 90, 99

Cassin Young, 212
Cates, Clifton, 197, 204, 207, 209, 224, 249, 290
Central Pacific Campaign. *See* Granite Campaign
Chappell, Edmund, 52–53
Chester, 127
Chicago, 96, 154
Chinese Exclusion Act of 1870, 18
Churchill, Winston, 23, 231
"Cinderella liberty," 5
Claggett, Bladen, 257–58
Cleveland, 234
Coleman, Henry, 285
Colorado
  joining task force, 146
  Kwajalein and, 198
  operating with forward main battery detectors, 158
  refit, 125
  Saipan battle and, 218
  San Pedro departure, 195
Colorado-class battleships, 58, 115, 154
Columbia, 279, 286, 292–93
Combined Fleet
  American amphibious forces and, 252
  First Striking Force and, 254
  Galvanic landings and, 180
  Philippines and, 251–52, 254
  Togo and, 16–17
  Truk and, 190
  Yamamoto and, 33–36, 80, 129
Condition Zed, 57
Conolly, Richard L (Admiral), 197, 226
Cook, Charles Jr., 73, 143
Coral Sea, Battle of, 130, 138, 139
Corn, William Anderson, 167, 170, 204
Costin, Louis, 121
Coward, Jesse, 262, 277–79, 282
Curtis, Lebbeus, 109–10
Curtiss, 55, 76
Cutler, Cy, 173

Dace, 257, 258
Daly, 280, 282, 286
Darter, 257, 258
Daves, Ray, 60
DeCastro, Julio "Lefty," 83–84, 85–86
December 6, 1941, 7–8
decisive fleet engagement, 21
decoding apparatus, 44
Denver, 213, 286, 292–93
Destroyer Repair Unit, 101
direct drive engines, 115
divers, navy, 91–92, 103–4, 110, 113, 120–21
Douglas, Archibald, 16
Downes, 73, 74, 90, 99
Dreadnought, 22–23
dreadnoughts
  construction of, 23
  defined, 22
  Eight-Eight Fleet, 27
  Japanese, 24
  Pearl Harbor, raising, 99, 123
  See also specific battleships
Duncan, Robert, 8

Edwards, 170
Eight-Eight Fleet, 27
Endicott, Ronald, 121–22
Engebi, 203, 206–7
Eniwetok Atoll
  about, 203
  beginning operation in, 202–3
  casualties, 208
  defenders, 207
  Japanese use of, 203
  landing force, 206–7
  Maryland and, 203
  Pennsylvania and, 206
  Spruance and, 205
  Tennessee and, 206
  transforming into air and sea base, 208–9
  use in campaign, 202
  See also Granite Campaign
Enterprise, 79, 127, 128, 135–36, 140, 148, 260, 273
Enterprise Task Force
  attack of Japanese, 126–27

composition of, 126
at Guadalcanal, 156, 161
Kwajalein, Wotje, and Taroa attacks, 126
to and from Wake Island, 46, 74

Farragut, 170
Fast Carrier Task Forces, 125–26, 140, 222, 246, 296
Fire Support Group, 183, 185, 192
Fire Support Unit Able, 234
First Carrier Strike Force, 131, 135, 136
Fisher, John "Jackie" (Admiral), 22
5:3:3 ratio, 29
fleet oilers, 149
Fletcher, Jack, 89, 93, 97, 126–27, 133, 147–49
Flintlock, Operation, 195–200, 202
Forager, Operation, 212, 215–26, 232
Forgy, Howell, 67
Formosa, 253
Frazier, 170, 187, 188
Fuchida, Misuo, 56, 81
Fuqua, Samuel, 65–66, 67, 70, 72
Furious, 28
Furlong, William, 100
Fuso, 27, 275, 281–82, 286, 291

Galvanic operation, 179–82, 190
Georgia, 41
Ghormley, Robert L. (Admiral), 151
Gilbert Islands, 179–82
Godwin, Donald, 91
Granite Campaign
Abemama and, 179, 180, 181
about, 177–78
Amphibious Recon Battalion and, 181
Betio Island and, 182–88, 191
Eniwetok Atoll and, 202–8
Flintlock operation, 195–200, 202
Galvanic operation, 179–82, 190
Gilbert Islands and, 179–82
Kwajalein and, 194–200
Makin and, 179, 180, 181
Marshall Islands and, 179
Spruance and, 178–79, 181
Tarawa and, 179, 180, 186, 189–94
Grant, 288
"The Great Marianas Turkey Shoot," 138, 222
"Great White Fleet," 14
Gruber, Stanley, 52, 64
Guadalcanal
casualties, 155
CINCPAC/COMINCH messages, 159, 160
fight for, as acid test, 152
Henderson Field, 148, 152–57
Japanese evacuation order, 161–62
Japanese troops on, 152
late summer/autumn 1942 and, 152
night combat, 155–57
OBBs and, 158
Tokyo Express and, 153, 158, 161
Guam, 88, 128, 226
Guerin, Bill, 6

Haggart, Robert Stevenson, 172–73, 174, 210
Halsey, William F. (Admiral)
background, 126
Enterprise task force, 46, 74
Guadalcanal and, 156, 157, 158, 160–61
Leyte Gulf and, 258, 259–60, 297–98
Philippines and, 231, 247–48, 253
rotational command system and, 230–31
Task Force 8, 126, 127
Hardeman, Bill, 53
Hart, Thomas C. (Admiral), 45
Haruna, 153, 253
Heffernan, John B., 233, 287
Helena, 75, 153
Helm, 204
Henderson Field (Guadalcanal), 148, 152–57
Hickam Army Field (Hawaii), 44, 56, 76
Higgins boats, 183, 185–86
Higuchi, Kiichiro, 168–69
Hill, Ed, 70
Hill, Harry (Admiral), 180, 184, 185, 197, 206

Hillenkoetter, Roscoe, 60, 68
Hiryu, 131
hit-and-run raids, 126–29
Hobby, William, 81–82, 83
Hoga, 72
Holland, Frank, 183
Holloway, James L., 283–84, 285, 288
Hong Kong, 33, 74, 97, 128
Honolulu
  desire for duty and, 39
  Japanese consulate in, 45, 79
  liberty in, 5–8, 72, 150
  Punchbowl Crater, 121
  "stewed, screwed and tattooed" in, 6–7
  See also Pearl Harbor
Honolulu, 75, 90, 122, 234
Hornet, 129, 135, 147, 149
Hosho, 28
Houston, 213–14, 241, 247
Hull, 173
Hutchins, 280, 286
Hyland, Everett, 73

Idaho, 43, 125, 174, 175, 209, 234
Imperial National Defense Policy of 1907, 26
Indianapolis, 180, 216, 217, 234
Iowa, 205, 302
Iowa-class battleships, 140, 196
Iroquois, 10, 15

Jaluit, 93, 127, 197
Jansen, Lenard, 68–69
Japan
  American xenophobia and, 25–26
  British design of naval stations, 16
  military and industrial base of, 15
  Operation K and, 111–12
  surrender in Tokyo Bay, 304–6
  US Navy as threat and, 24
Jarvis, 148
Johnson, Doir, 62
Joint Assault Signal Companies (JASCOs), 193–94
Jomini, Antoine-Henri, 10
Jones, Carl, 185
Jones, James, 76–77
Juhl, Howard, 51
Juneau, 155

Kaga, 53, 131, 136
Kahanu, George, 84–85
Kaiser Wilhelm II, 14
kamikazi tactics, 298–99
kantai kessen (decisive battle), 21, 35, 131–36
Karb, Joe, 4
"Kate" torpedo planes, 53, 90, 134–35, 221
Kawanishi H8K "Emily" flying boats, 111
Kelekian, Harry, 218
Kelly, Richmond (Admiral), 44
Kenworthy, Jesse, 57
Kidd, Isaac (Admiral), 3, 60, 75
Killen, 281
Kimmel, Husband E. (Admiral)
  about, 41
  in canceling moves to the Atlantic Fleet, 43
  CINCPAC, 41, 44, 45, 53
  as ensign, 41
  on fleet readiness, 42
  fleet training schedule and, 42
  imminent conflict messages and, 2
  Layton and, 45, 46–47
  November 27th dispatch and, 45–46
  Pearl Harbor need for resources and, 43–44
  reception of intelligence and, 44–45
  route to preparedness and, 42–43
  Wake Island and, 92–93
  witness of Pearl Harbor attack, 74
King, Ernest (Admiral), 39, 143, 158, 163
King, Thomas S. II, 143, 144, 167
Kingman, Howard F. (Admiral), 167, 183, 186
Kinkaid, Thomas (Admiral), 245, 260, 297
Kirishima, 156–57
Kiska, 130, 168–69, 173–75, 176
Kitts, Willard, 165–66
Knox, William Franklin, 92–93, 114, 214
Knyaz Suvorov, 19

Koga, Mineichi, 180–81, 190, 205, 222
Kongo, 27, 153, 253
Kovar, Mike, 290
Kurita, Takeo, 253–54, 256, 257–58, 259, 274, 297–98
Kwajalein
  about, 196
  amphibious operations, 196–97
  battleship deployment to, 195
  bombardment of, 197
  capture completion of, 200
  Colorado and, 198
  lagoon, ship operations in, 199
  Maryland and, 198, 199
  Nimitz on, 203
  observations of attack, 198–99
  Pennsylvania and, 197, 199
  Tennessee and, 198
  Underwater Demolition Team One and, 199–200
  See also Granite Campaign

Landcrab, Operation, 163
Langley, 28
Lawson, James, 66, 67
Layton, Edwin, 45, 46–47, 49, 97–98, 132, 149
Leahy, William (Admiral), 38, 227
Leak, Leslie, 62
Leary, 289–90
Leary, Herbert F. (Admiral), 151, 154
LeMay, Curtis (General), 226
"Lessons Learned at Tarawa," 190
Lexington, 79, 94, 114, 127–28, 130, 259
Lexington Task Force, 46, 93, 127
Leyte Gulf
  attack transports entering, 250
  battle plan, 262–63
  battleship patrol, 294–95
  California and, 241, 249, 250–51
  Center Force and, 273, 274, 297–98
  Close Covering Group and, 261
  Combat Air Patrol and, 258
  demolition teams and minesweeping units in, 249
  dreadnoughts and, 263–64
  engagements in, 297
  fleet travel to, 248–49
  Halsey and, 258, 259–60, 297–98
  Japanese assault on, 272
  Japanese battle plan for, 255
  Japanese force objective, 261
  Kurita and, 253–54, 256, 257–58, 259
  Maryland and, 241, 250–51
  Minesweeping and Hydrography group in, 249
  Nishimura and, 254, 256, 260
  Northern Force and, 273
  Oldendorf and, 261–62, 273–75
  Oldendorf entrance into, 249
  Pennsylvania and, 241
  PT boats and, 261
  routes into, 254
  Second Striking Force and, 269
  Task Force 38 and, 258–59
  Tennessee and, 241
  West Virginia and, 241, 250–51, 264
  "Leyte then Luzon" plan, 230
liberties, 5–8
liberty boats, 5
Lockard, Joseph, 49–50
Long Island, 152
Lott, Russell, 8
Louisville, 198, 214–15, 218, 234, 242, 272, 292

MacArthur, Douglas (General)
  Cavite and, 97
  invasion of Leyte, 245, 253
  "Leyte then Luzon" plan, 230
  Manus and, 238
  Operation Cartwheel and, 163
  at Pacific Strategy conference, 227–29
  return to the Philippines, 228–30, 243–45
  Southwest Pacific Area and, 151, 228
  Southwest Pacific Forces, 177, 238
  speaking on the *Missouri*, 304–5, 306
Macedonian, 11
Macon, 240, 241

MacPherson, Robert, 185
Mahan, Alfred Thayer
  about, 9–10
  book publications, 12–13
  lectures, 11, 12–13
  naval argument, 12
  Naval War College and, 11–13
  Roosevelt and, 13
  Sato and, 17
  Tsushima Strait and, 20
Majuro Atoll, 197, 204, 208–9
Makin, 179, 180, 181
Malcolm, Everett, 5
Manus, 238
Marcus Island, 128, 129
Mare Island maintenance, 171
Marshall, George C. (General), 39, 45, 228
Marshall Islands, 93, 111, 126–27, 131, 134, 148, 179
Maryland
  in Battleship Row, 3
  damage assessment, 89
  damage detail, 90–91
  departure to/from Puget Sound Naval Yard, 91, 92, 144–45
  Eniwetok repairs and, 224
  first moments on, 51–52
  Guadalcanal and, 157–58
  kamikazi attacks and, 299
  Kwajalein and, 198, 199
  Leyte Gulf and, 250–51
  off Betio Island, 183–84, 185, 186–87
  oil consumption, 149
  Oklahoma crew climbing aboard, 69
  Pearl Harbor dry dock (1944), 225
  Peleliu and, 234
  Philippines and, 241
  as remaining afloat, 78
  rescue parties from, 83
  Roi-Namur and, 200–201
  Saipan battle and, 218, 221, 222–24
  San Pedro departure, 195
  in Seeadler Harbor, 239
  Surigao Strait and, 287, 290
  torpedo attacks and, 54–55, 75
  travel to Bremerton, 141
  upgrades, 145
Mason, Ted, 7, 71–72
Mauna Loa, 204
Maya, 257–58
Maybee, George, 60
Mayer, Andrew de Graff, 210, 216, 219, 232–33
McCain, John (Admiral), 259
McCampbell, David, 258
McCarron, Jack, 60
McClintock, David, 257
McDermut, 278–80, 281
McElfresh, John, 276, 277
McGowan, 278–79
McGraw, William Francis, 200–201
McManes, Ken, 280
Meade, 186–87
Medusa, 88, 91
Meiji, Emperor, 15
Melvin, 278–79
Michigan, 23
Michishio, 281, 286
Midway, 130–31
Midway, Battle of
  AF Occupation Force and, 132
  American air attack and, 134–35
  American victory, 139
  Carrier Strike Force and, 131
  First Carrier Strike Force and, 136
  hit-and-run raids, 139–40
  Japanese Cruisers and, 136
  Japanese invasion force and, 134
  Japanese losses and, 137
  Nagumo and, 116, 131, 134, 136
  Nimitz and, 131–36, 139
  victory at, 80
Midway Island, 43, 46, 88
Mikuma, 136
Miller, Doris, 62, 63, 68
Miller, Jim, 5
Minneapolis, 232, 234, 279, 286, 292
Mississippi, 43, 125, 209, 234, 241, 287, 290
Missouri, 296–97, 304–5
Mitschek, Erwin, 57

Mitscher, Marc, 222
Mobile, 198
Mogami, 136, 269, 271, 275, 280–82, 286, 289, 291, 293
Monaghan, 64
Monssen, 278–80
Mount McKinley, 235
Mugford, 204
Musashi, 131, 253, 256, 259
Myoko, 259

Nachi, 291, 293
Nagato, 30, 259
Nagumo, Chuichi, 78–79, 81, 131, 205
Narwhal, 169
Nassau, 170
Naturalization Act of 1906, 18
Nautilus, 135, 169, 181
Navajo Code Talkers, 193–94
Naval Appropriations Act of 1891, 13
Naval War College, 9, 11–13, 26, 36, 133, 156, 178, 202, 213
Nevada
  in Aleutian mission, 165–66, 171
  Arizona survivors climbing aboard, 69
  in Atlantic Fleet, 301
  attempt to exit the harbor, 71–73
  Attu and, 165
  in Battleship Row, 3
  beaching of, 72
  casting mooring lines, 70–71
  casualties, 75
  construction as "super-dreadnought," 23
  design defects, 108
  early morning December 7th, 50
  as first to return to service, 166
  kamikazi attacks and, 301
  Kitts and, 166
  Mare Island maintenance, 171
  occupation duty in Japan, 302
  refit, 166–67
  sea trials and training, 167
  torpedo attacks and, 55, 71, 72, 102
  transfer to Atlantic Fleet, 171
  weight-trimming measures, 166–67
Nevada salvage
  afloat and back to channel and, 106
  alternative approach, 104
  ammunition/power can removal and, 104
  "Cheer Up Ship" and, 105, 106
  compartment dewatering, 105
  damage, 102
  damage assessment, 89
  electrical equipment and, 105
  hull breach and, 103
  navy divers and, 103–4
  patch attempt, 103
New Jersey, 87, 231
New Mexico, 43, 125, 146, 209, 220
New Orleans, 67, 89, 158, 205
New York, 41
Nimitz, Chester W. (Admiral)
  background, 94–96
  on Betio Island, 189
  canceling of "immediate operations," 232
  Central Pacific Campaign and, 177
  CINCPAC, 96
  as cruiser skipper, 96
  Distinguished Service Medal, 144
  as ensign, 95
  in First World War, 95–96
  Flying Boat accident and, 144
  future operations in Pacific and, 144
  Guadalcanal and, 154, 158
  inherited staff and, 96
  Knox and, 93
  on Kwajalein, 203
  Layton and, 97
  Midway and, 131–36, 139
  on the *Missouri*, 304
  morale restoration, 97–98
  Philippines and, 229–30, 231–32
  reputation of the party, 96
  rotational command system, 230
  Spruance and, 133–34
  viewing Pearl Harbor, 98–99
  Wallin and, 99, 123
"Ninety-Day Wonders," 42

Nishimura, Shoji, 254, 256, 260, 267–69,
271–72, 281–82, 293–94
Nishino, Shigeru, 289, 294
Nisshin, 30–31
Nomura, Kichisaburo, 34
Northampton, 127, 128, 166
North Carolina, 148
North Carolina-class battleships, 140, 150

OBBs ("Old Battleships"), 158, 162
Oglala, 70, 75, 100
O'Hare, Edward "Butch," 127–28
Oklahoma
in Battleship Row, 3
capsizing, 57, 59
damage assessment, 90
decommissioning of, 302
design defects, 108
entry points into, 84
first moments on, 51
killed and missing, 75
listing, 57
Lucky Bag, 85, 86
"parbuckling" operation, 302
repair priority, 99
rescue of trapped men and, 76
rescue parties, 81–86
sinking, 68, 81
torpedo attacks and, 54, 57
trapped survivors, saving, 81–86
Oldendorf, Jesse Barrett (Admiral)
about, 213–14
Coward plan and, 277–79, 282
Eniwetok anchorage and, 232
Leyte Gulf and, 249, 261–62, 273–75
message from Kinkaid, 260–61
Operation Plan 1-44 and, 233–34
Peleliu and, 233–35, 236–37
Saipan and, 218, 221, 226
Seeadler Harbor and, 238–39
Surigao Strait and, 277–79, 282–84,
289, 292–93
Task Group 32.5 and, 234
Task Group 77.2 and, 241–42,
262, 295
Underwater Demolition Teams and,
249–50
Olds, Clifford, 121
Operation K, 111–12
Opie, John N. III, 53
Ortolan, 101
Ozawa, Jisaburo, 222, 254

Pacific Bridge Company, 101, 110, 118
Pacific Fleet
Battle Force, 38, 77, 139
battle line destruction, 124
battleships and, 3, 146
decision to base at Pearl Harbor, 38
Readiness Condition Three, 55
reduction in strength, 36
route to preparedness, 42–43
"Unlimited National Emergency" and,
41–42
Pacific strategy conference, 227–28
Palau operation, 233–38
Panay, 32–33
Parry, 203, 207
Pearl Harbor
disadvantages of, 39
egress, 39
Ford Island, 2, 48, 50–52, 66, 76
map, 48
Navy Yard repair facilities, 79
Nimitz viewing of, 98–99
requests for more resources, 43–44
torpedo attacks and, 53–54
vulnerability to attack, 39
Pearl Harbor attack
afternoon of, 78
battleship casualties, 75
evening of, 79
first moments of, 51–54
Ford Island and, 65, 66–67, 77
hospitals after, 76
Navy casualties, 75
second wave, 70–77
steadfast devotion to duty and, 63–64
sunken ships, 75–76
torpedo attacks and, 54–57, 61, 65

torpedoes and, 54–55
See also specific Pearl Harbor battleships
Peleliu
"Bloody Nose Ridge," 237
bombardment, 234–35, 237
marines on, 235–36, 237–38
Nakagawa and, 236
Oldendorf and, 233–35, 236–37
as "rough but fast," 236
struggle for, 238
Task Group 32.5 and, 234, 235
Pennsylvania
in Aleutian mission, 169–70
bomb hit, 73
Bremerton repairs, 170, 175
casualties, 75
Cold Bay and, 168
command change in Long Beach, 167
damage assessment, 89
in Dry Dock Number One, 3
early morning December 7th, 50
Eniwetok Atoll and, 206
Hunter's Point dry dock and, 90, 143
joining Task Force 1, 143
Kwajalein and, 197, 199
leaving Pearl Harbor dry dock, 90
Leyte Gulf and, 301
Mauna Loa and, 204
Nevada and, 72–73
Parry Island and, 207
Peleliu and, 234
Philippines and, 241
powder explosions, 204–5
refit, 167
in South Pacific Area, 209
Surigao Strait and, 287, 290
in Sydney, 209–10
towed to Guam, 301
Philippines
about, 228–29
aircraft losses and, 246
American manpower and, 245
carrier raids, 246
central, opening attack on, 231
Combined Fleet and, 251–52, 254
Fast Carrier Task Forces and, 246
Halsey and, 253
Luzon, 229, 245, 254, 258
MacArthur and, 228–29, 251
"Main Body" and, 252–53
Nimitz and, 229–30
Palawan Passage, 257
Samar, 254, 298
San Bernardino Strait, 254, 256, 259, 272, 297–98
San Pedro Bay, 243
Sho-Go plan, 252–58
Sulu Sea, 256, 258, 260
Third Fleet and, 245
See also Leyte Gulf; Surigao Strait
Phoenix, 261, 262, 280
pilot training, Japanese, 137
Plan 1-44, Operation, 233–34
Plan Dog memo, 43
Porter, Gery, 61
Portland, 218, 234, 292
Port Moresby, 129, 130
Pownall, Charles (Admiral), 180
President Lincoln, 213
Princeton, 258–59
PT boats, 261, 265–67, 269–71, 275–77
Puget Sound Navy Yard, 140, 146, 240
Pullen, Weston Jr., 267
Puller, "Chesty," 236, 237
Pye, William S. (Admiral), 86, 87, 96–97, 139, 144, 151

Rainbow Five, 43
Rainbow series of war plans, 43
Ray, Herbert James, 194–95, 218
Rayleigh, 75
Raymer, Edward, 91–92, 117
Remey, 278–79
Reordan, Charles E., 146
rescue parties, 81–86
Richardson, James O. (Admiral), 38–41, 53
Ricketts, Claude, 58, 59, 62, 63
Rickover, Hyman, 114–16
Roberts, Howard, 85

Rockwell, Francis (Admiral), 163
Roi-Namur, 200
Roosevelt, Franklin D.
  Japanese aggression and, 33
  list of most competent officers and, 143, 214
  on Oahu, 227
  Philippines and, 228, 230
  Richardson and, 40
  "Unlimited National Emergency" and, 41
Roosevelt, Theodore, 13–14, 20, 26
Roscoe, Thomas M., 144
Royal Navy, 15–16, 22–23, 27, 41, 97, 142, 191
Rozhestvensky, Zinovy, 18–19
Ruddock, Theodore (Admiral), 262

Saipan
  about, 215
  coral shelf, 216
  declaration of secure, 226
  Garapan, 216–17, 220, 222
  large size of, 219
Saipan, Battle of
  bombardment, 216–17, 218, 219–20
  California and, 215–17, 220–21, 222–23
  Colorado and, 218
  Fast Carrier Task Forces and, 222
  final days of, 225–26
  Japanese coastal defense and, 219
  landing attack, 219
  landing ships, 218
  Maryland and, 218, 221, 222–24
  Oldendorf and, 213–14, 218, 221, 226
  Saito retreat and, 225
  Spruance and, 216
  Task Group 52.10 and, 214–15
  Task Group 52.17 and, 214–15
  Tennessee and, 215–16, 217, 220, 221, 222–23
  Underwater Demolition Teams and, 216–17, 218
Saito, Yoshitsugu, 222, 225
Salt Lake City, 127, 128, 153
Salvage Division, Navy Yard, 99, 109, 112–13, 123
San Francisco, 84, 88–89, 153, 155
San Pedro Harbor, 249
Saratoga, 79, 126, 148
Saratoga task force, 89, 93, 97, 161
Sato, Tetsutaro
  America and China and, 28
  Battle of the Yellow Sea and, 20
  5:3:3 ratio, 29
  History of Naval Defense, 24
  hypothetical enemy and, 24
  Mahan and, 17, 20
  Naval War College lectures, 17, 20, 21
Sato-Akiyama scheme, 27
Savo Island, 149, 153–54, 155
Schmitt, Aloysius, 64
Scott, Normal (Admiral), 153
Scott, Raymond, 63–64
Seabees, 189, 192, 199, 208, 226, 238–39
Sedberry, Bob, 70–71
Seeadler Harbor, 238–42
Shaw, 73, 74, 99
Sherrod, Robert, 176–77, 185, 186, 189–90
Shibazaki, Keiji, 182, 184, 188
Shigemitsu, Mamoru, 304
Shigure, 267, 269, 282, 283, 289, 293
Shima, Kiyohide, 248, 253, 271, 290–91, 293
Sho-Go plan, 252–58
Short, Leslie, 54–55
Short, Walter (General), 56, 93
shosu seiei shugi, 268
Singapore, 33, 74, 128
Smith, Holland (General), 178–79, 194, 225
Smith, Huston, 223
Solace, 71, 76
Solomon Islands, 151–52
Soryu, 131, 135
South Carolina, 23
South Dakota, 156, 157
South Dakota-class battleships, 140, 150, 171

Southern Plan, 35, 36, 80
Special Treatment Steel (STS), 150
Sprague, Clifton (Admiral), 298
Spruance, Raymond (Admiral)
  about, 133
  Central Pacific and, 163
  Eniwetok Atoll and, 205
  Granite Campaign and, 178–79, 181
  Nimitz and, 133–34
  promotion, 205
  Saipan and, 216
  Task Force 16, 133
  Truk Atoll and, 205–6
Stalemate, Operation, 232, 234
Stark, Harold R. (Admiral), 38, 39, 43–44, 49, 53, 142
Station HYPO, 44–45, 47, 111, 132, 138
steadfast devotion to duty, 63–64
Steele, James, 99
submarines
  in Aleutians, 169
  construction of, 29
  in hunting Japanese carriers, 222
  Japanese use of, 35, 39, 111, 141, 212
  in Leyte Gulf, 245
  patrols, 46
  See also specific submarines
Surigao Strait
  battle completion, 295
  battle map, 266
  California and, 287
  Coward's plan, 277–79
  DESRON 24 and, 262, 280, 286
  DESRON 54 and, 262, 277–78
  DESRON 56 and, 262, 283–85, 288
  DESRON X-Ray and, 262, 292
  Maryland and, 287, 290
  Nishimura and, 267–69, 271–72, 281–82, 293–94
  northern currents of, 274
  Oldendorf and, 277–79, 282–84, 289, 292–93
  as part of the Battle of Leyte Gulf, 297
  Pennsylvania and, 287, 290
  PT boats and, 265–67, 269–71, 275–77
  Shima's force and, 271, 290–92
  Sho-Go plan and, 254, 256
  Southern Force and, 272–75, 293
  Task Force 77.2 and, 262, 295
  Tennessee and, 285–86, 287
  West Virginia and, 282–83, 284–85, 290

Tarawa
  casualties, 189
  fight for, 186
  Galvanic fleet and, 180
  Joint Assault Signal Companies (JASCOs) and, 193–94
  lessons from, 188, 190
  naval gunfire changes after, 192–93
  naval gunfire support plan for, 190–91
  pre-D-Day bombardment after, 192, 193
Task Force 1, 139, 143, 144, 146–47, 149–51
Task Force 8, 126, 127, 149
Task Force 53, 176, 195
Task Force 61, 147, 149
Task Force 77.2, 262, 295
Task Group 52.17, 214–15
tattoo parlors, 7
Taussig, Joseph Jr., 64–65, 70
Tennessee
  Aleutian mission and, 173–75
  in Battleship Row, 3
  Betio Island and, 188
  Bofors and Oerlikons, 172
  damage assessment, 89
  Eniwetok Atoll and, 206, 223
  fire hoses deployment, 61
  fires, 68
  fledgling new sailors, 147
  freeing, 92
  heavy gun replacement, 146
  Kwajalein and, 198
  modernization of, 150–51, 210
  New Ireland and, 210
  new profile of, 171–72
  Parry Island and, 207
  Pearl Harbor dry dock (1944), 210–11

Peleliu and, 234
at Philadelphia Naval Yard, 301
Philippines and, 241, 300
Puget Sound Navy Yard and, 92, 141, 146
refitting, 171–72
remaining afloat, 78
rescue parties from, 83
Saipan battle and, 215–16, 217, 220, 221, 222–23
San Pedro departure, 195
sea trials (May, 1943), 171
Sherrod and, 176–77
in South Pacific Area, 209
steering casualty, 232
stump tower, 146
Surigao Strait and, 285–86, 287
as target of bombers, 61–62
torpedo attacks and, 75
West Virginia crew climbing aboard, 69
Tern, 83
Theobald, Robert (Admiral), 149
Thomas, Francis, 70, 72, 102
Thomas, Milton, 51
Thompson, Harold, 102–3
Tinian, 217, 226
Tirpitz, Alfred von (Admiral), 22–23
Tirpitz Plan, 23, 27
Tisdale, William, 4
Togo, Heihachiro, 17–18
Tojo, Hideki, 34, 35
Tokyo Express, 153, 158, 161, 273
Tokyo Rose, 246–47
torpedo attacks, 53, 54–57, 61, 102, 107
Towers, John (Admiral), 180
Toyoda, Soemu, 222, 251–52, 268, 293
Tripartite Pact, 33
Truk Atoll, 27, 161, 190, 205–6
Tsushima Strait, Battle of, 18, 20, 22
Tulagi, 148
turboelectric propulsion, 115–16, 122
Turner, Richmond Kelly
amphibious forces command, 164, 180
conquest of Central Pacific, 163
Kwajalein and, 200
as "the Navy's Patton," 149
Pye and, 144
Rocky Mount, 196
Saipan declaration and, 226
Task Force 62, 147
"Two Power Standard," 23
Tyler, Kermit, 49–50

US Navy, Alfred Thayer Mahan and, 11–14
Utah, 75

Vandergrift, Alexander, 147
Van Valkenburgh, Franklin, 60
Vestal, 5, 67, 83, 88, 91
Viti Levu, Fiji, 157, 160–61

Wachapreague, 270, 275
Wachusett, 10, 11
"Wahoo Cannonball," 5
Wai Momi ("waters of pearl"), 1
Wake Island, 46, 88, 89, 92–93, 96–97, 128
Wallin, Homer N
about, 86–87
after Pearl Harbor attack, 87–88
California and, 109, 110
citation, 123
as material and salvage officer, 77, 86
material shortages and, 100–101
Nevada salvage and, 106
new command, 99
Nimitz and, 96, 99, 123
salvage crews and, 123
salvage project and, 99
West Virginia and, 118, 120
Ward, 49
War Plan Orange, 43
Washington, 156, 157
Washington Naval Treaty of 1922, 28, 29
Wasp, 10, 148
Watchtower, Operation, 147
Weissman, Daniel, 82
Weller, Donald (General), 191
West Virginia
abandon ship order, 63

Arizona explosion and, 60
in Battleship Row, 3
counterflooding, 58–59
crew killed in action, 75
damage assessment, 89–90
early morning December 7th, 50–51
fires, 68, 82–83, 117–18
first moments on, 51, 53
kamikazi attacks and, 303
Leyte Gulf and, 250–51, 264
listing, 58, 59
modernization of, 150
occupation duties, 303–4
Philippines and, 241, 303
in Seeadler Harbor, 239–40
sinking, 75, 118
Surigao Strait and, 282–83, 284–85, 290
torpedo attacks and, 54, 61
working to save ship, 57–58
West Virginia salvage
damage detail, 117–18
debris removal, 119
dewatering, 120
to dry dock, 122
initial report, 118
main mast, 120
navy divers and, 120–21
remains discovery, 121
sealing patches and, 120
task of, 117
technical problems, 100
turboelectric drive cleaning, 122
Weyler, George (Admiral), 261–62, 282, 287
Whaley, F. C., 187
Wheeler Field, 56, 78, 112
Whipple, 213
White, William, 119
Widgeon, 83
Wiley, Herbert Victor, 240–41, 284–85
Wilkinson, Theodore "Ping" (Admiral), 232, 235
William B. Preston, 173

Yalu, Battle of, 16
Yamagumo, 279, 280, 281
Yamamoto, Isoroku
about, 30–31
on American economic pressure, 34
battleship destruction objective, 74–75
Combined Fleet and, 33–36, 80, 129
concern of homeland strike and, 129
as Deputy Navy Minister, 32
as gambler, 31
at Harvard, 31
Layton and, 45
misconceptions, 80–81
naval aviation and, 31–32
naval mission to Italy and, 54
Nimitz and, 131
as Sato student, 36
"short war" gamble, 80, 138
Southern Plan and, 35, 36
US and Japanese war and, 33
Yamasaki, Yasuyo, 170–71
Yamashiro, 267, 269, 281, 282, 284, 286, 287, 288–89, 291
Yamato, 131, 253, 256, 259
Yarnell, Harry (Admiral), 39
Yatsushiro, Sukeyoshi, 127
"Yellow Peril" ideology, 18, 25–26
Yellow Sea, Battle of, 17–20
YG-17, 69, 83
Yorktown, 43, 80, 130, 135–36
Young, Cassin, 67–68
Young, Stephen, 85
"young school" of naval defense, 16

Zero fighters, 56, 71, 134–35, 137, 253